By the same author

Lifeblood
Falling Off the Edge

THE RIFT

A NEW AFRICA
BREAKS FREE

ALEX PERRY

WEIDENFELD & NICOLSON

First published in Great Britain in 2015
by Weidenfeld & Nicolson

1 3 5 7 9 10 8 6 4 2

A CIP catalogue record for this book
is available from the British Library.

ISBN (hardback): 978 0 297 87122 4
ISBN (trade paperback): 978 0 297 87123 1

Typeset by Input Data Services Ltd, Bridgwater, Somerset

Printed and bound by CPI Group (UK) Ltd, Croydon CR0 4YY

Photographs © Dominic Nahr

Maps by John Gilkes

The Orion Publishing Group's policy is to use papers
that are natural, renewable and recyclable and made
from wood grown in sustainable forests. The logging and
manufacturing processes are expected to conform to
environmental regulations of the country of origin.

Weidenfeld & Nicolson
The Orion Publishing Group Ltd
Carmelite House
50 Victoria Embankment
London EC4Y 0DZ

An Hachette UK Company

www.orionbooks.co.uk

for Dominic Nahr, who always had a different angle
and for Tess, always

CONTENTS

PART III: The New Africa

SUB-SAHARAN AFRICA

APE VERDE

MAURITANIA

MALI
Kidal •
• Timbuktu

NIGER

Meroe •

Dakar • SENEGAL
GAMBIA
Bissau City •
GUINEA-
BISSAU
GUINEA

Sévaré • BURKINA
Bamako • FASO Niamey •
Ouagadougou •

Kano •
Jos • Maiduguri •

CHAD

Khartoum •

SUDAN

ERITREA

DJIBOUTI
Addis Ababa •
ETHIOPIA

SOMALILAND

SIERRA LEONE
CÔTE
D'IVOIRE
GHANA
BENIN
TOGO

NIGERIA

Lagos •

LIBERIA

CAMEROON

CENTRAL AFRICAN
REPUBLIC
Obo •

SOUTH SUDAN
• Juba

Malakal •

SOMALIA

EQUATORIAL GUINEA

SÃO TOME & PRÍNCIPE ⁶

GABON

CONGO

Kisangani •

DEMOCRATIC
REPUBLIC
OF CONGO
• Kinshasa

UGANDA
Kampala • Kogelo •
Kigali •
Goma • RWANDA
BURUNDI

KENYA

Dadaab •

• Nairobi

• Mogadishu

TANZANIA
• Dar es Salaam

SEYCHELLES

ANGOLA

ZAMBIA
Lusaka •

MALAWI

COMOROS

NAMIBIA

Harare •
ZIMBABWE
Masvingo •

MOZAMBIQUE

BOTSWANA

MADAGASCAR

MAURITIUS
RÉUNION

Johannesburg •
SWAZILAND
Brandfort • LESOTHO
SOUTH AFRICA • Durban
Mthatha •

Cape Town •

AUTHOR'S NOTE

For a European to write a book about Africa and freedom is an undertaking of precarious legitimacy. Europeans have a long history of exploiting Africans, and of getting Africa wrong. I have tried to avoid the latter but there is no doubt I am guilty of the former. A perfect stranger, I asked hundreds of Africans to entrust me with their stories without pay or other compensation, often in a detail that was indecent and at huge risk to themselves. These are not my stories, I borrowed them, even stole them, and I owe a deep debt to their true owners.

My highest ambition is that I have done them justice. That's also a reason why you won't find many old Africa 'hands' in these pages. Foreign academics and journalists tend to define Africa to the outside world by referencing or quoting other foreigners – aid workers or other academics. It is this presumptuous and incestuous process that has led to so many false conclusions. Even when foreigners alight on truth, too often speaking up for Africa has become speaking for it, and defending Africa's interests has become deciding them. While this book contains some conclusions of my own, they are a reporter's inferences, drawn from what Africans showed and told me. I wanted Africans to show and tell you their stories too, so you would hear what I heard and see what I saw, and that has required giving them space to do so.

But already I'm in danger of making the kind of generalizations that cause Africans to wince. Africa is the biggest and most diverse continent on earth and to speak of it or its people as a monolith is a grand folly. After all, we split the non-African half of the world's super-continent into three: Europe, the Middle East and Asia. I have drawn my own line across the Sahara, which remains such a barrier to culture, language, politics and economics that it is better to think of North Africa – Morocco, Algeria, Libya, Tunisia and Egypt – as part of Arabia and 'Africa' as the 49 countries to the south. Below the Sahara, the variation is still immense. I have tried to respect that by treating each country, and sometimes parts of them, as distinct. However my contention is that the nations and peoples of this vast land share some common themes. Many have a mutual history, most recently in colonialism and liberation, but before that in the experience of living in an endless and empty continent. That collective context means that the stories of one can hold true for many others and why, I think, we can speak meaningfully about Africans and Africa.

But here's the thing: not many of us. Given the dimensions of the place, most people in Africa, local or foreign, sensibly limit themselves to a corner or two. Even in my profession, almost no one attempts to cover the entire continent. The shrinking resources of the particular magazine for which I worked meant that, for close to a decade, that was my job. That's my best defence for writing this book. Africa is nearing the end of an epic quest for freedom that will revolutionize perceptions of it and change the world. Though I am not African, and though I was traversing the breadth of the continent merely because of the declining fortunes of a far-off employer, I turned out to be one of the few who could tell the whole story.

At the heart of Africa lie the Virungas, a chain of volcanoes that are home to the last of the mountain gorillas. Every few years one of the craters erupts, sending thick rivers of lava rolling down its steep slopes, sweeping away the misty bamboo thickets where the gorillas live, smashing through villages and burying farms. These local disasters are dwarfed by the continental cataclysm to come. The Virungas are fiery peepholes into a tectonic fissure – the Great Rift – that will one day rend Africa in two from Eritrea down to Mozambique. Seen from 3,000 metres up under a crater's lip, the distinct characters of these two future Africas are already apparent. To the west, spreading lazily down to the Atlantic, are a thousand kilometres of Congolese jungle, the canopy rolled flat by low, lumbering rain clouds. To the east is the high and rocky East African savannah, cool, grassy, blessedly free of mosquitoes and running clear over several horizons before plunging into the Indian Ocean.

A continental split happens in two stages. First, as the earth's plates move apart, they stretch the land's surface so thin that the earth's molten core bursts through and settles in monstrous pustules of cooling rock and ash. Later, as the partition widens further, the cones collapse and form a depression that, when the last one falls, fills with angry, hissing sea. From a distance, the division can seem to proceed peacefully. Africa's Rift is widening at the speed a fingernail grows and a process that began 100 million years ago will take at least another 10 million to complete. Up close, however, the separation can be violent. In 2002, the largest Virunga, Mount Nyiragongo, spat a stream of lava 300 metres wide into the middle of Congo's second city, Goma, carving the place in two and asphyxiating or incinerating 147 people. Three years later and several hundred kilometres to the north-west, a group of Ethiopian villagers watched helplessly as a crack six metres wide and 58 kilometres long opened up in the earth beneath their feet, swallowing huts, small hills and a herd of bellowing camels.

After a time I came to see the continent's seismic destiny as a metaphor for its more immediate human future. The Rift is a cauldron of violence and death. But it is also our source of life. Out of the devastation came insects, animals, then man, and now an entirely new land. And one day soon, this new Africa will break free.

PART I

GETTING AFRICA WRONG

ONE

SOMALIA

Nature creates drought but only man makes a famine, and in July 2011 a small group of men and women allowed the worst drought in southern Somalia in 60 years to plunge close to three million people into famine.

The catastrophe peaked in the capital, Mogadishu. After two decades of civil war, the city was already in ruins and occupied by tens of thousands of refugees. As the countryside emptied of several million people in a matter of weeks, Mogadishu was swamped by at least half a million more. By July, hunger was killing several hundred of the new arrivals a day. As measles and cholera took hold, that figure accelerated into the thousands. Soon the living and the dead were competing for space. Families moved into old graveyards, then fresh burial grounds. Mothers would return to the graves of children they had buried the day before to find a camp had materialized overnight. At the famine's height, 2.8 million people, two-thirds of the population of southern Somalia, were starving. Nine months later nearly one in 10 of them were dead, mostly babies, young children and the elderly, whom hunger kills first.

I flew up from Nairobi to Mogadishu with Dominic Nahr, a 28-year-old Swiss photographer with whom I often worked. We skirted the north-eastern edge of the continent, the beaches the colour of butter in the dawn light, the ocean empty save for the occasional foam trail of a pirate skiff. Touching down on the edge of the ocean, Bashir met us at the plane's steps and in one smooth movement pushed us through immigration and customs, out of the building and into one of his pick-ups. Within minutes we were approaching Banadir Hospital, one of the few functioning hospitals in the city. At the main entrance we were stopped by an exhausted-looking orderly in a dirty white coat, who made a show of trying to stop us, then gave up. We followed him through a door into a giant ward. The room, formerly a corridor, was filled with the warm, wet-hay smell of dysentery. Fifty beds were arranged in neat rows. Next to them were people. At first we wandered, distracted by the flies and by how well everyone looked, until we realized you had to walk right up to the beds to see the patients. Most were so thin and shrunken that a relative standing next to them or even a simple fold in their sheets could conceal them completely.

Khalima Adan was 38. She was dressed in a brown *abaya* under which she wore a silk dress – white, black and grey, with fuchsia-pink flashes – that might have fitted her once but now hung from her like washing on a line. She was leaning over her seven-year-old son Umar, fanning him with a piece of cardboard. 'We come from Kutubaray,' she said, naming a town 240 kilometres to the south-west. 'There was no food. The walk took 10 days and we arrived 12 days ago. I have six children. I had nine but three died: a two-year-old and a three-year-old on the way, and my nine-year-old boy from measles once we arrived.'

I asked if her husband was taking care of their other five children. She shook her head. 'His body swelled up on the way,' she said. 'He couldn't talk. Then he couldn't walk. We had to leave him there.'

Later in the camps I would hear accounts of a biblical exodus from the south, columns of tens of thousands of people abandoning the land *en masse*. Most had only a few bottles of water. They ate leaves. The bodies of those too weak to keep walking were left where they fell, to be eaten by vultures and hyenas. A 50-year-old who walked for two weeks described how he had seen seven people 'just sit down and die' by the side of the road. A 60-year-old farmer said he walked for hundreds of kilometres carrying his dying children in turn on his shoulders. 'When I realized they were dead, I would lift them off and bury them there, on the way,' the man said. He had lost two boys and three girls like that.

Mogadishu presented Khalima with fresh worries. All her surviving relatives were out scouring the city for a burial plot for Umar, she said, but their chances of finding one were slim. A doctor listening in said there was no more spare land. 'The refugees even built a camp over the hospital graveyard,' she said. 'We had to block all the gates to stop them coming in and camping here. They're still climbing over the walls.'

The new restrictions meant Khalima had had to leave her other five children at the gates. We stood there in silence for a moment, sweating and swaying in the heat. The doctor feared being overrun by the starving and homeless. Khalima was worried about leaving her children alone in a strange city of war and famine. I was wondering about Mogadishu's future. How could a city built over the bones of its people ever let go of its past? Clumsily, I asked Khalima how she felt. She didn't reply and, thinking she hadn't heard, I began to repeat myself when she interrupted.

'I don't have any grief,' she said. She was quiet for a moment. 'So many people are dying. I don't know where we're all going to live. I am trying to find a grave.'

Umar died while Khalima was talking. He hadn't moved for a while, and as Khalima wrestled with my questions, a nurse checked on the boy, then motioned to a male orderly. Khalima fell silent. The orderly picked up a worn orange and yellow cloth from the end of the bed and drew it over Umar's body. I looked over at Khalima and it was true: she had no grief.

The orderly picked up Umar's body. Khalima, Dominic and I followed the two of them downstairs and out into the grounds. In a corner was a small, whitewashed building, its walls splashed with rocket grenade bursts, its windows chiselled back to the brick by gunfire. Inside were a marble slab and two plastic buckets of water.

The orderly gently laid Umar down and, working systematically with a second man, unwrapped each part of his body, doused it with water, rubbed it, then re-covered it. The washing was meticulous. When the shroud became creased, the two men would straighten it with a smart tug. And as the thin wrap became steadily wetter and more transparent, the boy's silhouette was revealed: a pair of bone-thin feet attached to wader-bird legs, a waist as wide as my forearm, a torso the size of my palm, arms as thick as two of my fingers, all of it neatly concertinaed under his perfectly round head like the legs of a folding chair. How could there be no room in the city for *this*?

I ducked outside for some air. In the distance I could hear gun-fire. Bashir's men had set up a perimeter around the small morgue. Just over the hospital wall, I could hear children reciting verses of the Qur'an. A camp school, I guessed.

There was another sound, a monotone hum coming from above. I looked up, shielding my eyes from the sun. One of Bashir's gunmen saw me searching and walked over. Shouldering his gun and sticking his arm over my shoulder, he pointed up at a gap in the clouds to a tiny, slow-moving black dot.

'Predator drone,' he said.

Dominic and I spent most of the day in the wards at Banadir, and returned twice more on other days. I spoke to fathers, mothers, nurses, doctors, managers, orderlies, gravediggers and soldiers. No one had seen dying like it, not even at the height of the war. A Turkish doctor politely parried my questions then, when I remarked on what seemed to be a total absence of Western aid groups, exploded with rage at how the UN was stockpiling thousands of tons of food in giant warehouses at the port but, for reasons no one could understand, wasn't releasing any of it.

We spent hours in the tiny first-floor paediatric ward where we had met Khalima. The seven beds it contained seemed too few until, one day, the children began to die all at once: first one boy on a bed to our left, then a minute later another on our right, then a few minutes after that an older boy by the door. The room was ample, we realized. It was never long before a bed was free.

This, the dying, was what we had come to see. Still, how to be, surrounded by so much of it? I couldn't shake the thought of how, in that small ward, we must be sucking in the last breaths of the children dying around us. What strange last visions were we giving them in return, two white men with notebooks and cameras? At night, Dominic would flick back and forth over a set of shots of a boy he had watched die, searching for the moment. Had he distracted the boy's mother? Had I?

We didn't need to keep going back. I had scores of testimonies and Dominic had hundreds of pictures. But if we kept going, I thought, we might fix in ourselves the feeling of being there. I wanted the bruises to last, to remind me of a question I could ask on behalf of the dying and the dead. If famine was man-made, as all the experts said, then who, specifically, had made Somalia's?

Like every foreigner who travels to Africa, I arrived on the continent with some ready-made ideas of it. There would be famine, I supposed, and dictators and corruption. But thinking back now, I realize it was the war to which I was looking forward the most.

For many journalists of my generation, a few minutes on the morning of 11 September 2001 transformed a detached interest in war into a working life of it. Still, it was a choice, and my reasons for going to war were no better than most: an adolescent desire to experience the extreme; later, an appreciation for the clarity of combat, the way that, while it lasts, it can tidy the mind. Like a lot of reporters who cover conflict, I came to subscribe to a stubborn, circular argument: that all war is significant and important and must be covered – because it is war and people are dying. By that maxim, almost any war will do and on Boxing Day 2006, three weeks after I arrived in Africa, Ethiopia invaded Somalia. I was in Mogadishu in a week.

Ethiopia had invaded to overthrow a newly formed Islamist government, the Islamic Courts Union. Projecting power through its militia, al-Shabab ('The Youth'), the Islamic Courts had emerged as a pious and violent alternative to the destructive anarchy of Mogadishu's warlords. Finding out exactly what went on inside Ethiopia's invasion would take me back to Somalia more times than to any other country in Africa.

Even from the start, Mogadishu made all my other wars feel like mere preparation. Sixteen years of clan fighting had left every wall holed by a thousand bullets. Whole crescents of stucco villas spilled their stone guts into the street. The ash from a thousand fires and a million ruins coated the city with a grey, funereal dust. The roads were subsumed under two decades of compacted debris that had been shaped into rolling waves by the wind. As you made your way through the city streets, you rose and fell like a small boat on a big sea.

The destruction was so complete that life itself had become incongruous. In this monochrome, tropical Dresden, the mere colour of it – an overgrown pink bougainvillea, the turquoise of the sea, a scarlet headscarf half buried under rubble – was a shock. The act of living, too, took on strange forms. In the hungry years, 250,000 refugees would huddle in the city centre under egg-shaped pods of brushwood and plastic tied together with string. Inside the skeleton of the seafront Uruba Hotel, Ethiopian soldiers ate *tef* in shabby green tents jammed under chipped corniced ceilings. An hour's drive to the west of the city I once came across a riverfront palace belonging to a long-departed Arab prince where, in a walled garden of date palms and mango trees, the prince's staff were still caring for a lone, elderly pet ostrich.

The devastation climaxed in Mogadishu's centre. Just back from the seafront, a worn and scarred Romanesque arch announced the city in Latin to an empty harbour. Beyond it was Mogadishu's central square, now filled with great slabs of broken walls and piles of grey rubble. On one side, tottering twin towers framed the front of an Italianate cathedral whose centrepiece, a huge daisy-petal window, somehow survived intact. But walk through the wide wooden doors beneath and this grandeur was exposed as a façade. The great hall behind had been blasted back to its buttresses and now resembled a monstrous grey ribcage.

In time, I began to recognize the feeling of the long, slow descent into Mogadishu as something like falling. Nothing you could do but watch those scorched flatlands, with all their war and white heat, come up at you. But if setting out for Somalia was to step out into the abyss, Yusuf Bashir was the one who caught us. Short, slim, with a boyish face, dark glasses and never without three or four phones, Bashir offered an all-in service for US $300–$1,200 a day, depending on how well you knew him and how well he knew your finances. His deal included three meals a day and a room at his hotel, the Peace Hotel, with a bed, fan, power, wifi, a shared shower and Al-Jazeera on TV. Bashir liked to spoil his guests. The final dinner on a trip was often a platter of tiny lobsters. One night, for a French correspondent's birthday, Bashir produced a small chocolate cake decorated with five Kalashnikov rounds standing up like tiny missiles in the icing.

Control of Mogadishu was fluid. Parts of the city changed hands between clans and Islamist militias almost every week. The centre, continually captured but never held, was a no-man's-land. Freelance gunmen roamed, looking for something to steal or kill. Bashir had strict rules for moving around. You needed two cars: a pick-up in front filled with gunmen, then a second closed cab behind in which you travelled flanked on all sides by more guards. You wore a flak vest. You drove fast. You varied your routes. You might make vague arrangements for an interview but you were never specific, even for a president. You didn't crowd other cars, particularly ones carrying their own gunmen. Outside the car, you minimized your exposure, never stopping for more than 20 minutes. The strategy was to show yourself as little as possible and, when you had to, to look like too much trouble for anyone to want to fuck with. Bashir's guys had the look – the way they fanned out, the way they extended their forefingers above their trigger guards, the way they never smiled – and in all the years Bashir had been operating, no one ever had.

Mindful of other journalist hotels that had collapsed when reporters staying there were kidnapped or assassinated, Bashir maintained a spotless safety record. He would ask whom you wanted to see and where you wanted to go – though never why – then hit the phones, assessing security, planning routes, fixing appointments. His need for the latest information was urgent and constant. Bashir continued his research en route, juggling his many phones and a two-way radio over the steering wheel. If he couldn't get fresh information on a neighbourhood, he wouldn't take you. But once he had it, he could plan around almost anything. When the Islamists of al-Shabab counter-attacked and took most of the city in 2008, confining the Ethiopians, African Union peacekeepers and official government to a thin strip next to the airport, Bashir piled his staff, beds, tables, chairs, TVs, routers, cutlery, crockery and mosquito nets into a fleet of pick-ups, drove them across town through the rivers of refugees and opened up the Peace Guesthouse in a large villa inside the new security cordon that he'd identified months before. The message to his clients: Bashir's business, the business of keeping them alive, could operate even through an al-Qaeda onslaught. Here was a man with a plan, and also a Plan B.

But there were calm days, too. Sometimes Bashir took me sight-seeing in the city centre. A quick scramble up the wrecked central staircase of the Uruba Hotel to catch a view of the Ottoman castle on an adjoining headland. A short walk down an old Arab merchant street, past crenellated mud walls and heavy carved doors. A few snatched minutes inspecting the rubble inside the cathedral before Bashir urgently beckoned me back to the car.

For years I wondered why I loved Mogadishu's ruins so, guiltily worrying I took a grubby thrill from death and desolation. This was wild war, the most intense I had ever seen. But eventually I also came to understand it as craftsmanship. The tools – Kalashnikovs, RPGs, .50 cals mounted on pick-ups – may have been unconventional. But as every street was pummelled, then every house, then every wall and every brick, the city revealed itself as the canvas for the most painstaking work.

The Somali famine of 2011 was not my first in Africa. Even as Africa's economies took off in the new millennium, every year Africans still starved to death somewhere on the continent. One famine in particular, in the valleys of southern Ethiopia in 2008, had stayed with me. More than six million people had been going hungry and I'd watched the babies die then, too. But long after I'd forgotten their names and mixed up their faces, until I wasn't even sure whether I was remembering the living or the dead, I could recall the fields. The disaster played out in lush valleys swollen with grey-green *tef* planted in rich chocolate soil. The weather was cold and wet and the skies full of black rain clouds that burst several times a day. Moving around, our biggest obstacle had been mud. I couldn't make sense of it. So before I set out for another famine, I stopped for several days in Nairobi, the aid worker capital of Africa, to gather opinions on why people might starve to death even when food and water and lush farmland were all around.

Some said the simplicity of African farms was partly to blame. If American farmers could get through a bad year without starving, why couldn't Africans? The answer, said the aid workers, was that Africans' cheaper seeds, lack of fertilizer, rudimentary equipment and small scale made them less productive. They never grew enough.

But that didn't explain the fertile, unharvested fields. Or why, a quarter-century and hundreds of billions of dollars after Live Aid, Africans were still starving. If aid workers knew how famines began and how to prevent them, and if they had spent all that time and money trying to do it, why hadn't they succeeded?

Several aid workers confessed that while they knew the cure, they mostly only treated the symptom. One problem was the compassion on which aid was founded. Aid campaigns skilfully stoked public sympathy to attract donations. But asking for an emotional response was also to invite an irrational one. While the long-term solution to famine was investing in more productive farming – sending new seeds and tractors and building irrigation systems – donors presented with pictures of starving children insisted on feeding the babies; then, once the photographs stopped, they forgot all about the farming. Aid workers owed their jobs to kindness but it restricted them too. 'It's all just Band Aids,' said one relief worker.

Foreign food shipments also explained the fallow fields in Ethiopia. Because food aid was handed out for free, it killed the market for Africa's commercial farmers, who lost any incentive to farm. No farming then created more hungry people the next year. In that sense, food aid was addictive. The more the aid workers shipped, the more they had to.

Was it possible this continual disaster management had become a business in itself? Could aid workers' laudable desire to be useful in a crisis have suppressed, even subconsciously, their motivation to end it? Did the sheer size of the aid industry institutionalize emergency? Some thought so. At the time of the Somali famine, journalists and aid workers were passing round an essay by the British Africa scholar Stephen Ellis, *Season of Rains*, in which he wrote that aid, originally conceived as temporary emergency assistance, 'has actually turned into a way of life. Tens of thousands of Westerners, ranging from sandal-wearing volunteers through to the highly paid consultants found in five-star hotels, would have to look for a new line of work if Africa stopped needing aid. They collectively constitute a key lobby in Western relations with Africa and are the lineal descendants of the merchants and missionaries who influenced British policy in the nineteenth century.'

US emergency aid, in particular, was as much about the American economy as delivering food to the starving. US law required that nearly all the $2 billion the US spent annually on food aid be bought from American farmers, processed by American agribusiness and freighted by American shippers. This was commerce masquerading as charity. Worse, in an emergency where every dollar and day counted, food transported halfway around the world could take up to four months to arrive and was several times more expensive than buying locally.

Most aid workers I met were reasonable, well intentioned and driven. They knew these conundrums only too well but accepted their flawed system as the only system there was. Even if they rarely addressed the underlying causes, they were good at treating the symptoms.

So it was striking how uneasy many seemed to be about Somalia. There, they confessed, they were doing a terrible job even at handing out food. Quite how awful became fully apparent two years later in April 2013 when a UN inquiry found 258,000 Somalis had died over the 18 months of the famine. What's more, the disaster had been no surprise. Aid workers had known it was coming for a year. One senior Unicef manager sounded genuinely distraught. 'We are trying to work out how we ended up here, what we did wrong,' he said.

This is what we did wrong.

The night before I flew into Mogadishu I met an Australian aid worker, Tony Burns, in an empty Nairobi bar. Unusually for a foreign aid worker, Tony had eschewed the big Western agencies in favour of working for a small Somali aid group called SAACID. Chubby, sloppily dressed and grey-haired, he had the look of a man long ago disabused of his ideals. I tried to put him at ease by repeating some of what I'd heard about aid's shortcomings. Aid had grown from benevolence into a global business and that had introduced some contradictions. One of the worst was food aid, whose continued existence seemed to depend on keeping African farmers out of business.

Tony grunted. 'The food aid business *is* a business,' he said. But Tony spoke without animation, like a man repeating self-evident truths. He mentioned that day's news. After three years of block-by-block fighting in Mogadishu with Somalia's Western-funded government and their African Union protectors, al-Shabab's militants had abruptly pulled out of the city. Tony said many assumed that was good for relief. Al-Shabab had sometimes blocked aid and now, the thinking went, aid workers could once again deliver food across the city. They were wrong, said Tony. The US aid block was still in place. 'US policy is no food or resources to southern Somalia,' he added. 'The famine is proof of their success.'

It was a startling statement. I'd never heard of a US aid block. Catching my expression, Tony explained that the US had designated al-Shabab a terrorist group in its war on terror. Over the years, it had had some success assassinating al-Shabab's leaders with drones, missiles and helicopter strikes. But al-Shabab retained the momentum and, looking for other ways to squeeze the group, the State Department hit upon tightening its money. Al-Shabab's funding from the Middle East had been disrupted by the Arab Spring in 2011. One of its last remaining sources of funds was aid, which it blocked on some occasions but on others taxed and even stole. The argument could be made that foreign aid was a form of support to a designated terrorist group.

The State Department had made that case, said Tony. It approached the big aid agencies and told them that under US anti-terrorism law it was obligated to end all US assistance to al-Shabab areas. 'Which, incidentally, is all southern Somalia,' said Tony. The agencies objected. As long ago as February 2010, the UN Humanitarian Co-ordinator for Somalia, Mark Bowden, had accused the US of fighting its war on terror with aid. 'We're no longer involved in a discussion about the practicalities of delivering humanitarian assistance with proper safeguards [but] where assistance can be provided on political grounds,' he said. In response, the State Department reminded the aid groups it was their biggest donor. Tony said the aid industry groups strenuously objected but eventually opted to comply.

Tony was saying that a US strategy of blocking aid to a few thousand al-Shabab fighters had denied emergency food to a few million starving Somalis. In that sense, the famine was deliberate. It was US strategy. And, on its narrow terms, it had succeeded. Al-Shabab had pulled out of Mogadishu. The problem was that the plan had worked too well. 'There's a famine, for Christ's sake!' said Tony. 'Hundreds of thousands of people are going to die. And it's going to happen. Nothing can stop it now. It's too late.'

We considered that prospect for a moment as we were, in a bar a few hundred kilometres to the south where the menu offered 50 different cocktails and cuisine from five continents. Tony finished his Coke and made to leave.

'Can I? . . .'

'Quote me,' he said, anticipating my question. 'The UN, the aid groups, the Americans – fuckers all hate me anyway.'

The lack of food being sent to southern Somalia *was* striking. The 2011 drought affected 12.4 million people across all East Africa. One long-term foreign-funded project to fight hunger in Africa that did exist was the Famine Early Warning Systems Network, which monitored regional weather and harvests. It predicted as early as September 2010 that a famine was coming that would affect the entire region. Ever since, aid groups had been stockpiling massive emergency food reserves in Ethiopia, Somaliland, Sudan, Uganda, Djibouti and Kenya. Everywhere, that was, except southern Somalia.

Once I was on the ground in Mogadishu, I found further confirmation of what Tony had said. Several Western aid agencies had mounted press and billboard campaigns in Europe and the US asking for money to feed starving Somalis – an effort that would eventually raise a total of $1.8 billion. But I saw none of those organizations in the city. I did see Islamic Relief and Tony's group SAACID, plus a small reconnaissance team from Médecins Sans Frontières and another from the Red Cross. Inside the security cordon at Mogadishu airport the handful of Western aid workers who had arrived were staying put, limiting themselves to passing out individual bags of pre-cooked rice to Somalis to take out into the city. It wasn't close to being enough. All the aid being distributed in Somalia could sustain just a fifth of the 2.8 million southern Somalis in need of food. And yet the World Food Programme (WFP) was sitting on thousands of tons of the stuff. One day a Danish television crew slipped into one of its Mogadishu warehouses and filmed quite how much: 20-metre-high mountains of grain sacks stretching the entire length of a warehouse 50 metres wide and 100 metres long, enough to feed the city for weeks.

Back at the Peace, I went online and discovered that not being present at the famine hadn't stopped some aid groups from claiming heroic success in fighting it. WFP had broadcast a fundraising Twitter message on 9 August proclaiming: 'Airlifts launched to bring enough high-energy biscuits to Horn of Africa to feed 1.6 million people.' An accompanying press release clarified, like an insurance policy's small print, that these biscuits would feed 1.6 million people *for a day* and that the 'airlifts' were actually between Nairobi and Mombasa, hundreds of kilometres to the south in a different country.

There was also a BBC interview with an Oxfam spokesman called Louis Belanger. Speaking from a refugee camp in Dadaab in northern Kenya, a day's drive south of Somalia, Belanger reassured the BBC audience: 'The aid will make a difference. All the aid agencies are here on the ground . . . We're looking at 12 million people all across the Horn of Africa who are in desperate need of food, water, shelter and medication. That's why we need the funding. That's why we need the help.' I had also received an Oxfam Twitter message claiming the group was 'now reaching 880,000 people in Somalia and doing all we can to scale up. Hoping to reach 1.4 million.'

I was in Somalia. I knew Oxfam was not. I called Oxfam's Nairobi number. Belanger answered. How could he say Oxfam was reaching nearly a million people in Somalia when it was not even present? I asked.

Belanger admitted that there were no Oxfam staff present at the famine. He added that 880,000 people was the total number of people benefiting from Oxfam-funded projects across all Somalia – projects carried out by other charities subcontracted by Oxfam, in areas of Somalia not affected by the famine. Oxfam was mostly talking about long-term projects, he said, such as building latrines and irrigation systems, rather than emergency famine relief. Those types of initiatives were, he noted, the long-term solution to famine.

I'd heard the same thing when I was in Nairobi, I said. But wasn't a famine the definition of a short-term emergency? Didn't the starving need food? And if Oxfam was pretending to be addressing the famine, then funnelling the money it raised to other projects in other areas, wasn't it making matters worse? 'We don't mean to raise false hope,' replied Belanger. 'Massive food distribution is just not what we do.'

By then the disastrous consequences of the US plan were becoming apparent even to Washington. In late July, the US government had announced a temporary easing of its aid ban. But given that it took months to transport food around the world, Washington's change of heart came too late. In addition, the aid agencies treated the Americans' softening as a chance not to restart aid but to push back at their most demanding donor, insisting the US not just relax but repeal the anti-terrorism laws that restricted assistance. In effect, the aid block continued.

From Mogadishu, I set up phone interviews with officials from two of Somalia's biggest donors, Britain and the US. I asked them whether they knew of a reason why the famine was only affecting territory held by al-Shabab, a group against which both countries were at war? The answers I received were a study in disingenuousness. Andrew Mitchell, Britain's Secretary of State for International Development, said: 'Britain has made clear that it's conflict above all that condemns people to poverty. It's a terrible thing, when there is enough food in the world, even in the region, that a child should go through the horror of starving to death.' A senior US State Department official, who was willing to speak only if I didn't use his name, agreed it was no coincidence that the famine was entirely in areas 'managed, or mismanaged, by al-Shabab'. He added: 'There is a definite correlation.'

If Western powers were coy about taking credit for the famine, their allies in the Transitional Federal Government of Somalia were not. As I stood one morning outside Villa Somalia, the Somali government's offices in Mogadishu, I watched an American sedan pull up and a slickly dressed man in pressed slacks and green aviator sunglasses get out and enter the building. When he re-emerged, I introduced myself and we exchanged cards. The visitor asked me not to use his name but described himself as ethnic Somali and a Canadian citizen with some military experience. He had returned to the land of his birth in the hope that he might be of some use to the transitional government. I asked whether he thought famine relief had security implications.

'Some guys are saying: "Many people are dying. We should let the food in,"' he said. 'Personally I don't think we should be sending any food into those areas. We know al-Shabab will steal it and sell it. That's how they regroup.'

Soon I was called inside for my meeting with the Minister for Presidential Affairs, Abas Moalim Nur. The Minister was candid about the strategic benefits of withholding food aid. 'This famine is helping us,' he said. 'Al-Shabab is becoming weaker. They have problems inside [their group].' And if the famine was sapping al-Shabab, it was boosting the government. 'People know that the only place they can get food is a government place. I think in a few months, we can control all Somalia.'

Later that day Bashir drove three Spanish journalists, Dominic and me to Mogadishu's commercial heart, Bakara Market. Eighteen years before, Bakara had been the setting for a battle known as 'Black Hawk Down', in which 1,000 Somalis and 18 US Special Forces and Rangers were killed. Bakara was Somalia's biggest food bazaar, exporting camels and mangoes to the Middle East right through the war, and with al-Shabab's departure, any revival in Somalia's fortunes would be measured first in the market.

In the event, we were premature. None of Bakara's shopkeepers had returned. I wandered the streets. Dominic shot some pictures of wrecked buildings and the spidery tangles of downed power lines. Then we turned a corner and, suddenly, driving towards us was a Land Cruiser with smoked windows and a fur rug on the dashboard. The car stopped and out stepped the colossal figure of Inda'ade ('White Eyes'), more formally known as General Yusuf Mohammed Siad, Somalia's most notorious warlord.

Formerly al-Shabab's main commander, Inda'ade had switched sides a few months earlier to become Minister of Defence in the transitional government. Though I'd known of Inda'ade for years, it was the first time I'd met him. His size impressed me more than his eyes. He was tall, perhaps 6ft 4ins, with a cocked military beret accentuating his height. He was almost as wide, his belly surfing out over his trousers, pegged in by a green military shirt the size of a tablecloth, decorated with red and gold epaulettes. As Inda'ade planted his boots on the cracked pavement, his guards used their guns to jostle Dominic, the three Spaniards and me into a five-man crowd. A press conference, I realized.

Apparently feeling the need to justify his defection, Inda'ade explained he'd left al-Shabab because of their infighting. Also, they were bad Muslims. And it was their apostate behaviour that, in the divine way of things, had caused them to lose Mogadishu and would soon lead to their extermination. 'When I saw these guys didn't follow the Qur'an, I changed,' said Inda'ade. 'I know them well. And, *inshallah*, now we will finish every last one of them.'

Observing protocol, I held up my notepad and waited for Inda'ade to nod his assent. Why were the US and the Somali government blocking food aid to millions of starving Somalis? I asked.

Inda'ade replied there was a danger that al-Shabab would steal the food. His priority was killing them. The famine made his job easier. 'Right now, they have nothing and they cannot fight.' Only once they were all dead would food be allowed in.

'Is that the strategy?' I asked. 'To starve al-Shabab into defeat?'

'They used to have money,' said Inda'ade. 'Then they ran out and turned on the public. And when people run out of things, and they are left empty-handed, that's when they cannot fight and they can only run away from us.'

'But what about the other people who are also dying? The millions of ordinary Somalis also starving?'

Only now did Inda'ade catch my drift. 'Bakara Market is the biggest market in the whole of Africa and the most beautiful,' he smiled. 'Now what can you see? Utter devastation. Will the people who own this place let al-Shabab back in? No. Never. Their popularity is zero.'

And with a wave, Inda'ade stepped back into his Land Cruiser and drove away, the car bumping sharply over fallen telegraph poles as it made its way down the street.

Several days later, I was granted five minutes with Prime Minister Abdiweli Mohamed Ali at Villa Somalia. With me was a journalist from a Chinese state broadcaster. The Chinese reporter asked to have his picture taken with Ali. Ali beamed, hugged the reporter and talked about how much he loved China. I felt we were in danger of straying off-topic.

'Prime Minister, can we talk about the famine?' I interjected.

The Prime Minister disengaged himself and sat down. 'As you know, we are facing the worst drought for 60 years,' he replied. 'At least 2.8 million people are at risk of starvation. This is a calamity. This is a disaster. We have to help our people.'

The West had responded to Somalia's appeal for help, he added. So had Turkey and the Gulf countries. The aid agencies were trying their best. Then, without prompting, the Prime Minister changed tack. 'The more they are weak, the more we expand our reach. There is an opportunity in this situation to expand our reach.'

I looked up at the Prime Minister. 'The famine is an opportunity?'

The Prime Minister nodded. 'Every challenge comes with an opportunity,' he said.

Some think Africans starve the same way they think Russians drink, Arabs argue and Italians sing. The Somali famine took one of our most established images of Africa, the starving baby saved by Western charity, and inverted it. This wasn't about African helplessness prompting Western beneficence. It was Western ruthlessness prompting African annihilation. In pursuit of 3,000 guerrillas, the US and their Somali allies, with the reluctant complicity of Western aid agencies, had tipped close to three million Africans into starvation. In lives lost since World War II, it was a war crime that ranked behind only the genocides in Cambodia and Rwanda. But it was the perfidy of it, how assistance was transformed from charity into a weapon, which made it unique. Famine did not inevitably follow drought. So in the summer of 2011, a small group of foreigners and Somalis made sure it did.

The Somali famine showed Africa as a place of war, dictatorship, corruption and starvation – but for reasons entirely different from the ones we imagined. And in the way it upset our ideas of Africa and of ourselves, it was a précis of a continental story: how a changing Africa is overturning some of our most cherished perceptions.

After an eternity when disease and slavery kept Africa a vast and empty land, Africa is now becoming a vast and crowded one, where those great engines of human progress – private property, communication and cities – are becoming the norm. As a result, over the next decade and a half, hundreds of millions of Africans will pull themselves out of poverty. Africa's annual economic growth has been double the world average since 2003, with some countries growing 20 per cent or more in a year. In most years, Africa accounts for half or more of the world's 10 fastest-growing economies. If Africa sticks to that path, and there is little reason to doubt it will, the proportion of Africans defined as absolutely poor will fall from more than a half in 1990 to a quarter by 2030. By 2050, a typical African country like Zambia can reasonably expect to be, at worst, Poland and, at best, South Korea.

This transformation is bringing an end to poverty within sight. Its political and spiritual implications are just as profound. Half a century after Africans won their formal liberation, they are now winning the substance of it – and that will change humanity. It will bring closer the day when all human beings really are created equal. It will erase any lingering evidential foundation for racism: the belief that if attainment varies with race, it is no accident. Since Africa's new narrative will no longer be about weakness but resourcefulness, it should kill off for ever the notion that development is something rich people in rich countries do to poor people in poor countries through aid.

Massive social transformation is, of course, massively socially disruptive. In Africa, the inherent unevenness of development is creating a singular inequality that compresses all the stages of human progress into the same place and time. At the beginning of the twenty-first century, a naked pygmy hunter can be hunting a wild pig in a forest with a spear while, six miles overhead, an African billionaire crosses the continent in his private jet. Such contradictions raise essential questions of identity about who or what is African that, if mishandled, can stoke division, resentment and conflict.

Outsiders find this new Africa especially puzzling. Many still see the continent as one thing: either Africa Rising or a land of babies with flies in their eyes. But Africa today is a billion things, past and present, all at once. Old African tropes like autocracy and tribalism are mixed in with new ones like cashless economies and solar power. To lions, refugees and sunsets, now add sushi, billion-dollar banks and the world's biggest telescope.

Above all, a changing Africa challenges its old ruling order, a part of which is international aid. What originated as a compassionate impulse is today a giant global industry of unmatched institutional strength and reach. It comprises the UN, the World Bank, the International Monetary Fund, parts of the Pentagon and other foreign armies, hundreds of foreign aid departments, thousands of foreign embassies, tens of thousands of foreign aid agencies and more than 600,000 aid workers – who together make up a global trade worth an annual $134.8 billion. In Africa, where aid is valued at $57.1 billion a year, it is the biggest business on the continent, worth the same as the combined output from Africa's 20 poorest countries. Aid is, in effect, equal to close to half of Africa.

Inside the rich world, the debate surrounding aid is mostly dominated by arguments over how much. The rich assume Africa needs their help because they imagine Africans as helpless: sweet, poor folk with a fondness for drums and bright cloth but a sadly utilitarian attitude to killing wildlife and each other – all of which is thought to leave them as victims of, or accomplices to, disasters and despots. This is the foundation of the humanitarian imperative: helping those who can't help themselves. The question of whether aid can harm is rarely raised. As little thought is given to the paradox that haunts even the best aid: that by doing good, by finding a noble purpose in the lives of others, you can end up subtracting that purpose from those lives; that by trying to liberate others, you may diminish them.

An emerging Africa challenges such complacent conceits. Money gives ordinary Africans the ambition, authority and possibility to reclaim their freedom from those foreign aid workers who have supplanted them or made their assistance dependent on a long list

of conditions: take loans; pay debts; privatize industries; use con-
traceptives; celebrate women, children, wildlife or sexual diversity.
In the same way, Africans' rising autonomy means clawing it back
from African powers, such as the 'liberation leaders' who promised
Africans a new dawn only to set about looting their country and
suppressing their own people. Or fighting back against the continent's resurgent *jihadi* groups, who claim to be guiding Africans
towards a peaceful and prosperous future even as they bomb and
behead their fellow men.

What links these three ruling groups – aid workers, despots
and *jihadis* – is arrogance and hypocrisy. At their conferences
and workshops in Geneva and New York, aid workers note the
new hope in Africa, measure it against their press releases about
African need and conclude that reports about Africa's rise are
unhelpful. So it is that, even as Africa's economies have soared in
the new millennium, aid workers have quadrupled their funding
for Africa by claiming the place has never been worse. Likewise,
Africa's liberation heroes enjoy the continent's new wealth even
as they insist their people are children who need a father, while
liberation parties turn their countries into one-party states in the
name of freedom. Africa's *jihadis*, too, denounce Africa's modernization as a sin even as they broadcast their atrocities on YouTube
and earn billions from smuggling cocaine, and hail a new age of
spiritual harmony even as they open a new African battleground
in the global *jihad*.

This old Africa, a continent of aid, dictators and war, is one
with which you are likely familiar. There was even some truth to
it in the past. But the new Africa is a place swelling with an angry
assertion and pushing back at the false prophets who presume to
tell Africans who and how they are. Where once Africans fought
ruling powers, now they battle a ruling perception. Where once
they deferred, now they defy.

This great rupture is what I call the Rift. It is the story of how a
billion Africans will finally win their freedom.

*

On our last day in Mogadishu, Dominic and I found ourselves once more in Banadir Hospital. By now we had overstayed our welcome, certainly beyond all decency and maybe also beyond our ability to function. Still, the flight back to Nairobi wasn't for 24 hours and not working was unthinkable. So we went back to Banadir and I introduced myself to Ali Mohammed, a grey-haired, unshaven man standing next to a bed on which lay his four-year-old son, Yarow.

Ali's paper-thin cheeks were all sucked in and his fingers had the length and elegance of a pianist's. Yarow seemed almost dismembered by hunger, just a cranium, a rabbit's ribcage and spider's legs under a thin parchment of skin. I asked Ali how he and Yarow had come to this.

Ali considered me without expression. 'We had a farm in Baidoa,' he began, gesturing to the west. 'I had 40 cows and 28 goats. I used to grow olives for olive oil. And maize. And chickpeas, which I dried for *garbanzo*. There was plenty to go around.' For a moment Ali seemed transported back to the good years. Then he frowned. 'Now it hasn't rained for 24 months,' he said. 'Everything is dead. I planted, but nothing came up. I had some *garbanzo* saved. But now it's been nine months without much food.'

A month before, when his goats were all gone and the last of his cows sank to its knees and died, Ali, his wife and their eight children left Baidoa and joined the trek to Mogadishu. The walk took a week. Once in the city, they'd found a space in one of the camps where a local clan leader sometimes handed out bags of rice. But now measles had taken one son, two-year-old Usman, and Ali's wife and three of their children were sick.

Baidoa was 320 kilometres away. The family's walk, 40 kilometres a day with no food and little water, was an almost superhuman achievement. I tried to ask Ali about the journey but he didn't want to discuss it. He wanted to talk about *why* the family had abandoned their home, about what had happened to Baidoa. How people had turned on each other.

'It became so chaotic,' replied Ali. 'I can barely describe it. We never even used to lock our homes. Neighbours would come together, sit together, slaughter cows for each other. But now there are so many thieves. There are . . . Well, now we can't even talk to each other.'

Yarow wailed weakly. Ali lifted the boy's head in one hand and, with the other, brought a cup of water to his lips. Yarow sipped, coughed, spat, then began shaking. Under him, a thin, clear dribble of piss filled a small crease in his plastic mattress. Ali put his hands under Yarow's arms and lifted him over a bucket. In it was a puddle of cloudy water and rice. Cholera. Ali held his son there, suspended over the bucket as Yarow, now quiet, stared past his father with giant dark eyes. 'Look at him,' demanded Ali. 'Tell me how I am to keep my family together?'

It wasn't an accusation or even a plea. Still, I had no answer for him. After a while, Ali cleared his throat and spoke again. 'This is my first time in Mogadishu,' he said. 'I've never even left Baidoa before. All we can do is beg. This is my problem. I don't have any authority here.'

I didn't tell Ali what I'd discovered about who caused the famine. I didn't think he'd care. Even if others had decided that he should starve, in the end he was still ruined, and that seemed enough for anyone.

Later, however, I thought Ali might have sensed the bigger picture. He described the withering of his family as the onset of chaos, a loss of order and a death of personal authority. He had been robbed of the ability to feed his children. That was a symptom of a deeper loss: of choice, of independence and of dignity. Once he had controlled his fate. Now he was its beggar. To live by the charity of others filled him not with warm gratitude but hot humiliation. Aid was actually a perfect misnomer. Charity disabled him.

At first his words had puzzled me. Talk of liberty and personal sovereignty was not what I expected from a father caring for his dying son. But now, when I look back on my years in Africa, I realize I have been hearing the same chorus everywhere. Whatever the story, everyone kept coming back to freedom. What Ali was telling me, what Africa kept returning me to, was the story of the continent as it had been for centuries: the theft of freedom and the fight to regain it. Surviving and living are two different things, Ali was saying. Surviving is just the alternative to dying. But truly to live, you have to believe you can create your own future. You have to be free.

I wrote about the famine's real causes. But my report was drowned in a flood of more familiar narratives: aid campaigns for starving Somali babies and beautifully written newspaper trage-dies of African poverty, hopelessness and inevitable death.

It was proof, if nothing else, that this was not our story. We got it wrong. Years later, a few aid workers began to change their accounts. UN humanitarian co-ordinator Philippe Lazzarini said: 'We should have done more. These deaths could and should have been prevented. People paid with their lives.' Oxfam's Somalia chief went further, writing in the *New York Times* that the deaths of 260,000 Somalis 'should weigh heavily on the conscience of Americans' since 'US government counter-terrorism sanctions effectively prevented many humanitarian agencies from providing aid in the hardest-hit areas'.

Late and incomplete, these partial confessions went unnoticed, and the big questions were left unanswered. How had we come to this? How could famine relief workers help make a famine? How was it possible that all our fine principles, our good intentions, our compulsion to act and all the centuries of progress and righteous-ness we built with them – how had these things killed a quarter of a million people in Africa?

TWO

GENESIS

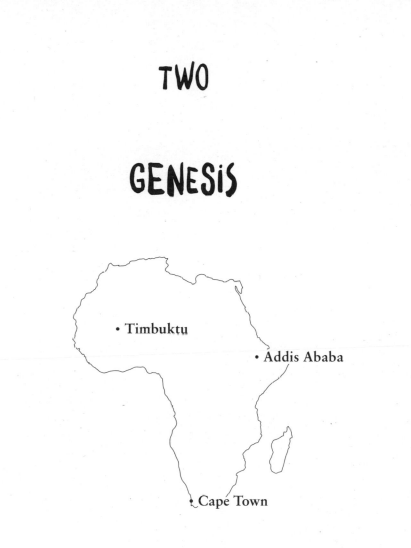

Africa is a continent created on a different scale. It is four times the size of Australia, three times that of Europe and more than twice Latin America, or India and China put together. A single African jungle, in the Congo, covers twice the area of Western Europe and a single African desert, the Sahara, is the size of the United States. Between the Sahara and the Cape of Good Hope are 49 countries, a quarter of those on earth.

I flew a million kilometres inside Africa, enough to go to the moon and back. Mostly I flew nights. When I lived in Asia, there was enough neon to sightsee from 30,000 feet. But when the sun went down in Africa, it was as if you'd flown into a void. At first I'd scan for lights out of my window, believing clouds were blocking my view. Then, once, I did spot a few yellowy flickers, and around the same time I saw NASA's famous picture of Africa at night, and I understood. It might take 10 hours to fly across the world's biggest continent, but in the twenty-first century it was still possible to do so without seeing a single electric light.

In a crowded world, Africa's wide-open spaces are the secret of its appeal. Imagine an African scene and you'll almost certainly conjure up a landscape or animals, not a city or people. Africa's size is the reason millions of tourists travel to Africa every year to take a *safari* ('journey' in Swahili) in one of the last places on earth where the experience is still possible.

Size also explains Africa's great attraction to foreigners. As though pulled in by gravity, outsiders have long been drawn to all that land, gold, rubber, slaves, diamonds and elephants. This is partly what economists mean when they say Africa is 'cursed' by abundant resources. Even after half a millennium of plunder, Africa still possesses 42 per cent of the world's gold reserves, half its diamond production, 60 per cent of its unused arable land and 80 per cent of its platinum, while new discoveries suggest Mozambique has more gas than Libya and Somalia more oil than Kuwait.

But Africa's grand dimensions have also been its best defence against acquisitive foreigners. Europeans and Americans spent much of the nineteenth century taming their own nations under great lattices of steel and copper: railway networks, electricity grids and telegraph cabling and, later, roads and airports. A second, related task for white settlers in the Americas and Australia was exterminating the indigenous population.

The scale of Africa mostly defeated similar ambitions there. Even the insatiable Cecil Rhodes, who dreamed of laying a railroad from Cape Town to Cairo, only achieved a fifth of that distance by his death in 1902, barely reaching Victoria Falls. European colonists did slaughter millions in Belgian Congo and even manage two African genocides, in Namibia in 1904–9, when, in a foretelling of the Holocaust, German settlers drove tens of thousands of Herero into the desert to starve, then collected thousands of Nama in death camps where they died of hunger and exposure. But Africa's great bulk was able to absorb even such extreme inhumanity. By the time empire ended, Africans still dominated Africa and the Europeans had succeeded in penetrating little more than its edges. To this day, many of Africa's colonial-era capitals huddle on its coasts and the only practical ways to travel across the continent remain to fly over it or sail around it.

Space made Africa rich. It was the key to its splendour and the guardian of its freedom. But boundless space can also be its own kind of prison. Sometimes I'd slip away from southern Africa at sunset, fly north for thousands of kilometres, rocketing right on through until dawn, and still I'd land back in Africa. Size explained so much in Africa. And staring out into those endless nights, I began to wonder whether it might also account for its poverty.

Eight hundred kilometres to the east of Mogadishu in the heart of the Rift Valley is Ethiopia's Afar Depression. It was here in 1974 that a group of palaeontologists dug up the skeleton of a 3.2-million-year-old hominid. They named the fossil 'Lucy' after the Beatles' song 'Lucy in the Sky with Diamonds', which was playing in their camp at the time. Not far away, in 1992 another dig uncovered Ardi, Lucy's 4.4-million-year-old ancestor. In 2000 a third team discovered the six-million-year-old fossil of a bipedal hominid, the oldest ever found.

DNA studies of human evolution show that the dozen or so species of hominid followed a similar pattern of emergence. They evolved and matured in the Rift Valley in southern Ethiopia, northern Kenya and western Somalia. Then, starting about a million years ago, they left. Why such wanderlust? Today we would call it climate change and poor resource management. Six million years ago, when the first human walked out onto the plains of East Africa, the Afar Depression was watery grassland, bountiful in fruits and animals. But early humans hunted too well for their own good, eating large animals to extinction almost everywhere they went. If they were to survive, they had to live on the move, hunting and foraging as nomads.

Moving mostly worked as a survival strategy. But every now and then the rains would slacken and the land became drier and the animals left, forcing a longer migration. Around 125,000 years ago the droughts began to last for years, then generations, pushing the latest hominid genus, *homo sapiens sapiens*, out of the Rift and eventually out of Africa. Wherever we wandered, we took our appetite for big animals with us. That explains the lack of woolly mammoths, mastodons, sabre-tooth tigers, giant bears and ground sloths in Europe, Asia and the Americas today.

With their prey exhausted, some human tribes died out. Others journeyed on, mastering shipbuilding and sailing to faraway lands, the last of which, New Zealand, was settled only 750 years ago. But around 9000 BC, in at least seven separate instances around the world, groups of humans stopped moving altogether and, by domesticating animals and sowing crops, invented farming. By eliminating hunting and maximizing gathering, they found they could produce 10 times more food from the same amount of land. In places several groups settled together. In time, these settlements became the first towns, then the first cities.

Those early days of human development set patterns for millennia to come. From the start, the impulse to improve was often as much the result of a deteriorating environment as the fruit of ingenuity. Something of a paradox was how progress often went hand in hand with conflict. By exchanging animals and crops and skills such as milling and brewing and baking, we created the first markets. By rewarding the entrepreneur, our rudimentary economies laid the foundations of a society based on individual liberty and free will, where human beings sought advancement in co-operation with each other, but also in competition. Occasionally things turned nasty. Once in a while that meant war. But, whether collaborating in peacetime or pooling strength in war, people achieved their best results in groups. For much of the human race, 'city' and 'civilization' was coming to mean many of the same things.

Everywhere except Africa. The continent was just too big and its population too small for human beings to run out of space or animals. Two thousand years ago there may have been 40–50 million Africans. Two hundred years ago, that number had barely changed. By 1900, there were only 11 African cities with populations of more than 100,000 and the continent was home to a mere twentieth of humanity. Africa, where humankind originated and which accounted for a fifth of the world's land mass, was becoming an also-ran in the human race.

One reason for Africa's low population was its lethal collection of diseases like malaria and yellow fever, which dispatched Africans in their millions. Another was the resilience of its predators. Africans have wiped out just two of their 44 large mammal species, a type of buffalo and a species of cow, compared to Americans' extermination of 70 out of 103 and Australians' dispatch of all but one of their 16. A third cause of Africa's emptiness was colonialism. Europeans gave Africans a new range of deadly illnesses to which they had no immunity, such as cholera, smallpox and measles, and new ways to spread them, like railways and river steamers. And while slavery had long existed in Africa, from the fifteenth to the nineteenth centuries European and Arab slave traders introduced Africans to industrial bondage, forcing 25 million of them, a quarter of the total population at the time, into lives outside the continent.

Disease, carnivores, slavery and oppression conspired to create a vast, open land in which that great motor of progress, the city, emerged far later than in the rest of the world. Africans lived apart, the sheer ceaselessness of the land muffling them from much contact with the rest of humanity or even each other. To this day Africans are the most diverse race on earth, whether measured by DNA or by language, of which there are 2,110 on the continent.

Such a small population in such a large space gave those Africans who survived the dangers of their land almost limitless freedom to roam and hunt. Until the twentieth century, most Africans never changed, never settled in cities, because they had never had to. That explained the great blackness outside my window. I wasn't looking out at nothing. I was passing over a million villages in which Africans rose with the day, slept with the night and hunted, fished and farmed without ever knowing much of the world or it much of them.

Serene symbiosis was Nature's great gift to Africans. The forest and the savannah provided for them so amply there was never a need to do things differently. But Africans' unchanging existence was also their great curse. Lacking the density that would place human minds and energy in close proximity, Africans forged no great advances in medicine or transport, technology or science.

As time passed, to exist as a human being in Africa and to live as one in Europe or Asia came to denote two markedly different experiences. And as Europeans moved steadily down the path of development, from farmland enclosure to the Renaissance and on to the Industrial Revolution, they used their advances to build boats and guns to pursue a global campaign of conquest. Africans, with only spears and arrows, were no match for the new arrivals.

This divergence between Africa and Europe was, in some ways, an early Rift. It shaped European perceptions of Africa. Europeans even took Africans' unchanging existence as evidence that they had discovered primitive man.

But a survey of Africa's ancient kingdoms suggests that it wasn't that Europeans didn't find civilization in Africa but that they hadn't recognized it when they did. In the second millennium, there were around 200 African kingdoms and empires. Some of them were remarkably durable. The Luba Kingdom in Zambia and southern Congo, in which power was shared between the king, a council of nobles and gatherings of clan elders, lasted from 1585 to1889. The federalism of the Wolof Empire united Senegal and Gambia for more than 600 years, from 1350 to 1890. Similarly the Kingdom of Kongo, Luba's western neighbour in Angola and southern Congo, which had a decentralized pyramid of power that included village chiefs, duchies and autonomous states, endured from 1390 to 1914. Though the Ashanti Empire was dissolved after two and a half centuries when Ghana became the first African country to break free of colonialism, its paved roads, national police forces and standing army of 200,000 – which saw off four British attempts at colonization in the nineteenth century – bear comparison with Imperial Rome.

Africa's empires distinguished themselves in other ways, too.

The discovery on an Australian beach of fourteenth-century coins minted in the Kilwa Sultanate on Africa's east coast suggests this was one African kingdom far ahead of the Europeans in exploration. The central citadel at Great Zimbabwe – an 11-metre-high dry-stone wall built in the thirteenth to fifteenth centuries – demonstrates impressive architectural achievement. Sculptures from the Benin Empire, which inspired what became Picasso's Cubism when they were exhibited in Paris in 1907, show exquisite artistry.

If Africans were as advanced as Europeans in many ways, the two continents differed crucially in character, however. Europe was a crowded place of finite limits, a collection of small countries with defined, if disputed, borders within which were known quantities of land and people. That environment led Europeans to develop ideas of private property, citizenship and even a fair distribution of wealth.

But endless Africa, which had no such confines, evolved differently. Kingdoms and empires rarely met and their edges were not so much borders as a gradual fading of influence. That meant citizenship was not a contract between individual and state like in Europe but a question of numerous overlapping loyalties to family, to village, then clan, region and empire, with culture, religion and language all commanding additional allegiances. Private land ownership wasn't necessary, so didn't exist. And if there was no limit on land or kingdom, there could be none on citizenry either. An African king could only guess at the number of his subjects. Not knowing how many citizens there were made a political system based on individual rights unworkable. Far more practical was a system based on collective rights. Property rights were commonly held, administered by a centralized monarchy or emperor. The centre ruled in communal fashion, not by drawing lines in the sand and counting citizens inside them but focusing on the whole, which remained a constant even if the numbers inside it varied. Outright autocracy was avoided by balancing the executive's powers with a second independent body: a council of elders, perhaps, or a separate clan structure or even a professional civil service.

This set of communal values is most commonly known today by its southern African name, *ubuntu*. If Europe's emerging individualism was summed up in the seventeenth century by René Descartes with *Cogito ergo sum*, 'I think, therefore I am', Africa's communalist counter was, 'I am because you are'. It is the idea that the individual is defined not in terms of himself or herself but by his or her membership of an inclusive community. I am because I belong, because I participate, because I share.

Ubuntu's record of stability compared well with Europe's turbulent history. More recently, its communalism has come to seem attractive next to the material excess of Western individualism. But *ubuntu* has its faults. Africa's long record of all-out tribal war shows what happens when one unified community meets another it doesn't like. Equally *ubuntu*'s suppression of individual freedom is profoundly illiberal. While the intention is consensual order, it is all too easy for benevolent dictatorships to slide into crude tyranny.

But the point is not to debate which – *ubuntu* or liberal democracy – is superior. Each was a product of its environment and each the more appropriate to it. And in that relativism is an important lesson about how different environments shape different outlooks on the world. Take the issue of dictatorship, which became such a phenomenon in Africa after independence. Perhaps remembering their own tyrants, Europeans tend to describe African dictatorships as a hollowing-out of democracy. But in an African context, dictatorship is perhaps better understood as a perversion of *ubuntu*, what happens when a leader crosses the fine line between creating consensus and enforcing it through absolutism. Take another perennial concern of Europeans in Africa: corruption. To any right-thinking European, corruption is abhorrent. But viewed through the lens of *ubuntu*, the corruption and nepotism of a government minister can seem like a social obligation, the conscientious *ubuntu* African sharing his good fortune with his clan.

These differing perspectives help explain European reactions on arriving in Africa. The explorers tended to see not an alternative system of government suited to the very different circumstances of Africa but an earlier, more savage stage of development akin to the Middle Ages. Here were a chief and his tribe living in the bush or forest. Here were nakedness and dancing. There was probably even a giant stewing pot in the corner.

This is how that early Rift would have begun to deepen. Different lives gave Africans and Europeans such different minds that they could look at the same object and see two entirely different things. Those contradictory visions have endured. A prominent example is the way Africans might regard as an imposition something Westerners intend as help. A more excruciating one is how the world might believe it was alleviating a famine in Somalia but never once ask who created it.

Our house in Cape Town sat among the vineyards of Constantia behind the most beautiful city centre of any on earth: a perfectly flat, near-vertical 900 metre-high block of granite and sandstone which burst out of the southern oceans 300 million years ago and which changed from grey to blue to black in the celestial light that bathed the bottom of the world. From Table Mountain, the city radiated out in easy scatterings across olive and tan slopes that plunged back into the sea, the South Atlantic to the north and west, the Indian Ocean to the south and east. South of the Table was the Cape Peninsula, a green and rocky spit which rose and fell like a serpent for 60 kilometres before diving 150 metres into the ocean at the Cape of Good Hope. This was the bottom of Africa; beyond was only Antarctica, and for the first European explorers five centuries ago it was the realm of monsters.

In time European settlers came to thank the restlessness of a place where two oceans met, in particular the way the seas gave Cape Town a near-perpetual sou'easter, which they called the Cape Doctor for its ability to blow disease out to sea. Even now the wind lends the city a sharp lucidity. The seawater is as clear and cold as ice, the summer sky is an infinite indigo and in winter rocks on the snowy Hex River Mountains 150 kilometres away are as sharp as a draughtsman's etching.

The setting makes for magnificent hiking, and to clear my head after Somalia I took to walking the paths behind the Table. For an hour or two, I could escape the day. Often that was best accomplished by disappearing into the past. One walk went through an abandoned mountain village once home to early Dutch settlers. A second looked down on Cecil Rhodes' old beach cottage, where the man who would have stolen a continent died at 48, exhausted by Africa's size. A third, on the flat back of the Table itself, threaded beneath the towering grey stone walls of the city's five reservoirs and the tin-roof shelters of the workers who built them. Sometimes I walked Cape Town's beaches in search of a Great White or a pod of dolphins or, in season, a Southern Right whale or an Orca nursing a newborn calf. On the coast were the ruins of a British World War II radio bunker and the ribs of a 110-year-old wrecked coal steamer and a plinth commemorating how, sometime in December 1488, Bartolomeu Dias, out of sight of land and blinded by a storm, unknowingly became the first European to round the Cape. North of my house was the botanical garden of Kirstenbosch where in 1660 Cape Town's founder, Jan van Riebeeck, planted a hedge of almond and bramble to mark his settlement's southern boundary and which today celebrates the *fynbos*, the Cape's unique heathland shrubs, of which there are more varieties – 9,000 – than all the plant species in North America.

Some of my favourite walks were through the vineyards behind my house. Dating from 1685, there was true grandeur there. Great avenues of oaks led to colossal Dutch longhouses around which were planted hundreds of agapanthuses, knee-high purple and white pom-poms bobbing in the wind. The architecture was uniform: thick, dark thatch hanging over sturdy white walls, stately windows protected by solid racing-green shutters. But there were indulgences too. One estate, Constantia Uitsig, featured a cricket oval sunk into the vines with a panoramic view of the peninsula. The upper gardens of the oldest estate, Groot Constantia, hid a 15-metre bath filled by a mountain stream that spurted from a stone bassoon held by the statue of a woodland sprite. Grapes grown on these slopes produce flinty, piercing whites and a floral dessert wine that, 200 years ago, was one of the most sought-after of its day. Crates were shipped to the royal courts of Europe. Napoleon, banished to the island of Saint Helena, a week's sail away out into the Atlantic and raging at his exile to 'this cursed rock', had 1,000 litres a year sent to him until his death in 1821.

Constantia's refined hedonism had a sobering edge, however. Overlooking several vineyards were large stucco arches on which hung the great bronze bells which once rang the changes in a farm slave's day. At the entrance to Klein Constantia stood the tomb of Sheikh Abdurahman Matebe Shah, last of the Malaccan sultans, exiled to the Cape by the Dutch in 1667 to live out his days among the profane vines, thousands of kilometres from his subjects. The graves in Groot Constantia's two cemeteries, meanwhile, recorded the colonial tussle over the Cape between the Dutch and the British. Names such as Clocte, Lourens and van Reenen dominated headstones dating from the seventeenth and eighteenth centuries. But by the mid nineteenth century these had given way to Dicksons and Joncses and Smiths. That change attested to the white-on-white annexation of southern Africa whose consequences would do so much to set the Afrikaner character. Between 1835 and 1846, thousands of Dutch settlers who refused to submit to the Union Jack or Britain's ban on slavery packed their women, children and possessions into wood-wheeled wagons and, in what became known as the Great Trek, pushed them out of the Cape to stake out a new life in an interior full of jagged mountains, desert wastes and Zulu *impis*. Two generations later, the antipathy between Dutch and English led to two wars. The Boers' lasting admiration for the stubborn audacity of the Great Trek also helped account for the way in which in 1948, just as the rest of the world was pulling back from white domination, the Afrikaners created an explicitly racist state.

To live in Cape Town was to live with the raw consequences of this history. English and Afrikaners still kept themselves largely apart, the former clustered around the city's southern winelands, the latter in newer suburbs to the north. Both also separated themselves from the non-white majority, which mostly lived inland on a 30-kilometre expanse of baking sandflats filled with tin shacks and social housing called the Cape Flats. Social standing in Cape Town was indicated by actual altitude. The further and lower you were down the mountain's slopes, the poorer and blacker you were likely to be. If you let slip your handbrake at the top of the highest streets in Cape Town, you could freewheel across one of the world's widest social divides in five minutes. It was these unmoving and bitter gradations that lay behind much of the city's social disintegration – the drugs, the gangs – and why, contrary to legend, Cape Town had a higher murder rate than the more integrated Johannesburg.

So it was a shock to discover, as I did out walking one day, that this deadly European history was blinding me to a much older African one. A sandy path near a summit looking out over False Bay led to a dry, soot-stained cave. A short walk away was another with a small entrance angled away from the wind leading to a chamber that had room for 30 or 40 people. Soon afterwards, on a beach, I came across some crumbled, waist-high middens of oyster shells and, rounding a rocky headland, a series of ancient stone-wall fish traps. My discoveries prompted a visit to the city's museums. There on display were rock drawings and stone hand-axes taken from other caves on South Africa's coast and, in a dusty case at the back of the national museum, the oldest evidence of *homo sapiens sapiens* ever discovered: a set of 117,000-year-old footprints, uncovered in mudflats two hours' drive north of the city.

Many South Africans claim the Cape was open country when van Riebeeck arrived in 1652. The truth could not have been more different. The Cape was not only inhabited, it had been so for longer than almost anywhere on earth. Cape Town's original inhabitants were San bushmen and three separate studies of their Y-chromosomes have found they have been there so long, and so separately, that they possess slightly different DNA to the rest of us. Nor were the San the Cape's only pre-European inhabitants. Around the fifth century AD they were joined by the Khoi, livestock farmers from the interior who brought with them sheep, goats and cattle. Sometimes the San fought the Khoi, sometimes the two tribes intermarried. But when the Europeans began to settle, the San and Khoi united to fight the incomers' attempts to enclose their cattle-grazing grounds, without which the Africans' social structures were quickly falling apart. By the eighteenth century those Africans who hadn't retreated north to the barren sanctuary of the Kalahari were working on European farms as labourers and slaves, where their owners, with a precision typical of the settlers, described their ethnicity as 'Khoisan'.

This wasn't just a case of history being written by the victors. The Cape's old African stories were so subtly recorded and blended so well with the landscape that reminders of the old ways had become easy to miss. You had to search for them on the walls of caves and cliff overhangs and low-tide beaches. On the other hand, you couldn't miss the Cape's European story. The Dutch and English transformed southern Africa's landscape. They built cities and ports and made thousands of little fenced kingdoms on the Highveld with enchanting whitewashed farmhouses at their centre.

The more familiar I became with the divide between the Africa of the cave and the Africa of the city, the more it seemed the European version of Africa's history was better known precisely because it was foreign. This was a tale about white settlers in a land of black nomads. It didn't fit. It stuck out. It was, perhaps, a distraction. So much had followed the Europeans' arrival in Africa. But even if you took all the vineyards and all the homesteads, all the slavery and all the wars, all the missionaries and charity rock concerts, next to a narrative that stretched over 100,000 years it was all just one noisy episode in a far longer existence.

Anyone in search of original Africa sooner or later finds themselves in Ethiopia. The birthplace of mankind and of one of humanity's oldest civilizations, Ethiopia is the one African country never colonized. High up in its shivery isolation in the mountainous northern Rift, Ethiopians celebrate their singularity with their own alphabet, their own religion and their own clock and calendar, by whose reckoning midday is 6 a.m. and the new millennium arrived on 12 September 2007.

The capital, Addis Ababa, is a modern metropolis in an old land, founded on the spot where the Empress Taitu discovered a hot spring in 1886. Its architecture is a compression of the city's short, unique life. Cobbled Victorian alleys lead past Italian restaurants recalling Ethiopia's brush with Mussolini in the 1930s. Parade squares dating from the Red Terror of the 1970s, when two million Ethiopians died in Mengistu Haile Mariam's orgy of Stalinist paranoia, are ringed by new office blocks clad in silver, gold and green-mirrored windows, built in the decade since 2003 when Ethiopia's economy has grown annually by 10 per cent or more.

Wandering the steep and slippery streets, I found other idiosyncrasies. Calling a neighbourhood 'Where the No. 22 Bus Turns Around' had a certain pragmatism. But only Addis' oddness seemed to explain why a leafy central district might be called 'Screaming in Vain' or an outlying suburb 'The Place of Crucifying Chickens'. The capital's musical tastes were just as eccentric. The rest of Africa loved hip-hop but Addis dug jazz, and on any evening of the week several jumping late-night clubs would fill up with goatee-stroking, weed-toking hipsters. I loved Addis for that, and for its intrigue. The combination of a Marxist government, a border with Somalia, a massive US embassy and the African Union's headquarters, plus a truly opulent Sheraton, had made the city a favourite for spooks. One day in a café just off Meskel Square I overheard a large Middle Eastern man in a well-tailored suit answer his mobile phone, laugh loudly, then boom: 'But, Ambassador! *Of course* I'll give the documents back.'

Addis revealed signs of Ethiopia's deep past. There were the striking similarities between the Amharic script and Hebrew and Armenian, two other early Christian tongues. There was also the veneration of Saint George. Wearing chain mail with a red cross on his chest and spearing a dragon from his horse, Saint George's image appeared on churches and schools as well as the team strip for Addis' Saint George football club and the label of the city's most popular beer, Saint George Premium Lager. In this Ethiopian version of the legend, England's patron saint is a black African and his dragon a Nile crocodile.

I became a regular at Addis' museums and second-hand book stalls. Exhibitions and out-of-print history books told the story of how some of the first human civilizations were the Kushite or Nubian Empire in Sudan, which existed 4,000 years ago, and the Land of Punt, later Aksum, later Abyssinia, which stretched across Eritrea, Ethiopia and Somalia, traded with Egypt as long ago as 2500 BC and shared a pottery style with ancient Greece. Ethiopians told a far more illustrious story of themselves than that found in any book. On an early visit, the Prime Minister's immaculately suited press aide, Bereket Simon, took me to dinner, and over dustbin lids of spongy *injera* laden with raw meat and piles of chilli and fenugreek he recited the Ethiopian emperors' lineage all the way back to Noah, a monologue that lasted three hours.

One of the greatest scions in this line was the Queen of Sheba, who ruled Ethiopia around 1000 BC. Sheba had a fleet of more than 70 ships and traded with Palestine, India and Greece. In due course, Sheba travelled to Jerusalem to stay with the Palestinian King Solomon, who converted her to Judaism and cured her of the ass's feet with which she had been plagued since stepping in dragon's blood as a child. In the Old Testament, the Bible affects a bashfulness on the question of whether Solomon and Sheba were lovers, rather lecherously referring to the 'royal gifts' the King gave the Queen. But soon afterwards Sheba had a son she named Ibn-al-Malik, or Menelik, and his return to Ethiopia is the basis for several claims of lost Jewish tribes in Africa. (Some of which Israel accepts. In the past 50 years, Israel has airlifted thousands of Ethiopians to resettle in their 'homeland'.)

Bereket said Menelik returned to Jerusalem as a young man, staying with his father, Solomon, for three years. When he returned to Ethiopia, he brought back with him the Ark of the Covenant, the gold-plated chest containing the Ten Commandments given to Moses on Mount Sinai and written on two tablets of stone. This he hid in the Church of Our Lady Saint Mary of Zion in the red-rock mountains of Aksum, where a priest guards it to this day. I examined Bereket. He was giving nothing away. I asked if the Ark was still there. 'People believe it is,' replied Bereket, carefully.

Menelik's descendants ruled Ethiopia for 3,000 years until 1974 through a succession of 237 kings. So venerable and divine is this line that it is often mixed in with legends of Eden and a Christian African king called Prester John, said to have been descended from one of the Magi and to have ruled over a Christian kingdom on the edge of paradise. Reverence for Ethiopia's emperors endures today, and not just in Ethiopia. In the Caribbean in the 1930s a new religion, Rastafarianism, sprang up among the descendants of African slaves who took the last Ethiopian Emperor, Haile Selassie, as their messiah.

Selassie's ancestry did not impress a group of Ethiopian army officers led by Mengistu, however. In 1974 he deposed Selassie, then the next year unleashed the Red Terror. Among the dead was Selassie, smothered with a pillow and buried under a lavatory in the palace grounds, from where his remains were recovered in 1992.

There are many flaws in this national narrative, not least several breaks in the Solomonic line. But the similarities between orthodox Jewish and Ethiopian culture leave little doubt that thousands of years ago, as two proximate powers, Ethiopia and Palestine shared culture, ideas and people. While Europe languished in its Dark and Middle Ages, Ethiopia was in its Enlightenment. At its height Aksum minted its own currency, developed its own script, erected obelisks bigger than any found in Egypt, traded with Rome, Persia, Arabia, China and India and maintained diplomatic outposts in Florence, Naples and Venice. Sometime in the fourth or fifth century AD, Aksum converted from Judaism to Christianity, making it the world's first ever Christian empire. In the twelfth and thirteenth centuries Aksum's emperors built dozens of the world's most remarkable churches at Lalibela and Tigray in northern Ethiopia, single pieces of stone, three floors high, carved straight down into the mountain rock.

The significance of Aksum was in how it undermined later European notions of superiority or of Europe as the hub of Christian civilization. The African Kingdom of Aksum was more sophisticated, more Christian, and far earlier, than any in Europe.

In the old story, God created Eden as a garden paradise fed by the headwaters of the Pishon, the Ghion, the Tigris and the Euphrates. In it he planted the Tree of Knowledge of Good and Evil, whose fruit he forbade Adam and Eve to eat. But a serpent persuaded Eve to disobey, she convinced Adam, and the pair lost their innocence, then their home. God cast them out into the lands east of Eden, where they founded the human race by having three sons, Cain, Abel and, after Cain killed Abel, Seth.

As an ancient account of our origins, the Fall of Man contains some geographic clues. The Pishon remains unidentified but the Tigris and the Euphrates are in Iraq and the Ghion, also known as the Blue Nile, is in Ethiopia, placing Eden somewhere in the upper Rift. As a parable about knowledge, however, the Fall is more enigmatic. It portrays learning as a sin, whose commission ushers in guilt, suspicion, fear and anger. Ignorance, on the other hand, it equates with a state of immaculate virtue. With bliss, in fact.

The longer I spent in Ethiopia, the more it seemed as though only the comforts of oblivion could explain how medieval Europeans had missed the civilizations that had grown up in the vast continent just 13 kilometres to Europe's south. Wandering the stalls in Addis' main market, Merkato, one day I came across an old and battered guidebook from the 1930s, which mentioned the first recorded foreign traveller to reach Aksum. Cosmas Indicopleustes was an Egyptian Christian monk from Alexandria who lived in the sixth century AD. He believed the world was flat and that heaven and earth were separate levels in an enormous celestial box, a theory he detailed with diagrams in his seminal work, *Christian Topography*. Cosmas' writing mixed excerpts from the Old Testament and outrageous self-regard with straightforward passages of travelogue and some surprisingly accurate orienteering. At one point he estimated the distance from Istanbul to southern Ethiopia at 9,600 kilometres, a miscalculation of a mere few hundred kilometres. In another passage, he described a white marble throne he saw on his visit to Aksum in AD 525. On it were carved sculptures of Hercules and Mercury and a description of all the conquests of the Ptolemaic Kingdom, which succeeded Alexander the Great in Egypt in 323 BC.

How far did Aksum's powers extend? Was the presence of a Ptolemaic throne in Ethiopia a clue to Aksum's reach or merely a lost piece of pharaonic furniture? Cosmas didn't care. He was more concerned with proving that the world ended at Ethiopia's southern edge and his travels, Cosmas crowed, proved him right. His simple-minded critics, he wrote, clung obstinately to the myth of a round world 'in preference to the truth and, in support of their vanity, advance conjectures, sophistries, and old wives' fables, no matter how false, inventing forsooth another zone further south . . . although no one has either seen or heard of such'. Clearly the world ended at Ethiopia, wrote Cosmas, 'for how could that be seen or heard of, that has never come within the ken of our senses?' The round-earthers should be exposed for the quacks they were, he concluded. 'The nonsense they babble cannot be accepted; for it is the jargon of mere novices in quibbling, and not of old adepts in that art.'

If the writings of a man who travelled the known earth and returned still believing it was flat teach us anything it is how easily perception overpowers reality. Another day I picked up a copy of the memoirs of a Portuguese priest, Francisco Alvares, who travelled to Ethiopia 1,000 years after Cosmas. More modest than his predecessor, he concluded a description of the churches of Lalibela in his book, *The Prester John of the Indies,* by saying that though he had seen wonders, he expected few Europeans to trust his accounts, convinced as they were of their own superiority. 'I weary of writing more about these buildings, because it seems to me that I shall not be believed if I write more,' wrote the priest, adding however that 'I swear by God, in Whose power I am, that all I have written is the truth.'

From the start, it seemed, Europe's relationship with Africa was defined by misunderstanding and, at times, wilful and arrogant presumption. Europeans knew next to nothing of Africa. On their maps, Europeans left blank spaces marked *Terra Incognita* south of the Mediterranean. Even after centuries of exploring Africa, they persisted in calling it the 'Dark Continent'. Most considered African poverty all the evidence they needed to conclude that Africans were inferior. On God's earth, there was Light and there was Dark and the blackamoor's salvation lay only in the white man's gift. Even as late as 1871, when German colonists 'discovered' the towering citadel of Great Zimbabwe, they concluded that the huge walls were evidence of Roman, Phoenician, Indian or Malay conquest, or even the remains of King Solomon's mines. The notion that Africans built such a magnificent capital never crossed their minds. Like Adam, Europeans preferred to live in a presumed paradise. And like Adam, when rude knowledge did intrude, they were immediately consumed by sin. In this case, greed.

*

In Africa sickness can fall as quickly as the night, and, arriving one overcast day in the Malian capital, Bamako, I caught a taxi to a downtown café, drank a glass of water and the sweat just poured out of me. I tried a couple of clinics but at each the diagnosis was vague and the treatment unfamiliar. When I felt my balance going, it seemed the best I could do was find a hotel and hole up. The fever took a week. Eventually it began to lift and, in need of a way to ease back into the world, I made a series of unsteady afternoon visits to the National Museum on a hill across the River Niger.

The museum related how one of Africa's greatest realms was the Mali Empire. It ruled much of West Africa between the thirteenth and seventeenth centuries with an army of 100,000 men, making it the second-biggest empire in the world after the Mongols. A federation of autonomous kingdoms, funded by three apparently bottomless gold mines and a lucrative trade in salt, Mali was con-structed as a bargain by whose terms the state delivered security in return for taxes collected and managed by a pyramid of vil-lage officials, county administrators, provincial representatives and imperial bureaucrats. At the top of this structure was the emperor, known as *mansa,* and a 29-member clan assembly called the *gbara.* While the authority of the empire was absolute, the power of in-dividual emperors was not. In AD 1275, when Malians discovered that their new Emperor, Mansa Khalifa, liked to amuse himself by firing arrows at passers-by from the palace roof, they killed him and a group of officials then held the throne in trust for 25 years until they were sure of a better replacement.

The *mansa* was at the apex of one of the richest, most expansive states on record. As it tends to, extraordinary success nurtured even wilder ambitions. We may never know whether Emperor Abubakari II succeeded in crossing the Atlantic from Africa to America in 1311, nearly two centuries before Christopher Columbus. But we know he tried twice, the second time disappearing after setting sail at the head of an armada of several thousand boats. Abubakari II's successor, Mansa Musa, told the Egyptian court about his cousin's voyages when he stayed in Cairo in 1324 en route to Mecca for the *hajj*. It was the Egyptians who passed these accounts on to the fourteenth-century Syrian scholar Ibn Fadl Allah al-Omari when he travelled to Cairo 12 years later.

As remarkable as this early odyssey was, al-Omari recounted that Musa's own travels made an even bigger impression. Passing through London a year later I caught another exhibition, on the *hajj* at the British Museum. This recounted how, a decade after Musa's stay in Cairo, the city was still buzzing with tales of his visit. Musa brought with him an entourage of no less than 8,000 servants – or as many as 60,000, according to some accounts – including soldiers, doctors, teachers, traditional *griot* storytellers and thousands of slave women in gowns of brocade and Yemeni silk to carry his equipment and furnishings. He also carried with him 15 tons of gold, loaded onto up to 100 camels. Mansa Musa, wrote al-Omari, 'flooded Cairo with his benefactions,' sending 'a load of gold' to the royal treasury and more to every courtier and royal office holder. So much gold did Mansa Musa spend or give away that the price of the metal plunged in Cairo's markets and 'has remained cheap till now'. Naturally, Cairo's traders did everything they could to relieve the West Africans of their wealth and soon Musa had spent all the gold he had with him.

It turned out that Musa had exhausted only his travel money. Contemporary estimates make him the richest man who ever lived, with a total wealth of $400 billion at today's prices. On his return to Mali two years later, Musa used more of his fortune to transform the city of Timbuktu into a centre of Islamic learning, building facilities that attracted scholars from across the world. These included a library of up to 700,000 manuscripts and a university which soon boasted 25,000 students studying mathematics, geography, history, physics, astronomy, chemistry, law and business, religion and philosophy. By the time he died in 1337, wrote al-Omari, Musa was 'the most powerful, the richest, the most fortunate, the most feared by his enemies and the most able to do good for those around him'.

Musa's legacy in Europe was less happy. In Islam's early years, Christians and Muslims saw each other for what they are: brothers in faith, with a God and saints in common. But their initial amity was quickly forgotten when Islam began to sweep Christianity away. Starting soon after Islam was founded in AD 652, and continuing for several centuries, Muslim soldiers advanced steadily across Europe, conquering parts of Spain, Italy and southern France. Even after Europe's Christian kings slowly pushed Muslim forces back in the second millennium, eventually ending Muslim rule in Europe in 1492, Christianity was still the lesser power, as the Ottoman capture of Constantinople and later Russia, Ukraine, the Balkans and much of eastern Europe underlined.

Under threat, Christians tightened ranks. Dissidence was not tolerated. From the twelfth century, the Inquisition in Spain, Portugal, southern France and northern Italy tortured suspected heretics. And if the Church used cruelty to keep its flock in line at home, it employed greed to encourage them to fight Muslims abroad. In 1095, Pope Urban II added a commercial incentive to Christian war against Muslims, instigating the first Crusade by granting *plenary indulgence* to thousands of European mercenaries. For attempting to restore Christian access to Jerusalem, the Pope would excuse all past sins – and, by implication, any sacking and pillaging of the Holy Lands the Crusaders undertook en route.

It was in that atmosphere, one in which Europe's Christian rulers were allowing expediency to corrupt all Christian principle, that news began filtering through to Christendom of a Muslim king in Africa of almost impossible wealth. Europe's reaction would set the tone for centuries of exploration to come.

In 1346, a large sail-and-oar galleass captained by Jaume Ferrer set sail from Majorca, headed south-west and, after clearing the

Straits of Gibraltar, tacked south. Ferrer is commemorated today by a statue in Majorca's capital, Palma. But very little is known about the man who inaugurated what Europeans came to call the Age of Discovery. He may have originally been a Catalan navigator called Joannis Ferne or a second-generation Genoese immigrant whose full Italian name was Giacomino Ferrar di Casa Maver. His identity might also have been assumed. His name, which translates into English as 'John Smith', feels almost designed for anonymity. Europe in the fourteenth century was a place of severe social restriction, but the high seas represented perfect freedom, and by sailing alone for unknown lands Ferrer identified himself, at the very least, as a maverick and adventurer and perhaps even a pirate.

If we have only the vaguest idea who Ferrer was, we know even less about how he fared. His only other mention in recorded history is 29 years later, in 1375, when he appeared on the Catalan Atlas drawn by the Jewish illustrator Abraham Cresques, also based in Majorca. Until then, Cape Bojador on the northern coast of the Western Sahara marked the southern limits of European knowledge. But in Cresques' map of the world – one of the first European atlases of its kind and by far the most detailed and accurate to date – he pictured Ferrer sitting in his galleass just off the Canary Islands, several hundred kilometres to the south. Whether Cresques knew his fellow Majorcan had reached West Africa or was merely speculating is not known. But Cresques did know why Ferrer had set out. He drew the mariner's boat at the mouth of a river of gold leading from the middle of the Sahara all the way to the Atlantic. At its source, sitting on his throne, was Mansa Musa, recognizable by his gold crown and sceptre and the fist-sized gold nugget in his hand.

Cresques was commissioned to produce his atlas by Prince John of Aragon as a gift to his cousin, Charles VI of France. For Europe's rulers 650 years ago, Africa and its riches had finally made it onto the map. The message was unequivocal. Africa was rich, and claiming its wealth would mean taking it from Muslims.

*

Ferrer's quest was a private venture. The cost of exploration more usually limited it to kings and nations. Initially the challenge of charting Africa fell to Portugal. Europe's foremost mariners, the Portuguese enjoyed an Atlantic coastline, were close to Africa, and in Henry the Navigator (1394–1460), third in line to the throne, they had the perfect leader.

Despite his moniker, Henry almost never sailed. But for most of his life, from the age of 21 until his death at 66, Henry was either planning a new expedition or awaiting his ships' return. The commercial objective of Henry's forays was to open up a sea passage to trade with Asia, with its silks and spices, and to those parts of Africa where gold and slaves were to be found.

Henry had a second mission. He was an ardent Christian, said by a court biographer to have emerged from the womb holding a cross, and as an adult he became governor of the Order of Christ, the successor to the Knights Templar. Henry's faith gave him a politico-religious zeal to bypass the Muslim world and its proprietorial trade routes, especially those controlled by the hated Ottoman Empire. And if relieving the Muslims of their monopoly on Asian trade meant killing a few of them as well, all the better.

In the event, Henry's methodical progress down the west coast of Africa gave him commercial, spiritual and military satisfaction. The capture of the trading port of Ceuta from the Moors in 1415 was a commercial boost for Portugal and a bloody score for Christianity against the Mohammedan. By 1444 Portuguese caravels had pushed far enough south to circumvent the Muslim trade routes across the Sahara and bring salt, gold and slaves direct to Europe. The first African slave market opened in Lisbon that same year. While Henry's court biographers stress his religious fervour over his commercial ambition, a more sober assessment is that the two more or less merged in his mind. Slavery, after all, was a form of conversion.

After Henry's death, the Portuguese continued pushing south. In 1488, Bartolomeu Dias finally rounded the southern tip of Africa, which he called the Cape of Storms, but his backer King Manuel, in a bit of rebranding to encourage co-investors, renamed the Cape of Good Hope. Dias' passage from the freezing waters of the southern Atlantic into the balmy currents of the Indian Ocean also put paid to attempts by a Genoese, Christopher Columbus, to secure Portuguese funding for a voyage to the East undertaken by sailing west. (Columbus did eventually persuade Spain to underwrite four trips. When he found land, he insisted on calling it the Indies.)

Dias' accomplishment made a sea spice route to Asia tantalizingly close. Exactly 150 years after Ferrer had first set out, the Portuguese ordered Vasco da Gama to complete what Ferrer had started. With crimson Crusader crosses on his sails, da Gama rounded the Cape of Good Hope in November 1497, spent Christmas off the south-eastern coast of South Africa – hence 'Natal', connoting the birth of Christ – then sailed up Africa's east coast to Kenya. There he found a pilot to take him to Calicut, India, where he arrived in May 1498 after a voyage that had lasted a total of 10 months.

Arabs, Asians, Africans and Latin Americans have long complained of the vanity of the term 'Age of Discovery'. The description suggests they barely existed, and anyway didn't matter, until they were noticed by Europeans. But even if we adopt an explicitly European view and accept that, for the sailors at least, these were voyages into the unknown, this was discovery of a most incurious kind.

Most of the early European explorers' diaries are composed largely of dry records of obstacles like winds, currents and hidden rocks to be negotiated in pursuit of material gain. The explorers expressed little interest in the inhabitants they came across beyond remarking on their primitive nakedness or assessing their usefulness as labour or sources of information. The latter they routinely extracted through torture. That the Portuguese expeditions were primarily conceived and executed as missions of mercantile and politico-religious acquisition is made clear by a 1449 document from King Alfonso V granting Henry a monopoly over all trade in the African Atlantic. The agreement made no mention of any high-minded ideals to discover the world or expand human knowledge. Instead, it seamlessly merges Mammon and God. 'He [Henry] has asked us to grant him the dues that belong to us on all merchandise and everything else that may be traded,' read the grant, 'because it is his intention to serve God and ourselves by working to bring it about that merchandise from the said lands reaches our kingdom.'

The biggest hurdle on the explorers' route to riches was Africa itself. While the Europeans were not averse to a little business en route, their true destination was always Asia. As da Gama proclaimed at his formal farewell to Portugal in July 1497: 'I, Vasco da Gama, [setting out] to discover the seas and lands of India and the Orient do swear on the symbol of this cross [that] I shall uphold it and not surrender it in sight of the Moor, pagan, or any race of people that I may encounter.' The first European to circumnavigate Africa was steadfast in his enmity to Islam. The continent itself he didn't even think worthy of mention. It wasn't until 1652, more than a century and a half after Dias rounded the Cape and three centuries after Ferrer first set out, that the Dutch established a permanent settlement in Africa, at Cape Town, and even then it was a mere refreshment station consisting of a basic hospital, a granary and a garden to supply Dutch East India Company ships en route.

Not only did the Europeans know next to nothing about Africa, they weren't much interested in learning about it either. Later European explorers would preserve this narrow-minded commercialism by naming new lands after what they sought from them: the Gold Coast, the Ivory Coast. The Portuguese were even more casual, apparently picking names according to the first thing they saw. 'Cap Verde' they named after its towering green mountains.

'Cameroon' is a derivation of the Portuguese word for prawns, *camarão*, which were abundant in its estuaries. 'Mozambique', a 2,500-kilometre stretch of East African coast, was named after an Arab sultan, Musa al-Bique, whom the Portuguese happened to meet there.

Such indifference towards Africa and Africans is explained by the deep religious chauvinism of the time. To Europeans and Arabs alike the Middle Ages were a binary era in which the world was divided between Christianity and Islam. Western Christianity's violent competition with Eastern Islam was the context of its adventures in Africa. In that environment, worshipping God or Allah in a rival fashion was bad enough, but not to pray to him at all was the definition of a savage. As da Gama said, the world beyond Christendom was inhabited by three kinds of people: Muslims, pagans, and others. When he arrived in India, da Gama immediately took the Hindu temples he found to be churches, therefore not Muslim, therefore proof that Prester John was close by. The phalluses and elephant-headed and blue-skinned gods he excused as local colour. 'Krishna' he heard as 'Christ'.

The most contentious part of Portugal's new trade route to Asia was the East African coast. Arab traders had been sailing, trading and slaving there for centuries and the Ottomans regarded the area as rightfully theirs. The Portuguese took a different view. The Indian Ocean was open water. On his way up the Mozambican coast, da Gama had already fought three battles with groups of Arab settlers.

It was to stake Christendom's claim to these seas that in 1541 two of Vasco da Gama's sons – the governor of India, Estêvão, and his younger brother Cristóvão – attacked the Ottomans at Suez at the head of the Red Sea. The brothers were outmatched, the attack was a failure and the Portuguese retreated to a frontier camp at the Red Sea port of Massawa, in what is now Eritrea, to make repairs and new plans.

It was at Massawa that the da Gamas received a plea for help from the Ethiopian Emperor, Gelawdewos. The da Gama brothers, whose father had eventually conceded that Prester John was not to be found in India, immediately took Gelawdewos to be the long-lost Christian king. What's more, he needed their help. Gelawdewos' messenger said his master was barely holding out against an invading Muslim and Ottoman-assisted force led by a Somali general, Ahmad Ibn Obrahim al-Ghazi ('the Left-Handed'). How fortunate, said the messenger, that the wise and benevolent King of Portugal, whom Gelawdewos called 'his brother', 'was accustomed to assist the impotent'.

The flattery would have appealed to the Portuguese. Just as important to the da Gama brothers would have been the chance to salvage some family pride, and maybe even finally unite Christendom against the Moors. They agreed without hesitation.

On 9 July 1541, the 26-year-old Cristóvão da Gama marched south into Africa, inaugurating the first ever European humanitarian intervention on the continent. The reason we know this is that the expedition can claim another first. Accompanying it was the original foreign correspondent in Africa, Miguel de Castanhoso. Castanhoso achieved that status not just by being an eyewitness to almost everything that occurred but by writing it down in dispatches as it happened. He set the mould for correspondents to come by being diligent with his facts, prolific in his copy and not shying away from editorializing when he felt the reader needed guidance. In this pre-headline era, he published his reports in a collection he titled *A History of Things that the Very Hardworking Captain Dom Cristóvão da Gama Did in the Realms of Prester John with Four Hundred Portuguese that He Took with Him; by Miguel de Castanhoso, Who Was Present Through All.*

Al-Ghazi the Left-Handed's war on Abyssinia was motivated by revenge. In the thirteenth century, just as Christians and Muslims fought each other elsewhere, so orthodox Ethiopian Solomonites had waged a series of devastating wars against the Muslim Berber

Sultanate in neighbouring Somalia. The Somalis waited centuries to retaliate but eventually in 1529 al-Ghazi declared a *jihad* on Abyssinia. The Somalis' retribution was devastating. In a few years al-Ghazi conquered three-quarters of Abyssinia, sacked the rock churches of Lalibela and reduced the Church of Our Lady Mary of Zion at Aksum to rubble.

By Castanhoso's account, Cristóvão da Gama was heavily out-numbered. Against 15,000 Mohammedans he had just 400 men, 130 slaves and 70 Indian mechanics. In what would become the pattern of Western intrusion in Africa, however, da Gama put his faith in a Christian God and bigger guns: around 1,000 match-lock arquebuses, the latest in sixteenth-century weaponry, as well as several siege cannon. Da Gama was young to command such a mission but, as a veteran of two trips to India and master of his own ship in the attack in Suez, not inexperienced. He was also, according to later colonial-era biographers, an extraordinary man. One British historian wrote in his 1902 translation of Castanhoso's diaries that da Gama was 'bold to temerity in action, chivalrous in his dealings with women, ready to share the burden of the common soldier, foremost in the fight and willing, though wounded himself, to do the work of the wounded surgeon . . . Dom Cristóvão stands out as a true leader of men'.

It's hard to miss the similarities between the qualities ascribed to da Gama – bravery, selflessness, graciousness and charity – and those to which European imperialists and even aid workers would also aspire. There are other parallels. According to Castanhoso, the locals were almost pathetically grateful to the Portuguese for their intervention. 'When they [the villagers] met Dom Cristóvão, they told him that . . . he was the apostle of God come to deliver them from captivity and subjection,' wrote Castanhoso. Da Gama did not deny the miracle of his arrival. Rather he 'consoled them much that with the help of our Lord they would quickly return to prosperity, as he had come to that land only to expel the Moors, and die for the faith of Christ'. Their saviour was at hand. 'The monks,' wrote Castanhoso, 'were much comforted by this reply.'

Castanhoso's account reveals that da Gama also made his plans with the same respect for local knowledge that would mark so much foreign humanitarianism in Africa. The Portuguese commander was 11 days into his march before he even thought to consult an African, whereupon he was told 'that then was not the season proper for marching, as the winter had begun there'. Rivers would swell, the mists would descend and the ground would freeze. Not two weeks in, and da Gama was forced to camp for four months. Even after they set off again, it wasn't for another five months that the Portuguese finally came across a small Somali contingent, which they easily defeated. In March 1542, almost nine months after da Gama had departed the coast, they finally confronted al-Ghazi's full forces.

As the far larger Somali army faced off against da Gama's diminutive band, al-Ghazi sent a messenger to da Gama giving him three choices: leave, join forces or be destroyed. Adding insult to injury, the messenger then teasingly produced a habit taken from a Christian monk. Castanhoso reported that da Gama sent a reply stating he had come to Abyssinia under orders from 'the Great Lion of the Sea' – the King of Portugal – and 'the next day he [al-Ghazi] would see what the Portuguese were worth'. The messenger then handed over a present from da Gama: a gift of 'small tweezers for the eyebrows and a very large mirror – making him [al-Ghazi] out to be a woman'. It was all getting rather childish.

Two battles followed, on 14 and 16 April. Incredibly – miraculously, Castanhoso hinted – the heavily outnumbered Portuguese won both. Al-Ghazi retreated, followed by da Gama. But more rain thwarted the Portuguese pursuit and al-Ghazi used the lull to send for reinforcements from Saudi Arabia. On 28 August, now bolstered by 2,900 Saudi musketeers, al-Ghazi counter-attacked. The Portuguese lost more than half their men. Da Gama was shot in the arm, then captured.

In al-Ghazi's camp, the Somali commander produced da Gama's tweezers and began to pluck his beard. Then da Gama was tortured in an unsuccessful attempt to convert him to Islam. Finally, al-Ghazi beheaded his adversary and tossed his head into a spring. That, according to Castanhoso, was when da Gama's true guise as a saint was revealed by another miracle. The spring waters immediately became capable of healing the sick.

If there was ever any doubt where righteousness lay, Castanhoso underlined the point in a final dispatch. Within a week, he wrote, the Portuguese attacked the Somalis once more, training their fire on al-Ghazi. Despite being mortally wounded himself, a Portuguese marksman shot and killed the Somali general.

So many straight lines can be drawn from that time to this. Heroic and high-minded in conception, bloody and uncertain in results, shaded by self-interest, disdain for Africans and hatred of Muslims, Cristóvão da Gama's short, suicidal expedition set the pattern for so much future foreign intervention in Africa. Above all, da Gama's adventures were marked by what would become the hallmark of so many incursions: ignorance and incuriosity and – what filled the spaces that those things left blank – prejudice, half-remembered legend and a presumption of primacy. By insisting on seeing the world simply, Europeans saw Africans as simple, or worse: half-human, half-ape savages unworthy of anything more than slavery or rudimentary engagement.

It was that mindset that allowed the colonists to regard European annexation of Africa as something that could only improve the place. Cecil Rhodes, who believed that 'to be born English is to win first prize in the lottery of life', wrote: 'I contend that we are the finest race in the world and that the more of the world we inhabit, the better it is for the human race. I would annex the planets if I could. I often think of that. It makes me sad to see them so clear and yet so far.'

Another consistent theme of Europe's adventures in Africa was

Church backing. With the same self-interest and self-deception Christian leaders displayed in the Crusades, European Christians portrayed their entry into Africa as not just materially and socially good for Africans but a selfless mission to save souls, whether that meant beating back the infidel Muslims or converting Godless heathens. This introduced a figure to Africa that crops up throughout Europe's sorties on the continent: the selfless, civilizing Christian hero. This character was first personified by Henry the Navigator, then Cristóvão da Gama, then missionaries such as David Livingstone as well as imperialists like Cecil Rhodes and General Charles Gordon of Khartoum.

With Church support for their decidedly unChristian plans, colonists were able to perform some truly gymnastic reasoning. Arrogance was presented as pre-eminence, avarice as selflessness, conquest as civilization and anti-Islamic prejudice as Christian righteousness. The missionary was a tool not of religious imperialism but of evangelical enlightenment. Much of this, of course, was founded on a bedrock of racism, which in the late nineteenth century was given a pseudo-empirical solidity by race 'scientists', who took Darwin's theories of evolution to mean that the displacement and even annihilation of less developed races was divine and natural progress.

Perhaps never before has one race estimated itself so far above another than at that climax of European colonialism. The King of Belgium, Leopold II, convened a conference in Berlin in 1884–5 in pursuit of an extraordinary goal: his personal takeover of an African fiefdom in Congo. Even more remarkable, by adopting the argument of civilization through conquest and parcelling out other parts of the continent to rival powers, he persuaded Europe to go along with his plan. Here the Europeans were again assisted by *ubuntu*. The ability of a colonial governor to strike a deal with a single chief and, at a stroke, extend his nation's rule over an entire land might have been tailor-made to grow European empires as fast as possible. In the process of dividing up the continent, Europe wrote its ignorance of Africa into the geography books once again. The conference participants took a continent of more than 150 nations with porous boundaries and redrew it – literally, applying rulers and pencils to a map of Africa – as a much neater collection of possessions with straight borders that turned at right angles, in defiance of all topography or genealogy on the ground. In the land of *ubuntu*, this arbitrary creation of nations was a disaster. The new borders split some peoples from each other and put others who had little contact or much in common inside the same nation. As in the Middle East, the imperialists set the stage for a hundred disputes and wars, many of which still rage today.

Europeans were able to discount African self-determination so completely because to European eyes Africans' traditional lives resembled their own past: feudal and archaic. Many seemed to conclude that if Africa resembled an earlier Europe, that was not because Africans were merely less developed but an earlier species. From the mid to late nineteenth century, explorers and settlers mostly subscribed to the race scientists' contention that there was a sacred genetic basis for white supremacy. What was it about the 'true curly-head, flab-nosed, pouch-mouthed negro?' the British explorer John Hanning Speke asked in 1864 in a now infamous section headlined 'Fauna' in his *The Discovery of the Source of the Nile*. 'How the negro has lived so many ages without advancing seems marvellous when all the countries surrounding Africa are so forward in comparison. Judging from the progressive state of the world, one is led to suppose that the African must soon either step out from his darkness, or be superseded by a being superior to himself.' Africans were trapped in poverty by their own nature, Speke wrote. 'His country is in such a state of turmoil, he has too much anxiety on hand looking out for his food to think of anything else.' Nor was there much prospect for change. 'As his fathers ever did, so does he. He works with his wife, sells his children, enslaves all he can lay his hands upon, and, unless when fighting for the property of others, contents himself with drinking, singing and dancing like a baboon to drive full care away.'

By now, what had started as ignorance, and then was infused with religious bigotry, had been distilled into full-proof racism: the belief that another people is genetically incapable of bettering itself. Racism leads to two possible paths. The first is that followed by the German explorer Carl Peters, who 'found' Great Zimbabwe and later became governor of German East Africa (now Tanzania). Peters described his feelings when shooting blacks as akin to 'intoxication'. Of the Maasai of the Serengeti, he wrote that the only thing 'to make an impression on these wild sons of the steppes was a bullet from a repeater'. Inevitably, Peters ascribed to the idea of a 'master race'. Dishonourably discharged for his barbarism from the German colonial office in 1897, he was rehabilitated posthumously in 1938 by the personal decree of Adolf Hitler.

The second path leads in an altogether kinder direction. Instead of killing, enslaving, repressing or excluding the 'inferior' African, the gentler response is to pity them and try to help. This is the white man's burden, the *noblesse oblige* of the missionary, colonist and development professional, who feel a duty to shepherd those unfortunate enough to be trapped in unenlightenment. Empire, declared the voice of French colonialism, Jules Ferry, in 1884, 'is a right for the superior races, because they have a duty . . . to civilize the inferior races'. Or as Speke wrote: 'Whilst the people of Europe and Asia were blessed by communion with God . . . the Africans were excluded from this dispensation. Whatever, then, may be said against them for being too avaricious or too destitute of fellow-feeling, should rather reflect on ourselves, who have been so much better favoured, yet have neglected to teach them.' Africans were sinners who 'know not what they are doing', wrote Speke. They were not, Speke insisted, a wholly lost cause. 'To say a negro is incapable of instruction is a mere absurdity. Among themselves, the deepness of their cunning and their power of repartee are quite surprising and are especially shown in their proficiency for telling lies most appropriately in preference to truth and with an off-handed manner that makes them most amusing.'

Castanhoso infantilized Africans. Speke thought they were mischievous and charming. But how different, truly, are today's aid campaign pictures of pretty, half-naked children? Even after Africans have thrown out imperialists, defeated apartheid and won their independence, Western aid workers and development specialists still talk about a 'third' or 'emerging' or 'developing' world that needs their assistance and guidance to face up to its enormous 'challenges' – much in the same way as they might talk about raising a child. The message is that Africa's problems are straightforward, if only Africans themselves could understand them.

The special and enduring appeal of racism is the way it makes the world comprehensible. Almost magically, by checking a simple colour code, all people and human events can be understood, and the future confidently predicted. As a tool for global generalization and simplification, racism is without par. In Africa's case, racism allowed foreigners to decode in an instant how a whole continent of people ought to behave and how, sadly, they probably would. The same miracle of generalization allowed them to abstract lessons from their own circumstances and set simple, universal and rigid standards of behaviour for all people, Africans and everyone else.

In the old days, colonial administrators who adjusted to local circumstances were said to have 'gone native'. Today we might describe someone who refuses to adapt to their environment as narrow-minded, the same phrase we would use for a racist. We see past attempts by explorers, missionaries and imperialists to 'civilize' Africans as so misguided they would be laughable if they hadn't been so ruthlessly pursued, and with such tragic consequences. We sympathize with notions of context and complexity and nuance, even of uncertainty: how one way of life may be inappropriate in one setting but suited to another.

How, then, should we describe those men and women of good conscience today who, in their offices in New York or Geneva, draw up rules for human behaviour, declare them applicable to all people everywhere and demand the whole world complies?

PART II

THE RIFT

THREE

SOUTH SUDAN

• Juba

A thousand kilometres from anywhere, among the empty flatlands and bare-rock hills that mark the Sahara's southern edge, Juba was a place of mud huts and plastic-bag roofs where buzzards lifted lazily on the afternoon heat and children washed in the muddy waters of the White Nile. When I first visited in early 2009, Juba had no landline telephones, no public transport, no power grid, no industry, no agriculture and precious few buildings; hotels, aid compounds and even government ministries were built from prefab cabins and shipping containers cut open at their ends and shoved together like tunnels of tin cans. There were a few businesses, a few hundred policemen, a handful of schools, one run-down hospital and several hundred bureaucrats. With the arrival of thousands of aid workers, there was also the occasional traffic jam of white SUVs on Juba's five tarred roads and a small clutch of bars filled with hustlers and hookers to soak up those expat salaries. But it hardly seemed to add up to the improbable reality then dawning on the place: barring war, famine or genocide – and all were possible – in less than a year, this sweltering, malarial shanty town would become the world's newest capital city in the world's newest country, South Sudan.

How could southern Sudan become an independent nation when it possessed so little of what defined one? Many Juba diplomats doubted it could. They coined a new term to describe its unique status: 'pre-failed state'. The US was the biggest foreign player in South Sudan, its influence memorialized by a leader, Salva Kiir, rarely seen without the Stetson given him by George W. Bush and a national seal of an eagle over the motto 'Justice, Liberty, Prosperity'. But the Americans were increasingly downbeat. Former President Jimmy Carter's Center had worked in southern Sudan for years trying to eradicate guinea worm disease, caught by drinking water containing parasites that eventually burrowed out through the skin. When I asked him whether the south was ready for independence, he replied simply: 'No'. General Scott Gration, US special envoy to Sudan, described his task as ensuring 'civil divorce, not civil war'. 'This place could go down in flames tomorrow,' he said. 'The probability of failure is great.' A US diplomat in the last month of his posting spoke even more freely. 'Damned if I know,' he replied when asked how he saw the future. 'There is an astonishing range of problems that are going to wash over this place.'

Any premature birth presents complications. For South Sudan, they were likely to be particularly severe. As it then was, Sudan was not only the largest country in Africa, it was also one of the least stable on earth. This was the pariah state where Osama bin Laden lived and ran al-Qaeda for five years in the 1990s and on which President Bill Clinton ordered air strikes in retaliation for al-Qaeda's 1998 bombing of US embassies in Nairobi and Dar es Salaam; where a genocide took place in Darfur a few years later; where the Sudanese President, Omar al-Bashir, was the first head of state to be indicted by the International Criminal Court for war crimes; and where two million people had died in two civil wars between north and south in 1955–72 and 1983–2005. A new country born into that kind of environment that, say, did not have clear frontiers or a functioning government or whose internal tribal division smothered any national spirit would likely spell disaster. And that was just the south. In the north, secession seemed certain to encourage other rebels, such as those in Darfur, or in the east of the country, or in the central-southern states of South Kordofan or the Blue Nile. Jimmy Carter downplayed a comparison many were making to Yugoslavia, where a centralized state splintered in secessionist conflict in the 1990s. Special envoy Gration was less sure. 'Disintegration is not a foregone conclusion,' he said.

With failure so likely, why was South Sudan pushing for independence? Why was the world helping it? One answer, as best as I could make out, was George Clooney.

It was a spring morning three years later and the staff were still wiping down the bar and clearing away the empties when Clooney ambled over to my table. He had a couple of hours before he headed north to the fighting and we'd agreed to meet by the Nile at the aid worker hotel where he stayed. The river was something to behold, a wide green trench filled with rain from the plains of Africa, cutting due north across the Sahara all the way to the Mediterranean. But Clooney ignored the view and instead surveyed the empty stools still grouped in convivial circles under the grass-roof bar.

'You been here at night?' he asked.

I said I had.

'So you know it gets pretty wild in here,' he chuckled. 'I've had some wild nights in here.'

He had just flown into Juba with John Prendergast, his fellow Sudan activist. In a few hours, the pair would be inside a war. To reach it, they would fly to a dirt strip beside a refugee camp in the far north of South Sudan, just below the newly made border with Sudan. There they would transfer to a battered, metal-floored SUV driven by Ryan Boyette.

Ryan was an American and a former aid worker who had married locally and never left. He had volunteered to drive Clooney and Prendergast illegally across the border and into the Nuba Mountains. The area was rebel territory. Ryan and his wife lived there in a stone house they built themselves, which had become Ryan's base for his project documenting atrocities by the Sudanese regime. A few months earlier, the Sudanese air force had dropped a bomb 100 metres from the house. The trio's route would take them up a dusty track that the planes were hitting almost daily. It was the bombings – barrels of oil attached to explosives rolled out of planes more than a mile up – that Clooney had come to see. 'It should be interesting,' he said. 'They're dropping those bombs from 6,000 feet so their effectiveness has been mostly to terrorize and less to actually . . . The bigger issue is violence on the road. Some guys just shot and killed and slit the throats of some people going up that road. So you have to be careful.'

I asked him if he was worried. He shook his head. 'It's OK,' he said. 'We've been in some sticky situations before and we're going with some guys who know what they're doing. And you know, you gotta do it.'

If we had to have celebrities, it seemed to me George Clooney was absolutely the best kind. It was nine months after South Sudan's independence and he was on his seventh trip there in as many years. In that time his activism had cost him hundreds of thousands of dollars. I could only imagine the angry conversations he must have endured with worried studio heads and Hollywood agents when he announced he was off to war in Africa. Now one of the biggest stars of his generation was about to fly to a spot about as far from a hospital as it was possible to be on earth, then drive up a dirt road in the hope of getting bombed.

By crossing the border, Clooney would be passing from Africa into Arabia. When it was one country, Sudan had straddled that line. In centuries past, like European Christians, Arabs had chosen to enlighten heathen Africans through slave-raiding, then conquest, then economic marginalization. After independence in 1956, the Arab-dominated Sudanese regime took its cue from this history, creating an autocratic state that exploited its regions for oil, then spent the money on itself in the capital. It was precisely that kind of behaviour that provoked the tide of African liberation in imperial times. So it was that Khartoum was soon confronting rebellion in almost every region, especially in its more Christian and African south.

Khartoum responded with repression and, after a military take-over in 1989, the kind of strident Islam that persuaded bin Laden to make Khartoum his home. Partly because of the sheer number of dead in Sudan's many conflicts, partly because Islamists became America's Enemy No. 1 after 9/11, partly because Sudan's contin-ued use of slaves horrified a nation whose own creation myth was so bound up in the trade, Sudan became a central cause for young American activists in the first years of the new millennium. And George Clooney, one of their favourite movie stars, became their champion.

Clooney's campaigning had evolved with the progression of Su-dan's various rebellions. Initially he spoke out against the Sudanese regime's atrocities in Darfur. After the US government designated that conflict a genocide in 2004, Clooney was among those who successfully campaigned to have the International Criminal Court indict President al Bashir. In 2005, the US brokered a peace agree-ment between Sudan and its southern rebels, the Sudan People's Liberation Army (SPLA). The deal included a referendum on se-cession and in the years that followed, Clooney's advocacy, which included interviews, television appearances, addresses to Congress, the Senate and the UN Security Council and talks with President Barack Obama, helped convince the world the south should be allowed independence. He was duly on hand in Juba in January 2011 when southern Sudanese voted by 98.8 per cent to split from the north. 'It was wild,' he said. 'I literally watched this 90-year-old woman vote for the first time in her life for freedom. There's something mind-blowing to see 98 per cent of the people voting. They consider it a duty and an honour and a privilege.'

Despite the peace deal, Khartoum never wavered from its preference for killing its opponents. Those included southerners, but also other rebels such as the Nuba who remained within its new truncated borders. Clooney was on an earlier trip with John

Prendergast trying to figure out ways to hinder the bloodshed when, lying out in the desert and looking up at the stars, the pair came up with an idea even more outlandish than helping create a new country in Africa: their own spy satellite. 'I was like: "How come you could Google Earth my house and you can't Google Earth where war crimes are being committed?"' said Clooney. '"It doesn't make sense to me." And John was, like, "I don't know. Maybe we can."'

On their return to the US, he and Prendergast contacted Google Maps and a satellite photography specialist, DigitalGlobe. They rented time on three of DigitalGlobe's satellites stationed in the stratosphere over Sudan and worked to process the images and overlay them with Google Maps in minutes. Speed was important, said Clooney. 'Then you can say, "Well, five days ago this is what this place looked like. And this is what it looked like two days ago."'

I told him I thought the idea was brilliant, if a little insane. The point, he said, was that it worked. 'If you're going to put 150,000 troops on a border, you're going to have a really tough time claiming this is all just rebel infighting if that's all going to be photographed by satellites, up close and personal. It makes it harder to get away with. It makes it impossible for the UN Security Council to veto action against Khartoum. We know it's effective because the government in Khartoum keeps saying what a rotten bunch of people we are and how it's not fair.' He laughed. 'I love the "It's not fair" thing,' he said. 'Literally stomping their feet. "It's not fair!" The Defence Minister came out and said: "How would Mister Clooney like it if every time he left his house there were people watching him with cameras?" And I was, like, "Man, I want you to enjoy the exact same amount of celebrity as me."' He laughed again. 'You can't please all the war criminals all the time, you know?'

You had to admire the inversion. George Clooney, whose privacy was routinely invaded in pursuit of trivialities, was violating the privacy of a dictatorial regime in the pursuit of saving lives. He was using his fame and fortune to try to effect positive change in a place that, without him, would have remained far more obscure. He presented a far less self-indulgent model of celebrity than usual and, with the way his stature in his industry seemed to persuade other stars to take up activism in Africa, could even lay claim to helping reinvent the whole notion and purpose of fame.

Clooney also knew his limits. He had a clear goal – prevention of human suffering – and a well-defined idea of his role. 'The reason I come is not because I'm a policy guy and not because I'm a soldier and not because I can do anything except get this on TV and in the newspapers,' he said. Nevertheless, publicity was key. 'The thing that's frustrating and disappointing – and you in the news organizations know this better than anybody – is that the assumption is always: "Well, if we know, then we do something about it." And that just isn't true. I mean we knew about Rwanda. We knew about Bosnia. We knew. But there was plausible deniability. So we're going to try and keep it loud enough so that at least they can't say they didn't know.'

George Clooney's efforts revealed imagination and depth. His campaigning was also effective. But in some ways, that only made it stranger. Because he was charming and handsome and famous and rich, he had been able to help engineer the creation of a vast new country in a faraway land. The fabulousness of one of Hollywood's leading men, normally used to sell movie tickets and watches and coffee, had changed millions of lives and the course of history. Good for him. But if this was how Western power operated in the twenty-first century, it was absurd.

At one point I asked Clooney if he'd ever met his northern Sudanese adversaries, whose consistent complaint was that Sudan's future wasn't the business of an American actor, no matter how cool he was. He replied that his one trip to Khartoum had been frustrating because the government obstinately refused to listen to him. As Clooney saw it, they forced him to play tough. 'We've tried carrots,' he said. 'I've been the first to talk about seeing if there's some door to open to allow these guys to step through and have an easier way of it. But carrots haven't been very successful with the government of Khartoum. They don't want to do it. So now we have to make it much harder.'

Clooney was not asking himself, as I was trying to, what any of this – Sudan – had to do with him. Rather, he was acknowledging that in practice it had had a lot to do with him, from the moment he decided it would. He had the clarity of moral obligation. Because he could, he should.

I felt his certainty was blinding him to something. With his campaigns, Clooney was acting on behalf of others. Inevitably, like when he rented a satellite, that sometimes meant instead of them. When I asked him about his role in making a new country, what I meant was: why should a Hollywood star wield such influence over a distant foreign land? Why should any outsider? How, really, could you foster someone else's independence? Surely the whole point with independence was that people had to do it for themselves?

Twenty-one months later, South Sudan imploded.

On 15 December 2013 there was an attempted coup in Juba by ethnic Nuer soldiers from the presidential guard. Or, as the Nuer had it, Dinka soldiers acting on orders from a paranoid Dinka President, Salva Kiir, tried to disarm them by force. A firefight erupted in the barracks and spilled out onto the streets. Around 500 soldiers died.

The violence reflected an unresolved split among South Sudan's leaders. All through their fight with Khartoum, the southern rebellion had been riven by ethnic rivalry, particularly between the Dinka, the biggest tribe, and the Nuer, the second-largest. During the civil war, more southerners had died fighting each other than the north. At times the Nuer leader, Riek Machar, even sided with

Khartoum. In a notorious attack in 1991, he had sacked the Dinka capital, Bor, massacring thousands of civilians.

At independence in July 2011, the Dinka took most government and army posts. Kiir made an effort to broaden the government's base by making Machar his deputy. But relations between the two never healed. In July 2013 Kiir fired Machar, along with his entire Cabinet, replacing them with Dinka loyalists. After that, another showdown was only a matter of time. The soldiers' firefight provided the spark. Within hours of that first clash, Dinka soldiers began carrying out pogroms across Juba, singling out Nuer soldiers and civilians and shooting them in their homes and in the street. Nuer mutinies erupted in army units across the country. Machar fled the capital and set up a command post in the northern bush. Nuer militias soon began their own series of reprisal massacres against Dinka.

In days, the conflict was threatening to widen into a regional war. Machar was receiving tacit support from Ethiopia and at times seemed to be angling to restart the north south war, making overtures to Khartoum about renegotiating the split the south paid it from its oil revenues. Kiir, meanwhile, welcomed reinforcements of several thousand Ugandan soldiers. Inside South Sudan, the conflict was tearing apart the new country's fragile national fabric. Nuer and Dinka mobs began attacking their neighbours. Militias went from house to house, demanding to know who was Nuer, who Dinka. Thousands were executed, their bodies left in the street. Children were shot as they ran. Fathers had their throats cut in front of their families. Women and girls were abducted and raped.

Coming on the twentieth anniversary of the Rwanda genocide, the bloodletting sharpened memories of how, a few hundred kilometres to the south, up to a million people had died in 100 days. With each new massacre, the parallels grew. Like Rwanda, families turned on each other. Like Rwanda, women and children who sought safety in churches and hospitals and schools and outside

UN bases were slaughtered *en masse*. When a Nuer militia fell on the town of Bentiu, massacring hundreds on 15 and 16 April, the UN reported that the killers were spurred on by broadcasts on local radio stations, just as they had been in Rwanda. And like Rwanda, the UN failed to stop the slaughter even when it happened right in front of them. The day after the Bentiu massacre, Dinka militiamen stormed a UN base at Bor and started shooting and slashing at Nuer refugees inside the perimeter, killing at least 58.

Twenty years before, the world had promised *never again*. Now newspapers around the world asked: were those empty words? Was it happening again? How could it be, when for a decade South Sudan's very creation had been a project nurtured and guided by the world's best intentions?

By the time I arrived back in Juba in mid April 2014, the violence had been raging for four months. Three provincial capitals had been razed. Up to 40,000 people were dead. More than a million of South Sudan's six to 11 million people (a measure of South Sudan's lack of development was that nobody knew the population for sure) had fled their homes and 250,000 of those had walked abroad. With no one left to tend the farms, the UN was warning that seven million South Sudanese needed food aid and 50,000 children could die of hunger in months.

George Clooney was now pointing his satellite at his former friends in the south, particularly the city of Malakal, a state capital, an hour's flight north of Juba. Nuer rebels had overrun Malakal three times. Three times the SPLA had recaptured it. The last period of rebel occupation in February had been especially devastating. Clooney's before-and-after pictures showed that where once there had been hundreds of tin shacks and thatched huts, now there were just blackened smudges. More fighting around Malakal seemed imminent. South Sudan's government depended on nearby oilfields for 98 per cent of its revenue. For his part, Machar was vowing to take those, then Juba, then overthrow Kiir.

Mading Ngor, a South Sudanese journalist with whom I worked, fixed us a ride to Malakal in the cargo hold of a government military resupply flight, a cavernous white Ilyushin packed with food and ammunition flown by seven portly Ukrainians. We sat on the back of a camouflaged, flat-back Land Cruiser, wobbling on the truck's suspension as the plane hit turbulence thrown up by the 45-degree heat below. Before we left, Mading and I had sought out a South Sudanese official who had just returned from Malakal. 'You will find mostly bones,' he said. 'They killed them in the streets and in the churches and in the hospital, then they burned the town to the ground. The dogs and the birds have been at the bones. Malakal isn't there any more.' Sure enough, when the Ukrainians threw open the Ilyushin's door at Malakal, I immediately smelled the bilious stench of bloating corpses.

We walked to the side of the runway. Around 200 people were gathered on its edge, apparently surrounded by everything they'd managed to save. Bedsteads. Bicycle wheels. Tightly packed suit-cases. Whole sheets tied up in great bundles. They told us they'd been there for weeks, hoping for a ride to Juba. The Ukrainians unloaded the trucks, pulled up the crew ladder and made ready to depart. Suddenly there was a cry and as one the crowd picked up their cases and mattresses and babies and ran to the open plane door. A stand-off ensued. The crowd remonstrated from the tarmac. The Ukrainians refused to lower the ladder. A dog began circling the nose wheel, barking at the pilots above. We left them to it.

With Malakal destroyed, we were staying at a UN base around a kilometre outside town. The road there was lined by hundreds of rope beds, set out like an endless open-air dormitory. Underneath were small piles of plastic bags, tin plates, car wheels and bamboo poles. People were busily adding to their piles, arriving from Malakal carrying wooden planks, plastic sheets, plastic chairs, more poles and more beds. Marabou storks as tall as teenagers strutted between the beds, stooping and picking.

We passed two SPLA technicals mounted with .50 cals and suddenly we were in a small market. Tiny mountains of tomatoes, onions, nuts and tamarind were stacked on the bare earth under sheets of plastic tied between poles. A hundred metres further on and we were at the gates of the UN base. We drove through to the other side to find more market stalls and thousands more people. At first I thought the UN had opened its gates to the refugees. But after another 50 metres we passed through a second set of gates, these ones ringed with razor wire and policed by a sentry checking IDs, and the people and the noise ended.

We were in a large yard packed with perhaps 100 giant white machines. Bulldozers, heavy-loader trucks, water-carriers, buses, a rubbish truck, a crane, a tank, an immense red fire truck and, beside it, 32 50-litre fire extinguishers still wrapped in cellophane. We turned into an avenue of prefabricated bungalows, perhaps 100 long and five rows deep on each side, around 1,000 cabins in all. Parked in front were hundreds of white SUVs marked 'UN' or stamped with the logos of international aid agencies: Médecins Sans Frontières, Solidarités, the Red Cross, the International Organization for Migration. A square air-conditioning unit stuck out from each bungalow. Most had a satellite dish on a metal spike out front. Some were surrounded by small gardens of aloe, neem and pink and white bougainvillea. Wooden boardwalks ran between the bungalows, flanked by concrete drainage ditches marked with red and white painted bollards. Every now and then the walkways would open up to small parks, in the corners of which were white rubbish bins and shelters protecting more fire extinguishers. Towering over the whole complex were several red and white radio masts and sodium street lights.

We wandered down the main street. Aside from a passing jogger dressed in Lycra with an iPod strapped to his forearm, the base looked deserted. We came across a cafeteria. Then came a bigger building on whose arch was written, 'Hard Rock Complex' in the style of the US chain. We passed a white UN pick-up with a dirt bike in the back. After that came a residential area, hundreds of cabins served by several shower blocks plumbed with hot and cold water and fitted with condom machines. Many of the buildings displayed UN posters. 'No to abuse in the workplace', said one over a photograph of a suited man in an office shouting at a woman through a megaphone. 'Sex with children is prohibited', read another.

Looking for someone to ask where to pitch our tents, Mading and I tried knocking on a few doors. We opened one to find three Ukrainians in air-conditioned cool looking up at us from computer screens. I asked if they knew where the base manager was. They looked at me blankly. 'This internet café,' said one. After a while we found a door marked 'Administration'. Inside a man sat at his desk, typing on his computer. He was bald and dressed in sandals, denim shorts and a freshly ironed short-sleeved shirt coloured in pastel checks. A badge around his neck announced that he was Imad Qatouni, UN general services assistant. 'No, no, no, we do not have any accommodation,' remonstrated Imad as we walked in.

I asked how things were. 'So far, so good,' replied Imad. I tried again, asking how many refugees there were. 'Maybe 22,000,' said Imad. 'They come and go. It changes every day.' Imad told us he would find someone to show us where to put our tents. Then he said: 'We are providing catering for everybody.' For a moment I thought he meant the refugees. He didn't. 'It's 20 South Sudanese pounds for breakfast, and 30 for lunch and dinner. Very reasonable. Out there even a tomato will cost you 15 Sudanese pounds. We even reduced the prices. Tonight you will get turkey, spaghetti, rice and soup.' Imad smiled. 'I am running this,' he said, opening his palms and indicating a pile of papers on his desk. 'Look at me. It's the weekend and all I am doing is going through the receipts. Thousands of them.'

I took in Imad's office. Shelves stacked with files. A kettle and coffee mugs. A water cooler, a fridge, a printer and a separate photocopier, piles of spare printer paper and toner cartridges. On

85

his desk next to his keyboard: a box of paperclips, sealed stacks of yellow and pink Post-It notes, a can of air freshener and a small bottle of hand sanitizer.

I asked about going into Malakal. 'There is no town,' said Imad. I said we'd heard as much. It was the destruction we had come to see. Imad said he couldn't help us. 'I have never been outside,' said Imad. 'I have nothing to do there. The military have to do it, so they do patrols. Some of the NGOs go with them. Maybe you could go on patrol too.'

The next morning Mading phoned a friend in South Sudan's military and a jeep came to meet us. On the way into Malakal we passed hundreds more people carrying more piles of belongings on their heads. At first, the destruction of the city announced itself quietly. A smashed doorway on the outskirts. A burned-out hut. A small stall spilling plastic and paper into the street. Then suddenly Malakal ceased to exist. In every direction was black earth, blackened stubs of walls and bent tin sheets. It was as though a hurricane of fire had passed through.

Mading and I got out. We began walking through the debris, sinking up to our ankles in the ash. A blackened fan. A blackened cooking pot. A rocking chair burned back to its metal frame. Cracked beer bottles. A small pile of melted medicine bottles. The warped back of a mobile phone. I came to a metal front gate, now standing alone, the walls on either side vaporized. Behind it was what had once been a front yard and a small flower bed, its borders marked with half-buried cans of Red Horse and Heineken. Beyond that a brick house still stood, though its windows were blown out and the walls around them were smudged with sooty eyeshadow. I peered inside. There were two small rooms. In each were three metal bed frames. There was a clothes dryer, a gas bottle, a hat stand with curled hooks, a shisha pipe, a spilled sack of rice, a pair of green flip-flops and a neatly stacked pile of tin plates and cups. Everything except the flip-flops was blackened and cracked, twisted or blistered. We were walking through incinerated lives.

Sleepless the night before, I'd ambled around the UN base and found scores of dogs lying in the road. Mindful of what the man in Juba had said about dogs and corpses, I'd watched one pack rummage through a garbage pile, tearing and growling and settling down to chew. Now I rounded a corner and saw more dogs. They tensed, snarled and bounded guiltily away. They looked well fed.

We climbed back into our truck and drove 100 metres before Mading said 'Oh!' and motioned for the driver to stop. We began walking again, stepping over a pile of mobile phone covers, then TV remotes, then around a large safe, its door wrenched open. I saw what Mading had seen: we were in the main market. Every store lock had been smashed, every metal door wrenched and everything inside looted. The signs, twisted and burned, took on a new, bitter tone. 'Tourist Restaurant 5 Stars', read one. 'South Supreme Airlines: the Spirit of a New Nation', read another. To one side was an old aid agency sign. 'Multi-donor trust fund for South Sudan', it said. 'Rapid Impact Emergency Project 2008: Rehabilitation of Market'.

The wreckage under our feet began to assume a medical theme – pill bottles, medicine sachets – and I looked up and saw a sign indicating we were outside Malakal Teaching Hospital. We walked through the front gates over a carpet of silver condom strips. Computers had been dragged out of the hospital's offices and smashed. Patient records littered the corridors. Outside the children's ward were hundreds of large paper sheets printed with the board game Ludo. Gold and purple Christmas tinsel hung on the walls. As we approached the operating theatre, a growling announced the hidden presence of another dog pack. On the walls outside were aid agency posters. 'Take an HIV test', advised Unicef. 'Fight for rights', said the UN. Next to them someone had written their name in blood: 'Bishok'. It was the last testimony to an existence presumably now erased. And maybe an accusation, too. What use, in the end, had health or rights programmes been to Bishok?

We drove to Malakal's river port. I'd read how in early January more than two hundred people trying to escape the violence had drowned crossing the Nile when an overcrowded ferry sank. Most of the dead were children. Now I saw some had not even made it that far. Just by the port gates a small skull lay next to a tiny shinbone. Inside there were more bones. An arm, a leg, another small skull next to a black silk hairband. As I walked over, I kicked something. A tiny coccyx skittered across the concrete.

Bar the dogs, we had seen no sign of life. But as we left the port and rounded a corner, we found a group of government troops encamped by the side of the road. We stopped to talk to some officers. 'Go to the church,' said one. 'You can get all you want.' A hundred metres further on and we were outside St Joseph's Cathedral. We walked through the front gates, across more piles of papers and garbage and up the front steps, stepping over a dark patch of blood. At first I couldn't understand what the soldier had meant. There were no bones here. Instead the floor of the cathedral was a sea of brightly coloured clothes, mixed in with a few plastic bowls and cups.

But there was something about the way the clothes were arranged. Small, neat piles. Perhaps 250 of them. We began stepping through the mess, picking up the clothes. Dresses. Skirts. Blouses. They smelled of washing powder and perfume. Tucked underneath were several collections of family photographs. A picture of a man relaxing on a picnic in a grassy field. Another of a woman with two girls, her daughters perhaps. A picture of a woman with triplets. A graduation portrait. Another of five children, aged about one to 10. These were the kinds of photographs mothers kept. They would have grabbed them as they fled their homes. Where were the women now? What had happened here to make them abandon their keepsakes?

We drove back to the camp outside the UN base and began asking around among the refugees. A rainstorm had broken and most were huddling under plastic sheets, tucking themselves up on their rope beds to keep out of the mud. Ernest Uruar was 52, spoke some English and wore a turquoise Unicef cap. 'I was in the hospital after Christmas,' he said. 'We ran there to save ourselves. My two boys, 16 and 14, died trying to get away when a canoe sank in the river on Christmas Day. So it was just me, my wife and my mother-in-law.

'We were there when the rebels came the third time. They were just killing people, even the wounded, even my mother-in-law. People ran and they opened fire. They were asking, "Who is Dinka? Who is Nuer?" If you were Dinka, you were shot. It didn't matter even if they were children. It was only being Dinka that mattered.'

Ernest was neither Dinka nor Nuer. He'd run with his wife to the cathedral. Hundreds of others did the same. 'The rebels were looting the town,' he said. 'Then they were coming to the cathedral to look for girls. They raped them. They would take girls in front of their mothers and fathers. Some were returned, some were not.'

I asked how long this went on for. 'Two months,' replied Ernest.

I looked at Ernest. 'Two months? The rebels used the cathedral as a rape camp for two months when there was a UN base full of peacekeepers ten minutes away?'

'Two months,' repeated Ernest.

A woman introduced herself as Asham Nyiyom. She said she was 50 and the mother of eight. 'The rebels came constantly to the cathedral,' she said. 'They were asking for money and taking young girls. They selected some people to be killed. They even shot one man dead in the church. My 18-year-old son is also missing.' A younger man who'd been listening interrupted. 'They would say: "You come, and you, and you,"' he said. 'They would take these girls and use them. One night they took seven and they did not return two. We don't know what happened to them. My sister was killed. And other relatives.'

The man caught his breath. He was trembling.

'Only I came out,' he said. Abruptly he walked off.

Ernest watched him go. 'It was a very bad situation,' he said.

'Even you cannot describe on this. How it became. How we became. They would kill people when they went to the river to fetch water.' The rapists did not spare mothers with babies, said Ernest. 'When they take the girls, if you are a man and you want to say something, they will beat you and kill you. It was two months of killings and abuses and rapes. And then the UN came. *After* the rebels had left. They did not risk until it became peaceful. They saw people dying and they did not move. They did not move until the government recaptured the place.'

I asked Ernest what he thought of the protection offered by the UN. He considered his reply. 'In a way, they had a hand in all this,' he said, eventually. 'They saved our lives *late*.'

Lunch back at the base was rice, lamb, broccoli and black-eyed peas. With most base residents cocooned all day in their air-conditioned cabins in front of their screens, mealtimes were some of the few occasions we got to see them. They would emerge in Bermuda shorts, T-shirts and sandals, shuffling to and from the cafeteria, perhaps stopping in at the Hard Rock Complex to use the gym or shoot some pool in the rec room.

I struck up a conversation with a Fijian policeman who was living in the bungalow next to my tent. He let me use his cabin to charge my computer, a gesture, he explained, of ethnic solidarity. I was British and Fiji had been a British colony. That made us allies.

After a while, I asked: 'Against whom?'

'Not all the UN people are friendly,' replied the Fijian. 'They lock the toilets and showers. They think they should be only for them.'

That morning an Indian soldier had reprimanded me for using his shower block. I told the Fijian. He erupted. 'This fucking guy and his fucking toilets,' he said. 'He write three times to the camp commander about this. He put his own locks. We go out at night and take his locks and throw them away.' The Fijian stewed for a moment, breathing heavily, rocking back and forth. 'These are not good people,' he said.

The uniform on the Indian from the shower block indicated he was a peacekeeper. I'd noticed he and many of his comrades wore surgical facemasks and asked the Fijian why. 'They say it is because Africans smell, because Africans are dirty,' he replied. 'This is not good. You see how these people are living. We are here to protect them. You should not wear a mask. Me, I talk to them. They offer their food and I eat it. I sit with them. These fucking UN people, they never eat Sudanese food. They never meet the people. They are not good with them.'

In the afternoon, Mading and I went to meet the SPLA general who had retaken Malakal from the rebels for the third time, Johnson Bilieu. En route, we passed hundreds of soldiers carrying furniture out of deserted houses and loading up trucks in the street. We mentioned it to the general but he was defensive, denying he had looters in his ranks. We let it pass.

The general said thousands had died. He apologized for not being more precise. Hundreds of bodies had been washed away by the river, he said. The dogs had dragged away those that remained. They split up the skeletons so it was impossible to make a proper count. I asked the general what he made of the UN's efforts to protect civilians. 'Slow,' he said.

Mading and the general began a long discussion about tactics and it was late afternoon by the time we left. Driving back to the base, we took a different route through town. I was thinking about the bodies. The general had said there were thousands but I'd only seen a few bones. The dogs couldn't have taken them all.

We passed an open field with a number of earthen mounds in it. It took me a few seconds to register what I had seen and I had to ask the driver to turn around and go back. The field turned out to be the town cemetery. Just inside the gate was a large expanse of freshly dug earth, perhaps 25 metres wide and broad. Behind it was another one, and behind that, and further on, and on either side, several more. I made a tour of the cemetery and counted 13 large mounds, 24 medium-sized ones and more than a hundred small ones. There was the same stink as at the airport. Sitting on one mound was a skull, half of its cranium missing. I asked our government driver if he knew how many people were buried in each large grave. 'About 20 to 30,' he replied.

Mading phoned General Bilieu. The graves weren't dug by his men, he said. But by then we already knew. In the earth were the tracks of fat-tyred heavy-lifting machines of the kind sitting at the entrance of the UN base.

The world had guided the South Sudanese to freedom. Two and a half years later, it was shovelling their bodies into mass graves with bulldozers.

The first modern celebrity activist was a child actor called Jackie Coogan, once a co-star to Charlie Chaplin. In 1924, aged 10, Coogan raised a million dollars for Armenian and Greek refugees left destitute by World War I. Coogan died in 1984. If you visit his grave in the Holy Cross Cemetery in Culver City, California, you might think you were standing before the tomb of a politician or civil rights leader. 'Humanitarian. Patriot. Entertainer', reads the stone. The last word is the only reference to the role for which millions knew Coogan: Uncle Fester in the 1960s comedy *The Addams Family*.

The accusation most commonly levelled at celebrities with a cause is that too often it is more about the saviours than the saved. This suspicion of self-interest is not new. In the late nineteenth century, the first attempt by outsiders to improve health in Africa was not even aimed at Africans but at European settlers, who were dying in droves in the continent's interior. It was Africa's particular misfortune that Europeans learned to beat many of the continent's diseases in the 1880s and 1890s just as their co-lonial ambitions peaked. Cures and treatments followed in quick succession, including those for yellow fever in 1881, tuberculosis in 1882, cholera in 1885 and malaria in 1898. If the Berlin conference gave Europe a plan for conquest, advances in tropical medicine – a bed-net to prevent malaria, salt, sugar and water to treat cholera – expedited them. In a few years, the Belgians had built rubber plantations across Congo, the Portuguese were growing coffee and sisal in Mozambique and Angola, the Germans were breeding cattle in Namibia and Tanzania, the French were farming groundnuts from Dakar to Niamey and Britons were planting wheat and fruit farms across Zimbabwe and Zambia, Ghana and Kenya.

Most of these farms formalized racist oppression. The white boss lived as a feudal lord in a palatial villa at the centre of his vast lands, ruling over hundreds of African men, women and children in the fields whom he kept in line with rhino-skin whips. If Africans benefited from their bosses' new mastery of disease, it was as an afterthought when the colonists, either out of conscience or a calculation that a healthy negro was a more productive one, let their workers have spare medicine and old bed-nets.

In the aftermath of the Second World War, the dying years of colonialism, the newly formed United Nations created two departments, the World Health Organization (WHO) and the United Nations Children's Fund (Unicef), and charged them with improving the health of the world's poor. But this lofty, universalist-sounding mission was also born of a pronounced Western bias. The term 'United Nations' was a front, invented by US President Franklin D. Roosevelt to give a veneer of internationalism to a pact of martial division: the 1942 Declaration by the United Nations, which committed all 26 Allies to global war until the Axis powers were defeated. As the Cold War took hold, the UN remained largely a Western political tool, dependent on American and European government funds and approval. Soon the US and Europe came to regard the UN's health agencies as an excellent way to convince the poor world that the capitalist West cared more for them than the Communist East. By the late 1950s, they were funding the new agencies plus their own government efforts with hundreds of millions of dollars a year.

The results were spectacular. In a decade, malaria, the most deadly disease ever to afflict mankind, declined from 350 million cases a year worldwide to 100 million. Eighteen countries became malaria-free. By the late 1960s, however, many of the UN's early successes were being reversed. The UN's malaria programmes withered and died as a new environmentalist movement questioned the toxic impact of the mosquito-killer dichlorodiphenyltrichloroethane (DDT). All the health campaigns also foundered on the realization that, once a disease was beaten back, it would take all but everlasting campaigns to keep it at bay. Perhaps most significant, the way the West had used aid to buy Cold War allies rankled the activists and idealists of the late 1960s who might have been expected to most approve of it. New non-government groups sprang up, proclaiming they were focused on people, not power, and declared their intention to be independent, politically neutral and benevolent to all. They gave themselves a name to capture this universal righteousness: humanitarians.

One day I made a request under Britain's Freedom of Information Act asking the Foreign Office to release secret files dating from 1967–8 on the Biafra civil war in Nigeria. The country's northern elite had been favoured by its British imperial rulers and had continued to dominate the country after independence in 1960. But in 1967 southern ethnic Igbos rebelled, declaring the secession of a new state they called Biafra.

If I had been looking for state secrets or tales of James Bond adventures in the British files, I would have been disappointed. British spies of the 1960s, it seemed, mostly extracted their intelligence by reading newspapers and taking reporters out to lunch. But as I'd suspected, much of the Biafran file was taken up with reports on a pioneering Geneva-based PR agency, Markpress, run by an American, William Bernhardt, who in a few short months laid the foundations of modern humanitarianism.

The Biafran rebels had hired Markpress to generate support in the West. MI6's file provided a methodical account of how, by co-opting celebrities and journalists, the agency created the first modern aid campaign. In a letter marked 'Confidential' dated 16 October 1968 and addressed to London from the Swiss town of Berne, a British operative who signed himself P. Arengo-Jones wrote: '[Markpress] has for over a year, we hear, been flying out groups of German and Swiss journalists. It has a member of the Associated Press office in Geneva working for it. I fear there is not much in this, if anything, which will be new to you but you may nevertheless like to have a sight of it.'

Despite his insouciance, P. Arengo-Jones was persuaded to persevere with his investigations. Over the months, his letters revealed a growing astonishment at how Markpress was able to generate unprecedented public interest in Biafra by presenting the need to get involved in the affairs of a far-off land as motivated less by political creed or national or commercial self-interest but by a higher human purpose. What so mystified Arengo-Jones was how, despite relying on journalists working on a commercial basis and being profitably contracted itself, Markpress was able to convince the public of the campaign's selfless, elevated ethics – of its own good intentions and of the public's need to act, the need to do something. 'We are finding it very difficult to isolate the mercenary involvement of people with Markpress from their humanitarian concern for the Ibos [*sic*],' wrote Arengo-Jones. 'One of them we know to be working with Markpress, a well-known broadcaster, makes frequent trips to rebel-held parts of Nigeria but is always able on his return to broadcast about what he claims to have witnessed as a radio man.'

The central aim of Markpress' campaign was to persuade the outside world of the need for a new type of Western intervention. This was not to be about killing others or seizing territory or protecting interests. It was to save lives, restore some morality to the exercise of rich-world power and rid it of the notoriety it had garnered propping up Cold War despots around the world. (Nigeria was a case in point. The British government was selling arms to the government.)

Though the campaigners would have been loath to admit it, their appeal to a higher calling drew on colonial precedent. Imperialists believed the exercise of European power necessarily improved a place. The Biafran humanitarians believed it would too, if wielded by the right people for the right reasons. The bad guys in Markpress' Biafran presentations would also have been familiar to any God-fearing colonist. They were Muslim, in particular soldiers of the Muslim-dominated Nigerian army and the Muslim mobs who beat and killed Christian Igbos. The campaigners described the crimes of these Islamist barbarians with a word which in later years would become a holy grail for those advocating humanitarian intervention around the world: genocide.

The most striking of Markpress' innovations was its creation of a campaign icon that would also echo through the decades: the starving African baby, on whose behalf action was required. But once again the agency drew on colonialism when it cast foreign campaigners as the hero-saviours in this African story. As it had been with missionaries and imperialists, the idea was to give the public a personal incentive to adopt what was otherwise a distant and obscure cause. By backing the campaign, you *became* one of the good guys. Who could dispute the bravery of the aid workers flying food into Biafra, 29 of whom were killed by the Nigerian air force and their Soviet allies? Who could doubt the sacrifice of American student Bruce Mayrock, who died on the lawn in front of the UN building in New York after setting himself alight carrying a sign that read 'You Must Stop Genocide'? Who could resist the chutzpah of John Lennon, who returned his MBE on 25 November 1969, explaining in an accompanying letter to Queen Elizabeth II: 'Your Majesty, I am returning my MBE as a protest against Britain's involvement in the Nigeria-Biafra thing, against our support of America in Vietnam and against "Cold Turkey" slipping down the charts. With Love, John Lennon.'

A million people died in the Biafran conflict, hardly a humanitarian success. It's a testament to both the tenacity and the introspective spirit in which humanitarianism was forged that Biafra remains a template today for the ideas, organizations and individuals it brought to prominence. Biafra saw the arrival of two concepts: the charity helper working under commercial contract; and the permanent charity built around a never-ending global mission to address crisis and do good that reserves for the charity the prerogative of deciding what, and where, is a crisis, and how good should be done. These concepts remain prototypes for the modern aid worker and aid group. Biafra echoes especially loudly in a certain type of swashbuckling aid worker who first emerged there. Unicef, Save the Children and Caritas were all on their first foreign ground operation in Biafra, and Oxfam only its second. Médecins Sans Frontières, the most glamorous of all aid agencies and the winner of the 1999 Nobel Peace Prize, was founded specifically for Biafra by Bernard Kouchner, the future French Foreign Minister. Kouchner was then a Red Cross worker who quit his organization in disgust at the way its neutrality prevented it from separating righteous from wrong. Another figure in this movement was a young French philosopher who liked to be photographed with his shirt unbuttoned to the navel, Bernard-Henri Lévy. A third was a Paris-based Brazilian student, Sérgio de Mello.

With no shortage of foreign crises onto which to project their vision, this small, charismatic group quickly grew into a worldwide movement. The new aid groups deployed to an earthquake in Nicaragua in 1972, a hurricane in Honduras in 1974, and set up refugee camps in Thailand for Cambodians fleeing the Khmer Rouge in 1975. In 1979, Kouchner filled a boat called *L'Île de Lumière* (*The Island of Light*) with doctors and journalists to sail the South

China Sea administering to fleeing South Vietnamese boat people.

In the 1980s in Afghanistan, where Médecins Sans Frontières and a crop of other relief groups were patching up those wounded in the *mujahedeen*'s fight against a Soviet invasion, the humanitarians made a second, crucial evolution. The new thinking was that Western military power could be good if exercised righteously and in the cause of liberty. Might – in Afghanistan's case the CIA's shipment of billions of dollars of arms to the *mujahedeen* – could be right. Wars could be just.

Around the same time the aid workers' ranks were swelled by a tide of celebrities. Famously, in 1984 the Irish singer Bob Geldof watched television news images of a famine in Ethiopia and underwent a conversion from angry rock star to curmudgeonly humanitarian. Geldof put together an all-star charity record, 'Do They Know it's Christmas?', which raised £6 million for famine relief. Six months later Geldof staged Live Aid, simultaneous all-star concerts in London and Philadelphia that raised more than $100 million. Famous friends boosted the humanitarians' impetus, and their self-regard. Do the right thing, stars urged in their campaigns. Be the right people. Be like us.

The spirit of Biafra was invoked once more in 1989 when a famine hit rebel areas of southern Sudan. In Biafra, civilian aid groups bringing in emergency relief had briefly made the landing strip at Uli the second busiest in Africa. Two decades later the UN and a small army of aid agencies did the same to a small airstrip in northern Kenya, Lokichoggio, using it as a base for Operation Lifeline Sudan, a mass airlift of millions of tons of food that ran for more than a decade.

The humanitarian cause suffered a setback in 1992–3 when a US mission to support a UN effort to address a famine in Somalia ended with 'Black Hawk Down'. Televised images of the bodies of two dead US soldiers being dragged through the streets of Mogadishu led to anguished questions. What were we thinking of? What were our boys doing there?

These were legitimate doubts. But 18 months later, when accounts of the Rwandan genocide began emerging, they were forgotten. Rwanda's government had ordered the country's Hutu majority to exterminate its Tutsi minority and in 100 days 800,000 people were killed, a tenth of the population. Though Rwandans had killed Rwandans, the horror of what had happened, magnified by a collective guilt at foreign inaction, persuaded many outsiders to focus on what they themselves had done wrong. Why had the world been so slow to step in? Why did foreigners always seem to fail Africa? *Never again*, the world resolved. Among the new disciples of international intervention was a young official at the National Security Council, Susan Rice, who had initially argued in favour of a UN pull-out from Rwanda. 'I swore to myself that if I ever faced such a crisis again, I would come down on the side of dramatic action, going down in flames if that was required,' Rice would later say.

If Rwanda seemed to make the case for forceful humanitarianism incontestable, the Balkans provided a first arena in which the world could demonstrate its new resolve. In 1999 in Kosovo, NATO bombed Serb forces out of concern for their Kosovan victims. It was no coincidence that de Mello, then Kouchner, both served as UN special representatives to Kosovo. Also present in the Balkans was a young reporter, Samantha Power. Based on her experiences, Power wrote a biography of de Mello and a Pulitzer Prize-winning book, *A Problem from Hell: America and the Age of Genocide*, in which she drew on Rwanda and the former Yugoslavia to sketch out a new emerging philosophy casting forceful humanitarian intervention as a moral obligation. A successful British operation in Sierra Leone in 2000 against rebels who used child soldiers to commit atrocities added further weight to the argument.

Though Power was initially moved by Serb persecution of Bosnia's Muslims, the humanitarians soon found themselves in regular opposition to Islamists. In 1999–2000, de Mello took a job as UN administrator in East Timor where he vigorously repelled attacks by Indonesian security forces and Muslim militias on the Catholic East Timorese. In 2003 Bernard-Henri Lévy became one of the few Europeans outside the British government to offer qualified support to the US war on terror on the grounds that fighting Islamism, with its restrictions on women and free expression, was a humanitarian cause. After Kouchner became French Foreign Minister under the centre-right administration of Nicolas Sarkozy in 2007, he reversed France's opposition to the war and the international fight against Islamist terrorism.

In the event, Iraq and the bloody sectarian chaos that ensued proved another setback. It also claimed de Mello's life. Working as the head of another UN mission, this time in Baghdad, he was killed in the bombing of the UN headquarters in 2003 by an al-Qaeda group that claimed it was avenging de Mello's actions against Muslims in East Timor. But the loss of one of their icons only redoubled the resolve of his peers. A UN World Summit in 2005 adopted humanitarian intervention – the 'Responsibility to Protect', or R2P – as official UN doctrine, vowing that never again would there be a Rwanda or a Cambodia or a Srebrenica.

R2P enshrined in international law the reason and duty for humanitarian intervention. This was a grand transformation in how the world worked. No longer would the UN issue empty criticism of repressive and incompetent governments. Henceforth if a government was excessively inhumane or inept, it would forfeit its sovereignty and the UN would be mandated to do better through diplomacy, sanctions or force. In many ways, R2P was a kinder, multilateral version of imperialism. Like imperialists, humanitarians presumed the West knows best. Like imperialists, they argued others' sovereignty could be overruled in the name of civilizing them. Like imperialists, over time their interventionist instincts bent them ever more in favour of using military force.

By this time the humanitarians were also making inroads into other parts of the Western establishment. The same year the UN approved R2P, Samantha Power, now in academia, began advising a young US Senator, Barack Obama, on another interventionist touchstone, the war between Darfuri rebels and the Sudanese regime in Khartoum. Sudan had been a focus since Operation Lifeline Sudan. After 9/11 the activists' numbers had been swelled by right-wing Christian Americans who characterized the conflict between south and north as one between Christian victims and Muslim oppressors. American evangelicals like Franklin Graham founded aid groups to which they gave names such as Samaritan's Purse to assist the south. Republican Congressmen began flying in with suitcases of dollars to buy Christian slaves from their Muslim overlords. George Bush's administration became the lead mediator in peace talks between Khartoum and Juba.

On Africa, Power worked closely with another rising US advocate of humanitarian intervention, John Prendergast. John had started his career in Sudan, writing excruciating reports for Human Rights Watch on the violence between rival southern militias. Under Bill Clinton, he switched to the government, working at the National Security Council as Director for African Affairs and as an advisor to Susan Rice in the State Department. After Clinton left, he switched back to non-government work, becoming an independent campaigner and publicist of some genius. He appeared frequently on television or before Congress, wrote books and editorials, and even advised the makers of the hit US television show *Law and Order: Special Victims Unit* on how to depict child soldiers and rape as a weapon of war. When he co-founded the Enough Project ('the project to end genocide and crimes against humanity'), John used his standing to reach out to another centre of Western influence, Hollywood, helping recruit George Clooney to South Sudan's cause, as well as his fellow actors Angelina Jolie (refugees), Matt Damon (water), Ben Affleck (Congo) and Don Cheadle (genocide and environment).

When Barack Obama was elected, the humanitarians' reach into the US government was assured. The new President appointed

Samantha Power as Special Assistant to the President in the State Department and a Senior Director at the National Security Council. He made Susan Rice Ambassador to the UN. John Prendergast became a frequent participant in White House discussions on Africa. In 2013, Obama promoted Rice and Power again. Rice became National Security Advisor and Power took Rice's old job at the UN.

The humanitarians' ascent to the highest office was complete. What began as an ideal inside the protest movement of the 1960s was, 50 years later, a cornerstone of Western foreign policy. This convergence between Western power and humanitarianism owed much to a mutual antipathy to Islamism. But it was also a credit to the commitment of its advocates, and there was no doubt, either, about the nobility of its goals: an end to suffering and war.

But even as the humanitarians were achieving new heights, South Sudan showed how short they could fall. International intervention had empowered a set of leaders whose behaviour quickly punctured any sense of triumph. The new ministers were accused of focusing on dividing up oil revenues among themselves. In 2011, several diplomats told me the government had stolen $14 billion in oil money since 2005, an allegation later repeated in public by Western diplomats and activist groups. In 2012, Kiir wrote to various government officials asking them to return $4 billion of it. In the same year, the south attacked the north and tried to steal the few oil wells Khartoum had retained after independence.

There were other signs of thuggery. Journalists were beaten, imprisoned and killed. A new constitution drawn up by President Salva Kiir granted him authoritarian powers. Worse, many southern leaders were turning on each other. Even before the Dinka-Nuer war erupted, thousands were dying every year in tribal clashes over land and cattle. The new government left aid workers to deal with some of the worst levels of health, education and poverty in the world – though, since two-thirds of the southern government was illiterate, that, at least, was partly justified.

For their part, the aid workers might have set an example with impressive results. They didn't. In 2005, South Sudan's donors had established a $526 million fund to get the country on its feet by paying for roads, running water, agriculture, health and education. Four years later, it had only spent $217 million of that. A World Bank investigation discovered its managers were apathetic and out of their depth. They had held up any spending for a year, for example, before explaining to the new government that it would need to open a bank account before payments could be made.

Then there was the UN, with its budget of $924 million a year and its 70 fortified bases across the country. It did not escape the notice of the South Sudanese that the single biggest infrastructure project in their new country – what South Sudan lacked above all else – was housing and offices for foreigners. Every time I returned to South Sudan, I heard ever more anger at these giant air-conditioned, razor-wired moon-bases on the edge of every town, which managed the neat trick of simultaneously focusing the UN's efforts and resources on itself while cutting it off from the people it was meant to assist. The bases seemed to symbolize the dilemma confronting all assistance. By designating one people as able to help and another as in need of that help, empowerment programmes could disempower. The very endeavour of trying to lift a people up could reduce them. With its riot fences and armed guards, the UN was presenting the South Sudanese with unassailable proof that it was on the wrong side of a line separating privilege from poverty.

South Sudan threw up other contradictions. It turned out that freedom, by its very nature, couldn't be shepherded on another's behalf. When South Sudan's leaders interpreted their new freedom as the freedom to kill each other, and the world reacted with horror, Kiir and others accused them of misunderstanding what they had helped create. Freedom meant freedom from everyone – from Khartoum, yes, but also erstwhile friends if they tried to take that freedom back. In this newly free country, even in a far from fully formed one like South Sudan, the world had much less influence than it imagined. President Kiir was especially intolerant of suggestions that he owed anyone. 'I am not under your command,' he told Ban ki-Moon in 2012 when the UN Secretary-General urged him to end his brief invasion of the north. 'I am a head of state accountable to my people. I will not withdraw the troops.' Likewise when the world demanded an end to the Dinka-Nuer fighting, Kiir's government staged mass rallies outside UN bases across the country demanding the foreigners leave. When Hilde Johnson, the Norwegian head of the UN Mission in South Sudan (UNMISS), protested at the way UN relief convoys were being harassed and delayed, Kiir accused her of trying to supplant him. 'Hilde Johnson and the UN are running a parallel government,' he said. 'They want to be the government of this country.' When aid agencies began warning of a looming famine, Kiir's government responded by telling the foreigners to leave. Four out of every five of the top jobs in foreign agencies and businesses would be reserved henceforth for South Sudanese.

It seemed possible that humanitarianism had reached a high-tide mark in South Sudan. In private, diplomats in Juba worried that if South Sudan was humanitarianism's fullest ever expression, its woeful failure put the whole doctrine in doubt. However noble the ideals, however high the ambitions, they were ruined by calamitous implementation. 'State-building was a total disaster,' one senior UN official conceded. 'It was just full of words and hardly any delivery, fragmented, weak and all over the place. It simply didn't deliver what the country needed.'

When I phoned him from Juba, John Prendergast said any expectations that South Sudan would experience a smooth birth ran counter to the violent norms of human history. But it was also true, he said, that South Sudan showed that the way the world pursued international intervention 'is crushingly flawed and will never make a difference unless it's altered. You have this plan where humanitarians are dispatched to help build a state – and they run smack up against political forces that have no interest in long-term peace and stability, that benefit from instability and no transparency. [The humanitarians] work on development before the war is over. They work with governments that are completely unreformed. The rebels are integrated into a national army without reform, so their predation continues. These are utterly fatal flaws. At this point in South Sudan, *everybody* has failed at their function.'

The world's weaknesses only became more evident once the violence started. In March 2014 the UN Security Council upgraded UNMISS' mandate from state-building to something more urgent: 'protecting civilians; facilitating humanitarian assistance; monitoring and reporting on human rights; preventing further inter-communal violence'. In reality, the UN seemed unable or unwilling even to protect its own bases, let alone venture out to stop the killing. 'These forces were sent for state-building, not war,' said John. 'You need to get troops that are willing to fight.'

The emergency aid effort was also insufficient. In mid May, when the rains began, cholera swept Juba, killing more than 130 and infecting close to 6,000, among them refugees camped outside the UN's main base. After that came an epidemic of malaria. Famine was said to be only months away. UN Secretary-General Ban ki-Moon warned that in a worst-case scenario, 'half South Sudan's 12 million people will either be displaced internally, refugees abroad, starving or dead by the year's end'.

Maybe, sighed a few veteran diplomats in Juba, the answer was simply to pull out. Asked what the world had accomplished in South Sudan, one Western diplomat with three decades of experience in Sudan replied: 'I would say we have saved a lot of lives.' But it was fair, he said, to wonder whether two generations of efforts to teach South Sudanese leaders how to care – how to provide food and education and health – had had the opposite effect. Had aid taught South Sudan's leaders they didn't need to bother? Had it enriched them and allowed them to build the forces now slaughtering their own countrymen? 'Did we create this?' asked the diplomat. 'If we had bailed out 20 years ago, would the country be more politically mature now? Probably, yes.' At one point, I noticed the man was struggling not to cry. Seeing Mading and me out through the steel gates of his high-walled compound in Juba, he said: 'I honestly don't think anybody here has any answers any more.'

Humanitarianism was being ruined by incompetence and indifference within the rank and file on whom it relied for implementation. But among its leading advocates in the UN and aid industry, I began to see humanitarianism's problem as one of character – or, rather, a problem of *great* character. Its disciples believed in freedom. They strove for the poor and unfortunate. They took on projects of almost impossibly high ambition and often put the happiness and welfare of strangers before their own. This idealism was admirable. But it made them easy meat for the lesser characters in whom they placed their trust. 'They get caught up in the romance,' said Peter Adwok, a former Cabinet minister fired by Kiir. 'They believe the best of people. They can't imagine their friends ordering people thrown out of the back of a helicopter.'

The humanitarians' high ideals seemed to limit not just their effectiveness but their imaginations too. By positioning themselves as the protectors of all, they set themselves up for certain failure. And yet their character was such that, whatever the doubts and misgivings and setbacks, there was no question of quitting. Confronted by catastrophe in South Sudan, I heard scores of US diplomats, UN officials, aid workers and activists accept responsibility, confess they should have done more – and refuse to be deterred. Failure was no reason to doubt the cause. On the contrary, the history of how humanitarianism grew from the margins to become orthodoxy proved the value of steadfastness. Almost all their suggestions for South Sudan were about doing more of the same: more aid, more peacekeepers, firmer sanctions on South

Sudanese leaders, a bigger UN presence. Hilde Johnson stressed the enormity of the task still ahead. 'A peace agreement is just a few signatures on a piece of paper,' she said. 'Actual peace starts the day the signatures are dry.'

Frustrated by those they had tried to help, it was easy to see how the urge to do something might become an urge to take over. To hear some talk, the best way forward was to take South Sudan back to an earlier era. When I called her in Washington, the US Ambassador, Susan Page, initially insisted foreigners should be confined to a supporting role but soon switched to talking about how to impose international will. 'Right now [the question is] how do you get a country of 10 million people to reconcile even when war and ethnic conflict continue to exist?' she said. Some diplomats in Juba were discussing restarting Operation Lifeline Sudan. Many were passing round an article in the *Atlantic* magazine that argued for a kind of humanitarian colonialism, doing away with South Sudan's government altogether and creating a UN or US protectorate until South Sudan could be trusted to rule itself. 'The solution to these problems is not to send in more peacekeepers . . . or hammer out a power-sharing agreement between the warring parties – or rather, not only to do these things,' wrote Pascal Zachary, an Arizona University lecturer in African affairs. 'The response to South Sudan's turmoil should be crafted with a set of policy tools that were popular in the 1950s . . . the process known as "trusteeship", whereby a newly independent nation is granted special forms of assistance and special constraints on sovereignty. In some cases, the former colonial power sought to administer the trusteeship, and in other cases an international coalition or the United Nations did so.'

Even before South Sudan fell apart, George Clooney had had his doubts about how things would turn out. 'I've spent a lot of time with the South Sudan government,' he said. 'I have faith in them. But could it fail? Without question.' But, like his fellow humanitarians, his uncertainty only redoubled his conviction. 'What I do know is it will most definitely fail without the entire world's effort in trying to help it,' he said.

When I asked Clooney why he kept coming back, he admitted it was partly about what he got out of it, the way it made him feel. 'The truth,' he said, 'is I think any human being, once they participate in something that's bigger than themselves and something that you can't fix yourself . . . the idea that you wouldn't continue . . . you would feel as if you had done something terrible, you'd abandoned them. So you have to continue.'

After World War II, Africa rose up against foreign interference. Since the turn of the millennium, a new wave of African assertion has once more gathered pace. But there will always be those Africans who, for their own reasons, ask foreigners to intervene. Clooney mentioned that one South Sudanese official to whom he was close was Ezekiel Lol Gatkuoth, South Sudan's former Ambassador to the US. In 2014 Ezekiel was on trial in Juba for treason, accused of helping instigate the violence in December. He was being kept under lock and key except for the occasional court appearance. One of those fell on a day when Mading and I were in the city.

We arrived early, positioned ourselves at the court entrance and, as Ezekiel swept past in a cloud of soldiers and assistants, Mading slipped a note I had prepared into the hand of his lawyer. I had written down a handful of questions, chiefly about what Ezekiel thought the world should do next. 'Some say the world should pull out,' I wrote. 'Some argue for more intervention. What do you think?'

The lawyer returned the note the next day, with Ezekiel's replies scribbled under my queries. The disaster in South Sudan had a clear solution, said Ezekiel. 'George Clooney must get more engaged now to help shape the future of this country,' he wrote.

FOUR

UGANDA AND THE CENTRAL AFRICAN REPUBLIC

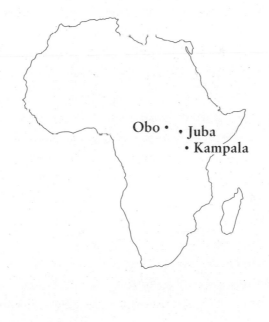

Obo · · Juba
· Kampala

Leaving Juba and travelling due west towards the centre of Africa, humanity thins then all but disappears until the world seems to be nothing but thorn forest and scrub, stretching in every direction to the horizon. After 700 kilometres, you come to the town of Obo, which lies in the bend of an unknown river in a nameless forest in a country whose name – Central African Republic – is generic. A few kilometres from Africa's Pole of Inaccessibility, its furthest point from any ocean, it is about as remote a place as exists in the world. Obo's 15,000 residents build houses of cane and palm thatch, have neither power nor running water, and come together at the town church to which the priest still summons them by banging a stick on a wooden drum. Outside town, in any direction, are hundreds of kilometres of unbroken forest, home to nomads, pygmies and hippos.

There were almost no cars in Obo but there were motorbikes. Dominic and I hired a pair and followed the single road through town to its western edge. A sidetrack led past a police post to which a baby chimpanzee was tied by a string. Past it, the path ended on a bluff overlooking the river on which there was a new construction: a two-metre-high reed fence inside which were several grass huts. There was a guard outside. I scribbled my name on a piece of paper, handed it to the man and asked him to take it inside. Seconds later two stern white faces popped up on the other side of the fence. 'You're not allowed in here,' said one, in an American accent. 'Speak to public affairs in Entebbe.' And the faces disappeared.

What were 30 US Special Operations soldiers doing in one of the most far-flung places on earth? Special Ops' customary secrecy notwithstanding, their mission was on public record. In May 2010, Congress passed the Lord's Resistance Army (LRA) Disarmament and Northern Uganda Recovery Act, mandating President Barack Obama to 'eliminate the threat to civilians and regional stability' posed by the LRA. In response, Obama said he would back African efforts to 'apprehend or remove' LRA leader Joseph Kony. He duly deployed 30 Special Operations troops to the Central African Republic and 70 more to Uganda, Congo and South Sudan. Two years later he doubled the force and equipped it with four Osprey search aircraft.

To which a reasonable question was: why?

The Lord's Resistance Army had its origins in a devout Christian group called the Holy Spirit Movement founded by a woman called Alice Auma in Gulu, northern Uganda, in the early 1980s. Alice belonged to the Acholi tribe and earned her living as a spirit medium, diviner and healer. In 1985, at the height of a bloody civil war that would see Yoweri Museveni win power, she was possessed by the spirit of a dead Acholi soldier whom she called 'Lakwena', meaning 'messenger'. Lakwena instructed Alice to give up her work, which Lakwena said was pointless in war, and concentrate on trying to end the bloodshed. She was to do this by forming the Holy Spirit Movement, with which she would recapture the Ugandan capital, Kampala, from Museveni.

In 1987 Alice marched south towards Kampala. She had thousands of followers and picked up more support en route from other anti-Museveni rebels. But Lakwena had instructed his followers to arm themselves only with sticks and stones and smear themselves with shea nut oil to protect themselves from bullets. Outside Kampala, the movement was obliterated by Museveni's artillery. Alice fled to a life of exile in a Kenyan refugee camp. Joseph Kony, one of the movement's commanders, gathered up the few survivors, led them back to the north and disappeared into the forest, where he renamed his force the Lord's Resistance Army.

Kony's *modus operandi* was terror and his brutality made him a grotesque caricature of a bloodthirsty African rebel. He ordered his fighters not just to rape and murder but to mutilate and eat parts of their dead enemies. Most of his soldiers were children and he sustained his forces' strength by pillaging villages to abduct more. That was also how the LRA leader found his wives, of which he soon built up a harem of a few dozen.

Evil isn't a useful word – it is dismissive and obscures under-standing – but in Kony's case it was a description he embraced. One LRA deserter in Obo, 33-year-old Emmanuel Dada, said he had been abducted by Kony from his village and forced to fight and kill for the LRA for several years. Dada remembered a sermon the leader once gave. 'Kony told us: "The Bible says if you are going to do good, do good all your life, and if you are going to do evil, do evil all your life,"' recalled Dada. '"I chose evil and that's what I will always do."'

Kony had long since given up trying to oust Museveni. Over the years the LRA had wandered from Uganda into South Sudan, Congo and the Central African Republic. After a December 2008 assault on the LRA's main base in Congo, Kony split the LRA into tiny groups and scattered them as far as Darfur. He pursued a bloody campaign of annihilation against any villagers he came across, not just stealing food and abducting children but carrying out a series of massacres too. 'I killed too many to count,' Dada said. 'They forced me to kill an old man. He was just doing nothing, just sitting there, and I beat him to death with a stick.'

After 26 years of marauding through the central African bush, the cumulative damage inflicted by the LRA was staggering. Despite never mustering more than a few thousand fighters, and generally no more than a few hundred, the UN said the LRA had killed tens of thousands, abducted 30,000 and displaced 1.5 million.

Of all the rebel groups on the continent, the LRA conformed most closely to rich-world nightmares of African savagery. Perhaps it should have been no surprise, then, that it attracted some peculiarly imaginative Westerners to fight it. One day I visited an orphanage in a town called Nimule on South Sudan's border with Uganda. The place was a crumbling collection of 18 windowless brick and tin-roof buildings including dormitories, school halls and a cafeteria housing around 200 children. A sign indicated it was run by the World Mission Shekinah Fellowship, an evangelical church in Central City, Pennsylvania, with support from other charities. There was nothing to suggest the presence of the man who founded it, Sam Childers, aka the Machine Gun Preacher.

Childers has written two books. He titled the first *Another Man's War: The True Story of One Man's Battle to Save Children in the Sudan.* The second he called *Living on the Edge – Something Worth Dying For, the Children of Africa.* The first book was made into a movie, *Machine Gun Preacher*, starring the Scottish action hero Gerard Butler. The books, the movie, plus Machine Gun Preacher T-shirts, caps, shot glasses, dog tags, keyrings and beer coolers, as well as a selection of photographs showing Childers on his Harley-Davidson in checked shirts sawn off at the shoulder, chewing a toothpick through his walrus moustache, are available on Childers' website. The subject of all this merchandise never varies: Sam Childers.

Childers is a former drug dealer and biker turned born-again Christian who in the late 1990s made it his one-man mission to save 'Africa's orphans' from the LRA. The poster for *Machine Gun Preacher*, the movie, depicted a stern-faced Gerard Butler in black jeans, black T-shirt and black beard, his legs astride an African shanty town, one hand gripping a Kalashnikov, the other protecting an African urchin in rags. In the film, Butler growls to a

Sudanese boy with whom he is sitting outside a mud hut: 'Helping you kids 'sbout the only good thin' I 'ver dun 'nthis life.' A few seconds pass. 'You got no idea what 'msaying, dooya?' says Butler.

It turned out that few of the villagers living around Childers' orphanage had any idea who he was, either. I went to five or six huts, then asked around in a few shop stalls. Everywhere I drew a blank. Nobody knew the *kawaja*. Some said they had seen him once or twice but added he only came to the orphanage every few years. No one could give any credence to Childers' claim to be single-handedly fighting the LRA.

Eventually, I found Festo Fuli Akim sitting out in his front yard taking the afternoon air. Festo was 80. He knew Childers. He thought the orphanage was a good idea. Festo had helped Childers obtain the necessary permissions to start it. He found him a plot of land. He gave him several truckloads of bricks. And at first, the orphanage seemed to fulfil a need. But within a few years, it was collapsing. Festo claimed Childers was struggling to finance the place. The orphans were malnourished and had only rags for clothes. Other aid agencies began bringing in food and shoes. 'The children were always breaking out and eating my mangoes and guavas,' said Festo. 'They were in bad shape.' Childers denied the orphans suffered and blamed others for misusing funds.

After an LRA attack on Nimule, however, Childers hit upon a scheme to raise attention and money. 'He took the orphans to a river camp some way away from here,' said Festo. 'He trained them. He dressed them in camouflage uniforms. He armed them. He pretended that one group was LRA and that he was trying to rescue children from the LRA. He took pictures of himself. He had a documentary made about himself.' But when they returned to Nimule, the children told the villagers what Childers was up to. Policemen raided the orphanage and found four guns. Childers was asked to leave. Festo sighed. 'Sam is a complicated man,' he said. 'He always talked big, big big. He thought he would become famous. A commander.' Childers has denied these allegations.

I wanted to hear Childers' explanation for his actions but he ignored my attempts at contact. I did find some account of his motives in the opening pages of his second book, *Living on the Edge*. It began with 'I, Sam Childers, the Machine Gun Preacher' riding his Harley to a Hollywood Oscar party, celebrating the release of the film. 'It's a movie about a man who does his best to take care of people who can't take care of themselves,' wrote Childers. At the entrance to the party, Childers described how his appearance – 'big moustache, biker tattoos, leather from head to toe' – gave the doorman pause, only for his eyes to widen in amazement when Childers pointed out the words 'Machine Gun Preacher' on his guest list. The doorman then stepped aside and Childers strutted into the party. 'In a few minutes, I was shooting the breeze with George Clooney,' he wrote. 'It made perfect sense to me.'

Over the years, Africa has received its share of foreigners on a quest for what Carl Jung called individuation: discovering themselves by being out in the world. It is an old story – the stranger who becomes a hero to the people of a faraway land – and in the rich world, it is generally regarded as a laudable rite of passage. And, it is true, the desire to make a difference can sound commendable.

The problem arises when questions of who to help, and why, are left as secondary. This is how Africans become bit players in their own story. There is no room in this picture for Africans who can look after themselves or control their own destiny. There is no recognition of the zero-sum maths of how fulfilling Westerners' desire to do something can rob Africans of the ability to do it for themselves. There is little understanding of how viewing Africa simplistically encourages some dangerously simple solutions. Feed people. Clothe them. Starve the terrorists. See how straightforward Africa's problems have become.

Most aid workers laughed through *Machine Gun Preacher*, which became a kind of cult hit on the NGO circuit. But how different was it from *The E-Team*, a 2014 documentary on the 'high-stakes work' of Human Rights Watch's 'emergency team'? 'Though they are very different personalities, Anna, Rwigema and Peter share a fearless spirit and a deep commitment to exposing and halting human rights abuses all over the world', read a publicity release featuring a poster of the three, looking every bit as rough-travelled and righteously furious as Gerard Butler. One of them was Peter Bouckaert, 'a savvy strategist and fearless investigator . . . "the James Bond of human-rights investigators"'. I knew Peter, who had been a neighbour in Cape Town. He was dedicated, good company and publicized appalling acts in tough spots. I can't say he ever reminded me of James Bond.

The humanitarians' licence to honour themselves derived from their assertion that they were championing universal values. The justice of their causes was undeniable, they said. And the way humanitarians presented them, it was hard to object. How could you be *against* Saving the Children?

The trouble was the way the children – actually fully formed adults, in the main – insisted on leading more complicated lives than black-and-white didactics allowed. Take the vow from clothes manufacturers like Nike, H&M and Walmart's Baby George line that they would only use organic cotton, and thus instantly transform the fortunes of Uganda's low-tech cotton farmers who would become prosperous, green pioneers. Was there a better win-win? Unlikely, it seemed, until you considered that Uganda's central villages also had the world's highest concentration of malaria, and that organic certification required a ban on mosquito-killing insecticides. A trip I made to the most malarial town on earth, Apac in northern Uganda, confirmed a dreadful suspicion: African babies were dying so that Western babies could wear organic.

Simplification can aid understanding. It can also impede it. And in the imaginary, curiously flat Africa of the humanitarian, the people are one-dimensional objects awaiting rescue or upliftment by kindly foreigners. Any recognition of them as fully realized individuals with normal, intricate lives is lost. Africa becomes an exotic, bizarre, violent place, without past or context, a place of good guys and bad guys, simple problems and universal solutions. It's only a short step from there to regarding Africa as a place that is essentially negative, where half-humans live half-lives, life is somehow cheaper and where foreigners shrug at black misfortune as another example of 'TIA' – This is Africa. This Africa is a place without history, where wars erupt out of nowhere, over nothing, and Africans fight and die all the time, for no good reason. War just is, because Africans are. The more incomprehensible and cease-less the dying, the more heroic the effort to help. This is an Africa where, as the *New Yorker* correspondent Jon Lee Anderson puts it, the people have become 'killable'.

After Obo, I flew to the US to find out why the government had decided it should try to kill Joseph Kony. It was then that I first met John Prendergast. John said the reason for the US interest was down to an extraordinary new 'social movement of mostly young people attempting to address a moral issue halfway round the world which had little or no ramifications for them'. John thought it was amazing. 'How many people responded to the call!' he said. 'It's revitalizing.'

The movement was Invisible Children. It was founded by three Californian students: Bobby Bailey, Laren Poole and Jason Russell. They set up the group in March 2003, a time when they were, re-spectively 21, 19 and 24. Invisible Children's origins were easy to trace because, with some foresight, its three founders had filmed them for their own documentary. At the beginning of the film, they gave charmingly inarticulate explanations for why three hipsters with goatees and baseball caps might be setting off for Africa to make a film about a 47-year-old civil war that had cost two million lives. 'We are naïve kids that have not travelled a lot and we are going to Sudan,' said Bobby Bailey. Laren Poole rambled about how 'media is life, it defines your life. So it's an obvious choice for three kids who want to find the truth . . .'. In a voice-over,

Jason Russell added: 'None of us knew what we were doing.'

As the documentary recorded, the three made it to Sudan but failed to find the fighting. After filming themselves vomiting, setting anthills on fire and chopping a snake in half, they followed a trail of Sudanese refugees south across the border into northern Uganda. When they approached the town of Gulu, a truck in front of them was shot at and two people were killed. Forced to stay in Gulu overnight, they filmed as thousands of children showed up after dark, sleeping on street corners, in a bus park and in the corridors of Gulu's hospital. 'Needless to say,' narrated Jason Russell, 'we found our story.'

The three friends had stumbled across the fallout from the LRA's war: thousands of children too afraid to sleep at home because of the risk of being abducted. The Californians stayed two months and ended by vowing, on camera, to return. Back in San Diego they cut their documentary and called it *Invisible Children*. To maximize its impact, they took their film on the road themselves, screening it to hundreds of thousands of students at high schools and college campuses across the US.

So far, so do good. But Invisible Children was different from other campaign groups. Young, privileged and goofy, their DNA was more selfie than selfless. They broke with convention, horrifying old Africa hands by making a film that was as much about themselves as the war, discarding any notion of neutrality and paying no lip service to concerns about interfering in the sovereign affairs of a foreign country. While military action was anathema to most of the aid world, Invisible Children demanded it. When I spoke to Jason Russell and Ben Keesey, Invisible Children's 29-year-old CEO, the pair said the established model of international intervention, addressing needs for food and shelter but ignoring the political cause, was merely a way of 'managing pain' but not fixing it. Ben said even the most aggressive form of foreign intervention, UN peacekeeping, had been ineffective in Darfur, Congo and Sudan because it was done by developing-world armies with no stake in the fight and no peace to keep. That left robust Western – preferably US – military action.

In many ways, Invisible Children was humanitarianism taken to its logical end point. Its philosophy and supporters were largely Christian. The self-absorption the group displayed – and which Sam Childers had taken to such delirious heights – had dogged the humanitarian movement from the start. The question of deploying armed force was another long-standing paradox. It was the most forceful way of enforcing international goodwill, but it also meant giving up the moral high ground and that, for most, was a step too far. Childers didn't care about any of that, nor did Invisible Children. 'That's really old-school,' said Jason. Invisible Children wanted action. The ends justified the means. 'What's more humanitarian than stopping a war?' asked Jason. 'I understand the conviction that violence begets violence. But either you just go on pulling people out of the river or you go upstream, find out who is pushing them in and stop them. And that's not about Kumbaya concerts for world peace.' Jason said he would prefer Kony captured alive and tried, not killed. But he was realistic about how unlikely that was. 'This is a war,' he said. 'We're not hoping for rainbows and butterflies.'

Invisible Children wanted US military action to finish off the LRA. They were surprised when they didn't immediately get it. Their film did generate impressive support, though, enough to provide funds for eight further documentaries. A team of what grew to 60 volunteers then toured across the US, screening their new films to total audiences of up to a million, drumming up more support and more donations. Within a few years, Invisible Children had made the LRA a key foreign issue for American students. But however much publicity the group garnered, it didn't solve anything. 'In our world,' Jason said, 'abducting children, cutting people's faces off, making children eat their friends – that just doesn't happen. We thought: "Once people know about this, it's going to end in a year.'" It didn't. Which was when Invisible Children linked up with John Prendergast as their big gun in Washington.

By the time of Barack Obama's election, John's links to the celebrity world were without equal. Perhaps more than anyone, he had helped kick off a new era of superstar advocacy. When a Republican president gave way to a Democrat one in 2009, it sealed John's influence. His ties to the new administration were manifold. He was a former advisor to Susan Rice, by then US Ambassador to the UN. From their work together on Darfur, he was also friends with Samantha Power, by then advisor to the National Security Council. John had also co-founded the Enough Project with Gayle Smith, now Special Assistant to the President and Senior Director at the National Security Council. The President was even a former community organizer himself.

With the access and influence at his command, John took the energy that Invisible Children had stoked and focused it on Washington. He drew up a punishing schedule of meetings with Senate and Congressional leaders, and White House staffers. John's stance was unequivocal. The LRA should be bombed, he said. By 2009, John and Invisible Children had made impressive progress and were helping draft a Congressional Act demanding presidential action against the LRA. By early 2010, a time of corrosive partisanship in Washington, the anti-LRA group had secured cross-party Congressional backing for the LRA Act and in the Senate co-sponsorship from conservative Sam Brownback and liberal Russ Feingold. Whenever the legislation hit a speed bump, Invisible Children overcame it through sheer numbers. At one point Senator Tom Coburn, a Republican known as 'Dr No' for blocking legislation on budgetary grounds, tried to kill the bill. That was a cue for 100 Invisible Children activists to sleep in the car park outside his office for 11 nights in snowy, midwinter Oklahoma until he relented.

*

At first glance, the saga of how three Californian backpackers persuaded Obama to deploy 100 Special Operations soldiers to central Africa seemed the ultimate wag-the-dog story. If that was the case, it raised some profound questions about the US political process and, in particular, how America decided to go to war.

But as the LRA campaign gathered pace, John said that though the White House shared his humanitarian goals, Obama was revealing he had additional reasons for backing it. One was smart politics. Throughout their lobbying, John said he and Invisible Children were quietly encouraged by the White House – by Power, Rice and Obama himself. 'You make it an issue for young people, a community who vote, and he will take that seriously,' said John. 'He's very aware of the scope of movements.'

Another motive was smart counter-terrorism. At the heart of Obama's remade US foreign policy was a belief that after the Bush years, in which American soldiers had garnered a reputation as hegemonic, vengeful bullies who loved oil and hated Muslims, it was in the best US national interest to present America itself as the ultimate humanitarian, an all-round international good guy. In another era, aid groups in Afghanistan had argued that the humanitarian project could be writ large, and extended to governments or armies. Obama was reaching back further still, to the pre-humanitarian Cold War, and arguing, once again, that being righteous had strategic benefits for the West. And in the twenty-first century, he proposed that the US military would take a leading role. They would continue to protect the US directly with force. But they would also do so indirectly, by representing America as a benign force out in the world, doing good by being good.

In April 2013, the Sudan scholar and former Africa activist Alex de Waal wrote that he had become 'rather uncomfortable' with the humanitarian movement, 'not because I had diluted my personal commitment to working in solidarity with suffering and oppressed people but because a group of people, in whose company I didn't want to be, were claiming not only to be activists but to define "activism" itself'. De Waal decried the policy lobbyists and 'designer activists' in Washington who now endorsed African causes. 'It was no accident,' continued de Waal, 'that their purported solutions placed the "activists" themselves at the centre of the narrative, because many of them were Hollywood actors – or their hangers-on – for whom the only possible role is as the protagonist-saviour.' And if the way these activists supplanted Africans as guardians of African interests was plain wrong, said de Waal, a new low was how the actions they proposed all had one thing in common: 'using more US power around the world'.

John and Invisible Children had been pushing at an open door. By the time Congress passed the LRA law, Obama was telling John he planned to stretch its wording as far as possible – even to the extent of interpreting the words 'eliminate the threat' to mean US boots on the ground. John didn't particularly care what anyone's reasons were for joining the fight. Whatever worked. That didn't mean he hadn't noticed them. 'We suddenly got the feeling that anything was possible. We never asked for troops on the ground. But they went further than anything we were advocating. And this is not a decision by underlings. This is a decision by the President.'

This was what de Waal meant when he said activism had been hijacked in the name of US power. It was the kind of thinking that led Rice, Power and Obama to push the argument inside the White House in favour of attacking Muammar Gaddafi's regime in Libya to protect pro-democracy rebels. The operation against the LRA was an even fuller example of the US military's new righteous pose. In early 2012, just as I was travelling to Obo, Obama chose the National Prayer Breakfast to give a detailed explanation of his new thinking on how to wield US power overseas. 'When I decide to stand up for foreign aid, or prevent atrocities in places like Uganda,' said Obama, 'it's not just about strengthening alliances, or promoting democratic values.' It was also about 'the Biblical call to care [and] projecting American leadership around the world. It will make us safer and more secure.'

At its most damaging, humanitarians' self-regard encouraged them to appropriate African autonomy. They defined Africa's problems and imagined their solutions. What was meant to be about them ended up being about you.

Employing the US military as armed humanitarians wrote that in stone. Constitutionally, the President could only use the US military for US national defence. This is how foreign military adventurism and foreign compassion, two belief systems that might at first sound very far apart, could come to intersect. This is also how a group of aid workers might get themselves mixed up in an American plot to cause a famine in pursuit of a few thousand Islamists.

On 5 March 2012, Invisible Children released a 29-minute internet film, their tenth, called *Kony 2012*. The idea behind it was to encourage Invisible Children's followers to make Kony the most famous war criminal on earth. That would, they said, raise the necessary political will to arrest or kill him.

The film was well made, slick and emotive. It featured Jason Russell's five-year-old son, Jake, as he grappled with the notion of Kony's killings and kidnapping of child soldiers. Another star was a Ugandan boy, Jacob, who cried as he called for Jason's help. Jason duly pledged it. Invisible Children had wanted 500,000 website hits. They got a million in 24 hours. After 48 hours they had a million every 30 minutes. Six days after its release, 85 million people had watched the film, by then translated into 50 different languages.

Depending on your view, *Kony 2012* was either stunningly innovative, a whole new type of campaign, or recklessly manipulative and inaccurate. There was no doubt that conventional aid-group campaigning, the old black-and-white pictures of starving babies, suddenly looked desperately tired. Effusive backing came from a host of American Senators, Congressmen and celebrities. International Criminal Court Chief Prosecutor

Louis Moreno Ocampo told the BBC: 'They've mobilized the world.'

The contrary view was that Invisible Children had made a film glorifying their own desire to save others and, in the process, simplified and sensationalized the LRA conflict. Academics and bloggers, particularly Africans, criticized the group for overstating the threat – with 150–200 mostly barefoot fighters, the LRA had never been weaker. Older, more established campaigners grumbled that Invisible Children's support for armed intervention conflicted with the foundation of a human rights organization. By personal-izing the narrative of *Kony 2012* with Jason Russell's own family, they added, Invisible Children had exposed their true motive: self-aggrandizement. Ugandan video-blogger Rosebell Kagumire became a web hit herself when she attacked Invisible Children for casting themselves as 'heroes rescuing African children' and Afri-cans as 'hopeless, voiceless'.

Jason now became the target of a deeply personal, bullying online 'takedown'. I called him eight days after *Kony 2012*'s release. He told me he hadn't slept for a week. The film was 'changing the world', he said, but at the same time 'people are calling me the devil'. Three days later, Jason was found by the San Diego police naked and kneeling on the side of a busy highway, raising his palms to Heaven and slapping the pavement. He was diagnosed with exhaustion and admitted to hospital.

Six months later Invisible Children released a new Kony film. Jason, now out of treatment, featured as extensively as before. He embarked on a series of prime-time interviews, including an appearance on the *The Oprah Winfrey Show*, to explain his be-haviour. He looked well, if a little chastened. But the breakdown had done nothing to dim his enthusiasm for the mission. On the contrary, he seemed to view his collapse as a wondrous, terrifying breakthrough. 'I literally thought I was responsible for the future of humanity,' he told one interviewer.

In the autumn of 2013, Invisible Children convened what they titled a Fourth Estate Summit at the University of Los Angeles campus in California. For $495 for an all-inclusive four-day ticket, participants could take part in an event 'where the future of justice is shaped by you'. Jason was MC. The star speaker was Samantha Power. A new addition to the Invisible Children leadership was Jedidiah Jenkins, described on the group's website as its 'ideas maven'.

On stage, Jedidiah talked about how Invisible Children saved him from law school – 'I felt the liberty of it, I couldn't get it out of my system, I became addicted to it' – and was now 'empowering' him to bicycle from Florence, Oregon, to Patagonia, South America. 'I'm on that search for identity, what makes us who we are,' he said. 'Once you know that you are worthy, and that you matter, you are *so* liberated to liberate others. We want to make sure you guys know what's up, what it's all about. Because when you fight for Jacob, when you fight for zero LRA, you're discovering yourself, you're building your heart.'

Jason introduced Samantha Power. Over a short film of her life, he narrated how the 'world-famous' holder of 'one of the most important positions in the world' had 'discovered her passion for human rights' in Bosnia. 'What she saw there changed her for ever and inspired her to dedicate her life to ending extreme human rights abuses.'

Power appeared in an orange and black evening dress to a standing ovation of cheers, claps and camera flashes. She clapped back. 'OMG,' she said. 'Right back atcha. I had a hunch that this would be inspiring. But this is something else.' Over another round of whooping and whistles, she began: 'So as you heard, I just began serving as US Ambassador to the United Nations . . .' – more applause – '. . . and I thought: "Where should I give my first speech?" There was only one answer. As you know, you are not just any group of young people. You are young people who take very seriously the charge to love your neighbour as yourself. Young people with a moral imagination. Young people on a mission.

Young people who are determined to leave this world kinder than the world you found.

'Though the odds are against you, you're going to offer whatever you have, your voice, your time, your creativity, your skills, your determination to try to help people. Because it turns out *you* have the power! If you've ever doubted that your activism matters, thanks to you the State Department is offering the first cash rewards to bring the LRA killers to justice!'

At that, the cheering began to raise the roof. 'That's you! You! The most powerful weapon of all is you! We need your positive moral vision more than ever. We need your vision of justice to win over those who fear it. We need your vision of freedom to overwhelm those who rely on repression. We need your vision of equality and tolerance to overcome those who propagate division and terror. And we need you to act so that that vision, your vision, prevails. You're not just activists. You're leaders. You're diplomats. It is your time!'

Power spoke for 20 minutes. When she finished, the crowd jumped to its feet for a second standing ovation. Jedidiah and Jason appeared on stage behind Power, raising their hands and applauding. Jason seemed entranced. 'I used to think that God did not make perfect people,' he said. 'I'm very wrong tonight.' Jedidiah might have been in love. 'Justice has a new face, and it is perfectly symmetrical, with red hair,' he said.

There followed a dance gala during which Jason brought his son Jake on stage. Then Jedidiah closed the event by introducing a last video that returned to his theme of saving the world through introspection. 'You being you is changing everything,' he said. 'You guys are everything.'

The lights dimmed. Images of ethnically mixed young people appeared on screen. 'There is only one vision, one life,' intoned a voice-over. 'It's your turn to carry that torch, to realize you were born to ignite the world. You are worthy.'

*

Judging by what former LRA fighters had said in Obo, Joseph Kony was astonished by the international campaign to kill him. One of his former wives was Guinikpara Germaine, who had been abducted from Obo when she was 15 in March 2008 and had spent three years as one of his three 'senior wives'. 'He used to laugh and enjoy himself,' she said. 'But now he recognizes he is weak. He says everyone must fight to the end, even if they are all killed. When he thinks about what he wants and his ambitions, he's like a man on drugs. He stays in his room and watches DVDs.'

I wondered whether Kony's depression had lasted. At the time the villagers of Obo expected him to meet an imminent and spectacular Hollywood end, in a drone strike, perhaps, or a helicopter raid. But by early 2015, three years later, the US team had yet to confront the LRA leader. And if US commitment to killing Kony depended on the hype Invisible Children mustered, that, too, was fading. The group never again matched *Kony 2012* for attention. Traffic to their website slowed and all but dried up. In the last days of 2014, the group announced it was folding.

If Kony remained at large, Invisible Children's main legacy would be telling thousands of American college kids that they could change the world if they only looked into themselves hard enough. *That* message did seem to have struck a chord. In November 2013, when a UN force routed a group of eastern Congolese rebels called the M23, another California-based group called Falling Whistles achieved new heights of narcissism when it announced on its website: 'We Stopped M23!!!!!!!!!!!!!' Under the slogan 'Be a whistle-blower for peace,' Falling Whistles sold tin and brass whistles over the web for $38–$58. For another $25, it would mail out a magazine called *Free World Reader*, 'built to be bravely displayed on coffee tables and bookshelves around the world'. It had been this – selling tin whistles and arranging magazines on coffee tables – that had stopped Congo's war.

At night in Obo, Dominic and I would watch the villagers dance and sing around giant wooden xylophones and congas. One new composition went:

> *The Americans are here*
> *Our saviours are here*
> *Our hope is here*
> *Let's dance.*

One night we noticed one of the drummers wearing something familiar, a 2008 Obama campaign shirt bearing the slogan 'Change You Can Believe In'. The people of Obo did believe. But I worried they would be disappointed. When humanitarians in Africa used the word 'change', I'd noticed, they'd mostly been talking about themselves.

FIVE

RWANDA AND CONGO

Goma • • Kigali

For an event with such wide consequences, the Rwandan genocide is poorly understood. The terms *Tutsi* and *Hutu*, for instance, have had different meanings at different times. Today Rwandans will tell you they denote distinct ethnicities, identifiable by discrete features. Tutsis are typically towering in height and have a long nose. Hutus are stockier and have a flatter nose. But in history, the terms also delineated different roles in the Rwandan royal court. In the fifteenth century, the Rwandan monarch was from the Tutsi minority, a semi-deity who ruled with the advice and consent of an autonomous council drawn from the Hutu majority.

That *ubuntu* power-sharing arrangement lasted until the nineteenth century when a series of expansionist Tutsi kings began pushing their kingdom deeper into eastern Congo. At home this militarism translated to a new Tutsi autocracy. The kings first marginalized the Hutu council, then all Hutus, by taking ownership of all land and demanding tithes from their subjects. This unwinding of Rwanda's delicate distribution of power likely provoked considerable Hutu resentment. But in the way it refashioned the Hutu-Tutsi relationship as an economic one, it had an unwitting benefit. A Hutu farmer who prospered could become a Tutsi and a Tutsi cattle herder who lost his animals to disease could become a Hutu. The lack of Hutu rebellion suggests the new social porousness eased the sense of exclusion Hutus must have felt.

When Europe divided up claims to Africa at the Berlin conference in 1885, there was no recognition of such subtleties. The Social Darwinism of the time held that colonialism was human evolution in action and the displacement or extermination of 'inferior' races by 'superior' ones was inevitable and sanctified progress, and therefore moral and desirable. In Congo, King Leopold II of Belgium oversaw the killing of millions of Congolese labourers, whom the colonists worked and beat to death. When Germany forfeited its overseas possessions with its defeat at the end of World War I, Belgium acquired Rwanda too. Blind even to the possibility of African nuance, the Belgians took Hutus and Tutsis simply as separate races and postulated that the Tutsis' higher wealth indicated they were superior, probably of Ethiopian or Mediterranean blood or even, as Speke had claimed, descended from Noah's son, Ham.

In 1932, the Belgians made Rwanda's ethnic division official and permanent. Belgian priests travelled the country measuring the width of their subjects' noses with callipers, then recorded the ethnicities thus determined on identity cards. The colonists further stoked Hutu resentment by favouring Tutsis with jobs. If divide and rule was standard practice for European imperialism, nowhere were the consequences graver than in Rwanda. As President Paul Kagame said when I first met him in 2007: 'The seeds of genocide were planted when the Belgians introduced the identity card.'

Kagame was born into a Tutsi family in 1957 in a hillside village called Tambwe in the green and terraced hills of southern Rwanda. By then, the legacy that Belgian rule might leave in an independent Rwanda was already apparent. Liberation was sweeping Africa and in Rwanda the Hutu majority, now supported by the Belgians in a last-minute spasm of conscience, began violently asserting its claim to power. In 1959, three years before independence, Hutu mobs butchered tens of thousands of Tutsis.

Kagame's family fled this first genocide, settling in a refugee camp in Gahunge in south-west Uganda in 1962. That same year, the departing Belgians handed power to a Hutu regime in Kigali, the capital. Growing up as a refugee, Kagame remembers asking his parents why they were stateless. 'I thought they must have done something,' he said. 'They explained to me the whole history. And I saw that I had nothing to do with my circumstances and how I was living. That builds something in you as you grow up. You question. It's on that basis that we, young people, thought of organizing. Even if it meant fighting, we would do that.'

Kagame's best friend in the camp was Fred Rwigema. The two young men decided that, to be successful revolutionaries, they required experience. In 1980, aged 22, Kagame and Rwigema were among the original 27 recruits to Museveni's guerrilla army in Uganda. After six years of bush fighting, in 1986 Museveni took Kampala with Kagame and Rwigema at his side. Kagame, an introvert, became Museveni's head of military intelligence. Rwigema, an extrovert, was appointed Deputy Minister of Defence.

By day, the pair built a new Uganda. At night they plotted revolution in Rwanda as founders of the Rwandan Patriotic Front (RPF). It was in Kampala in 1987 that Tito Rutaremara first met Kagame and Rwigema. Two decades later, Rutaremara was a portly, grey-haired senator in Rwanda's parliament with a taste for bright-patterned Mandela shirts. But in the 1980s, Rutaremara was a wild-haired dissident in London, protesting against Margaret Thatcher, American imperialism and apartheid. He became a regular visitor to Kampala, where he would discuss rebellion with Rwigema and Kagame.

The three men agreed that Africa's earlier, anti-colonial revolutions offered some lessons. The way so many of their fellow liberators turned tyrant on achieving power showed that strong self-criticism was needed to avoid corruption, factionalism and authoritarianism. And if African rebels had been too overbearing with their countrymen, they had been too deferential to foreigners. Many had imported Western ideas wholesale and allowed themselves to be sucked into the Cold War, usually by accepting military and financial aid from one side or another. The RPF, the three men resolved, would be different: self-reliant, internally democratic and never beholden to foreign ideas or finances. 'We were always digging into our culture to see if there were things to help us,' said Rutaremara. 'We wanted to be masters of our own destiny and of our own philosophy.' Kagame added that while the trio admired many European ideals – democracy, free speech, universal suffrage – some of these goals would have to remain aspirational for Rwanda for a generation or two. 'Everything is contextual,' Kagame said. Nineteenth-century America was not as free or liberal as it was today. It made no sense, argued Kagame, to expect Rwanda instantly to transform itself into a modern, twenty-first-century democracy.

In the event, the RPF's revolution was nearly over as soon as it began. In 1990 Kagame accepted a US offer of military training at Fort Leavenworth in Kansas. The impetuous Rwigema decided he couldn't wait for his friend. On 1 October, Rwigema crossed from Uganda into Rwanda at the head of 2,000 men. He was killed within hours.

When Kagame caught up with the RPF in northern Rwanda days later, it was disintegrating. Swallowing his grief, Kagame marched the surviving RPF forces high up into the Virunga volcanoes, organized supplies of food and ammunition and drilled discipline back into the ranks. 'Fred was Kagame's friend,' said Rutaremara. 'Of course he was affected. But we needed him. He was the right person at the right time to save the Struggle.'

By 1991, a remade RPF was taking territory. By 1992 it had beaten back the national Rwandan army almost to Kigali. Peace talks were under way by April 1994. But on 6 April a plane carrying the Rwandan and Burundian Presidents, both Hutus, was shot down over Kigali. Disputes over who fired the fatal missile continue to this day. But the double assassination acted as a signal to Hutu soldiers and militias to start the apocalypse that, it soon became apparent, they had been preparing for months. As reports reached him of the bloodbath erupting to his south, Kagame accelerated his advance. In three months he captured all Rwanda and pushed the Interahamwe over the border into eastern Congo. By then, however, between 800,000 and a million people were dead.

One remarkable aspect of the genocide was that most of it was accomplished by hand, with machetes. It was hard work. Even a determined group of several hundred *génocidaires* would take days to dispatch several thousand Tutsis and dissident Hutus. The killers worked in shifts, sometimes collapsing in exhausted sleep on the ground next to the bodies they had felled. One way to accelerate the killing was to urge Tutsis to seek shelter in churches, then throw grenades through the windows. Afterwards the killers would wade through the pews, butchering any survivors.

Many of the churches had been left untouched. On my first visit to Rwanda, I drove an hour south from Kigali to the village of Nyamata. Years after the event, you could still see the blood on the church walls where the babies had been smashed up against the brick. There was more blood – wide, brown stains of it – on the altar cloth. Grenade-blast patterns twinkled like stars in the roof. Against a side wall were 20 new-looking coffins and, next to them, a cloth on which were laid ribs, femurs and broken skulls. More than a decade later, new bodies were still being unearthed every week.

Outside the church, a narrow staircase sank into the ground, leading to a crypt. I descended, my shoulders brushing against the earth sides. At the foot of the stairs was a narrow, gloomy chamber lined on each side with bare and dusty wooden shelves. I squeezed between them. On each shelf were thousands of skulls. There was something about their eyes, small pools of Styx with their own insistent and impenetrable mysteries of murder. I tried to count them but kept losing my place. It became hard to breathe. I ran back up the stairs. The man who'd let me in said there were 50,000 people down there.

Close by the church I met Jacqueline Nyiramayonde, brushing

leaves off the dirt path in front of her house. Jacqueline was 42. She had been a young mother living in Kigali when the killing started. She spent a week with her boy and girl hiding behind a cupboard in a neighbour's house. When the Interahamwe reached their street, the neighbour drove her and her children to a military camp, hoping they would be safe. But the *génocidaires* followed them and stood outside the gates, asking for Jacqueline and her children by name. So the neighbour bought passage for them on a truck heading south to the city of Butare, hiding them under sacks of rice. Jacqueline and her children were discovered en route at an Interahamwe roadblock. That might have been it for them if the truck driver, who was sympathetic, hadn't bought their freedom. Once in Butare, they were reunited with Jacqueline's husband and another son. The family hid out in the city for three years. Finally, in 1998, with their home in Kigali destroyed, Jacqueline and her husband judged it safe to move to their families' ancestral village, Nyamata. They found the place still littered with the bones of their relatives. 'My three brothers and two sisters had been killed,' she said. 'My uncle was killed with all his children. My husband also lost all his brothers and sisters.'

Such a toll on one family was not unusual. Six out of every 10 people living in Nyamata were killed. Across Rwanda, surveys found that more than two-thirds of the genocide's survivors had witnessed at least one killing and close to nine out of ten had come across dead bodies, or parts of them.

Though no one said it explicitly, when the UN adopted R2P in 2005, few imagined sending peacekeepers to Asia or Latin America, or Russia or China, or the Middle East, and certainly not to any first-world nation. Everyone, however, expected to be sending them to Africa. Rwanda had been a particular spur to R2P. And after Kagame drove the Interahamwe across Rwanda's western border into Congo, the war had continued there.

Still, it was curious timing for the rich world to be pushing through a new code of intervention in Africa just as much of Africa was showing a rising ability to take care of itself. I wanted to witness one of these new 'just wars' up close to see whether, as R2P required, the world did a better job than the government it displaced. In October 2008, in Congo, I got my chance. A few thousand ethnic Rwandan rebels had advanced on Congo's second city, Goma. Aid agencies were proclaiming an imminent disaster. The only thing standing between eastern Congo and catastrophe, it was said, was the UN.

From Kigali the road to Congo threaded west through steep hills. Every slope and gully was cultivated in a patchwork of red and brown and green and gold, the frontiers of each smallholding marked by towering stands of silvery eucalyptus. In almost every village there were real, actual signs of trouble: hand-painted sign-boards marking the sites of massacres during the genocide. Here 212 were killed. There 318. Here 532. The word JENOSIDE was painted in scarlet capitals. As we wound down through the valleys to Lake Kivu, where the bloodshed had been concentrated, the signs indicated an escalation from mere massacres to attempted eradication. Several put the toll at '+/− 5,000'. The earth was a coppery-red. I couldn't help but think of all the blood that must have soaked into the soil in those 100 days.

The different paths Rwanda and Congo had taken since the genocide were never clearer than at the border. In Rwanda peace and prosperity reigned. Next to the genocide markers were signs of progress: boards indicating new hospitals and schools and government signs exhorting Rwandans on to a new future of virtuous prosperity. 'YES TO INVESTMENT', they read. 'NO TO CORRUPTION'. But, crossing the frontier, I passed from a new Africa of shopping malls and wifi into an old one that would have been familiar to Burton, Speke and Stanley. The asphalt stopped and turned to mud and grit. Here were grass-roofed huts and wood-wheeled bicycles, smoking volcanoes and jungles home to gorillas and pygmies, a vast land of giant suns, blood-red moons and war, which had continued unabated since Kagame pushed the *génocidaires* over the border. The first Congolese citizen I met, a border guard, shook me down for $50 then pressed the number of his friend into my hand, instructing me to employ the man as my fixer and translator.

Even without the fighting, poverty and corruption, it would be possible to think of Goma as a cursed city. At first glance its position, deep in the cradle of the Rift, seemed beautiful. To the south, placid Lake Kivu stretched away to green hills, Rwanda on the eastern shore, Congo on the west. To the north was the perfect black cone of one of the world's biggest volcanoes, Nyiragongo.

But Goma's residents regarded their surroundings more with fear than affection. Nyiragongo's crater was over three kilometres high, one and a half kilometres across and two and a half deep, and contained a lava lake that could cover all Manhattan in four and a half metres of lava. The mouth produced 50,000 tons of sulphur dioxide a day, more than all the industry, power stations and cars in the US and enough to produce acid rain of such concentration that it could burn the eyes and skin on contact. The seismic idiosyncrasies of the Albertine Rift had also created a dissolved bubble of methane and carbon dioxide 300 metres below Lake Kivu's surface that, at 300 cubic kilometres, was the same size as all the crude oil on earth. Occasionally lava from Nyiragongo heated the water, and carbon dioxide from the bubble escaped in a concentrated cloud. Heavier than air, the gas lurked in ditches at a height just tall enough to cover a child's head. Around 100 children suffocated that way every year on the lake's shores.

The threat of a true apocalypse was also ever present. Goma and Lake Kivu are in Nyiragongo's eruption path. In 2002, a river of lava rolled through town at 100 kilometres an hour, killing 147 people, splitting the town and burying two-thirds of the runway at its airport before sliding to a halt at the water's edge. Since then, volcanologists have discovered that Goma sits directly over a second fissure and a build-up of lava under the city indicated an eruption was approaching. That alone would likely kill tens of thousands. But if a poison-gas bubble and a killer volcano weren't enough, try to imagine what might happen if they met. Should the lava stream ever touch Lake Kivu's underwater bubble and release all the gas – as has happened at other volcanoes with similar geology – the consequences would be almost inconceivable. If 500 million tons of carbon dioxide or 230 cubic kilometres of methane were released at once – and in the latter case, ignited – they could blow much of the water out of Lake Kivu, depositing it onto the two million people living on its shores.

So far, however, it is Congo's political disasters that have proved the deadlier. When he pushed them out of Rwanda in 1994, Kagame had hoped the Interahamwe would melt away. Instead they found shelter in scores of refugee camps set up by aid groups, where they regrouped and rearmed, then counter-attacked across the border. By 1996 Kagame had had enough. He invaded Congo to fight what now rebranded itself the Democratic Force for the Liberation of Rwanda (FDLR). In 1997, Kagame's troops pursued their bloody advance all the way to Kinshasa, deposing the ageing autocrat President Mobutu Sese Seko and installing in his place an obscure Congolese rebel leader living in Tanzania called Laurent Kabila.

Kagame effectively ruled both countries for a short while. His Defence Minister, James Kabarebe, was simultaneously Kabila's Chief of Staff. But Rwanda had not killed off the FDLR and ordinary Congolese objected to Rwanda's overbearing influence. Under public pressure, in 1998 Kabila sacked Kabarebe and threw the Rwandans out. That proved to be a signal for pogroms to begin in eastern Congo against an ethnic Rwandan tribe, the Banyamulenge. Once more Rwanda and Uganda intervened and started moving on Kinshasa. This time, however, Kabila used promises of access to Congo's riches to attract reinforcements from Zimbabwe, Namibia, Chad, Libya, Sudan and Angola. Rwanda and Uganda then fell out, fighting over control of the inland river port of Kisangani. By 1999, Congo's war had degenerated into a pan-African smash-and-grab for Congo's minerals and timber.

Through ceasefires and negotiations, massacres and coups, the fighting in Congo has never stopped. And if Congo's wars never quite matched Rwanda's for bloody intensity, the sequel has proved bigger, longer and immeasurably more complicated. By 2008, the fighting was in its fifteenth year. It had spawned a plethora of rebel groups broadly aligned with one or other side of the Rwandan-Congolese divide. A string of small militias known as 'Mai Mai' had also sprung up, founded on a mix of tribal grievances and criminal intent. Everyone – government, army, Hutu, Tutsi, Congolese, Rwandan, Mai Mai – fought everyone else.

The UN first intervened in 1999 when it sent 90 liaison officers to try to bolster one of Congo's ceasefires. When that failed, in February 2000 it created the UN Mission in the Democratic Republic of Congo (MONUC), later renamed the United Nations Organization Stabilization Mission in the Democratic Republic of Congo (MONUSCO). Initially the mission had 5,537 soldiers. By 2008 it had more than tripled in size to 17,000 men, making it the world's biggest peacekeeping operation and ensuring it outnumbered by seven to one the biggest Congolese rebel group, the 2,500-strong, ethnically Rwandan Congrès National pour la Défense du People (CNDP). With an annual budget of $1.1 billion, the UN was also far better equipped. Against the rebels' Kalashnikovs, rocket grenades and ancient artillery pieces, the blue helmets had helicopters, planes, tanks and armoured personnel carriers. Finally, MONUSCO's mandate was the most aggressive in peacekeeping history, allowing it to 'forcibly implement' ceasefires and use 'all means deemed necessary' to protect civilians and improve security.

For all that, the Rwandan rebels were making all the running. When they advanced on Goma, Congo's underpaid, poorly equipped and ill-disciplined government soldiers abandoned their posts without a fight. The UN said a million civilians, a quarter of the eastern population, had fled their homes. If the rebels tried to take Goma, a key base for aid groups in Africa, foreign assistance would collapse and Congo might even split in two. It was exactly for this type of scenario that the Responsibility to Protect was created. The UN was ordered to step in.

I caught a motorcycle taxi to the UN base next to Goma's airport and found my way to the press office. 'You're not in London now,' grinned a Ugandan UN officer from behind his desk. 'This is war. You are in a war zone at this moment. The front line is five miles away. Our threat assessment right now is four out of five.'

I looked around. The office was quiet. It was lined with neat shelves of files. Aside from the border guards, I hadn't seen a single gun since entering Congo. I told the press officer I hadn't realized I was in such danger.

'You are in a war zone right now,' he repeated. 'This is a war zone.'

The officer said that, at any time, the UN had up to 10 patrols out in Goma. It maintained bases in both government and rebel areas. Its soldiers mostly came from India, South Africa, Benin and Uruguay. Their mandate was to protect people and the UN was doing that by allowing refugees to settle in camps outside the gates of its bases. 'We do whatever we can,' said the officer.

I filled out some accreditation forms in triplicate, had my picture taken and, as the officer processed them, wandered around the base. There were several public noticeboards that had been turned into displays of photographs. 'Guardians of Peace', read a banner over some pictures of Indian soldiers driving past a column of refugees. Two more banners over more photographs of peace-keepers sweeping by refugees read: 'We Are Here for the People' and 'Do Not Worry, We Are There'. Some of the displays had a military theme. 'Artillery lends dignity to what might otherwise be a vulgar brawl', read one. There were others. 'Without cavalry, battles are without result.' 'It's not big armies that win battles, it's good ones.' This all seemed sound advice, though perhaps for a different war. MONUSCO had no artillery or horses and in eight years of operations it had fought no battles either.

A large display, entitled 'Beyond Mandate', caught my attention. This was an account of how, on 6–8 July 2007, Indian peacekeepers retrieved the body of Ms Sui Yan Cecilia Cheung, a hiker from Hong Kong who had been overcome by the fumes on Nyiragongo, and died. The soldiers were pictured putting on masks, lifting Cheung's body on a stretcher and grinning proudly as they reached an ambulance. There was even a letter of thanks from the Hong Kong government. From the size and prominence of the display, I gathered that the recovery of the body of a single dead Chinese tourist was the proudest moment to date for the biggest peacekeeping force in history.

The fixer whom the border guard insisted I employ turned out to be the best in Goma. Albert Kambale was one of the few journalists permanently based in the city. He normally filed for Agence France-Presse but it was my luck that he'd had a row with his editors the day before I arrived and, to show them he had options, he was temporarily freelancing.

At a café by Lake Kivu, Albert pulled out a map. North of Goma eastern Congo was connected by a single dirt road that ran for 200 kilometres between the Virungas, from government territory to the rebel area to Mai Mai village and back again. The rebels had advanced to within sight of its southern terminus, Goma. If we called ahead to warn his contacts we were coming, Albert said we could still move freely along the full length of the road. I said I wanted to see as much as I could. Albert said we'd need a week, and a car and a driver, and went off to arrange them.

We drove out of Goma the following morning. Barely two minutes outside the city and we were at the front line. At the government checkpoint, hung-over soldiers in dirty and torn uniforms asked for money. A minute further on and we were at a rebel

The Great Rift Valley. Out of devastation comes life.

(*above*) A mother and child camping in the ruins of Mogadishu cathedral.

(*left*) One of the many camps erected by Somali refugees across Mogadishu during the famine.

(*below left*) Walking through Bakara Market – Mogadishu's commercial heart – with Yusuf Bashir's guards.

(above) The centre of Mogadishu in August 2011,
and *(below)* the view from the Uruba Hotel on the seafront.

(left) Children's graffiti on a hut wall in Obo, Central African Republic.

(below left) The ancient Malian mosque at Djenné, south of Sévaré, Mali.

(above right) South Sudanese president Salva Kiir.

(right) The body of a Sudanese soldier lies next to an oil installation during South Sudan's brief invasion of the north in 2012.

(below) Independence celebrations in Juba, South Sudan.

Illegal Zimbabwean migrants crossing the Limpopo river border into South Africa.

(above left) Congolese army tanks
manoeuvre during the 2012 war with
Rwandan rebels outside Goma.

(left) Paul Kagame heads for a
round of Africans-only negotiations
on the future of Congo, 2012.

The UN on patrol in Goma, 2012.

The French war against al-Qaeda in the Islamic Maghreb in Mali, 2013.

checkpoint, where a smartly dressed guard checked my passport and noted down the number. We drove on through lush fields of maize and coffee. We saw plenty of civilians on the road. Most told us they slept in the refugee camps at night but returned to work their farms by day. Albert knew an astonishing number of them. No one seemed to have moved more than a couple of hours' walk from their homes.

In two hours we were in Rutshuru, the main rebel town. Adjoining it was Kiwanja, where the UN had a base. Camped in front of the base gates were thousands of refugees, just as the UN press officer had said. Their plastic sacks and cases and mattresses were piled high on the ground or on wooden bicycles. But the press officer had been wrong about the protection the UN was offering. The Indian soldiers at Kiwanja didn't seem to want anything to do with the refugees. They peered out at them from behind their razor wire, levelled their guns at them and shooed them off an adjoining helipad. 'The UN does nothing for us,' said one Congolese man camped against the base fence with his family. 'The rebels take our young boys and rape our women. Even then the UN does nothing.'

We'd stopped at Kiwanja because I'd heard about a massacre there a few days before in which 150 villagers had been killed in a series of attacks by a succession of fighters – first Mai Mai, then rebels, then the government. The refugees told me they'd heard the gunshots. But despite their pleading with the Indians to intervene, despite it being the UN's Responsibility to Protect, the peace-keepers – complaining they were short of men and equipment, and unaware of the attack anyway – had not set foot outside their base.

I slipped inside the gates to try to talk to the Indian commander. I was immediately confronted by a guard, my request for an interview denied and I was asked to leave. Behind the guard were several rows of white trucks, tanks, cranes, water tankers, ambulances and tents. There were flowers planted around the officers' mess tent. Another well-tended flower garden sat next to a car park marked 'VIP'. On a wall, a neatly painted regimental crest displayed the Sikh soldier's motto. 'Nische kar apni jeet karon.' 'With Determination I Will Triumph.'

Back outside the gates, I described what I'd seen to a 22-year-old fruit seller called Meshaq Shabani. He nodded. 'They can fight,' he said. 'With all that equipment, they can do whatever they want. But they are just in their base. They never let us in, even when there is fighting. They just watch us being killed off, one by one.'

We drove on to Kirumba, a town of 60,000 people two more hours to the north. The land here was wilder and less cultivated. At some undefined point we passed back into government territory. The Congolese army, whom the UN was supporting against the rebels, had just retaken Kirumba. When we arrived, hundreds of government soldiers were sitting around in the street.

The place was filled with women and children. Initially I assumed these were civilians from the town. But after watching them with the soldiers, I realized the Congolese soldiers had brought their families with them: wives, sons, daughters, infants and, piled up on the ground next to them, what seemed to be all the mattresses and chairs and cooking pots they could carry. The soldiers were busy adding to the piles, breaking into shops and ransacking them. Afterwards they would sit in the smashed doorways of cigarette stalls and food shops, sifting their loot, while their women lit fires in the street and cooked stolen food.

Just off the main highway through Kirumba were two bodies. One man had been disembowelled, his white and green-purple guts lying stinking in the dirt next to him. The other had had his foot blown off and it sat strangely unmarked and intact beside him, like an ornament. Both cadavers were blackened. Albert said all sides in Congo's wars had developed a habit of shooting their enemies, then setting them alight.

It's best to move slowly in the aftermath of a fight. Soldiers don't like sudden movement, and if you walk too fast and breathe in the smell of a corpse too deeply, you'll throw up. Albert and I toured

Kirumba bit by bit, taking our time to pause in the patches of clean air. We were stopped in one alley by a small man with an insistent expression who pulled us aside and introduced himself as Kambale Rahera, a Baptist priest. 'Even at this time, they are looting,' whispered Kambale. 'They have nothing. They come into your house and say, "I want food." The soldiers are the worst. This is the second time they've looted us.' The troops' appetite for medicine was voracious, he added. 'They even looted the hospital. Everyone depended on that here. Now there's not even a single tablet of medicine in this town. If you get sick here now, you just die.'

Albert and I walked down a hill to check the hospital and, sure enough, there was a group of soldiers standing in front of its smashed central doorway. One was holding a sickly-looking baby in a torn pink dress in one arm and a red cassette player in the other. He asked if we had any malaria drugs. 'There's no medicine or doctors here,' he complained. The baby girl climbed into the crook of her father's arm and fell asleep. I noticed all the other soldiers had children with them. The man talking to me looked like he had been crying. Albert apologized for having nothing to give the soldiers. Maybe they should ask their comrades who looted the hospital, he suggested. 'If the others looted, we did not,' sulked the soldier. 'Why are our children going to die for this?'

Back on the main road we found the commanding Congolese officer in town, Colonel John Tschibangu. He was tall, smartly dressed and standing in the middle of the street with his legs wide apart, smiling broadly. Albert seemed to know him and they hailed each other, embraced, and chatted. After several minutes Albert introduced me and we shook hands. 'We are here to protect the people, to observe the ceasefire and to reorganize our soldiers for another mission,' announced the colonel.

His assessment was surprising. Around us hundreds of his men were looting the town, many of them in plain sight. There was also a government signpost a few metres from where we stood which read: 'Lots of women and children are raped every day in this region. What if it was your mother, your wife, your sister or your daughter? Everyone against sexual violence! Respect the law!'

I asked the colonel whether he considered lawlessness to be a problem among his men and whether, as it seemed, his forces were so underfed that they had to steal to live. 'There have been some soldiers who looted and we are taking them to justice, where they will be punished,' said the colonel. 'But we do not need to steal. We are well supplied by the government. It's a government army. It *must* be well supplied.'

There didn't seem much point continuing. The Baptist cleric was listening in. We thanked the colonel, walked into a side street and beckoned to the priest to follow us. I told him about the colonel's double-speak, how he talked about protecting the people even as he watched his soldiers lay waste to the town. It dawned on me that this was also a problem for the UN. The UN and the Congolese army were allies. But the UN was also meant to stop war crimes and many government soldiers were plainly committing them. Years later, in 2013, the UN would finally issue a report accusing the army of summary executions, targeting civilians and 'being a significant source of sexual violence, notably against minors.' I asked the priest if the UN ever took action against the army. 'The UN passed by one day,' he shrugged. 'They did not stop.'

A shopkeeper who was listening chipped in. 'Are we people or are we animals?' he asked. 'Are we even insects?' The man was upset. The priest tried to calm him. But the shopkeeper would not be calmed. The UN was meant to help them, he railed. Instead Pakistani, Indian, Russian, Moroccan and Uruguayan peacekeepers had been caught in a string of scandals, which the man methodically listed. In 2005, the UN expelled 63 of its soldiers for paying refugee children for sex. A separate internal inquiry the same year found that Pakistani peacekeepers had sold weapons to militias in exchange for gold. 'It would be better for the UN to kill us instead of letting us suffer,' he concluded.

The priest, embarrassed by how the shopkeeper was bad-mouthing foreign peacekeepers to a foreign journalist, tried to explain. 'You see, we don't see the point of the UN,' he said. 'They have no point in this town.'

Driving back to Goma two days later, I watched a column of 20 Mai Mai child soldiers as young as 12 carrying Kalashnikovs and RPGs file past the front gates of a UN base. The following morning I went to a UN press briefing in Goma where I heard a spokesman deliver an operations summary in which he claimed this column had been stopped. When I said I had seen something else, a British UN officer angrily interjected. To think that what I had seen on a 'cursory visit to observe' in any way compared with information gathered by the UN's 'information and verification mechanisms' was 'absurd', he said. He did not dispute what I had seen. Rather he was saying he possessed superior truth.

In time, I came to realize that gathering the facts was never going to be enough in Africa. For many outsiders, the truth about Africa was not something they learned from mere observation; it was a position to be arrived at via a far more sophisticated process of assumption, imagination and interpretation. It had been like that since Cosmas Indicopleustes found the edge of the earth in Ethiopia. His descendants were the foreign academics, aid workers, diplomats, soldiers, journalists and militants who understood Africa not by travelling to it but by digesting data and reports in their offices in Washington, London, Geneva or Abbottabad. From these virtual voyages, they deduced arguments of exemplary simplicity and marvellous consistency – aid was good; aid was not good; this was what Africa needed to do now – which they set out in newspapers, books and videos that were not distributed in Africa and speeches and seminars not presented there.

In this way our most physical of continents, with its thousands of mountains and rivers, its great forests and deserts, its great wide plains and its billion people, became an abstraction, an idea or even a conviction to be debated free from the distractions of its raw existence. High on this lofty plane, events in Africa did not simply happen and were not merely witnessed. Rather, everything in Africa had to be perceived.

The West's fondness for intervening in Africa reflects the power of a favourite perception: that humanitarianism is an undeniable good. In the twenty-first century this benevolence increasingly manifests itself as military force. In the second half of the twentieth century, however, it arrived more often in the form of foreign aid. When records began in 1960, all overseas aid to Africa was $596.4 million, or slightly more than $2 per African per year. Over the next 50 years it doubled every few years. By 2013 it had increased nearly a hundredfold, equating to more than $50 for every African every year, and around the world employing three times the numbers working in US oil and gas, the world's biggest commercial industry.

On the face of it, that immensity speaks well of the rich world's conscience. But with a little examination, it raises some awkward questions. With so much aid and so much of it concentrated on Africa, why was most of Africa still so poor? Why did so many Africans complain they saw so little of the hundreds of billions of dollars sent to them?

The explanations were various. Sometimes aid went unnoticed because it was spent on intangibles like civil service training or successful efforts to fight an outbreak of disease or – often the biggest item in a developing country's aid funding – the billions of dollars a year spent servicing foreign debt. Sometimes aid had benefited Africans in tangible ways but so long ago it had been forgotten, such as with the UN global health programmes of the 1950s and 1960s.

But another reason for aid's invisibility was the most obvious one: it never reached the people for whom it was intended. Since 1960, billions of dollars in aid has been misspent or stolen or held up in interminable bureaucratic procedure. Especially noticeable on the ground in Africa were the billions of dollars every year that aid groups spent on themselves. To take one example of this largesse: the UN operates the biggest airline in Africa, running to 200–250 aircraft for its peacekeeping operations alone. How this extravagance was viewed in Africa became clear to me one night watching a Kenyan soap opera. The stock character of the roguish ladies' man with a flashy car, shades and seducer's apartment was rounded out by the backstory of a job with a foreign NGO.

In wealthier parts of the world, aid is generally measured by generosity: by funds raised and donations made. In the poor world it is measured by how that money is spent – and from that perspective the picture can often look very different. The houses, the parties, the conferences at beach resorts, the free private schooling for aid workers' children, the tax-free salaries – it all adds up to some of the most generous pay and perks in Africa. At times, aid can seem like nothing so much as a get-rich, live-well scheme run by aid workers for aid workers. Aid workers were Africa's 1 per cent. Viewing the scrums of white Toyota Land Cruisers outside the finest restaurants from Maputo to Mauritania, it was hard to argue that aid assisted Africans more than it assisted aid workers themselves, or to dispute two common African refrains: that aid was one of the best gigs going; and that aid was just the old Western arrogance in a white SUV.

Congo was a case in point. In 2013 the package for a UN middle manager in Goma included a tax-free salary of $75,099–$301,443, a $75,000 car, a hardship allowance of $23,250, rent subsidies for a lakeside villa that could go for $10,000 a month, all travel and most living expenses, business-class flights home, and school fees paid anywhere in the world of up to $25,129 per year per child, for an unlimited number of children. For a UN staffer with a couple of kids who was in Goma to, say, oversee the situation in Kivu province with regard to refugees or nutrition or internal UN logistics, the total came to nearly half a million dollars a year. That was more than was paid to the US President or, for that matter, most people on earth.

All this money had fashioned one of the most morally vexed cities in creation. Goma boasted refugee camps for the starving and homeless and, on its main drag, a choice of French, Italian, Mexican, Lebanese or Indian restaurants for the aid worker. Entering the clapperboard roadside stalls I found the usual African staples of rice, salt, sugar and manioc and the usual Parisian ones of Bordeaux, goat's cheese and three types of extra-virgin olive oil. When Albert and I returned from our trip upcountry, I checked into a lakeside hotel to catch sight of an aid worker water-skiing on Lake Kivu behind a scarlet speedboat playing loud rock, whooping and carving out nifty turns in front of Congolese soldiers and refugees.

All this would matter a lot less if aid groups were able to present concrete examples of where they were helping. In some cases, they can. A distribution of a new drug or treatment can save hundreds of lives – tens of thousands in the case of Médecins Sans Frontières' 2014 efforts to contain Ebola in West Africa, or millions, in the case of those first UN health campaigns against malaria. A new seed can allow subsistence farmers to become commercial. Improved education can allow children to progress beyond their parents.

But aid's relation to development is often indirect. The precise link between, say, a malaria bed-net distribution campaign and a town's prosperity or the installation of an irrigation pipe and a decline in malnutrition or the impact of an effort to improve macroeconomic stability – these are all but impossible to quantify. Much aid work also happens in places where even the most basic statistics, such as population, are unknown, making it hard to measure results. The awkward truth about aid to Africa is that, 70 years after the UN was first founded, economists are still unable to say in more than the most vague terms how helpful it really is.

Worse, when the numbers are known, they can be unflattering. In 2002, basing his calculations on the World Bank's own figures, the aid sceptic William Easterly discovered it took $3,521 in aid to raise a single poor person's income by $3.65 a year. Likewise, between 1981 and 2001, despite hundreds of billions of dollars in aid, the number of Africans living on $1 a day or less doubled from 164 million to 316 million. The 1980s and 1990s, in particular, saw a series of disastrous 'structural adjustment' programmes foisted on Africa by the World Bank and the International Monetary Fund, in which the creditors forced debtor governments into programmes of wholesale privatization which quickly led to the collapse of whole industries, dragging down economies and employment. As President Kagame said: 'In the last 50 years, the West has spent $400 billion in aid to Africa. But what is there to show for it?'

But the Biafran rubric requires heroes, and heroes need results. And in their search for success, many aid workers benefited from the patchiness of the data and their distance from their audience. In this information vacuum, there was little to stop them from claiming good results or even awesome ones. Over time, standard aid agency procedure has become to make a guess at the population in an area where the group was deployed, then flatly suggest that was the number of people being assisted. 'We are working in Congo/Somalia/Niger,' read the formula of several hundred press releases I received every year, 'where one/two/three million people are affected by famine/war/drought.'

Heroes also need battles. So barely a week went by, either, without a new aid agency press release announcing a fresh disaster. There were imminent refugee crises in Congo and Somalia, a looming outbreak of disease in Uganda and Malawi and the forthcoming starvation of millions in Niger and Mali and Zimbabwe. It was hard not to notice how few of these debacles ended up happening. Was it too cynical to wonder whether crisis equalled opportunity in the aid world?

Congo hardened such suspicions. What had begun as a

temporary mission to shore up a ceasefire had become institution-alized and permanent, and big money. In 2012–13, MONUSCO's budget was $1.48 billion. Annual aid spending in Congo was an additional $449–$646 million, shared out among Goma's 80 or so resident agencies.

This process didn't look much like altruism. It looked like busi-ness. Aid groups competed as rival enterprises, vying for contracts to assuage human suffering. Like any good business people, aid workers were adaptable and pursued growth. Carefully drawn lines between emergency help and development assistance became blurred as some aid groups took on both, presenting all their work as urgent and life-saving and expanding in whichever direction promised most funds. Aid workers also branded their clients, decorating refugee camps with logos on flags and tents and even dressing refugees in aid agency T-shirts.

Like all advertising, the messaging was often distorted. But the Markpress principles held that maintaining image *was* the business. Donations would dry up unless aid agencies promoted themselves as selfless, efficacious saviours. In that sense, an effective aid campaign didn't just encourage self-regard, it required it. It also required a disaster. So Congo was described not just in dire terms but as the greatest apocalypse mathematically possible. At the first sign of any influx of refugees, Oxfam would declare two million Congolese were on the move. Women's rights specialists referred to Congo as 'the rape capital of the world'. One infamous piece of aid agency exaggeration by the International Rescue Committee announced that Congo's wars had claimed the lives of 5.4 million people between 1996 and 2008, an average of 45,000 a month, or 1,500 a day. That allowed enterprising journalists to call Congo the 'Deadliest Conflict Since World War II'. Which would have been impressive – the population of Las Vegas every year! – were it not for other estimates putting deaths at a few tens of thousands.

Over time many aid agencies had dispensed with their founding specialisms and expanded into whichever areas promised most funding. So it was striking how none had taken on the task of ending the fighting. In the name of securing access to the suffering, aid workers refused to get involved. That sounded noble. But by not confronting a conflict's political causes, they also ensured they were no help in fixing it. The Goma aid industry also depended on the war continuing. Was there a connection? The American chronicler of the Rwandan genocide, Philip Gourevitch, was clear. He described the Goma aid operation as 'not fixing conflict, but catering to it'.

Rwanda's geography borrowed from both sides of the Rift, blending jungle and lakes, mountains and moorland into a symphony of green, brown and grey. The capital Kigali sat in the centre of Rwanda, and if Paul Kagame was a figurehead of the new Africa then Kigali was his showpiece, a living symbol of his determination to replace the bloody chaos of Africa's past with a future of peace and order. Plastic bags were banned. Government ministers led the population in a mass street-sweeping once a month. Traffic lights were not only observed, they counted down the interruption to your journey to the second.

The presidential offices sat on a high ridge overlooking this sea of calculated calm, a series of whitewashed bungalows surrounded by a garden of banana trees, giant palms and open lawns. One dark-wood building contained an open-sided deli serving inventive salads and chilled pastas to Kagame's young staff, many of whom were American graduates. Another, the room in which I was to meet Kagame, was styled as a European business centre: grey walls, drawn burgundy curtains, recessed strip lights, a polished rosewood boardroom table and a giant teleconferencing screen. The effect of such a complex in central Africa was disorientating and, I suspected, deliberate. Kagame was the first president I met after arriving in Africa and it was precisely because of his habit of confounding expectations that I returned to see him more often than any other.

I waited in my accustomed seat to one side of the table's head. Presently there was a commotion outside, Kagame's press aide stiffened and the President strode in. Kagame's lankiness was as arresting as ever. He was tall, perhaps 6ft 3ins, and so bony that the arms of his suits hung hollow at his sides. As he sat and crossed his long, slender fingers in a cat's cradle, I couldn't help but be reminded of Steven Spielberg's glowing alien digit.

It was 2012 and Kagame was under unprecedented attack. UN monitors in Congo were accusing him of sending men and weapons to ethnic Rwandan rebels north of Goma, just as he had done in 1996 and 2008. The rebels named themselves the M23 after their abandoned 23 March 2009 peace deal with the Congolese government. Their implicit threat was to establish a breakaway state in the east of the country. They were led by a man nicknamed the Terminator, who had been indicted for war crimes by the International Criminal Court in The Hague.

Rwanda had been accused of puppeteering Rwandan rebels in Congo before. This time the allegations were set out in a comprehensive 48-page UN report. Taking their lead from the blue helmets, the foreign press had duly characterized the M23 as a Rwandan proxy and denounced Kagame as a bloodthirsty authoritarian with the usual African despot's designs: power and money, in this case the wealth buried in eastern Congo's mines of gold, diamonds and coltan. Several donors, including the US and Britain, had suspended aid.

Kagame had always struck me as all business, all the time. So after we greeted each other and I introduced Dominic, I got to the point. 'I'm not here to portray you as a saint,' I said, 'but I wonder how you assess the recent press coverage calling you a tyrant?' Kagame didn't blink. 'I don't want to be a saint,' he said. 'I don't even attempt to be. It wouldn't make any sense. It would divert me from my responsibilities. Concentrating on being a saint would end with me doing nothing that I was supposed to.'

Kagame then spoke without interruption for 42 minutes. His

tone was one of controlled exasperation. He picked holes in the charges against him and pointed out gaps in his accusers' knowledge of history. He took strident issue with the idea that Rwanda was the primary source of Congo's troubles, rather than Congo's own kleptomaniac, indifferent, dysfunctional government.

The President was most troubled by a deeper problem. The affair showed something was wrong with the way the world worked, he said. The outside world insisted it needed to take care of Africans. But at a time when much of the world was in financial crisis but Africa itself was booming, it was ever more apparent that Africans could take care of themselves. Moreover, when foreigners did intervene, their record was appalling. When he beat back the *génocidaires*, Kagame found he was also fighting several hundred French paratroopers supporting the murderous Hutu regime. A few months later the same foreigners who had ignored the butchery went on to clothe, feed and house the very people who had carried it out in refugee camps in Congo. Those efforts allowed the killers to rebuild their strength and counter-attack across the border into Rwanda. After that, the UN had failed – repeatedly, endlessly, despite the presence of what, by 2012, was 19,000 peacekeepers and an annual cost of $1.4 billion – to bring peace to Congo. 'Have they even made a dent in Congo's problems?' asked Kagame.

Kagame felt he had something to offer the situation. As a rebel commander, he had rescued his country from annihilation in 1994. As a president, he had led Rwanda to a stunning rebirth. In the decade to 2012, economic growth in Rwanda had averaged 8.2 per cent, aid funding of the national budget had fallen from 85 per cent to 41 per cent, child mortality had halved and primary school attendance had tripled. Inside Africa, he was recognized as one of the continent's most outstanding leaders. Outside it, businessmen hailed him as the embodiment of a new Africa bursting with opportunity that, in a few years, had relegated aid to a subplot. Why wouldn't Congo want to learn from Rwanda and follow it out of the abyss? And yet the wider world – the UN, the aid agencies and foreign governments – had not sought Kagame's assistance. Far from asking him to help solve the problem, it accused him of *being* the problem.

Kagame was angry. But he was also dumbfounded. 'These are enlightened people,' he said, 'people who always tell the world how well intentioned they are and how they want to see global security and fairness and justice, and who are respected by all. And they are the ones who are turning everything upside down.'

I spent a week shadowing Kagame, talking to him for several hours a day. I spoke to his staff and ministers about the allegations against him and Rwanda. Some were easy to dismiss. The UN said Rwanda's actions had displaced 53,000 people. Oxfam's Congo director, Elodie Martel, made that 500,000 and on Twitter Oxfam said the figure was '2 million+'.

Given Rwanda's history in Congo, it was plausible that Rwanda was backing rebels there. Over several days in M23 territory I talked to scores of people who said they were sure it was doing exactly that. But I found no proof. The UN report was also less than conclusive. Though it quoted 80 testimonies, almost all were M23 deserters, none of them were named and none of their allegations were corroborated. It was all anonymous accusations from a group with an axe to grind, released by an organization – the UN – whose competence and purpose Kagame frequently called into question.

To Kagame, the controversy of whether or not his government was backing the M23 was an artificial scandal intended to distract from the bigger issue: the mess the UN, aid agencies and the Congolese state had made of Congo. 'If they were talking about the situation in Congo as it might involve Rwanda, then fine,' he said. 'But they are just talking about Rwanda, which betrays everything about their intention. Their intention is *not* to pay attention to the problems of Congo.'

*

Kagame had experienced the genocide intimately. Years later, he still struggled with what he had seen. 'Some of the things that were done, I still cannot speak about,' he said. 'Fathers were killing their own children because [they] resembled their wife, who was a Tutsi. How do you explain that?' Even before the genocide, Kagame had been profoundly mistrustful of human nature. 'I know people,' he told me. 'Betrayals, lies, dishonesties. I have seen these. I understood very well from the beginning, I think.' But even such deep cynicism had offered him little protection during the genocide. His friend and fellow rebel Tito Rutaremara told me Kagame was so disturbed – and so disorientated by his inability to distance himself from the vengeful rage sweeping the RPF's ranks – that he stopped visiting massacre sites. 'He wanted to avoid his judgement being influenced,' said Rutaremara. 'If you saw those thousands of bodies, you could only think about revenge.'

In the aftermath of the genocide, Human Rights Watch accused the RPF of killing 25,000 people in its own reprisal massacres. The allegations, well substantiated, became a central plank of the group's aggressive campaign against Kagame, denouncing him as not a visionary of the new Africa but a tyrant of the old one. Kagame growled that the real story was how many people the RPF *didn't* kill. 'We had to battle extreme anger among our own men,' he said. 'So many had lost their families and they had guns in their hands. Whole villages could have been wiped out. But we did not allow it.'

In some ways, Kagame's resolve echoed the interventionists: *never again*. But whereas the foreigners wanted to stop others perpetrating atrocities, Kagame's focus was on ending the bloodshed among his own people. He wasn't shy to point a finger at Belgian colonists or foreign indifference. But anyone who denied that Rwandans were primarily responsible for the genocide was deluding themselves, he said. 'We have to look into ourselves. We have to work out why this happened in Rwanda.'

This was the difference between Kagame and the humanitarians. The outsiders believed Rwandans had to be stopped from killing each other. *They can't help themselves.* For Kagame, too, the issue was one of character. But to him 'never again' was an introspective imperative. To heal Rwandans' divisions and to end the ease with which they were so disastrously manipulated, he proposed instilling in them a new self-confidence, a self-discipline, an unyielding self-determination and sense of citizenship that would allow Rwandans to trust themselves and walk their own path. Rwanda was to discover in itself a new pride and spirit, something that one day might become Rwandan patriotism, binding Hutu and Tutsi together and liberating them from their past.

Kagame saw the international attack on him as an attempt to thwart such plans and an attack on the whole notion of African autonomy. As a rebel leader, freedom had been Kagame's ultimate goal. After the genocide, freedom became the standard by which he measured almost everything. African prosperity and African dignity could only come from free African enterprise, he argued. Shared prosperity was a way to release Rwandans from hatred. 'If people are thinking about how to move forward, if people see the benefit in associating with one another . . . you really have no time to hate one another. You start valuing one another instead.'

It was a vision wholly at odds with dependence on foreign charity. Kagame allowed that foreign aid was welcome in the short term while Rwanda's own finances did not match its needs. But he insisted it was given freely, without expectation of foreign control. Even then he added that, though aid purported to be 'about helping people to stand on their own, about self-determination', one of its great contradictions was that the more aid a country received, the more its freedom was undermined. Regarding another human being as less successful or capable than yourself necessarily belittled them. When that intersected with race, as it had done so often in Africa, that could be the spark for the kindly racism of the patrician – the reverse of setting someone free. 'Where does it all end?' asked Kagame. 'With them thinking this is their territory, that they are the ones who are right and the ones who must shape things? Is this what the international system has become?' With aid groups and UN agencies who pursued their own interests, 'even at the expense of whole countries?'.

Kagame concluded the real reason the outside world still reserved the right to intervene in Africa was that it kept faith with an old prejudice: that Africans were inferior. Foreigners still exhibited the same self-centred paternalism, the same habits of discounting African freedoms and lives, the same stealing of Africa's destiny that the continent had known throughout its contact with Europe. 'There is always this assumption,' said Kagame. '"These people do not know human rights."' In reality, said Kagame, Africans knew more than most about 'what it means to be free, to express yourself, to have justice, to be treated fairly' precisely because of the way the West had 'shaped and destroyed' Africans' lives in the past. Now that Rwanda had pulled itself back from disaster and become an African success, it still found it was 'wrestling with an international system which says: "There are some people who should stay where they are and we are the only ones who can determine"' how they might progress.

Kagame sighed. 'This is what Rwanda is facing, the same struggle every day,' he said. 'I believe it is contempt. I believe it is absolute contempt.' Only prejudice could explain how the opinion of a self-selected, Western-staffed, New York-based activist group like Human Rights Watch was valued higher than the elected government of Rwanda or any of its people. It was Human Rights Watch who defined Rwanda to the world, and that was fundamentally anti-democratic. Human Rights Watch was, in effect, stealing *his* human rights. 'If you are really talking about freedoms, then why not listen to me?' he asked. 'Are you not committing the same offence you accuse me of? If Ken Roth is the one who feels everything for me, then he has taken away my rights.'

Ken Roth was the Director of Human Rights Watch. I called

him in New York and relayed a summary of Kagame's comments. Initially Roth was dismissive. 'I don't think anyone takes *that* seriously,' he scoffed. But when I pressed Kagame's argument that groups like his would never attempt similar campaigns with richer nations, Roth conceded Kagame had a point. 'If he's saying the world is unfair, yes, that's true,' said Roth. 'We tried to put pressure on the US because of Bush's use of torture and it was hard. Rwanda is not as powerful as the US and, yes, is more susceptible to pressure.'

The inconsistency was unintelligent, said Kagame. Unintelligent and unacceptable. What was presented as selflessness in the rich world in Africa revealed itself as self-regard. If Africa was truly to master its fate and achieve real freedom, 'if Africa is finally to write its own future,' that had to change. The belief that Africa could not take care of itself had to be exposed for what it was: racism. If racism shaped the workings of the international community, those structures must be reformed. The UN had to be remade or abolished. Aid, all of it, must go. Only by breaking out of this prison of misconceptions would Africa ever be free. 'Telling the wrong story about us has consequences,' he said. 'Telling the right story, our own story . . . it's an issue of our rights. This is about overcoming our past. We are not going to abandon these years of self-determination or self-respect, of survival and living for our people and our country.'

This was why Kagame's disagreement with the humanitarians often seemed so personal. Because it was. Kagame was demanding Africa finally be allowed to master its own fate and achieve real freedom. By doing so, he was calling into question not just the integrity of the UN mission in Congo and aid and all foreign intervention in Africa, but their very existence.

Kagame was only too aware of the mistakes of other African liberation leaders who had won freedom from white rule only to govern so badly that they gave the outside world every justification to intervene once more. He also said he knew that even if aid groups and foreign governments agreed in theory to let Rwanda run its own affairs, it would be naïve to believe that they would do so in practice. Africa had to prove itself, he said. 'We cannot just claim our rightful place. We have to deserve it.'

It's difficult to imagine how Rwandans might have made a stronger case. From utter devastation, they patched together one of the world's feeblest economies and, in two decades, transformed it into one of Africa's most sophisticated and one of the world's fastest-growing. Economic growth, once an almost unimaginable concept in Rwanda, peaked at 11.5 per cent in 2008 and now averages just below 8 per cent, handily beating China and India. The World Economic Forum used not to bother ranking Rwanda at all. Now it places it as the ninth-easiest country in the world in which to start a business.

As Kagame hoped, a robust and free economy led to a generalized improvement. Advances in Rwanda's health and education accompanied and reinforced its growing prosperity. Rwanda's infrastructure is now one of the best in Africa. Roads are pothole-free, the entire country is connected with fibre-optic broadband and a new multibillion-dollar, 3,200-kilometre, 130-kilometre-an-hour railway is due to connect Kigali to Uganda and the Kenyan port of Mombasa by 2018. Rwandan health is especially improved. Malaria is down two-thirds and maternal deaths by 92 per cent. Meanwhile Rwanda leads much of the world in areas as diverse as gourmet coffee production, primary school attendance and women's representation in parliament (the world's highest at 53 per cent).

Rwanda's progress was all the more remarkable in the context of the genocide. That, said Kagame, was precisely the point. 'It has been a struggle,' he said. 'We had to wage a war. We had to go through the aftermath of the genocide. We had to rebuild the country. And we did this not by begging. We sacrificed. Look at what we went through. A country where a million people have been lost. A country which has really been shattered beyond what you could imagine, where three million people were displaced and every institution completely destroyed. Starting not from zero, but below, from the most difficult situation ever witnessed. We had absolutely nothing. We *lacked*. Many countries, if they faced what we faced here, would have simply failed. We did not.'

Through Kagame's eyes, Rwanda and Africa were locked in a furious global reckoning between privilege and disadvantage. At its heart, this was an assertion of freedom. It was a reclamation of sovereignty from the once powerful by the once excluded, a demonstration that ideas and innovation were limited not by birth but only by brilliance and a demand that economic growth translate to political and personal liberty for all. In this final struggle for dignity, human beings were moving from division to harmony, from inequality to opportunity, from narrow to global and from injustice to liberty. The new mood among the poor was not helplessness but resourcefulness. The new response among the rich had to be not to impose but to ask.

At times, Kagame could sound like Africa finding its voice. Just as often he seemed to provoke controversy for its own sake. He delighted in offending foreigners' sensibilities and dismissed meetings at the UN and other global events as irrelevant and stupefyingly dull. 'I have learned a technique for these meetings,' he confided one day. 'I am there, you see me there. But really, in my mind, I am not there at all.'

It was Kagame's response to accusations that he killed his opponents that especially outraged the rich world. Between 1996 and 2014, a total of 14 Rwandans – eight politicians, three former army officers and three journalists – had been murdered, nine of them inside Rwanda, five outside it. There were other unsuccessful assassination attempts too, including three in four years on a former Rwandan army chief living in South Africa.

Fourteen dead enemies over 20 years was a low count for any government, African or otherwise. But when Kagame was asked about the deaths, rather than expressing remorse or promising an investigation or simply prevaricating, he would scandalize his interrogators by saying the dead men had it coming. 'If you have somebody out there saying, "I wanted to carry out a coup" and later on he is shot, maybe he deserves it, you see?' he told me. 'A coup means he wanted to kill people here. You are really indicting yourself by saying I want to kill people to make a change happen. It's like you are declaring war on a country.' When the former head of Rwanda's intelligence was strangled in his hotel room in South Africa, Kagame didn't hide his satisfaction. 'We didn't do it but my question is: "Shouldn't we have?",' he asked. 'If someone feels no shame in destroying what we have built over a period of time, I for my part will not feel shy of protecting what we have built. Treason brings consequences. No one will betray Rwanda and get away with it.' Defence Minister James Kabarebe was just as unsympathetic. 'If you choose to be a dog, you die like a dog and cleaners will remove the trash and dump it where it is supposed to be so that it doesn't stink for others,' he said.

Statements like those sent foreign observers into a kind of apoplexy. Correspondents would write a stream of articles that essentially said: 'He admitted it! He's a tyrant! Stop him!' They were backed by hysterical press releases from Human Rights Watch and others. A spokeswoman for the US State Department said Washington viewed Kagame's comments with 'deep concern'. UN Special Rapporteur Maina Kiai said they sent a 'chilling and unacceptable message'.

I thought I knew Kagame well enough to know that the message was aimed as much at the West as his domestic opponents. Many heard the voice of an unapologetic killer in his words. I did too. Kagame often spoke about how he preferred the bloody certainties of battle to the half-victories of politics. But Kagame's words were also those of a free man. He was incensed by the way the rich world routinely rated its judgement above that of Africans. He was incensing it right back, giving offence to what offended him, conspicuously placing his judgement on Rwandan affairs above that of foreigners. By refusing to do what the UN wanted in Congo or saying he was glad when his opponents died, Kagame was demonstrating as explicitly as he could that he couldn't care less what others said. He wasn't so much rejecting the West's opinion as rejecting its right even to have one. 'We draw a line on the basis of what is wrong and what is right for us,' Kagame said. 'And not just on something we have read in books, but on the basis of what we have lived, our experience, our history. We do not accept that other people's views and values must always prevail over us. No. We are people who think also. We are people who can think for ourselves.'

And, really, beyond the rhetoric, Kagame was only asking for equivalence. Every leader killed opponents, even in the West. The US President killed far more often and with far less precision but very few of his opponents would claim Barack Obama did so because he was black. Kagame was demanding the same courtesy. Celebrating his opponents' death might have been poor taste. But if he did kill people, he was saying he didn't do it because he was African but because he was President and sometimes, in the defence of their nation, to rid it of those who would tear it down, that's what presidents did. 'For being single-minded, focused, for expressing my views, for putting myself on a par with anybody – if this is what I am accused of,' said Kagame, 'then I am guilty.'

Kagame said what he liked. Mostly his energy was ferocious. But at times his never-ending fight with the world seemed to be taking a toll. Then his face would hang slack in an expression of wide-eyed exhaustion and he would seem to have trouble structuring his thoughts. After we had talked for hours one day, there came a moment when he trailed off and stared into space. I glanced at him and quietly put my pen down on my notebook. Dominic saw me and followed suit, dropping his camera to his side. Thirty seconds passed. When Kagame resumed, his gaze was still fixed on the middle distance and his voice was low and hypnotic, almost as though it were his subconscious talking.

'From our side,' he said, 'there are things we want to live for and are ready to die for – things we cannot deviate from. We will do what we feel and what we believe. You cannot threaten us. There is no threat anywhere that can change our minds. We have had worse things. We have already sunk to the lowest level and we can't go lower. This is about our rights. It's about how we survive, how we live on. And nobody is going to do it for us. Nobody is going to do it for us.'

Two months later, with the M23 rebels still on the outskirts of Goma, the UN peacekeepers in eastern Congo finally took decisive action. They fled.

An M23 tank had fired a single shell into Goma. Around 1,000 guerrillas began advancing on the city. The UN immediately abandoned the civilian population, retreating in convoys of trucks back inside their bases or moving clean outside the city. The rebels took Goma that afternoon without firing a shot. By the evening, crowds were gathering in front of UN bases, demanding those peacekeepers who had not left to do so forthwith. 'You could not defend us,' shouted Amani Muchumu, 18. 'You are useless. You are dismissed.'

In theory, international intervention was infused with a noble neutrality. In practice, with nothing at stake in Congo's wars, the peacekeepers were unwilling to take risks on behalf of a people they didn't know. 'I have a wife and a son back home,' said a Uruguayan platoon officer. 'My men have families too. I want us to get out there but it's not safe. I have to make the right decision for everyone concerned.' Apparently 'everyone' did not include the African refugees the UN was meant to protect.

A new atrocity then coming to light in a village outside Goma illuminated the consequences of the UN's timidity. In September, a small militia called Mai Mai Cheka captured the town of Pinga, in which there was a UN base. The militia commander, 'Colonel' Cheka, apparently wanted the peacekeepers gone. To that end, he concocted a plan to force them from their base, so he could chase them out of town.

According to several aid workers who visited Pinga, Cheka ordered seven civilian leaders decapitated. His men then paraded their severed heads on sticks outside the base gates. They also threw several of the heads at the gates while Cheka shouted 'Come out!' to the peacekeepers inside.

Cheka and his men likely thought it was a display of barbarism no peacekeeper could ignore. They had overestimated the UN. The peacekeepers never even opened their gates.

SIX

ZIMBABWE

The freest man I ever met was a Somali pirate called Fingers. Skinny and sun-creased for his 32 years, Fingers dressed in a *kikoi*, plastic sandals and a dirty T-shirt. He told stories of how the Indian Ocean was full of little plastic boats filled with dead pirates who had run out of fuel or food or water. He said one crew he knew had eaten their friend to survive. Fingers laughed. 'It's not a crime if you're about to die,' he said.

Fingers had made a success of piracy, earning $350,000 in ransoms from two ships alone. 'When I need a ship, I go out and take one,' he said. 'When I want a woman, I give her money and she becomes my mistress. No one can stop me. No one controls the sea. My life is as wide as the ocean. I don't depend on anyone.'

I looked at Fingers. Even $500 was a fortune in Somalia. Fingers had earned several hundred times that and here he was wearing all of $5, squatting on the floor like an East African deckhand. Even his phones looked old.

'Fingers,' I asked, finally, 'where did all the money go?'

Fingers laughed again.

'You blew it all?'

'I bought houses and cars. I bought a couple of Land Cruisers. I spent the money on friends. I enjoyed it, but now it's gone. That's why I'm still a pirate. I need the money.'

Fingers shrugged. Then he gave me a look that said: 'What did you expect from a pirate? Responsibility?'

*

The in-flight entertainment to Harare featured a documentary about five young black Americans discovering Africa. The film-makers' tone was wondrous revelation. Despite what you'd heard, Africa was OK. There was hope in Africa. There was even money. It wasn't all war and disease and poverty. At one point, the five were hustled into a room to meet Africa's richest man, Aliko Dangote, a billionaire Nigerian cement-maker. Everyone agreed the world got Africa badly wrong. 'It's just that people are too lazy to find out whether Africa is good or bad,' said Dangote. The identity of these indolent ignoramuses was clear: Western journalists like me.

It was July 2013 and I was heading to Zimbabwe in a final attempt to figure out the good and bad in Robert Gabriel Mugabe. In his early days, Mugabe's life had had some similarities to Paul Kagame's. Mugabe, too, was an intellectual and a rebel leader whose forces won a devastating war against a racist regime, in this case the white minority government of Rhodesia. For the generation after independence in 1980, he also presided over Zimbabwe's transformation into a star of Africa: a thriving economy and food exporter whose people were among the healthiest and best educated on the continent.

There were differences, though. Twenty thousand people died in Zimbabwe's civil war, most of them black nationalists, and Mugabe killed almost as many in the years afterwards when he sent his troops into areas dominated by a rival rebel group. By the time Mugabe began his third decade in power, rising corruption, theft and mismanagement, followed by the violent appropriation of white-owned farms, had caused the economy to collapse in hyperinflation, prompting the mass emigration of more than a million Zimbabweans, among them many of the country's wealthiest and best educated.

Mugabe's accelerating autocracy and incompetence represented the only possible argument for continued foreign intervention in

Africa: that the continent's freedom movements had delivered a false dawn. Liberation had meant nothing of the sort. Africans couldn't handle freedom. They screwed it up when they got it.

The argument, naturally, was a racists' favourite. It was simplistic, ignoring the part played by Western businesses and governments who continued to exploit Africa's resources and who helped the continent's new rulers funnel billions of stolen dollars into Swiss bank accounts. But as one African country after another produced a despot in the decades after colonialism, the notion that Africa's independence leaders were not nurturing freedom but wrecking it seemed to hold an uncomfortable truth. What freedom fighters fought for in the name of the people, they then took from the people upon victory. As their reward for freeing nations, they stole those nations whole. From Mozambique to Mali, Africa's liberation heroes assumed the same oppressive powers and crushing wealth they once fought against. Within a few years, much of the continent was ruled by a line-up of new African Cecil Rhodeses: Mobutu Sese Seko in Congo, Idi Amin in Uganda, Haile Mariam Mengistu in Ethiopia, Hastings Banda in Malawi and Jean-Bedel Bokassa in the Central African Republic. Some ruling families – the Kenyattas in Kenya, the dos Santoses in Angola, the Bongos in Gabon, the Owings in Equatorial Guinea – even became quasi-monarchies, with power passing down the family line.

Mugabe was the last of the great African liberation dinosaurs still in power. By 2013 he was 89 and in his 33rd year as head of state. And yet he was running for his seventh term as President, with a view to handing over after the poll to his wife, Grace, famous mostly for her lavish overseas shopping trips.

Mugabe's opponent, as he had been for more than a decade, was Morgan Tsvangirai, 61, a former trade unionist who headed the Movement for Democratic Change (MDC). The consensus in Zimbabwe was that the actual vote was less important than the question of whether the President would allow a fair one. Tsvangirai and the MDC were thought likely to win in a free contest, as they had in 2008. So Mugabe and his Zimbabwe African National Union-Patriotic Front (Zanu-PF) were expected to rig the vote against them. Several pro-democracy groups claimed the fix was already in. Votes of older, rural Zimbabweans – Mugabe's most consistent supporters – would be double-counted, they said. Millions of younger, more urban Zimbabweans would be disenfranchised.

Still, perhaps mindful of how isolated his violence made him, even among African leaders who were once his disciples, Mugabe was striking a new, conciliatory tone. In the past, he had egged on his thugs to beat and kill his opponents. Now he was urging the comrades to be peaceful. He was also campaigning in earnest, speaking for hours at a time at 10 'Star Rallies' across the country, which would end with the 'Mother of All Rallies' in Harare three days before the vote.

I had been trying to interview Mugabe for years. Given reports about his advanced prostate cancer, I was running out of time. The rallies, I decided, would allow me to write around Mugabe's reticence. From his speeches I would stitch together a portrait of the man who, more than anyone, seemed to personify the paradoxes at the heart of Africa's struggle for freedom.

Mugabe's first rally was in the central town of Masvingo, just north of the ruins of Great Zimbabwe. The drive south from Harare had its hazards: a narrow, deteriorating road, giant oncoming trailer trucks, several burnt-out cars and wandering cows and vervet monkeys. As I drove, I listened to state radio, the Zimbabwean Broadcasting Corporation. Though Tsvangirai and the MDC were not mentioned by name, they were the target of persistent abuse. In one election advertisement, two young women discussed their vote.

'Hey, chick, would you vote for a man who supports sanctions that hurt us all?' said one woman to her friend.

'No way!' replied the friend.

'Would you vote for a man who in this age of HIV does not use a condom and runs around impregnating people's daughters?'

'Uh-uh,' replied the friend again. 'No way.'

'Vote Team Zanu-PF, the People's Party,' intoned a voice-over.

There followed an interview with a Zanu-PF member about his new book. The author, whose name I couldn't catch, said he was trying to fight tribalism in Zimbabwe, something he argued was created by the British to divide and rule. 'Cecil John Rhodes tried to divide us, but it's all lies,' he said. 'I encourage people to go back to the past to find out who we are. Look at Great Zimbabwe. These silly fools who tell us we were not civilized. We came from Egypt. We taught the Egyptians hieroglyphics! They learned it from us!'

There were regular police checks on the road to Masvingo. My heart beat a little faster when I was called over at one but the officers just wanted a lift. A sergeant climbed into my front seat and three large female cadets squeezed into the back. We introduced ourselves, and Sergeant Mnungwe asked me what I was doing in Zimbabwe. Business, I said. 'Ah, it is good when you come for business,' said Mnungwe. At the next checkpoint we were waved through. 'You are lucky you are with policemen,' smiled Mnungwe. 'Some of these people, they don't like . . .'

'Whites?' I asked.

Mnungwe and the cadets erupted in laughter. I had mentioned the unmentionable.

'Ha!' said Mnungwe, tears streaming down his face. '"Whites?" Ah!' Eventually, when Mnungwe regained his composure, he said: 'Yes. Whites like you.'

I dropped off the police officers and drove on to Masvingo. Pulling into a gas station, I asked directions for the rally where Mugabe was speaking. The attendant found me as funny as Sergeant Mnungwe. 'Ha!' he laughed. '"I want to see Bob speak." Ah! Serious?' The attendant told me the way and soon I found a stream of cars and trucks plastered with posters of Mugabe. After a while the line stopped moving. I wound down my window to ask a tall man in a neat striped shirt and gold sunglasses if he knew where I could park. He walked over, we talked and he said he would help me find some parking.

Chris Charumbira was 37, a former primary school teacher with a wife and three children. At first, the family had lived together in Masvingo. But when Zimbabwe's economy imploded, Chris followed the great trek south to South Africa, settling in a township outside Port Elizabeth on the south coast where he worked in construction and tree-felling. In 2010 his elder brother, Tiwone, came to visit. A few days after he arrived, Tiwone was stabbed and killed in a street fight. 'I had to collect my brother's body and bring it back,' said Chris. 'They had to embalm it for the journey because it was too hot. But we had to bury him in our place.' The experience of hauling his brother's decaying body across Africa had traumatized Chris. He was thinking of coming home. There was more money in South Africa, he said, but given the choice between corruption and violence abroad or at home, Chris preferred to experience it where he understood it. 'In South Africa there is a lot of madness,' he said. 'They will kill you just for your phone.'

Charumbira was an illustrious name in Zimbabwe. Chris had grown up herding cattle around Great Zimbabwe, which stood on his ancestral land. His cousin, Fortune, was president of the national council of tribal chiefs. That made Fortune a big shot in Masvingo and a Zanu-PF stalwart. Chris said Fortune would be sitting on the dais next to Mugabe.

Thousands of people were streaming past us. 'The thing about Bob,' said Chris, 'is that even if there are a lot of bad things about him, his values are African values. Africans first and foremost believe in their culture. They go to church but they also practise African culture. There are Western things that people do not value.

'Let me go straight to the gay issue,' said Chris, warming to his theme. Africans did not like homosexuality, he said. They didn't want it. 'On the Western side, there is this gay thing. On the African side, there is polygamy. It's different cultures.

'Let's go to the farm invasions,' he continued. It wasn't good just to take someone's land, said Chris. But 'as Zimbabweans, we have been living in the mountains. There should be land for everyone, not just for the top man, not just for the white. We want whites. We need them. Zimbabwe should be a mixed grill. But we want to live in a fair land.'

Chris was a rousing speaker. But I noticed he sometimes dropped his voice to hide his words from the crowd streaming past us. He flinched at my more direct questions. Finally, when I suggested we head to the rally, he confessed he was afraid for me. 'We should get you a cap and a T-shirt,' he said. Chris hailed a group of passing Zanu supporters and asked them for a red cap decorated with a picture of Mugabe and the Zanu-PF insignia and a yellow Zanu-PF T-shirt. 'You just wear it,' said Chris, catching my expression. 'Everybody just wears one. No one is fooled by them. It's just on your head, not in your mind.' Chris laughed at his joke, then was quickly serious again. 'You know what?' he said. 'When they are doing the slogans, you should just do it too.'

We walked with the crowd. Everyone was wearing yellow and light-green Zanu-PF T-shirts. On the back were four words: 'Indigenize. Empower. Develop. Employ.' I was handed a 'Team Zanu-PF' manifesto warning of '3,000 regime-change' aid groups working inside Zimbabwe. Rejecting foreign assistance as a Trojan horse was a central Zanu-PF message, part of a broad goal of re-claiming Zimbabwean sovereignty and asserting African freedom. Of 22 Key Goals of the People set out in the manifesto, the first six – independence, sovereignty, unity, security, respect for the values and ideals of the liberation struggle, patriotism – concerned self-determination.

Zanu-PF's plan for liberating its countrymen hinged on its pro-posal that 51 per cent of every company in the country be owned by Zimbabweans. Nationalizing the 1,138 foreign companies in this way would 'unlock' $7.3 billion. In other good news, Zanu-PF said it had identified $10.8 billion 'idle assets' held by the state, which it would set free in similar fashion. The party would also create a new Zimbabwean-only stock exchange, which would block the West's 'sustained regime-change onslaught'. Zanu-PF predicted that the financial surge generated by these three initiatives would remake Zimbabwe at a stroke, creating more than two million jobs, pushing annual economic growth to a blistering 9 per cent and funding massive expansion in social housing, industry, markets, clinics and schools plus the construction of a new parliament building. In such ways, the manifesto concluded, Zanu-PF would 'restore sanity'.

I took all this in as Chris and I were jostled towards the rally. From just under a kilometre away, the music on the sound-system speakers was already deafening. Suddenly, we heard a thudding, then a high decelerating whine, and a white helicopter split the cloudless blue sky perhaps 150 metres over our heads. A second helicopter followed, then a third, the last painted in military camouflage. The crowd cheered and whistled. We turned a corner and before us I could see at least 100,000 people. They filled an entire valley. At the crowd's edges, hundreds of people sat on walls and hung from trees. Some had placards. 'Down with Agents of Imperialism', read one. 'Zimbabwe is Not for Sale', read another. They were all facing a wooden lectern fixed with three microphones that sat in the centre of a small stage hung with a green and white striped garden canopy.

Chris and I were steadily making our way to the front when suddenly there was a cheer behind us. We looked around to see Mugabe and Grace perhaps 100 metres away. Both were in outlandish suits made out of a green and yellow cloth printed with a picture of Mugabe. They were standing on the back of an open-sided pick-up, waving and driving slowly through the crowd. Someone yelled 'One-party state! One-party state!' over the sound system. The crowd parted as the Mugabes made their way to the stage. When the pick-up neared the front, it stopped, Mugabe briefly disappeared, then reappeared ascending the stage to more cheers and whistles. In front of him, a choir in purple robes sang the national anthem. I saw a group of reporters and cameramen standing in a cordoned space in front of Mugabe. I told Chris we should head there. 'OK,' he said, doubtfully.

We advanced ten more metres before we were stopped by a line of party officials. 'Who are you?' asked one man in wrap-around sunglasses and Mugabe cap and T-shirt. 'I'm a writer,' I said brightly. 'I'm writing a book about Africa.' I beamed again.

Sunglasses was impassive.

'*I'm* not writing anything,' said Chris.

Chris had spotted his cousin, Fortune, among the Zanu-PF VIPs. He told Sunglasses he was Fortune's assistant. Sunglasses said nothing.

'I just want to hear the speech,' I said. 'Can I go and stand with the press?'

'*I* don't want to stand with the press,' said Chris.

Sunglasses ignored him. 'Do you have accreditation?' he asked me.

Shit, I thought. *Again.*

From outside Africa, Mugabe was seen as the most prominent in a long line of baby-eating African dictators. What was there to understand? Mugabe was a tyrant. When he accused the West of wanting to overthrow him, the West's response was that *of course* it wanted him gone. Mugabe forfeited his right to rule and all but justified foreign intervention when he ruined his country and killed his people. The man was a murderer and a thief and likely a sociopath too, a mad genius whose diabolical masterpiece was the ruin of Zimbabwe.

Inside Africa, many took a different view. Mugabe might be arrogant and vicious and an economic illiterate. But he stuck it to the West. The last of the great liberation leaders, he was a living embodiment of African freedom and an unbending warrior in the unending fight against white domination. Because, make no mistake, that fight went on. As Mugabe always said, Zimbabwe might have won its freedom but the oppressors had far from given up.

Mugabe's speeches are worth reading, not least because their clarity challenges the Western caricature of an ageing madman. But they were often extremely verbose, so let me offer this précis of his main themes.

Mugabe would often start by declaring Zimbabwe to be a beautiful country. It was rich in diamonds and bounteous land. Naturally, Britain wanted it back. What else but white greed explained why, after independence, the descendants of British settlers, perhaps 2 per cent of Zimbabwe's population, held onto millions of acres of the more fertile land stolen by their colonial ancestors? Why else had Tony Blair's government cancelled Britain's underwriting of the handover of Zimbabwean land from whites to blacks? Britain wanted its colony back and Mugabe gone. It derailed the land redistribution to destabilize the country. These attitudes were intolerable but not, said Mugabe, unfamiliar. If you added up the question of the land, Blair's plotting and the centuries of theft and abuse by white men in Africa, you saw 'this is the same fight we have always been fighting'. This was about rights. This was about freedom. 'Zimbabwe, which we fought and died for, must never be a colony again,' he said.

Zimbabwe was still fighting for its freedom. And in a liberation war, the rules were different. You gave no quarter. You took decisive action. You did not prevaricate. Taking over white farms by force was regrettable but necessary. Crushing the MDC was just as essential. The opposition was 'the creation of Blair', formed from unions and pressure groups funded by foreigners. Zanu-PF, on the other hand, was the 'people's party'. Sometimes, 'if the people make mistakes', it had to 'correct' them. Once in a while, that might entail violence. Only a fool would play nice against such a cunning enemy. This was war! Zimbabweans had to fight! To beat Britain's malevolent greed, Zimbabwe needed a leader of steel. Mugabe did what was necessary. He protected the people. Praise God let Mugabe stay for ever! One-party state!

Mugabe's conclusions might have been self-serving but there was logic to his arguments, and accuracy too. For whites to hold onto millions of acres of Zimbabwe's best land after independence was an anomaly. Blair's cancelling of the land redistribution process did renege on the treaty that inaugurated Zimbabwe's independence. The MDC did receive foreign backing. Blair's own autobiography confirmed that he saw derailing land redistribution as a way to build pressure on Mugabe.

But there was no denying that Mugabe's rhetoric seemed stuck in the past, nor that the country he ruled sometimes seemed to be going backwards in time. When I first touched down in Zimbabwe in April 2007, flying into the southern city of Bulawayo, living standards were back at their 1953 levels and life expectancy had regressed to 34 for women and 37 for men. There were roads but few cars. There were shops but only bare shelves. Clocks were everywhere but all of them had stopped. Telephones didn't work, power was out, there were no cars at the gas stations and the factory stacks were blackened but sent out no smoke. There was something terrifyingly post-apocalyptic about the way the concrete rails on the bridges had been smashed open and the steel mesh ripped out. People still gathered in town centres, but they had nothing to do or say and nowhere to go even if there had been a way to get there. And how thin they were. When they sat down, they folded themselves up. When they walked, they looked like they were being blown by the wind. Outside Bulawayo Cathedral, I met a lawyer. I remarked on the willowy figures shuffling past in the street and asked him what people ate. 'Good question,' he replied.

One thing of which Zimbabwe was in no danger of running out was pictures of His Excellency Comrade Robert Gabriel Mugabe. Uncle Bob looked down from framed photographs in every store and every office, a small man in gold glasses with a vertical Hitler moustache in the nasal groove above his upper lip. Mugabe was front-page news in every newspaper too. His response to the collapse of the country he had ruled for close to three decades could be summed up in one word: Britain. Britain had brought Zimbabwe to its knees through sanctions. Britain was paying the 'so-called' opposition to overthrow him. As long as he was around, Mugabe vowed Zimbabwe would never surrender to its old colonial ruler, particularly now that it was rotten with gays. In his curiously *pukka* English, Mugabe said Britain could 'go hang' for plotting 'monkey business'. His opponents deserved a 'bashing'. And they were getting one. A few weeks before, riot police had split open Morgan Tsvangirai's head with a truncheon. Thousands of opposition members had been beaten and a small number killed.

On that first trip to Zimbabwe, I also drove south, to the gold-fields of the Great Dyke where I'd heard thousands of Zimbabweans were trying to scratch a living mining with bare hands. Driving into the small town of West Nicholson, I pulled over to talk to an open-faced man walking down the street. Trynos Nkomo said he owned several mining concessions and would be happy to talk at his house a street away. He sat me down in his living room, made us both a cup of tea, then excused himself on a short errand.

Ten minutes later he returned with two policemen. The officers marched me to a police station 100 metres away and charged me with working as a journalist without accreditation. When I read my charge sheet, I saw the officers had described me as 'a dedicated and clandestine journalist on a secret mission'. In the looking-glass world of Zimbabwe, that was enough to get me two years.

I wasn't beaten or tortured or even held for very long, just five days in the end. I had no food or anything to drink, but after lock-down I learned to force the rusty door on my cell and walk to the showers to suck water from the pipes. One day a slip-up meant I was allowed to wander freely around a police station for an hour, an extraordinary opportunity to rifle through drawers and copy documents and maps onto scraps of paper that I stuffed into a smuggler's zip pocket on the inside of my belt.

But there was still no food, the rank prison blanket had given my hair lice, my teeth ached and the skin on my arms and legs was flaky with dirt and tight and shiny with mosquito bites. Lying on the bare concrete bunk under unblinking strip lights, I didn't sleep more than an hour or two at a time. The iron shackling ring bolted to the floor of my cell suggested things could get a lot worse. And I was alone. Some strange jail apartheid meant I had my own cell while next door 14 black men were crammed into an identical concrete tank. My neighbours had to endure each others' stink and the humiliation of an open toilet. But alone in a concrete box in southern Zimbabwe, with no idea of how long I would stay there, I was having a hard time not collapsing in on myself. My fourth day in prison was a Sunday. In the evening my neighbours held a service. For two hours, they sang African spirituals of suffering and acceptance and unbroken beauty. Slave songs. I stuck my hands and feet in the bars and swayed back and forth like a chimpanzee in a zoo.

I did learn something about the inside of Mugabe's security machine, however. The policemen who had arrested me did not have fuel for their car. When they moved me to a bigger police station, I drove. Five officers crowded onto the back seat. Every few minutes, they would ask me to stop. Eventually I asked why. 'Bush meat,' said one, pointing to a small shack with a sign.

Arriving in the town of Gwanda, I was shown into a room containing several detectives. Detective Inspector Moyo introduced himself and said he was in charge of my case. He started his interrogation by telling me he saw nothing wrong with a good beating if the crime demanded it. A junior officer grinned and volunteered to 'manhandle' me. Another opened that day's newspaper and pointed me to a report detailing the murder of a Zimbabwean journalist. I had been planning to write 'negative' stories about Zimbabwe, one man said. 'Do you think I can just come to your country, start asking questions and write anything I want?' he demanded.

The next morning, and every morning after that for the next four days, our cell doors were unlocked and we were asked to line up before the station's officers. They shouted at us. They slapped my fellow inmates. Most of these, I gathered, had been arrested for minor offences: selling fuel, illegal mining, trapping porcupines. We were then marched back to our cells. At some point every day, Moyo would have me fetched for another interrogation. He was angry that I would not talk without a lawyer. My refusal to confess was arrogant, he said. 'I am educated,' he would say. 'And you do not co-operate.'

Absolute hierarchy ruled the station. Junior officers almost never spoke. Senior officers like Moyo could not give me permission to visit the toilet or brush my teeth without approval from their superiors. There was an obsession with paperwork. Every remark I made was noted down in longhand and typed out in triplicate. I was finger-printed in quintuplicate. Moyo wanted to ensure I had no complaints. He often reminded me he hadn't beaten me. 'You cannot say anything against me,' he said.

My money was a constant worry for him. Before my arrest, I had changed $400 into Zimbabwean dollars which, at 19,000 to the dollar, meant I was carrying more than 7,000 notes in several taped bricks. Each night, when I handed over my watch, belt, shoes and jacket, the money was counted out note by note and placed in the station safe, a process which took half an hour. Each morning it was counted out again and handed back to me.

One day Moyo left me alone in his office. I studied the directives on the walls. On one, there was a list of crimes in order of priority for the Criminal Investigation Department. Number one was 'insulting or undermining the authority of the President'. Another directive reminded Moyo that it was the CID's mission to 'investigate all cases of a political nature, suppress all civil commotion and gather political intelligence'. On a facing wall, a large map highlighted 'areas of political activity' with red pins. That turned out to be every town and village on Moyo's map.

On my fourth day in jail, a human rights lawyer, Simba Chivaura, came to see me. Simba advised me to plead guilty and helped me prepare a statement. Moyo relaxed after that. There was still no food. But I'm not sure the detectives had any either. In quiet moments, some would ask me if I could help them with a British visa. 'I cannot lie to you – the situation is very bad,' said Moyo one day. 'You can see for yourself. The country is ruined.'

Court was set for my fifth day. On the way there, Moyo took me to a gas station café for breakfast, my first meal since my arrest. As we entered, I was amazed to see a blackboard offering English breakfast: sausages, eggs, toast and coffee. I walked to the counter, ordered, then sat down. Moyo and another junior officer sat at another table over in a corner. I beckoned them to join me, indicating the free seats at my table. They demurred. I became aware of another table at which sat three large, middle-aged white men and a large, middle-aged white woman. They were discussing the price of private planes. '$75,000 for a Cessna is really nothing,' said one.

I looked over at Moyo. He had ordered a black tea and was sipping it slowly. A black man in a suit then asked if he could sit at my table. He introduced himself as Ben, a manager for a Christian food aid organization. He expressed shock at the price of breakfast ($3), apparently three times the day before. I asked him about the harvest.

'There's zero,' said Ben. 'There's no crop. We're covering five districts here with 3,000 people in each, but we're asking for permission to expand to all 19. There's millions of hungry people, and our maize sacks are all there is.' I asked him whether people were starving. Ben looked at me like I was a white man who had just stepped off a private plane.

I finished breakfast and went to court. In the end I was fined 100 Zimbabwean dollars – half a US cent.

*

Jail gave me an unprecedented view inside Mugabe's regime. While I could follow his reasoning, I'd also seen the gaping flaws in his repression. Killing, ruin, a national exodus – there was precious little freedom at the end of Mugabe's freedom fight. Even Mugabe seemed to know that. A year later, I returned to Zimbabwe and spent a week hiding out at a friend's house in Harare, making surreptitious trips to meet Morgan Tsvangirai and others. One day, as I was returning from an interview, the car radio began live broadcasting the funeral of an old independence war hero and Mugabe came on.

'I have delivered to my nation, my people, a Zimbabwe that is free,' the President intoned. In the manner of a father reading to a child, Mugabe then listed the evidence for his claim. 'We call ourselves Zimbabweans and we never called ourselves Zimbabweans before. We never had a flag before, did we? No. We never had a national anthem before, did we? No.'

That was it. A name, a banner and a song.

A year later I found myself in Mutare in eastern Zimbabwe. In 2006, the citizens of Mutare had discovered there were billions of dollars of diamonds under their feet. As word about the diamond fields spread, 30,000 people descended. They were followed by Zimbabwe's security services. In late 2008, the army used two attack helicopters to storm the diggings, killing 200 miners. Then they marched the survivors back into the digs again to work as forced labour. The Zimbabwe fields were soon producing $1.7 billion in diamonds a year, about a fifth of annual global supply.

In Mutare I met Gamma, 29, who worked in one of the Zimbabwean army's mines. He had once found a million-dollar stone, 23 carats, but after agreeing a price for it and handing it over to a dealer, he had never been paid. I told Gamma that in the West diamonds were associated with marriage and beauty and love. I had to repeat myself, twice. I think the words just sounded too strange to him. Eventually Gamma replied: 'It's very different, what a diamond means to you and what it means to me. Here a diamond means beatings and shootings. Here it means trying to get something just to survive. And there is no choice. There is no choice here.'

This wasn't the freedom for which Mugabe claimed to be fighting. This was a criminal state securing its power and wealth through a blood-diamond industry that killed and enslaved its people. It was every reason the world would ever need to intervene once more in Zimbabwe, and for Africans themselves to doubt African rule.

In the end, Mugabe had come to have much in common with the imperialists he so vilified. Both stole Africa's wealth. Both refused to share it with Africans. Both oppressed and murdered the people they claimed to be protecting. Mugabe was correct that colonialism had been abominable, but his solutions seemed designed to keep Africa in the same past, when the continent's leaders ruled as potentates.

Mugabe also shared something with humanitarians. Like them, he was blind to how Africa was changing. If Africa had ever been a monochrome of suffering, it wasn't any more. Beyond rural Zimbabwe, even in parts of Harare, it was taking off, and Africans were no longer willing to accept authoritarianism, whether foreign or home-grown. The similarities between Mugabe and his enemies could even make you wonder whether the anger and accusations Mugabe traded with the West were all that real. After all, Zimbabwe still received more than $700 million in foreign aid a year, more than half of it from the West. It felt like a marriage where the partners hated and needed each other in equal measure.

One thing of which Mugabe had no need, however, was intrusive foreign journalists. And at that 2013 rally in Masvingo, I was travelling without proper credentials once again. How could I have been so stupid?

Mercifully, after a lengthy examination of my passport, Sunglasses let me pass. I walked across the front of the crowd and took up a position directly facing the stage. There was something under my feet and I looked down and saw that I was on a piece of red carpet. I dimly registered that this was the carpet down which a star speaker might walk as he ascended the stage. I followed the carpet away from my feet and across the small piece of dusty ground to the stage. At the other end were two small feet in shiny black shoes.

It was Mugabe. He was staring at me. I held his gaze for a second, trying to betray no expression. As casually as possible, I turned around and looked out across the crowd behind me. He *was* looking at me. He couldn't miss me. I was the only white face in a crowd of 100,000 and I was standing at the front.

I tried to find Chris. He was suddenly invisible. Several more Zanu-PF officials sidled up to me and asked for my accreditation. I smiled. I explained that I was not strictly a news journalist because, the thing was, I was writing a book. I smiled again. The men looked doubtful and wrote down my name.

By now, however, it was too late to hustle me away. A pastor was introducing Mugabe on the dais. He based his message on Joshua 1:6. 'Be strong and courageous; for you shall put this people in possession of the land that I swore to their ancestors to give them.' In front of me, two men hauled a small wooden lectern onto the stage. Mugabe stood up, walked forward, put an iPad on the lectern, rested his elbows on either side of it, locked his arms together and leaned into the microphone.

He started with a long introduction, thanking the local organizers. His voice was strong and mellifluous. He enunciated slowly, precisely and playfully, rolling his Rs, cooing his Us, slurring his Zs and smiling wide for his Es. If I hadn't known he was teetotal, I might have thought he was drunk. The way his arms sometimes hung loose at his sides, the way he curled his fist and banged the back of it on the podium, the way he clapped his languid hands together, the way he suspended an open palm over his head like a shower-head – it was, I'm afraid, strikingly simian and all too easy to imagine the kind of prejudices Mugabe might stir in his opponents.

I don't speak Shona, but as Mugabe reached the meat of his speech, I picked up the gist from the odd English word. '1960 to '61,' he said, 'Ghana . . . Algeria . . .'. He did an imagined back-and-forth canter on Algeria's independence negotiations half a century ago, playing both parts. 'Algeria is part of France,' Mugabe said, affecting the voice of colonial France. 'Ah!' Mugabe replied, now a confused Algerian, 'part of France?' 'No, it's part of France,' said French Mugabe. 'Ah!' replied Algerian Mugabe. 'I want to become independent.'

The story continued: '1963 meeting . . . Addis Ababa . . . liberation committee . . . guerrilla forces'. This part was about the tide of African independence that swept the continent 50 years ago. We moved on to Zimbabwe's own tortured route to freedom. '1976 Geneva conference . . . 1977–8 Anglo-American proposals . . . 1979 Lancaster House. October, November, December, Christmas Day . . . British . . . Carter administration . . .'. We had finally arrived at the drawn-out negotiations at Lancaster House in London which created an independent Zimbabwe.

I looked around at the crowd. They couldn't have cared less. Most were sitting on the ground, hugging their knees, their eyes closed or cast down. Some were chatting but most seemed to be quietly daydreaming as they endured the midday heat. And why would they have listened? This was ancient history. Most were born after these events. I looked at my watch. Mugabe had been speaking for more than half an hour already. I had a sudden realization. Mugabe was a war bore. Like Europe's 'Greatest Generation', he was going on and on about the war to a younger generation who could barely be less interested.

I smiled at my joke, then immediately regretted it. Mugabe was looking straight at me. I busied myself with my notebook. But when I snatched a glance, I could see he was still staring at me. I suddenly had the idea that he was talking to me. The English was coming more frequently now, and while I was far from the only person in the crowd who spoke it, I was almost certainly the only person who didn't speak Shona.

'You cannot ask our poor people to buy their land back which was never bought from them in the first place,' said Mugabe. Zimbabwean ownership of the Zimbabwean economy – 'indigenization' – was imperative. 'Start your own businesses, run your own businesses, be employers in your own right, own the wealth of the country – like the farmers are doing,' he said. 'What in our Gross Domestic Product is really our own? What goes out? GDP should contain 80–90 per cent of our own income. Otherwise it means nothing. It means wealth for people outside.'

That brought Mugabe to his nemesis. 'Blair said: "We are calling for regime change in Zimbabwe." What right have you to do so? Whoever calls for regime change in Britain? Regime change in Zimbabwe is the task of Zimbabweans. It's they and they alone who have the responsibility, the sole right to change the government, to change the leadership.'

Mugabe paused. Out of the corner of my eye, I could see he was still looking at me.

'One-party state, one-party state!' he yelled.

Still looking at me.

'Ah! These journalists!' he exclaimed.

My adrenalin surged. I looked up.

'The journalists even support the errors, the mistakes, the blunders,' he said. 'What is the conscience of the journalist? That sense of truth, sense of honesty? It does not exist.'

Mugabe was glowering at me now.

'We will never accept a person who is impudent and non-compliant and irresponsible and who wants to impose himself on others. We will not accept an imposition.'

The crowd cheered. By now I'd graduated from shame to fear.

But abruptly Mugabe caught himself. 'We must be peaceful,' he said. 'We should not hear of any incident of violence. Let us demonstrate to the world that we are peaceful. Demonstrate to the British.'

Mugabe punched the air with his fist. 'Vote Zanu-PF!' he said. 'One-party state!'

And he sat down.

At the next rally, before a crowd of 25,000 in the central city of Gweru, I decided to stay hidden and sat at the back of the crowd, watching them but listening to Mugabe on my car radio. He ran through the same history of African and Zimbabwean independence. He spoke just one full sentence in English, declaring homosexuality a Western abomination.

In Bulawayo, an opposition stronghold, Mugabe spoke in English throughout. He was on form. He pointed out that since 1980 the number of health clinics in Zimbabwe had risen from 318 to 1,105 and the literacy rate from 62 per cent to 94 per cent. He told people he felt their pain. 'You have no money,' he said. 'The people have no employment. People are hungry. There is water only three days a week. The electricity is off-on-off-on.' He blasted Blair for creating the MDC 'to destroy our country' and spoke of the need for every Zimbabwean to unite 'in the defence of your land, of your sovereignty, of your freedom'.

'In the name of all those we buried in mass graves in Zambia, Tanzania, Mozambique and Botswana, Zimbabwe must never be a colony again, never fall prey to imperialism and colonialism again,' he said. Since colonialism Mugabe and his party had fought the same enemy, 'not the colour of their skin but the evil they brought with them as they preached from the Bible'. 'We are a free people,' he continued, 'masters of our own destiny, with a country that has great natural resources and we must ensure they are ours for ever. For a true Zimbabwean, a lover of his or her own country, there is no choice at this election.'

It was Mugabe at his best. But still he struggled to keep the crowd's attention. At the back, there was a constant loud hubbub of conversation. People were leaving by the score. Far more interesting to the crowd in my section were a couple of drunks arguing over whose turn it was to get more beer. It felt like a day out in the park with the chance to see someone famous, if rather dull.

Mugabe's fourth and final rally was held at the national stadium in Harare before 40,000 people. Introducing the President as an evangelical pastor, Andrew Wutawunashe also invoked Joshua: 'Now Joshua was old and advanced in years and the Lord said to him, "You are old and advanced in years, and very much of the land still remains to be possessed."' God required Mugabe to 'finish the job', said Wutawunashe. 'You must change our way of thinking to show us black people that we have value among the nations. This land must be for the people of Africa and the resources must benefit them after so many years of slavery and oppression.'

After that came a football display that seemed to be a daringly candid metaphor for a Zimbabwean election. A single unopposed team of 11 players passed to each other, then shot and scored in open goals at each end, to wild celebrations and group hugs of congratulations on the pitch. The crowd looked on with mild interest. But the moment Mugabe stood up to speak, thousands started trooping out. Alarmed policemen locked the exit turnstiles to prevent an exodus. It looked like the crush might turn fatal. Mugabe wasn't helping by giving his most tedious speech yet. Dull in tone and content, it featured interminable detours into chemistry and the mechanics of suicide bombing. A soliloquy on the dilemma of matter, as posed by the action of mining, was such gobbledygook that I wrote it down verbatim.

'When you dig it out, you leave a cavity,' intoned Mugabe. 'You can never cover that hole with anything that is satisfactory. It's a minus. It's irreplaceable. You must go to another place and get soil from that other place. But then what happens to that other place? How do you fill that other place? And that other place is no longer what it was. It is what it was, minus what has been subtracted from it.'

It was literally a speech about nothing.

Mugabe was not a free man. He was trapped, a prisoner of the past. His speeches centred on a struggle four decades before. Like a punch-drunk boxer, that fight had formed him so completely that he had somehow missed everything that came after. Even after winning freedom, Mugabe had never left the battlefield.

The criticism of him was often overdone and factually incorrect. He was right that the whites should have given up at least some of their land. He was right that Britain was wrong to cut the subsidizing of land handovers. Nor, contrary to reports, had seized farms been ruined in black hands. In 2000, 2,000 white farmers farmed tobacco, growing 522 million pounds that year. In 2012, 60,000 black farmers grew 330 million pounds, a decline in total production but, in that it earned 60,000 families $6,000 a year, an immeasurable boost to equality and dignity.

But Mugabe's despotic methods suffocated any merit in his arguments. In addition, in a post-*ubuntu* Africa, freedom came from development and Mugabe had reversed that. Kagame said Africa had to prove its case. Mugabe had demonstrated the opposite: Zimbabweans often *were* helpless.

Before she died in August 2012, I met Mugabe's best biographer, Heidi Holland, at a café near her home in Johannesburg. As a young white liberation activist in Zimbabwe, Heidi had once fed Mugabe dinner at her house while he was living underground and on the run, the basis for the title of her book *Dinner with Mugabe*. What was it with Mugabe? I asked. Why had this illustrious and intelligent freedom fighter never been able to liberate himself? Why had he won freedom for his countrymen only to spend three decades trampling all over it?

Heidi told me how, after Mugabe's father left when he was young, he was raised by his mother and educated by an Irish missionary priest. This Western assistance, this aid, cleaved Mugabe in two. Mugabe had fought white imperialism but in an earlier life he had benefited from it – and the tragedy of Mugabe, and Zimbabwe, was that he never reconciled the dissonance. Heidi discovered that Mugabe would tell his children, 'The British Empire was once the greatest kingdom in the world – and the way they did things was the civilized way'. Even as Mugabe hated the idea of foreign rule over Africa, another part of him had been seduced by the way a foreigner had taken care of him. He despised his oppressors, the more so because he admired them. 'He's half British and half African,' said Heidi, 'and the two halves hate each other.'

On 31 July 2013, more than six million Zimbabweans voted at a fresh election. Many queued at the polling booths in the winter chill from before dawn and they were still there at midnight and again the following day. They brought their own pens, worried by rumours that Zanu-PF had equipped the booths with ones whose ink would fade, allowing them to change the vote.

In the end, none of it mattered. The fix *was* in. In Harare, police caught 20 Zanu-PF members with 6,000 fake voting slips. Not far from my old jail in Gwanda, voters discovered Zanu-PF had built an entire fake polling station. Far more professional and large-scale was Zanu-PF's tampering with the electoral roll. The independent Zimbabwe Election Support Network said that more than a million of the 6.4 million voters had been missed off. The Zimbabwe Election Commission announced Mugabe had won his seventh term as President with 61 per cent of the vote. Mugabe hailed a victory over the 'British and their allies'.

Back in Masvingo that first day, I had told Chris I wanted to see Great Zimbabwe and he offered to show me around after the rally finished. We drove to the site and climbed the steep, narrow steps between the giant boulders to the citadel, built to protect the emperor from attack. The dry-stone granite walls, as thick as a man and as high as three or four, were perched on the edge of a precipice still displaying perfect straight lines and right angles.

Next we explored the Valley Complex, at whose centre was the Great Enclosure, another dry-stone wall, this one 250 metres long, as wide as three men and as tall as seven. Inside it was a construction known as the 'conical tower': solid, round and 10 metres high. Beyond some regal significance, no one knew exactly what it was for. I had seen the tower before, on the Zanu-PF flag. I asked Chris why the place held such importance.

'The tower, the walls, they show solidarity and strength,' he replied. 'They show that together we can build this one strong thing. Just imagine how many stones were carried here to make this wall, and this tower, and how many people it took to carry them. People took stones from all the hills around. Everyone was coming together to build one thing, and a huge thing, which would stand for a long time.'

We sat down in front of the tower. It was late afternoon, the wind had died and the afternoon sun was picking out strands of gold in the long grass. We talked about Mugabe's fixation on the past. I suggested that maybe he was still fighting the old battles because he had never really won his freedom, from himself as much as his enemies. Maybe the curse of a true revolutionary was that he never stopped fighting.

Chris looked up at the tower. 'Why does anyone fight?' he asked. 'You fight for what you believe in. You fight for freedom. And Mugabe was right. I believe that. But after you win, you stop fighting. You come together. You build.' Chris regarded the ancient citadel where he grew up. 'In the end, I believe you fight for peace,' he said, getting to his feet. 'So I believe it's time to move on now.'

SEVEN

SOUTH AFRICA

• Johannesburg

Mthatha • • Durban

Durban was an African Miami, a city of beaches and apartment blocks painted in bubble-gum pastels where the summer never ended and the surf was always up. Way back from the strip, past the Victorian bungalows, past the low-rent estates, past the warehouses and the truck depots, up into the townships that were scattered like litter across the green foothills of the Zulu uplands, the world's most legendary freedom movement was fighting a new war. Fighting, and dying. Between 2010 and 2012, South Africa's police said 15 ANC members had been killed in the city. They were lying. A leaked internal ANC document put the true figure at 38. A Durban University crime researcher put the total at 40. That meant a comrade was being gunned down in Durban at least every month, mostly, according to the newspapers, by other comrades. What was happening to the ANC?

In a crowded coffee shop at the end of one of Durban's piers, Sifiso sat down with his back to the water. Large, tall, with dread-locks, Sifiso was a former aide to Sbu Sibiya, who had been the ANC's provincial leader in Kwazulu-Natal until he was assassinated in July 2011.

A friend in the police had let Sifiso see the files on his former boss's murder. Sifiso said the evidence suggested Sbu's killers did not care if they were seen. All day a lookout had sat in the crowded waiting room outside Sbu's office in the ANC's Durban headquarters. In a suburb across town, a hitman had sat in the shade of a hedge outside Sbu's house, cradling a 9mm pistol.

At 8.30 p.m. Sbu left work. The killers' phone logs showed the lookout alerted his partner across town. There were a further 18 calls between the two. An hour later Sbu pulled into his driveway and waited for his electric security gate to open. The gunman walked up to the driver's window and shot Sbu in the shoulder, then behind the ear, then in the heart. Sbu slumped over the wheel. His foot jammed on the accelerator. The car surged forward and rammed his garage wall, collapsing the building on top of it. The assassin fled, briefly calling the lookout once more. Then both men phoned several senior leaders in the Durban ANC.

'Sbu had five kids,' said Sifiso. 'And his wife has no work.'

We sat in silence. It was a bright, clear day. The seagulls were wheeling on the wind and out on the water a flotilla of dinghies was racing. After a while, Sifiso said: 'The police know who they are. *I* know who they are.' He took a long drink of Coke. 'I still have to work with some of them.'

Sifiso shook his head. 'Sbu was my brother,' he said. 'He was everything to me. He always said, "If I die for the ANC, it's OK. Even if I die, the ANC will live."'

Sifiso wasn't sure his friend was right. Sbu hadn't been killed for a grand cause. The modern ANC had no ideology, he said. Anyone could join. The wrong people had. 'It becomes no longer about changing the lives of the poor or building a society that is equal. People join because the ANC has state power and access to resources.'

One time, said Sifiso, Sbu had found five billion Rand missing from state finances. At others he discovered tenders that were awarded to friends, or paid twice for the same job, or for nothing. The legend of the ANC once made it seem immortal. Now corruption was killing everything it had stood for. Sbu had exposed the rot. 'So they removed him,' said Sifiso. 'They killed him.'

*

The Archbishop and Nobel Peace Prize winner Desmond Tutu lived a few miles from me in Cape Town. Tutu liked to tell a parable about the most corrosive legacy of apartheid: self-doubt. In the 1970s, he had obtained rare permission from the South African authorities to visit Africa's most populous nation, Nigeria. For weeks, he swept around the country, marvelling at the cacophony of black freedom all around him. African politicians! African businessmen! African engineers! African doctors! One day he boarded an internal flight and felt his pride surge when he saw two African pilots in the cockpit. After the plane took off, however, it hit turbulence and Tutu was seized with panic. 'I thought that was it,' he said. 'I thought: "Those *blacks* at the controls are going to crash!"'

Sbu's death provoked the same awkward reaction in Sifiso. 'People, even our own people, have begun to think a black man cannot lead,' he said. Sifiso was acknowledging the heartbreak of Africa's post-colonial years: how so many African independence movements had won the war only to mess up the peace.

One of the most striking contradictions about African liberation movements' assumption of power was how inequality often grew back to levels as obscene as anything experienced under colonialism. By 2011, seven out of 10 of the most iniquitous countries in the world were African. Fourth on that list, after the Seychelles, the Comoros Islands and Namibia, was South Africa. There inequality had worsened significantly *after* it had been a legal requirement of a white supremacist state. European visitors often expressed shock at the persistence of white racism in post-apartheid South Africa, but the truth was that the decades after apartheid were a golden time to be a racist. *Told you so*, Ian Smith, architect of white Rhodesia, would crow to journalists visiting him at his retirement home next to Rhodes' old beach cottage in Cape Town.

Smith believed the ANC's sorry record in office revealed its political immaturity and racial inferiority. Sifiso thought there was a problem with the freedom fight itself. Freedom fighters fought the law. Under an oppressive state, breaking the law *was* freedom. It was freeing your mind and snatching back your authority. And if you were breaking the law, why not work with the experts? In its fight with apartheid, the ANC, and its Durban branch in particular, had worked in close alliance with black organized crime.

The problems began once the Struggle was over. Once they *were* the law, many of Africa's freedom fighters saw no reason to stop breaking it. It was who they were, after all: free thinkers and revolutionaries, righteously radical entrepreneurs who took what they wanted and, in that act, found their liberation. It was a mindset well suited to rebellion. But it made for horrible rulers. Once in power, numerous ANC revolutionaries who had fought to better themselves made sure they did, helping themselves to state finances, often in alliance with their old criminal friends. With power so lucrative and used so unscrupulously, comrades were soon killing each other over housing deals or government contracts or simply because they thought it was their turn.

This was the paradox of liberation and democracy, said Sifiso. The ANC may have fought for democracy. But to do so effectively, it had had to become profoundly undemocratic. The Struggle had required discipline, hierarchy and a willingness to safeguard the movement above all else. When it took power in 1994, the ANC should have adjusted. 'But we did not,' said Sifiso. 'We did not deliver to the people. We continued to deliver only to ourselves.'

Before he became South Africa's fourth black President, Jacob Gedleyihlekisa Zuma lived in a villa on a street not far from Nelson Mandela's home in central Johannesburg lined with purple-flowered jacaranda trees. It was a time when most South Africans assumed Zuma's misconduct had effectively barred him from government office. Zuma was from Durban and had once been head of the ANC's intelligence wing. In that role he had forged the links with organized crime that helped the ANC smuggle weapons and people in and out of South Africa. Zuma maintained his contacts after apartheid ended. In 2005, one of them was jailed for

15 years for soliciting for Zuma a total of 783 bribes amounting
to $400,000 over 10 years. As a result, Zuma himself was due to
stand trial on four counts of corruption, one of racketeering, one
of money-laundering and 12 of fraud.

Zuma's reputation had already been tarnished by another trial,
for rape. Though he was acquitted, his testimony that he washed
off AIDS in a shower had scandalized South Africa's liberals, who
noted it was precisely that sort of ignorance that had given South
Africa the world's largest HIV/AIDS population. Nor were such
concerns assuaged when the trial revealed the extent of Zuma's
polygamy – three wives, two fiancées and 17 children – or by his
contention that by marrying some of his girlfriends (the list later
grew to five wives) he was being socially responsible.

President Thabo Mbeki had sacked Zuma as his deputy in
government. But it was the ANC rank and file, not the party president, who decided party positions and they had retained Zuma as
the party's No. 2, giving him a platform from which to fight back
against Mbeki. Zuma was popular with the party. His earthiness
contrasted well with the aloofness of Mbeki, who had spent 30
years in pipe-smoking British academia and spoke beautifully
about being African but never once looked comfortable *in* Africa.
Zuma was also highly motivated. Losing to Mbeki meant, very
probably, going to jail. The young militant ANC leader, Julius
Malema, then a close Zuma ally, said Zuma's showdown with
Mbeki 'was very personal . . . informed by the fear of being arrested and going to prison. In that situation, you fight because you
have nothing to lose.'

Zuma's very private inspiration weighed against his ability to
unite South Africans in the manner of Mandela. Mandela reached
out across the country's many divides. Zuma stuck to his supporters, whom he saw as an army, paid by patronage, with which he
could fight his persecutors, be they Mbeki, the newspapers, whites
or anyone else. His was not a subtle campaign. A halting and awkward public speaker who had not finished three years of school,

Zuma largely confined his public appearances to singing the Zulu war anthem 'Umshini Wam', which translates loosely as 'Bring Me My Machine Gun'.

Foreign dignitaries often described Zuma as a warm man at ease in his own skin. But when he appeared for his interview – tall, broad and bald in a white shirt, cream trousers and Polaroid glasses – I wondered whether they had been merely reaching for something positive to say. Zuma was distant and guarded. When I asked what he stood for, he was evasive. When I raised racism in South Africa, he interpreted my question as a racist affront. '*You* are asking *me* about race?' he asked. When I asked if he would run for President, he said I didn't understand. 'I cannot *run*. The system that we follow, it's never *running*.' The ANC was not an open society, said Zuma, but an exclusive members-only organization whose inner circle decided who was to be deployed as President. 'And I have never refused a deployment by the ANC.'

Zuma's intent was to describe himself as a humble party servant. But his account of how South Africa's next President would be chosen not by popular vote but appointed by the closed club of the ANC's top ranks went to the heart of its post-apartheid quandary.

The legend of Mandela and the Struggle had given the party such a lock on power that it rendered the democracy which it inaugurated all but meaningless. At the ballot box, voters' disappointment at the ANC in power was consistently trumped by their loyalty to its legend. The ANC's vote had never dipped below 60 per cent.

And since the ANC wasn't made to care, it didn't. Its performance was dire. Though the government had stopped releasing many of the more damaging statistics, most independent research put unemployment at around 40 per cent, the HIV/AIDS population at five million, a rate of 10 per cent, and violent crime, at 45 murders a day, among the worst in the world.

In many ways, little had changed since apartheid. For most

whites, the post-apartheid years had been an unqualified boon. More money, less guilt. For blacks, out of a total population of 50 million, 8.7 million still earned $1.25 or less a day. Most continued to live in the same township shacks, travelled inside the same crowded minibuses and, if they had jobs, worked in the same white-owned homes and businesses as they had before the revolution.

Most of the lives truly transformed by the ANC's victory were those of the party's own leaders. Many ANC councillors and ministers built empires of patronage and self-enrichment. The biggest single corruption case occurred in 1999 when overpayment in a $3.6 billion arms deal saw billions of dollars sprinkled across the ANC's upper echelons. Only one ANC leader was ever held to account. Many seemed to view the public purse as their own private bank account. Counting spending on luxuries and privileges by ministers and their wives between 2009 and 2012, the opposition Democratic Alliance said the total had reached $550 million. It took exceptional brazenness to stand out in this orgy of graft, but those that managed to included a state security minister's wife who was convicted of running an international drug ring and a local government minister caught using public money to fly first-class to Switzerland to visit his girlfriend, also in prison for narcotics.

That set the tone for the party's lower ranks. Every national, provincial and local tender for every road, school and social housing project was a new opportunity. By 2012, South Africa's anti-corruption police, the Special Investigating Unit, reckoned that up to a quarter of annual state spending on goods and services – $3.8 billion – was being wasted through overpayment and graft. The independent Council for the Advancement of the South African Constitution added that a fifth of South Africa's annual GDP – a towering $81.6 billion – was being lost to corruption and crime. The Auditor General said a third of all government departments had awarded contracts to companies owned by officials or their families. In one ANC-ruled province, the Eastern Cape, three-quarters of all contracts benefited officials in this way.

The criminality, and the violence that went with it, climaxed in Zuma's home state, Kwazulu-Natal, and its capital, Durban. KZN accounted for 1,103 of the 1,640 cases on the Auditor General's desk.

Even at these lower levels, few party members were punished for their crimes. As long ago as 1996, Zuma made clear he considered the ANC above the law and 'more important' than the constitution. His assertion reflected how the party had set about ensuring that the state served it instead of the people. Penalties for corruption either evaporated entirely or were so diluted by parole and medical discharges that they became meaningless. Few corruption cases had as high a profile as that of Zuma's advisor, but even he was released after serving just 28 months of his 15 years.

Nor were the police much better. In Durban in 2011, all 30 members of an elite organized crime unit were suspended, accused of more than 116 offences, including theft, racketeering and 28 murders, many of them contract hits ordered by politicians. Twenty-seven were later convicted of various offences. As in politics, the corruption went to the top. Two of South Africa's post-apartheid national police chiefs were sacked for corruption. One, Jackie Selebi, who also happened to be head of Interpol at the time, was jailed for 15 years in August 2010 for taking bribes from a notorious mob boss and drug smuggler. Selebi was released on health grounds after serving just 229 days.

In theory, wayward ANC members might still have faced censure from the party's own ruling body, the National Executive Committee. In practice, its membership made that unlikely. In December 2007, when it elected Zuma the party's president, seven of its 80 members had been convicted of offences such as corruption, drink-driving and kidnapping; seven more were being investigated by police for offences including fraud and culpable homicide; three had faced internal ANC censorship for an array of scandals; and another eight were accused of a variety of further improprieties. Some of the cases were pursued, but most were quietly dropped.

One drawback of such impunity for rank-and-file ANC members with ambitions to rise up the party was the way it encouraged their superiors to hold onto their positions for as long as possible. With little turnover of personnel, they had no way to join this orgy of self-enrichment.

No way, perhaps, except killing the incumbent.

For anyone wanting to lead the ANC, the way forward was to buy enough supporters. Likewise, the best leader for corrupt ANC members was one who was as interested as they were in making government office pay. The risk of a leader's exposure made him less likely to want to expose others.

As I left Zuma's house, his press advisor pulled me aside and cautioned me against giving too much weight to the scandals surrounding Zuma. His support among ANC members was the only thing that mattered, she said, and that was rock-solid. She opened a hardback accountant's book listing all the ANC branches and regional organizations in the country and started counting them off. 'Kwazulu-Natal, Limpopo, Mpumalanga, Eastern Cape ... we've already got them,' she said. 'We've already got enough.'

'*Got* them?' I asked.

She closed her book and smiled. 'It's a done deal,' she said.

It was. I saw Zuma again in May 2009, 18 months after he deposed Mbeki as president of the ANC and a month after the ANC's fourth election landslide made him South Africa's President. Perhaps because he felt untouchable, Zuma was more candid about the ANC's failings. 'There has been weakness in implementation,' Zuma said. 'After 15 years, people are saying: where is the delivery? We are aware of our shortcomings. These challenges are based in reality.'

It was unusual for an ANC leader to admit to any mistakes. I asked Zuma if that's how he would describe them. 'That's the reality,' said Zuma. 'You lose nothing by admitting where there have been weaknesses.' Still, in reality Zuma was being modest.

By 2009 barely a week was passing without a new protest about state failure to provide water or roads or books or houses. The corruption scandals were continuing to pile up. Desmond Tutu, who had fought apartheid peacefully alongside the ANC's guerrilla war, was calling the regime built by his former comrades 'worse than apartheid'. The way Zuma portrayed it, however, the party was the unwitting victim of its own popularity. 'After a decade or so in power, the success of liberation begins to challenge you,' he said. 'We are too strong. Such support and power can intoxicate the party and lead you into believing that you know it all. The situation tests your clarity, your understanding.' Many other African liberation movements had failed the same test, he said. The ANC had come to the same point 'where we might turn into something else'.

That wouldn't happen, said Zuma, because he had a plan to restore the ANC's moral authority. His government would record such a spectacular performance that all doubts would be erased. He would create 11 million jobs, he promised, build two universities and several railway lines, deploy an extra 1.3 million health workers and install five million solar heaters. The truth was that in power the ANC 'might have fallen' but, through determination and results, it would regain its stature.

It's possible that Zuma may even have been sincere. He made similar promises a few months later to the South African parliament. But he kept none of them. What actions Zuma did take in power suggested that the preoccupations of patronage and protecting his position quickly became overwhelming.

As party president, he flung open the gates of the ANC in a recruitment drive among his supporters in Durban and Kwazulu-Natal that doubled membership from 600,000 to 1.2 million and gave the party a marked pro-Zuma character. As national President, he neutered the criminal justice system by appointing close allies as his ministers of justice, police and state security.

(It was the state security minister whose wife was later convicted of drug-smuggling. The police minister was also soon exposed as a beneficiary of a government slush fund.) Zuma dismantled the Scorpions, the elite police unit which had pursued him for corruption. He appointed an unqualified ally as chief national prosecutor. He replaced the head of the supposedly independent Special Investigating Unit with a close advisor.

Those critics that he could not replace, silence or buy off, Zuma attacked. He sued journalists and cartoonists who questioned him and his supporters even demanded an artist destroy a portrait of him showing his penis (a comment on his polygamy, according to the artist). The ANC-led parliament then passed a law that allowed the state to jail for up to 25 years journalists and whistle-blowers who divulged state secrets. Precisely what defined a state secret would be up to the government to decide.

In 2012, an investigation by the opposition Democratic Alliance claimed Zuma and his family had cost the taxpayer close to $100 million in the previous five years, much of it spent on flights and private homes and $10 million in 'spousal support' going to Zuma's wives. In November 2013, the Public Prosecutor found that the state had also spent $20 million on upgrades to Zuma's sprawling private home at Nkandla, north of Durban, including 79 additional buildings, a pool and a cattle *kraal*.

None of it shook the ANC's hold on power. In May 2014, despite a wide consensus that he should probably be in jail, the party reappointed Jacob Zuma for a second term as South Africa's President.

ANC politicians confronting the difficulties of the present tended to reach back to the black-and-white certainties of the past. There the ANC was for ever the party of glorious and righteous revolution, the party of Nelson Mandela that freed South Africa and inspired the world. It was this past party that was still winning the present one its crushing election majorities.

This electoral trump card made the ANC fond of anniversaries and the biggest was 18 July, Mandela's birthday. It was as good an occasion as any to visit Qunu, the small village where Mandela was raised and now lived again, a few hours south-west of Durban, on a bluff overlooking the rolling prairies of South Africa's Eastern Cape.

Under apartheid, the Eastern Cape was where South Africa's racial engineers had created two autonomous black homelands, the 'Bantustans' of Transkei and Ciskei. The disingenuous injustice of that marginalization, making a pale mockery of black freedom by confining it to two small half-states of chilly, thin-soiled and treeless hills, fuelled a wave of righteous rebellion from which many black leaders emerged: Mandela, Oliver Tambo, Walter and Albertina Sisulu, Chris Hani, Govan and Thabo Mbeki, and Black Consciousness leader Steve Biko.

Despite the region's ties to the ANC, two decades after the party took power life in the Eastern Cape remained as desperate as ever. The statistics described true deprivation: the HIV/AIDS rate was 33 per cent; unemployment was 70 per cent; 78.3 per cent of the population had no running water; 88 per cent of people were below the poverty line; 93.3 per cent had no sewers, prompting intermittent outbreaks of cholera; and murder was three times the national average. The rape rate, that prime integer of social collapse, was jaw-dropping. In 2008, surveys of the rural Eastern Cape found 26.7 per cent of men admitted to being rapists. Of the victims, close to half were under 16, nearly a quarter under 11 and 9.4 per cent under six.

The morning of Mandela's 94th birthday I drove into Mthatha, the regional centre. I'd visited two years before and found every lamp post plastered with flyers advertising the mobile phone numbers of surgeons offering same-day back-street abortions. Parents were keeping their children out of school for fear they would be raped as they walked to class. Two years on, the place hadn't improved. At one set of traffic lights, a young beggar with filthy clothes and a dirty face knocked on my window, distracting me so his two companions could open a rear door and rifle my bag. At another junction, a boy of perhaps 14 stood in the road, stared at me through unseeing red eyes and urinated through his hands onto his ripped trousers and bare feet. When I pulled over to ask for directions to Laura Mpahlwa's house, a woman said she would take me and got in. 'You shouldn't be out here alone,' she said. '*Tsotsis* [gangsters] are everywhere.'

I'd arranged to meet Laura because I wanted to hear how life had changed for Mandela's home-town contemporaries. Laura was born in Johannesburg in 1929. She was among the first to move to Soweto when it was designed as a black dormitory town under apartheid in 1948. Mandela's struggle had taken him from Qunu to Johannesburg then Soweto but Laura had gone the other way, moving to Mthatha to work as a nurse in 1953.

With Transkei's government little more than an apartheid puppet, the revolution was as fierce in Mthatha as Soweto. Laura's first son spent five years on Robben Island for subversion, her second fled into exile, her third was tortured and Laura herself helped ANC leaders move in and out of South Africa. Living in the Eastern Cape was a daily reminder of what they were all fighting for. 'Back then, it was mud huts all the way to Durban,' said the 83-year-old.

Laura remembered how the mood in Transkei was transformed when apartheid collapsed. 'People got lights,' she said. 'Some got water. Work started on roads. There were social grants.' Still, when the ANC asked Laura to become an MP in the new parliament, she declined. 'I was scared,' she said. 'Deep down I knew in my heart it was too big a position. I wasn't trained for it. I wouldn't cope.'

Other ANC members did not share her humility. Soon, the new ANC government was performing as poorly as she had feared. In the Eastern Cape, it still left its people short of what they needed – books, teachers, medicine, roads, houses, jobs – and failed to protect them from what they didn't. 'Drugs, high rates of teenage pregnancies and HIV/AIDS,' said Laura. 'There was mismanagement, misuse and, very disappointingly, a lot of fraud.'

Two of the few white people Laura knew in Mthatha were an American Episcopalian missionary couple, Jennie and Chris McConnachie. Chris was a surgeon and set about building Transkei's only orthopaedic hospital. Jennie established a clinic in a squatter camp in the city whose Xhosa name, Itipini, meaning 'In the Dumps', described it physically and spiritually. When work on Chris's hospital finished in 1996, Mandela himself came to open it. In his speech, the President said: 'Nowhere has the legacy of apartheid been more shocking than in the state of health care in the former Transkei region.' He described the hospital as 'the difference between life and death' for the people of the Eastern Cape. The new hospital, created 'against all odds' by an inspiring spirit of 'partnership which has come to characterize our young democracy', was an example of how a united South Africa would 'build a better life for all'. Jennie showed me a cracked photograph of a smiling Chris with Mandela. 'It was the proudest day of his life,' she said.

Chris died in 2006. By then the hospital could run without him. The same could not be said of the rest of the Eastern Cape, however. Itipini, in many ways, was the lowest of the already very low. Shacks were built from scrap metal and cardboard. There was no sewerage, transport or power, and just two taps between 3,000 people. Unemployment was near-universal. As well as the clinic, Jennie's mission ran a snack hall, a homework club, a soccer team, a recycling operation, a choir and a vegetable garden. She stayed on in Mthatha after Chris's death because she was needed but also because, despite everything, Itipini was a community.

The rest of Mthatha took a different view. As a place of tiny alleyways and hidden corners, Itipini had a reputation for muggers and junkies. Years of simmering resentment exploded in April 2012 when a group of Itipini men murdered a liquor store owner in the neighbouring suburb of Waterfall. Two days later, the two communities held a meeting overseen by the police. Waterfall residents demanded Itipini be demolished. Several threatened to burn it down. Watched by police, they gave the Itipini residents one week to vacate.

A few nights later a group of Waterfall residents set fire to some shacks in Itipini. When the police arrived, they did not try to arrest the arsonists but instead beat and arrested the residents. Itipini's families began moving out. A week after that the police returned with rifles and announced through a megaphone that all residents had to leave. They returned with bulldozers the next day. By evening, Itipini no longer existed.

The authorities, it turned out, had no plan for how to rehouse Itipini's 3,000 people. Thousands wandered into Mthatha, seeking shelter from relatives or friends, hitching rides out of town or sleeping rough. A total of 268, including 24 children, moved into an empty Rotary Hall one and a half kilometres away, which the Waterfall residents immediately threatened to burn down as well. The authorities fed the Rotary group for two weeks, then stopped, complaining of the cost. Jennie had stepped in but was unsure how long she could continue. 'How can I fundraise for a community that does not exist and a project that has been flattened?' she asked.

Apartheid was built on an insistence that blacks were to be viewed not as individual human beings with rights and freedoms but collectively as an inferior class. The poverty of places like Transkei was taken as self-evident proof of black inadequacy. Blacks were backward, a race who couldn't help themselves. And if whites and blacks were separated by mental ability and culture, it made sense to divide them by geography too. Blacks as a group were the problem. So blacks as a group were moved elsewhere.

It was that kind of thinking that had led Pretoria to demolish troublesome townships in white areas, such as the Johannesburg neighbourhood of Sophiatown, telling blacks to go back to the village. Twenty years after apartheid, Mthatha's police were doing the same. Was Mthatha regressing towards apartheid? Had the ANC turned against freedom? Laura seemed to think so. 'Look at this town now. Mthatha is more threatening now. You used to be able to walk around alone at night. Now you can't talk to people, can't even look at them or they'll stab you and take whatever they want. It's so sad. It wasn't a better life for all.'

I drove to the Rotary Hall where some of Itipini's survivors were gathered. Living there was another contemporary of Mandela, 78-year-old Thandeka Nani. With seven children and so many grandchildren she had lost count, Thandeka spent all day every day trying to find food. 'It's not the same as apartheid,' she said, anticipating the question. 'It's worse.'

We were surrounded by about 20 men and women who were sitting on small piles of their belongings and listening to our conversation. When I asked Thandeka whether she had celebrated Mandela's birthday, they angrily chorused: 'No!'

Thandeka smiled, embarrassed by the younger generation's directness. 'We're still waiting for our celebration,' she said.

In the new South Africa, freedom had become indistinguishable from unrestrained criminality. The ruling party, the ANC, seemed to have particular difficulty telling them apart. Violence dominated much of the party's language. Zuma sang 'Bring Me My Machine Gun'. Julius Malema sang 'Shoot the Boer' and told supporters they should be prepared to kill for Zuma. When the metalworkers' union broke off its support for the ANC, a party leader wrote on the Facebook page of the union's boss, Irvin Jim: 'We must deal with you to the extent of killing you. No apology.' In Cape Town, the one South African province where the opposition Democratic Alliance held power, the ANC abandoned discussion in favour of flinging faeces at DA politicians, emptying buckets of the stuff over the steps of the provincial legislature and holding rallies which quickly degenerated into a smash-and-grab at street stalls in the city centre. Tutu was among 86 Capetonians who signed a public letter urging the ANC to wage its campaign of opposition 'without resorting to violence, without fomenting hate'. In the provincial city of Pietermaritzburg I met a group of ANC members who had protested against the corruption of their own provincial leaders. Those leaders had promptly dispatched two assassins to shoot them. Both had been arrested, but a 42-year-old man called Phelele said the group's luck couldn't hold. 'We expect to be killed,' he said.

Some South Africans were learning from the ANC's example. In the Eastern Cape, nurses protesting low pay kidnapped their managers and held them hostage as a negotiating tactic. Schoolchildren angry at the poor state of their school buildings burned them to the ground. There was a rash of murders on South Africa's university campuses. And every few months the country's townships would erupt in racist violence in which South Africans would lynch Somalis or Bangladeshis or Zimbabweans or Nigerians – whoever they accused of taking their jobs or being where they weren't wanted. In the worst of these race riots in 2008 more than 60 people died. The police did little to stop the killing. When I looked into an anti-Somali mob lynching in Port Elizabeth in which one man had died, a white police captain told me: 'Immigrants should expect a little difficulty from locals. Maybe they should weigh it up and if it really is that bad here, go back.' Like their political masters, some police officers seemed to see violence as part of their job. Nine hundred prisoners died in police custody every year. In 2013 in Daveyton, east of Johannesburg, nine police officers were filmed dragging a 27-year-old Mozambican taxi driver down the road, his feet tied to the back of a police van.

Even South Africans were shocked, however, when on 16 August 2012 a squad of riot police gunned down 34 striking miners at a platinum mine at Marikana, north-west of Johannesburg. Miners' strikes occupy a hallowed place in the legend of the Struggle. There were few injustices more evocative of apartheid than a black miner, digging into his ancestral land to enrich his white bosses while enduring low pay, lung disease, prison-like hostels and the occasional collapsing mine shaft. Under the leadership of the young head of the National Union of Mineworkers (NUM), Cyril Ramaphosa, miners' strikes helped push the apartheid state towards collapse.

Come 2012, however, Ramaphosa was an ANC leader, a prospective successor to Zuma and one of the richest men in Africa, worth at least a billion dollars. Much of his wealth derived from his 9 per cent share in Lonmin, which operated the mine at Marikana. The 3,000 Marikana rock drillers armed with machetes, clubs and home-made pistols who had walked out were members of a new breakaway union that accused Ramaphosa's old one of being in hock with the bosses. The strike quickly turned violent. Within days, eight people were dead. The strikers left the body of a suspected informant lying in the open, his head split open, his body arranged in a crucifix.

On 15 August 2012, Ramaphosa wrote an email to Lonmin's chief commercial officer. 'The terrible events that have unfolded cannot be described as a labour dispute,' he said. 'They are plainly dastardly criminal and must be characterized as such . . . there needs to be concomitant action to address this situation.' The next day, the police began herding the miners into an area away from the mine. The miners pushed back. The police fired tear gas, rubber bullets, stun grenades and water cannon. When a group of miners charged, the police, who were being filmed by a number of television news crews, opened fire with automatic machine guns. More than a dozen protesters were killed. Off camera, the police pursued the miners into a rock gully where they executed at least 14 more at close range. The total number of dead and injured was 34 and 78 respectively. Many had been shot in the back.

The comparisons to apartheid were only compounded two weeks later when state prosecutors announced they would be using the apartheid-era law of incitement to charge 270 miners with 34 counts of murder and 78 counts of attempted murder. The state was saying the killings were the miners' fault. They had murdered themselves.

The question people always asked about Zimbabwe was why Zimbabweans had not staged a second revolution against Mugabe. The same question haunted South Africa. There, too, the freedom that was meant to follow revolution had not materialized. What would it take for the people to rise up against the ANC?

One day, comparing the numbers of dead from South Africa's crime with some of the tolls from Africa's wars, I realized that maybe they already were. In its annual survey of global crime in 2013, the UN Office of Drugs and Crime reported South Africa had the highest murder rate in Africa and the sixth-highest in the world. At 16,250 murders a year, South African crime was around 10 times more deadly than the civil war in Somalia. South Africans couldn't bring themselves, yet, to attack the ANC regime. But in their frustration and marginalization, they were waging war on each other.

It was hard to know where this new war began and the old struggle had ended. The beginning of the end of apartheid came in 1976 when Soweto, and then all South Africa's townships, rose up in a tide of insurrection sparked by students refusing to learn Afrikaans. Forty years later large urban areas of South Africa remained no-go areas for the police. In his 2008 book *Thin Blue*, for which he spent 350 hours on patrol with South Africa's police, the South African writer Jonny Steinberg described the relationship between the country's police and its criminals as part 'negotiated settlement', part 'tightly choreographed' street theatre. Criminals, he observed, made a show of running away and officers half-heartedly pursued them. His thesis was that 'the consent of citizens to be policed is a pre-condition of policing' and in South Africa, for two generations, that consent had been lacking.

Other countries experienced violent crime as a temporary upsurge after a sudden shock, like a recession or the opening of a new drug route. In South Africa it had lasted for two generations – and that had shaped a nation. Unable to rely on the state, South Africans had learned to cope with crime on their own. Policing had become a private concern. In the townships there were hundreds of vigilante killings a year. More salubrious areas, like my own white-dominated neighbourhood, relied on South Africa's 411,000 private security officers, whose number more than doubled that of policemen. Residents cocooned themselves in security estates. In the nineteenth century, South Africa's Afrikaners had circled their wagons in an impenetrable *laager* when faced with attack. At the Battle of Blood River in 1838, 470 Afrikaners slaughtered more than 3,000 Zulus, at a cost of just three injured of their own. The security estate – walled-off clusters of houses protected by razor wire, electric fences, motion detectors and guards – was the twenty-first-century *laager*. Its purpose was the same: separation from danger, from the other.

What a racist regime once made mandatory, crime now made desirable. What prejudice had divided, inequality now atomized. In the first years after apartheid, Tutu had spoken about a Rainbow Nation. The new South Africa turned out to be no harmony of colour and, with its electric-fence partitions, barely even a nation. Freedom, in South Africa, was really a murderous free-for-all. The struggle against apartheid, rooted in black solidarity and an end to discrimination, had, in the end, led to fragmentation. South Africans lived apart and, ultimately, alone. And individuals couldn't stop a country falling apart. From behind their barricades, they just got to watch.

EIGHT

MADE IN AFRICA

· Nairobi

On the corner of Moi and Haile Selassie in downtown Nairobi is a small garden where office workers on a lunch break stretch out on the grass and hawkers sell them fried chicken quarters for a dollar. It's a rare corner of peace in the gridlock and skyscrapers of the Kenyan capital and that, one suspects, was its creators' solemn intent. If you were to dig down a foot or two into the turf, you'd find broken and charred evidence of a cataclysm that, a generation ago, changed the world. Contrary to legend, it was here on 7 August 1998 that the opening shots were fired in a conflict that would become known as the war on terror.

That Friday, inside the five-storey, sand-coloured US embassy, hundreds of diplomats and their staff were working the last hours of the week before taking off for the game-park trips and country-club parties that fill the expat weekend in East Africa. It seems unlikely anyone was aware that the day was the eighth anniversary of the stationing of American troops in Saudi Arabia. It is all but inconceivable that even one suspected that, as a result, hundreds of people in Africa were about to die.

At 10.30 a.m., two men drove a truck up to the embassy's back gates. The truck, a Toyota Dyna pick-up, was loaded with 900kg of TNT wired to a detonator under the dashboard. One of the men, a Saudi, shouted at a security guard to open the gate. When the guard refused, the man shot at him, threw a stun grenade, then leaped out of the truck and ran off. As he did so, his accomplice flicked the detonator.

The blast blew the face off the embassy building. A neighbouring secretarial college collapsed. A packed commuter bus in the road was incinerated. Every window within 400 metres shattered. A total of 201 Kenyans died, most of them passers-by. Twelve Americans were also killed. Several hundred kilometres to the south in the Tanzanian capital, Dar es Salaam, a second team of bombers, led by an Egyptian known as 'Ahmed the German' for his light-brown hair, killed 11 more people outside a second US embassy when they detonated a similar device. The total number of injured from both attacks ran to several thousand. They included the surviving Nairobi bomber, who was arrested when doctors examining his injuries realized they had to have been sustained by someone already running away from the blast as it detonated.

Thirteen years after the attacks, I was in Nairobi on the morning in May 2011 that a US Special Operations team helicoptered into northern Pakistan and shot dead Osama bin Laden at a house in Abbottabad. Nairobi and Dar had lit a fuse that led to 9/11, Afghanistan, Iraq and beyond. These were the wars that had shaped the world, and my professional life. With bin Laden finally gone, I wanted to mark the moment at the spot where it all began.

At first glance, Nairobi seemed to have long moved on. Bin Laden's death prompted no public remembrances, nor even any private ones that I could see. But on the walls of a small museum at the back of the small park were written commemorations of the dead and, among them, testimonies of those who survived. Here was bitterness to last an age. Douglas Sidialo, whose sight was taken in the bombing, wrote that for years he had been overwhelmed by a desire for revenge. 'If I had met bin Laden,' he wrote, 'I would have skinned him alive.'

The Prophet Muhammad was born in AD 570 in Mecca in what is now Saudi Arabia. Though high-born, he was orphaned at six and as a boy Muhammad earned his keep helping his uncle, who was a travelling merchant. This unusual upbringing, in which he experienced privilege and poverty, gave Muhammad a unique outlook. He was a social rebel, who married a much older woman for love and treated her as an equal. He was also a reformer who – guided by the divine visions he began receiving at 40 – fought against the inequality, immorality and tribal lawlessness of seventh-century Arabia.

After Muhammad's death in 632, his followers set about formalizing his teachings in a canon of holy custom and law. That work is still ongoing but its central elements include the Qur'an, God's collected revelations to Mohammed; the *Hadith*, sayings which describe *sunna*, Mohammed's way of life, taken as a guide by his followers; and *sharia*, which is Islam translated into law. It was in these scriptures that the term *jihad* first appeared.

Most scholars agree that *jihad* denotes lawful and justifiable war. It is founded on notions of sacred duty, righteousness and sacrifice. It applies most commonly to a war for freedom and against oppression, especially one defending Muslims persecuted by unbelievers. It is that idea, coming to the aid of fellow Muslims and the obligation and global brotherhood that implies, on which the figure of the wandering foreign *jihadi* is based.

In Islam's first few centuries, *jihad* described the Arab conquest of the Middle East, North Africa and parts of southern Europe. That empire is to what many Muslims are referring when they talk of the Caliphate and is the context for an explicitly military and expansive definition of *jihad* that denotes holy wars of liberation. After the Mongols sacked Baghdad in 1258 and European Christians began pushing the Caliphate back, eventually expelling Muslims from Europe, *jihad* came to have a more introspective meaning in much of the Muslim world, referring to an internal struggle for virtue and freedom. Only in the eighteenth century did a new doctrinaire movement on the Arabian peninsula, Salafism, emphasizing literalist adherence to ancient texts and the purifying absolutism of fire and sword, restore *jihad*'s violent side in the Middle East.

In Africa, however, *jihad*'s connection to war never wavered. The age of European exploration was, in part, the latest manoeuvre by Christians in their global conflagration with Muslims. By inaugurating a sea route through which not just trade but Christianity and European values flowed to Asia, Vasco da Gama put a southern cinch on the frontiers of the Caliphate. The world's wealth would henceforth flow not overland via the Muslim merchants of the Middle East but via sea traders to Christian Europe.

Africa's Islamists have never forgotten the injury. Much of the history of Africa over the last five centuries can be told as a never-ending conflict between Muslims and Christians as the *jihadis* tried to restore Islam's pre-eminence. The Sahara has been a particular front line. With Islam established in North Africa and European Christians making inroads from the south, the two faiths met in the desert and from east to west, for thousands of kilometres, they have never stopped killing each other. Today's Muslim-Christian butchery in Nigeria, Sudan, Chad and the Central African Republic, and the eternal rivalry between Somalia and Ethiopia, are the latest episodes in this ancient confrontation.

This is where Africa's long fight for freedom merges with its history of *jihad*. The Christian fighters in Africa were often foreign colonists. Africa's Islamic warriors, by contrast, tended to be home-grown, the descendants of African converts with a lineage stretching back to Muhammad's first followers whom the Prophet sent to Ethiopia in 615. In West Africa, the struggle against French rule was led by Sufi *jihadis* of the Tijani order. In Sudan, General Charles Gordon was cut down in Khartoum in 1885 as he tried to face down the *jihadis* of a self-proclaimed Mahdi, or messiah. Even as late as 1920, the Royal Air Force was carrying out air strikes on another champion of African Islam, the poet and guerrilla fighter Mohammed Abdullah Hassan, whom the British called 'the Mad

Mullah' but whom Somalis revere to this day as the embodiment of the independent Somali spirit.

In the West in the twenty-first century, we live in a post-imperial age in which Africa's freedom fighters are lionized but also a post-9/11 one in which Islamists are demonized. To African Muslims, this is a contradiction. To them, the connection between *jihadi* resistance fighters of Africa's colonial past and *jihadis* fighting US forces in Somalia or French ones in Mali is manifest. For Westerners, who see a world divided between defenders of freedom and Muslim terrorists, the awkward truth is that Africa's great liberation leaders and its Islamist militants have often been one and the same. Perhaps that myopia goes some way to explaining why many in Europe and the US also fail to see how, from the start, Africa was a key battleground in their war on terror.

Osama bin Laden suffered no such blindness. Bin Laden came of age in the 1980s as an Islamic warrior among the Afghan *mujahedeen*. The Afghans' barefoot defiance of a global superpower won them worldwide sympathy, including billions of dollars in funding and arms from the CIA – and even the support of America's most famous fictional avenging knight, John Rambo, whose third adventure, *Rambo III*, was set in Afghanistan.

When the Eastern bloc collapsed in the aftermath of the Soviet defeat, for a time the West convinced itself that victory was permanent and even, in the title of Francis Fukuyama's book of the time, that history was at an end. But a true *jihadi* fights not for power but paradise – in this life, an unattainable and never-ending task. Some Afghan *jihadis* soon found new wars, especially against the USSR's former Serbian allies in Bosnia and its Russian successors in Chechnya. But for bin Laden, the defeat of one apostate superpower was a cue to turn on the next.

Bin Laden formed a new group composed of old Afghan hands and new young radicals. He named it al-Qaeda ('the Base') after a *mujahedeen* training camp in Afghanistan and made the US its prime target. But for its formative years, when his nascent group was developing its character and outlook, bin Laden chose to base it where Islam's first followers had also found their feet and where al-Qaeda could draw on centuries of righteous *jihad* against Christians: Africa. Bin Laden stayed five years in Sudan, from 1992 to 1997, developing al-Qaeda's philosophy and organization. After he returned to Afghanistan and, in 1998, publicly declared a *jihad* against the US, it was his original disciples in Africa who first made good his threat.

The East Africa bombings had grim legacies. They were al-Qaeda's first attacks on the US. They were also the first truly indiscriminate terrorist assaults in living memory. Before East Africa, political militants such as Hezbollah or the Irish Republican Army (IRA) or the Fuerzas Armadas Revolucionarias de Colombia (FARC) or the Basque Euskadi Ta Askatasuna (ETA) mostly attacked soldiers or state buildings and, if they killed civilians, made some attempt to limit casualties. The East Africa attacks were different. Secure in their righteousness, the bombers were less concerned about the legitimacy of their targets than attracting attention to their cause, something they decided was best accomplished by killing as many people as possible. Al-Qaeda slaughtered civilians not by accident or as necessary, regrettable sacrifices but by explicit design.

Terrorism has its fashions. With its first attacks, al-Qaeda broke taboos on the mass-murder of innocents and took terrorism in a new self-absorbed direction. Henceforth bombers would strike out of the blue and aim for the widest possible carnage. They wanted the world's notice and sought it with outrage. Any crowded place was a possible target, especially chokepoints like hotels, shopping centres and public transport. Whom they killed was all but immaterial. It was a blueprint followed by those who bombed a nightclub in Bali in 2002, trains in Madrid in 2004 and buses in London in 2005.

This narcissistic bloodlust made al-Qaeda deeply unpopular. It could hardly have been otherwise. Still, the revulsion they inspired seemed to come as a shock to bin Laden and his lieutenants. These were men who believed they were divinely guided. Their miraculous defeat of the Soviets in Afghanistan, against overwhelming odds, precipitated the Godless empire's collapse. In 2001, they toppled the Twin Towers in New York in equally unexpected manner. In a videotaped dinner conversation with Saudi visitors to his home in Afghanistan a few weeks later, bin Laden said: 'All we had hoped for was at most three or four floors.'

After 9/11, however, the brothers' blind faith was tested. They were prepared for denunciations from the West. What they hadn't predicted was that most of the rest of the *ummah* would not only refuse to join their *jihad*, but even fight against them. Around the world, Islamic leaders issued *fatwas* against terrorism. In Yemen, tribes rose up against al-Qaeda. In Iraq by late 2007, al-Qaeda's killing of thousands of civilians had prompted Sunni militants, who previously fought with the group, to start fighting with the Americans against it, decisively changing the course of the war. No one had expected *that*.

Letters recovered from Abbottabad after bin Laden's death show the Sheikh was beginning to rethink the entire al-Qaeda enterprise. He wouldn't allow himself to say that East Africa or 9/11 had been mistakes. America remained the Great Satan and there was no turning back the clock on the age-old blood feud between Muslim and Christian. But bin Laden was wondering about the wisdom of indiscriminate killing, in which Muslims inevitably died as well, and the near-universal public resentment of the Islamist totalitarianism that al-Qaeda sought to impose. Al-Qaeda was losing any claim to virtue. Its unpopularity, bin Laden wrote, might 'lead us to winning several battles while losing the war'.

In his attempts to rebuild the group's reputation, bin Laden turned once again to Africa. In his letters to the growing number of al-Qaeda groups on the continent, he sketched out a new plan for the *jihad*. Stop so much killing, he wrote. Stop talk of a global

Caliphate and the imposition of medieval laws. Align with popular uprisings. Focus on how the West was oppressing the poor and the hungry, and offending all decency with its pornography and homosexuality. 'We are not yet ready to cover the people with the umbrella of Islamic rule,' bin Laden warned.

In this remade *jihad*, he added, Africa would be vital. With its history of anti-colonial *jihad* and the way imperialism echoed in its present-day injustices, not least in the arrogance of aid and corruption of Africa's liberation leaders, the continent represented one of al-Qaeda's best hopes for refashioning itself as a catalyst of noble revolution. As it had been from its founding, Africa would be key to al-Qaeda's success.

NiNE

GUINEA-BiSSAU AND MALI

Bissau City • • Bamako

In a small village on Africa's western tip a 62-year-old woman stood outside her wooden, grass-roof hut and described how one night a plane landed on the road in front and unloaded several tons of South American cocaine.

It had been December 2011 and Quinta Balanta was taking the night air on her veranda at the edge of the village of Amedalae in the tiny country of Guinea-Bissau. Without warning, around 9.30 p.m. a group of 20 soldiers and 10 men in plain clothes arrived in a small convoy of pick-ups. Some of the soldiers set up a roadblock outside her house. The others took off down the road that leads out of Amedalae and ran dead straight for several kilometres across endless fields of flat, treeless rice paddies. Two and a half kilometres away, they set up another roadblock. Between the checkpoints, the soldiers unloaded hundreds of aluminium cooking bowls and placed them in parallel lines down each side of the road. Finally they filled the bowls with paraffin and lit them. 'The light was amazing,' said Quinta. 'You'd have thought you were in Europe.'

Their preparations complete, the soldiers asked Quinta to go inside. 'I refused. I said: "This is my house, something's going on and I'm going to sit on my veranda and watch." And at midnight I heard a plane coming from the sea. It went overhead, did a slow circle, turned back and started to land.' The twin-prop touched down, taxied right up to Quinta's house, then turned side-on. The

231

pilot cut the engines and threw open the cargo door. Pulling up in two trucks, a few of the ground crew pumped fuel into the plane's tanks while the rest unloaded the cargo. 'The plane was full of big, white sacks – the kind you take to sell second-hand clothes at market,' said Quinta. 'They filled one truck, then another, then covered both trucks with tarpaulins.'

The entire operation, landing, refuelling and offloading perhaps two tons of cocaine, took 30 minutes. As soon as it was finished, the pilot started his engines, rumbled back down the road, took off and banked away to the west, towards the Atlantic. The soldiers and civilians left immediately as well, in the direction of a nearby farm owned by General Antonio Indjai, then head of Guinea-Bissau's army.

There might have been a time, perhaps before dawn, when Bissau City hustled but I never saw it. There was never a breeze and the sun and humidity meant your shirt was scalding-wet across your back before you'd walked a block. The city subsisted in a state of exhausted collapse. Every wall was covered with black fungus and green moss and every pavement was buckled by the heat and shattered by decades of evening downpours.

The one benefit of this torpor was that Bissau City took no time at all to get to know. The need to move as little as possible meant everyone arranged themselves within a kilometre of each other in the city centre, around a handful of cafés and restaurants serving bottles of chilled water and *vinho verde*. I met a European honorary consul who greeted me on the first-floor balcony of a building that he used as his home, his office and a warehouse. 'We've had so many coups,' he said, stretching out a hand from his easy chair, 'and apparently we're going to have another one.'

It was September 2012. General Indjai had overthrown the government in April, the second coup in three years. Political calamity was followed by economic. The price of cashews had plummeted, and Bissau's entire economy was tied up in 60 million tons of raw nuts that, since they could now only be sold for a loss, were rotting on the docks. 'It's like Saturday every day,' said the honorary consul. 'We don't even bother opening in the afternoon.'

The depression only made the cars more incongruous. Parked in the broken road outside a neighbourhood restaurant a block from my hotel were a bright-yellow Hummer, a brand-new Range Rover, an Audi SUV and a Bentley – more than half a million dollars in cars all told. Inside, their owners included a bald Eastern European man talking on a satellite phone, his shirt open to show a gold medallion the size of a CD, and seven neatly bearded young Lebanese men silently sipping water. 'Nobody even pretends any more,' said the honorary consul. 'It's the only business in town.' Diplomats estimated the amount of cocaine moving through Guinea-Bissau had doubled to 60 tons a year since Indjai's coup. At that kind of volume, the trade was worth twice Guinea-Bissau's official GDP.

At his offices in a side street just back from the centre, I met João Biague, the 44-year-old National Director of the Judicial Police and, as such, Guinea-Bissau's lead anti-narcotics officer. João had no money to run an effective operation. One year the UN Office of Drugs and Crime had given his squad five cars but they had suspended their support after Indjai's coup and, without it, the judicial police had no gas money. João did have about a dozen mobile phones and around 20 men, whom he deployed in the bars and cafés around town like the Kallista and Papa Loco's. He also watched the cars. 'I know how many Hummers there are in Guinea-Bissau,' he said. 'If I see them moving, I know something is happening.'

With no resources to stop the trade, João spent his time studying it. Cocaine, he discovered, had been transported across the Atlantic for thousands of years. In 1992, tests on several 3,000-year-old Egyptian mummies found traces of cocaine and nicotine, both of which originated in the Andes, suggesting not only that the transatlantic drug trade was several millennia old but that Egyptians or Africans crossed the ocean 2,500 years before Christopher

Columbus. In the nineteenth century cocaine was used by doctors as an anaesthetic, prescribed by Sigmund Freud as a mood enhancer, dispensed to children as a treatment for toothache, mixed with wine in a blend given divine endorsement by Pope Leo XIII, used by the Antarctic explorers Ernest Shackleton and Captain Robert Scott and even included in the original recipe of Coca-Cola, which fused the drug with the kola nut. Southern American plantation and factory owners also used cocaine to improve the productivity of their black workers. By the early twentieth century that led to a string of stories in the *New York Times* about 'Negro cocaine fiends' who murdered and raped at will.

The backlash and cocaine's prohibition in 1914 in the US suppressed its use for half a century. But in the late 1960s, Colombian growers began tapping a new American appetite for drugs. By the turn of the millennium the cartels discovered that their business growth in the US was flat-lining, not because of the US 'war on drugs' launched by President Richard Nixon in 1971, but simply because the market was saturated. It was then, said João, that the cartels realized the European market was still comparatively underdeveloped and that halfway to Europe, within range of small planes and fishing boats, were a series of eminently corruptible African countries with little in the way of law, government, air forces or navies.

In 2004 fishing trawlers, go-fast powerboats, small jets and cargo twin-props with custom-enlarged fuel tanks began shuttling across the Atlantic. 'Highway 10', so called because the route roughly followed the 10th parallel, was born. At the beginning of the decade, Europe's cocaine market was a quarter of its American equivalent. By its end, the two markets matched each other at 350 tons a year. By 2014, there were 14–21 million cocaine users in the world, equating to one in 100 Westerners, rising to around three in 100 in Spain, the US and the UK. In Britain cocaine became as middle-class as Volvos or farmers' markets.

The Africans rarely owned the drugs they were moving,

something their Latin American, Middle Eastern and European bosses tended to reserve for themselves. But transporting was lucrative work and the syndicates quickly recruited customs officials, baggage handlers, soldiers, rebels, government ministers, diplomats, even a prime minister and president or two. The cocaine was flown in by small plane, then taken overland to another African country and flown out in the stomachs of human mules. It was shipped in by speedboat and freighted out again in a sea container stacked inside a pile of others. It was imported in the stomachs of African exchange students returning home from Brazil for the holidays, then re-exported hidden under tons of iced fish or even driven north across the Sahara in convoys of fat-tyred super-charged pick-ups.

To keep ahead of the law, the traffickers switched routes constantly, and quickly extended their reach across the continent. Soon every African country with a language in common with Latin America – Angola, the Azores, Cape Verde, Equatorial Guinea, Guinea-Bissau, Mozambique – was a trafficking hub, as were all of Africa's biggest airports – Nairobi, Lagos, Johannesburg and Cape Town. Among the airlines, Royal Air Maroc, which linked Brazil with North and West Africa and Europe, became a smugglers' favourite, as did Africa's biggest, South African Airways. In 2009, in the first of five cocaine busts on the airline in two years, an entire 15-person SAA crew was arrested at Heathrow accused of smuggling close to half a million dollars' worth of the drug. One crew member was later jailed for seven years for trying to smuggle 3 kilograms of the drug in her underwear.

When it came to African countries, the cartels especially liked Guinea-Bissau. It had a coastline of a thousand hidden creeks and 88 islands, some with their own colonial-era airstrips. But with a population of 1.5 million and an average per capita income of $500, the country was too small and too poor to afford boats for its navy or planes for its air force.

When the traffickers first arrived around 2004, said João, 'they called themselves businessmen. At first we didn't understand because there was no business for them to do here.' The first most people in Guinea-Bissau heard of cocaine was in 2005 when farmers on the coast found sacks of white powder washed up on the beach and, thinking it was fertilizer, sprinkled tens of millions of dollars of the drug on their crops. The plants died. But within a year, cocaine was a thriving mainstay of Guinea-Bissau's economy. In December 2006, Dutch customs at Schiphol airport arrested 30 passengers on a single flight arriving from Bissau City, all on allegations of having swallowed several bags of cocaine.

Perhaps the biggest hindrance to João's work was that as a state employee, ultimately he worked for Guinea-Bissau's biggest cocaine smuggler, General Indjai. It was an isolating existence. João had had death threats and rarely slept in the same place twice. When I met him, he looked exhausted and told me he was on the point of quitting not just his job but his country, too. 'Look, I don't know about the future of the country,' he said, 'but I can tell you what I plan for my future. No country that has been through this has been able to fix it and if I cannot achieve what I want, there's no need for me to stay.' A few months later I heard he had quit and moved to Italy.

If Guinea-Bissau's transition to a military-led narco-state was a tragedy for its people, the collapse of one of Africa's smallest states had little strategic importance – even the US didn't keep an embassy there. But as traffickers moved out across West Africa, so the criminality and instability they brought with them spread through the region. Between 2008 and 2013 West Africa saw six coups (two in Guinea-Bissau, and one each in Guinea-Conakry, Mali, Mauritania and Niger), two attempted coups (Gambia and Guinea-Conakry), two civil wars (Cote d'Ivoire and Mali), one popular revolution (Senegal) and a string of assassinations.

The scale of the drug-smuggling through Mali had been clear since 2 November 2009 when an ancient Boeing 727 was found burnt out in the middle of the desert near Tarkint in north-east Mali. Investigators from the UN Office of Drugs and Crime discovered that the smugglers flew the large Bissau-registered jet from Venezuela across the Atlantic to Mali. Touching down on a rocky desert strip, they unloaded perhaps 10 tons of cocaine, then, finding they had damaged the landing gear, torched the plane. Villagers around Tarkint said they'd seen other planes landing and taking off again for the best part of a year. The UNODC's West Africa chief, Antonia Maria Costa, warned this new 'larger, faster, more high-tech' smuggling, plus the revelation that smugglers could afford to burn planes, showed that drug-trafficking in West Africa was attaining a 'whole new dimension'.

The flag had been raised. Few chose to heed it. In Bamako in 2012 I couldn't find a single diplomat who, beyond the bare facts of 'Air Cocaine', knew much about African drug-smuggling. 'Nobody knows what the heck is flying over, or has any idea of what is coming in or coming out,' was one American's sunny summary. Cheikh Dioura, a Malian journalist who had written about cocaine for Reuters, told me he had had the same experience. Despite signs of an exploding trade in illegal drugs-smuggling to Europe, he said most diplomats were preoccupied with managing generous foreign aid programmes.

That reflected the story foreign donors preferred to tell about Mali. Before President Amadou Toumani Touré abruptly quit in April 2012, diplomats described Touré – known by his initials 'ATT' – as an army officer who overthrew a dictator in 1991, then handed power to a democratically elected civilian president, then, 10 years later, legitimately won an election. It was an unusual narrative of democratic African leadership and Westerners loved it. Foreign aid rose to 50 per cent of the government's budget under Touré. Aid workers held up Mali as an example to the continent. US Special Forces also conducted annual counter-terrorism training with the Malian army. 'The country is considered one of the most politically and socially stable countries in Africa,' read the

World Bank's 2007 assessment. 'One of the most enlightened democracies in Africa,' said USAID in 2012.

Cheikh Dioura, the Reuters stringer, had a different take on his former President. 'Amadou Toumani Touré,' he said, 'was the biggest drug trafficker of all.'

Cheikh had a friend in the Malian secret service, a colonel who had been posted to Gao and Timbuktu and was covering the region when the 'Air Cocaine' plane was discovered in the desert. The colonel agreed to meet in an empty Chinese restaurant close to my hotel. A small man in scruffy plain clothes, the only clue to his identity was a neat military moustache. Cheikh warned me the colonel did not much like journalists and had even less time for ignorant foreigners. To open him up, Cheikh suggested I played up to the colonel's predispositions.

I began by remarking that the stories I'd heard of the scale of trans-Sahara cocaine-trafficking seemed too wild to be true. The colonel snorted. 'There are convoys every Friday!' he said. The colonel described trans-Saharan processions of 15 to 22 cars that followed the old Tuareg caravan routes across the desert. In each cab was a driver and a fighter. As many as three convoys were moving at any one time. 'Everyone knows this!' exclaimed the colonel.

The colonel's description tallied with that of a 32-year-old convoy driver Cheikh had taken me to meet in a dusty Bamako back street. The driver talked about taking three or four days to cross the Sahara. The trips were done in convoy, he said, guided by a Tuareg who knew the old routes from Mali and Niger into Algeria, Libya, Egypt, the Middle East and Europe. Like the colonel, the driver said half the cars in a typical convoy carried drugs and half provided security. Assuming a light load of half a ton per truck, and a minimal schedule of one convoy a month, that was still 48 tons of cocaine a year, worth around $1.8 billion in Europe.

Like Guinea-Bissau, the cocaine trade in northern Mali was

more or less open. The driver said the man who ran it from Mali's easternmost city of Gao was an Arab called Oumar. Oumar had gathered around him 100 young men in pimped-out 4x4s who liked to smoke hashish and tear around Gao in their cars. 'The drivers are gone for a week,' said the driver. 'When they come back, they have big parties in the desert – girls, music, roasting sheep over big fires, spending money like water. Then they're gone again.' In an attempt to lower their profile, Oumar built 25 high-walled villas in a neighbourhood in Gao to house his drivers. The plan backfired. The townspeople of Gao immediately nicknamed the place Cocainebougou, or 'Cocaine City'.

Especially worrying for Mali's foreign aid donors was that Cheikh, the colonel and the driver all maintained that the smugglers were in business with government officials and Malian soldiers. 'This is very well organized,' Cheikh told me. 'Mayors are involved. Police are involved. Politicians in Bamako are involved. There are links to security people and officials in Algeria and Niger and Morocco and Libya.' When the colonel said something similar, I feigned shock. Surely he wasn't suggesting corruption inside the Malian state? 'Of course!' bellowed the colonel. 'There is very high complicity! There were times when we were prevented from going out on patrol. Our superiors told us not to go. I sent reports up the hierarchy asking: "What's going on? Why are you preventing us from doing our work?" But I got nothing back.'

The driver said the corruption went to the very top. 'Oumar called President Touré direct if he had any problems,' he said. The colonel agreed. 'It went all the way to Touré,' he said. The colonel added, however, that he considered Mali's former President something of an accidental drug baron. Mali's Tuaregs, most of whom were extremely poor, had staged intermittent rebellions in the north throughout Mali's 50-year history. Touré had tried to buy them off. He recruited Tuareg commanders into the army and gave them fat salaries and plenty of perks. After a Tuareg mutiny in 2006, Touré gave the Tuaregs even more, allowing them to run their territory as a highly corrupt, semi-autonomous state. The clan leaders diverted aid money intended for schools, roads and irrigation projects. They also took a cut from the cocaine trade.

Once the Malian state was sanctioning criminality, it wasn't long before it was taking part in it. Hundreds of millions of dollars were kicked back to government officials and soldiers. As head of state Touré found himself, in effect, in business with drug smugglers – as did, by extension, the foreign donors who funded him. That was what Touré was referring to when, in a candid moment, he called Baba Ould Cheikh, the mayor of Tarkint later convicted of cocaine-smuggling, 'mon bandit'. 'Lots of people witnessed Baba Ould Cheikh talk to ATT on his Thuraya,' said a second driver I met. 'He called him "le grand patron". If he had any problems with the police or security services, he would call ATT and say: "Your people are disturbing us. You need to speak to your men here and tell them to get out of our way." Baba was Pablo Escobar.' In 2012, the UN estimated West African smugglers either earned or helped launder around $500 million. Much of the money was spent on villa compounds like Cocainebougou that materialized along the smuggling route from Morocco to Mali and the building sites that suddenly spread across West Africa's regional capital, Dakar in Senegal.

With corruption at the highest levels, Mali's government became a business. Judges sold verdicts. MPs auctioned legislation. The rot destroyed the army's command and control system. The colonel said that even if soldiers could properly identify their duty, they no longer had the means to perform it. 'The Malian army has these old Chinese AKs from the 1960s,' he complained. 'They don't even fire. There's no food. The Malian army doesn't have a map of northern Mali. War is knowledge and war takes money, and they know nothing and they have nothing.'

*

West Africa was rotten with drugs and corruption, wildly unstable, its governments were crazily unpopular and many of its Big Men were supported by big Western aid. Mali, especially, was all the proof anyone needed that Africa's foreign humanitarians and its nationalist leaders were false prophets. The democracy held up by foreigners as an example to others was in reality a narco-state and its President, even if by default, a crime kingpin. It was perfect territory for bin Laden's repurposed Islamic revolution. Al-Qaeda even had a branch in northern Mali, al-Qaeda in the Islamic Maghreb (AQIM).

This was the context for the snowballing disaster that was to overtake Mali. That, and the fall of Colonel Muammar Gaddafi in Libya. In the first decade of the new millennium, AQIM had made between $40 million and $65 million kidnapping and ransoming tourists in the Sahara. As tourist numbers predictably dwindled, the group switched to cocaine-smuggling, earning millions more dollars escorting the convoys of 4x4s across the Sahara. When Gaddafi was killed by a mob in October 2011, thousands of Gaddafi's men, many of them ethnic Tuaregs from Mali and Niger, fled south into the Sahara. With them they took their weapons, including armoured vehicles, artillery, surface-to-air missiles, grenade launchers and thousands of Kalashnikovs. In Mali and Niger they met willing and flush buyers in AQIM.

In early 2012, a group of low-ranking officers in the Malian army staged a mutiny to protest about corruption in the upper ranks. To their surprise, Touré abruptly quit and flew to Senegal, tired, so diplomats said, of the endless squabbles inside his regime. The soldiers first denied they were taking over, then declared they were, after all. In the confusion, an alliance of northern Tuareg rebels and AQIM used their new firepower to overwhelm and rout the Malian army, seizing the entire north of Mali in just three days, including the cities of Timbuktu, Gao and Kidal. A few months later, the Islamists turned on the Tuaregs and kicked them out of the country. Suddenly, in the middle of the Sahara about an hour's flight south of Europe, there was a de facto al-Qaeda state the size of France.

The colonel predicted the Islamists would advance south towards Bamako within months. On 7 January 2013 convoys of AQIM fighters duly moved out of Timbuktu and, meeting no resistance, seemed to be heading for the capital. France had spent a fruitless year trying to marshal the creation of a West African intervention force to push back the Islamists. With Mali's takeover by al-Qaeda imminent, Paris acted. French warplanes were bombing the Islamists within days.

On my return to Bamako, I found the diplomats and aid workers as clueless as before. 'I don't think anybody expected an Islamist offensive,' said one. Now the advance had happened, however, the city was flooded with aid workers arriving to address an expected refugee emergency. In reality, there was none. A team from the International Medical Corps told me they were pulling out after two weeks of driving across Mali in which they found plenty of refugees but, since many northerners had gone to stay with relatives in the south, not a single one who needed help. Their assessment did nothing to deter a team of Oxfam press officers deployed to Bamako, who held a news conference declaring that 800,000 Malians needed 'immediate food assistance' and the world should send Oxfam as much money as possible.

All this seemingly wilful misreading of Mali left crucial questions unanswered. For one: what did the Islamists want? I found some answers from the first refugee I came across. Rama Koné was 32 and lodging at a relative's house in Bamako. Rama had sold cigarettes on the streets of Konna, a small town of 5,000 about 12 hours north of Bamako. On the morning of 10 January, Rama was walking the main road through town when a convoy of 100 4x4s and pick-ups mounted with heavy machine guns and al-Qaeda's black flags swept into town. Rama said he saw Malians and Arabs. The convoy drove to Konna's police post and opened fire.

The shooting last four hours. 'At 2 p.m. the military ran and the Islamists went around town shouting, "Allah Akbar,"' said Rama.

The Islamists then gathered around a man that Rama recognized instantly as Amadou Kouffa. 'I have come here with a message for the people of Konna,' Kouffa shouted, as the crowd gingerly stepped around the bodies of 50 Malian soldiers lying in the street. 'There is no commandant for this town. There is no mayor. The government is not here today. From now on, all your issues are in the care of the imam of Konna.' Gesturing to the south and the garrison town of Sévaré, 60 kilometres away, he added: 'And, *inshallah*, on Friday I will pray in the mosque of Sévaré.'

I asked Rama how he knew Kouffa.

'Everybody knew him,' he replied. 'He used to be a famous singer.'

The idea that the latest African *jihad* had been started by a former *marabout* was intriguing. Mali's *marabouts* wandered from village to village reciting Islamic verses and performing folk music, precisely the kind of homespun departure from the Qur'an that a doctrinaire *jihadi* would consider heresy. What had driven an artist into the austerity of fundamentalism?

I drove north out of Bamako for central Mali. Kouffa came from a village near Konna that was also called Kouffa. In the regional capital Sévaré I tracked down one of his neighbours, a 35-year-old livestock trader called Niama Tutu. Niama said Kouffa had played the *n'goni*, the Malian guitar made from cord strung over a calabash covered with goatskin, and sang stories about the Prophet. Kouffa was a good storyteller and well respected. He also ran a small school. While his manner was ascetic and religious, it was also moderate. 'His music was good and what he said was good,' said Niama. 'Everybody liked him.'

But as Kouffa entered his fifties, he began to change. His songs took on a political tone, decrying state corruption and brutality, especially the cocaine trade. One day in 2007 in Sévaré there was a conference of the Dawat-e-Islami, a conservative Islamic movement headquartered in Karachi, Pakistan. Kouffa attended and met its organizers to ask for their assistance in his campaign against the government. By this time, Kouffa's popularity had grown to the point where he had a position in a Sévaré mosque. The Dawat, impressed with Kouffa's following, agreed on condition that he give up the *n'goni* and instead begin preaching the Dawat's far stricter version of Islam. They had a deal.

In time, Kouffa made trips to Dawat seminaries in Egypt and Tunisia. While in Mali, he was often accompanied on his travels by an Arab or Nigerian imam. But Kouffa took pains to show his new status had not gone to his head. He gave away the car the Dawat gave him, then two more, preferring to walk from village to village. His modesty contrasted well with the self-enrichment of the state, which remained the main target of his sermons. His followers soon numbered in the tens of thousands. Another friend, Oumar Fofo, 55, said Kouffa became a kind of Pied Piper figure. On his walks, he would often gather around 50 to 60 children whom he called *Talibé* – Taliban, or 'students'.

Kouffa began proposing Islamic revolution as the only solution to the criminality of the Malian state. Only Islam could turn back the clock to a time before Western modernization opened the floodgates to greed and degeneracy. 'Kouffa used to say that in the old days, before they had been led astray by all these modern things, men and women respected themselves,' said Oumar. 'He talked about corruption and the power the soldiers had taken from people. He would say: "I'm telling you this will all finish one day. Either you leave these things willingly, or you will be made to."'

When AQIM and their Tuareg allies swept the north of Mali, Kouffa evidently decided that the day of salvation he had long predicted had finally arrived. He moved to Timbuktu and joined AQIM's Islamic police.

*

For the West, the intricate and astonishing cause-and-effect of this disaster were damning. The same Malian government to which the West gave hundreds of millions of dollars and which the US was training in counter-terrorism had been business partners with an al-Qaeda group that kidnapped and ransomed Westerners and smuggled billions of dollars of cocaine to Europe. The Islamists had then used their earnings to buy Gaddafi's guns and create a new terrorist state. 'You know, this is not some small game,' a Western diplomat in Guinea-Bissau had told me. 'This is about financing terrorism on Europe's southern border, about drug money from Guinea-Bissau and Mali being used for a bomb in London.'

But AQIM's revolution was not the great liberation Kouffa had foreseen. Its Islamic police spent their days closing down Timbuktu's tourist bars and nightclubs, forbidding women from leaving their homes and children from playing, stoning adulterers and smashing Timbuktu's centuries-old Sufi tombs, some of which dated to the time of Mansa Musa. It was precisely the kind of alienating and authoritarian takeover that bin Laden had warned his followers against. Months later in Timbuktu, Associated Press found a six-part letter from Abdel-Malek Droukdel, AQIM's leader, admonishing his men for their over-zealousness. 'One of the wrong policies you carried out is the extreme speed with which you applied *sharia*, [which] will lead to people rejecting the religion, engender hatred towards the *mujahedeen* and lead to the failure of our experiment,' wrote Droukdel. 'Your officials need to control themselves. Like our Sheikh, Osama bin Laden, may he rest in peace, says in a previous letter, "States are not created from one night to the next."' The brothers should adopt more 'mature and moderate rhetoric that reassures and calms' and focus on local concerns. 'Pretend to be a "domestic" movement,' wrote Droukdel.

If their authoritarianism wasn't bad enough, the Islamists were just as criminal as the Malian state. Shortly before I'd met the colonel in Bamako, I'd spoken to an Islamist leader who denied any involvement in trafficking. 'As Muslims, we are the first to fight cocaine,' he said. But his denial was undermined by scattered reports of Islamist fighters freely using cocaine. When I remarked to the colonel that it seemed unlikely that pious Islamists were involved, he thundered: 'Have you even been listening to me at all?! It's all done in the Islamists' vehicles! The Islamists and the drug traffickers are the same!' The colonel said the Islamist leader to whom I'd spoken was a small merchant from Timbuktu before he moved into cocaine. He became an Islamist as another commercial move, so he could continue his business after the Islamist takeover. It was good cover, said the colonel. 'When the smugglers come to town,' he said, 'they come as Muslims with turbans, as preachers, and they slaughter sheep and say the money is from Saudi Arabia. They invite people to eat and pray with them and everyone is happy. That's how they get people to support them. But it's money from drugs! They're traffickers!'

In the end, it was not the desire for a purifying revolution that had spurred Mali's Islamists. It was the money they earned from trafficking cocaine and ransoming tourists. The Islamists' involvement in crime was a perfect hypocrisy. By combining the self-righteousness of aid with the criminal despotism of Africa's tyrants, they might have been purposely setting themselves up for failure. Sure enough, with no public support, their rebellion collapsed within days of France's attack.

In the aftermath of the French assault, Kouffa's fate was uncertain. Some reports said he fled overseas. Malian national radio announced his death. Another newspaper said he was wounded and captured, which likely also meant dead: as they retook territory, Malian soldiers routinely executed any Islamists they captured. Videos being passed around cell-phones in Sévaré showed the soldiers leaving a group of Islamists out in the desert to bake in the sun, their hands and knees tied behind their backs.

The state's predatory brutality, which had fired Kouffa's anger and inspired thousands to follow him, was back in force. The cocaine convoys soon resumed too. So did foreign aid, which grew to new heights in May 2013 when foreign donors pledged $4 billion to a new government led by a 78-year-old career politician. In Sévaré I had become friends with a travel agent who used to take tea with Kouffa. I was with him on the day state radio broadcast the new government line-up, filled with the same old faces. 'Kouffa may have proposed the wrong solution,' said the agent. 'But he identified the right problems.'

One day in Sévaré my friend from Reuters, Cheikh Dioura, introduced me to a skinny man in his thirties with a small beard and scar above his left eye who went by the assumed name of Hayballa Ag Agali. Hayballa had been a cocaine convoy driver, then briefly joined the Islamists, and was now driving cocaine across the desert again. Hayballa said the war had only briefly disrupted the trade and there were now two main cocaine-smuggling groups in northern Mali, one dominated by Tuaregs and the other by Arabs. The Arab cartel was run, once again, by Oumar and Baba Ould Cheikh who, despite being arrested and jailed for cocaine-trafficking, was running his operation from his 'jail', a villa inside a Malian military compound in central Bamako.

Hayballa worked for the Tuareg group. He said that, if anything, cocaine-trafficking had become more organized since the French arrived. He described a smuggling route more than 1,000 kilometres long that ran between three desert relay stations across northern Mali, beginning near the Niger border in Mali's far east and ending at the Algerian border in the far north. At each way station was a well-equipped logistics base containing generators, refrigerated food, underground storage tanks for water and fuel, cars, camouflage nets, even bulldozers to bury vehicles in the sand away from aerial surveillance and paint shops to paint the cars desert-yellow. 'There's everything at these places,' said Hayballa. 'If you are going for a job, they give you a car and a package, and you take it from one place to another. They give you a Thuraya and a GPS to track you. You go in convoy with maybe 50 other cars. The cars are all new, 4x4 pick-ups from Dubai, Toyota Land Cruisers mostly. When they have cocaine to move, the convoys run once or twice or week. Each car will take around half a ton. You arrive and a guy meets you. You don't know him but he knows you because you have the Thuraya. They pay you $8,000 to $14,000. Sometimes they even give you the car too.'

On the road north to Sévaré, I had passed a two-kilometre-long French military convoy heading south. After nearly two years, by late 2014 the French were pulling out. But many Malians were left wondering what, precisely, the French intervention had achieved?

If the French had any doubts about the connection between cocaine-smuggling and the Tuareg and Islamist rebels, the smuggling camps dispelled that. One was run by a Tuareg commander, another by an AQIM lieutenant who had kidnapped and killed two French journalists in November 2013 and the third by a group of rogue Algerian generals and colonels who allowed AQIM a safe haven in the south of their country. Hayballa said hundreds of Islamist foot soldiers like him had also found work at the cocaine bases. But the French soldiers never once disturbed the traffickers. 'They say it's not part of their mission,' said Hayballa.

For the French to see cocaine as unconnected to instability or Islamist militancy took an especially tight set of blinkers. The fluid identities of northern Mali meant the same individual could simultaneously be an Islamist, a Tuareg nationalist, a cocaine smuggler and a Malian official. Even peace talks had multiple meanings. 'When you hear about a deal between the MNLA and some other group, it's not a political thing, it's two cartels doing a business deal,' said Hayballa. 'They just put a political hat on it.'

The French ignored these nuances and deceptions. They treated the Islamists and the Tuaregs as monolithic, exclusively political groups. Their plan was to replace the former with the latter. In effect, their intervention empowered the Tuareg cartels over the Islamist ones – though all the Islamist ones had to do was fly a Tuareg flag and the French would let them pass too. By allowing the cocaine business to thrive, the French were letting billions of illegal drugs continue on their way to Europe. They were also leaving in place the financial engine of all the armed groups in northern Mali, including the Islamists they had come to fight. That was allowing the smugglers to entrench themselves. To contrast themselves with the Malian state, they were even digging irrigation trenches and building schools and opening clinics. On my return to Bamako, I looked up the colonel. 'They make out like they're the real humanitarians,' he said. 'Like Pablo Escobar. If you're out there in the desert, this, the big boss, the cartel, this *is* your state.'

Worst of all, by leaving the cocaine smugglers untouched, the French were fuelling the popular frustration at crime and corruption that had facilitated an Islamist revolution in the first place. The colonel asked me to imagine how a northern chief reacted on a visit to Bamako on which he saw aid money intended for the north disappearing instead into villa complexes and $100,000 cars. 'The chief thinks: "This system cannot help my people. I'm going to fight this system." So he buys a few cows to show them to foreigners as proof of their aid programme and the rest of the money he uses to buy guns and prepare for a revolution. Because one day he is going to stop this rotten system and the state behind it.'

Trouble seemed imminent. As the French pulled out, large unidentified desert convoys of hundreds of 4x4s had been spotted moving in behind them. Gao was in a state of panic, the town markets deserted and families locking themselves in their houses. UN peacekeepers were coming under attack from unidentified insurgents: eight had been killed. Suspected government informers were also turning up dead. 'AQIM took five guys from Timbuktu and yesterday we found one of them strung from a tree in the desert outside the city,' said the colonel. 'They'd beheaded him.' He felt another Islamic insurgency in Mali was inevitable. 'Sooner or later it's going to be the same thing all over again,' he said.

*

One day in Bissau City I was having lunch with a friend when he answered his phone by saying: 'Ah! My Taliban friend.' I asked for an introduction and sure enough, Sheikh Mohamed Aziz arrived at my hotel room looking uncannily like an African Osama bin Laden. He was as tall as the former al-Qaeda leader, perhaps 6ft 4ins, and wore a white turban, a long grey bread, brown leather waistcoat and white robes, and carried a string of worry beads in his hand.

Guinea-Bissau was 50 per cent Muslim but inside that broad affiliation was considerable variation. In 1985, the Sheikh had converted to the same doctrinaire Saudi strand of Wahhabi Islam followed by bin Laden and other Sunni literalists. He had gone on to form the Youth Association for Social Integration, which proselytized to the young and built mosques, Qur'anic schools and health clinics with funding from Saudi Arabia and Kuwait.

The Sheikh was a loud, cheery man, quick to laugh and given to wide-eyed expressions. He said his association was experiencing terrific growth. He was building a new mosque and drawing thousands of new followers every month. The movement was popular, he said, because it tried to fill the gaps created when a 'corrupt, selfish, thieving, lying' government of cocaine smugglers fell short. 'People's frustrations are not addressed by the state,' said the Sheikh. 'So many say: "Let's try an alternative." And most of them choose Islam.' Ultimately, the Sheikh's movement promised its supporters freedom. 'The only orders I obey come from the sky and the only one I trust is God. A man cannot be free if he doesn't eat or he is sick or has no home. What I feel is complete independence, total freedom – and I share that with people.'

The Sheikh said it was part of his job to control the young men in his group. But he was candid about the direction in which it might be heading. 'For sure, if our movement is increasing, it becomes a threat to whoever is in front of it,' he said. Personally, he considered al-Qaeda to be fanatics who had perverted his faith and hadn't fully thought through the consequences of their actions.

'*Jihad* is a double-edged sword. You fight corruption. But your killing is another problem.' But he conceded that his views were increasingly in the minority. 'I tell them they have to be patient,' said the Sheikh of his supporters. 'Only if you have tried all other means can you use violence. But young people always want to solve problems with force.'

Whether or not the coming revolution was violent, the Sheikh was convinced it was imminent. 'I'm optimistic,' he said. 'If one group oppresses others in their own interests, you can be sure that this group's days are limited. The corruption is too much. The lies are too much. This selfishness is getting worse every day. All this can push people. Our organization is increasing. People are even afraid of us. These are good signs.' The Sheikh whooped and clapped his hands at the prospect of West Africa's next Islamist upheaval. 'This time is victory time for Islam.'

TEN

NIGERIA

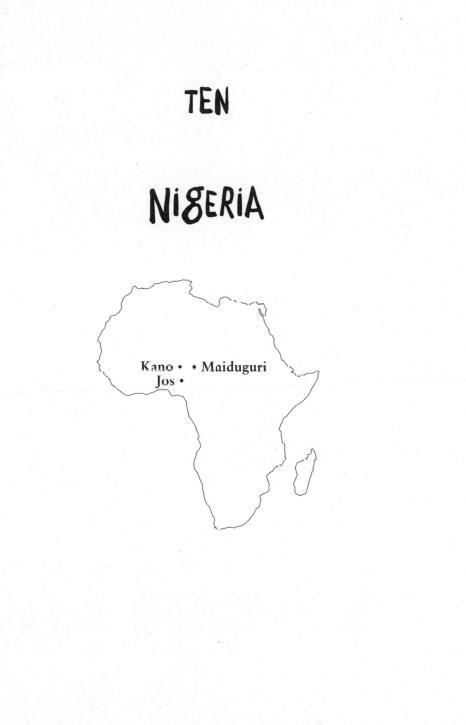

Fifty days had passed since Boko Haram had kidnapped an entire school of 276 girls in north-eastern Nigeria and the general wanted me to see what he was up against. He invited me to his office in the capital, Abuja, and opened his laptop.

The general clicked on one folder entitled 'Abubakar Shekau'. A first clip showed the future leader of Boko Haram in his years as a preacher, in a white cap and white *babban riga*, the traditional Nigerian pyjama, tunic and cape. A second was more recent, from 2013, and showed Shekau in a clearing in the scrub looking far bulkier and in full combat camouflage, an ammunition vest across his chest and a Kalashnikov in his hand.

The general clicked on a folder called 'Bama Attack'. The first clip showed Shekau's former No. 2, Abu Sa'ad, a few months before his death in August 2013. Abu Sa'ad was giving a speech to his men on the eve of an attack on an army barracks in Bama, a town on the Nigeria-Cameroon border. The fighters, who appeared to be mostly teenagers, grinned shyly at the camera. Abu Sa'ad, dressed in camouflage with a scarf tied under his eyes and a Kalashnikov across his chest, said the attack had been long planned and that most of its architects were dead. 'You should look for victory or martyrdom, which is victory in the eyes of God. There is nothing more beautiful than martyrdom. A martyr knows he is going to die, knows there are enemies, but goes to the battlefield anyway without fear of death because he loves God and he knows God will smile on him.'

The attack began at dawn. Hundreds of Abu Sa'ad's men were filmed strolling through the bush. They began firing. When they started receiving return fire, they did not change pace or even look for cover. They kept walking almost casually into the fusillade. Bullets whistled over the cameraman's head. 'Allahu Akbar!' he shouted. 'Allahu Akbar!'

All around, the fighters were being cut down. Ten made it to the base fence and took cover behind a toilet block. The cameraman filmed one fighter shouting back at his comrades. 'Stop firing from behind,' the man yelled. 'You're hitting us.' Suddenly the camera went down on its side. 'They've killed me,' said a voice. The general whistled. 'I've never seen anything like it,' he said. 'Just walking into death.'

He opened another video. This time, Abu Sa'ad was standing in front of the black flags of al-Qaeda surrounded by 20 boys, all in headscarves, all carrying guns. The boys looked as young as four. The heads of the smallest just reached Abu Sa'ad's waist. 'You must wage war,' he said, his hands resting on the boys' heads. 'You must perform every violent act you can.' 'Allahu Akbar!' cried the boys. Abu Sa'ad turned to the camera. 'You can kill us,' he said, 'but these children will continue. Children are the future.'

The general found another clip. Two men in the black uniform of the Nigerian police were on their knees in the bush in front of a black banner held up by two militants which read in Arabic: 'There is only one God and Muhammad is his prophet.' Abu Sa'ad stood to one side, holding a book. Several dozen fighters were gathered around. All were wearing scarves across their faces. The video featured a soft soundtrack of Islamic chants.

The cameraman asked the two policemen to speak. The first gave his name as Corporal Mehmud Daba. 'I know mine has ended,' he said. 'My legacy is to ask my wife to please bring up our children in Islam. Let my mother hear this and pay all my debts for me.' The second policeman said his name was Sergeant David Hoya, a

Christian. He did not raise his head and mumbled into the ground. 'What is your message for your wife?' asked the cameraman.

'That she should take care of my children.'

'In Islam or as unbelievers?'

'I'm not an unbeliever,' said David.

'How can they see you if your face is down like that?' asked the cameraman. 'Lift your face up!'

The camera turned to Abu Sa'ad. 'I want to give an explanation for what we are about to do,' he said. 'We are punishing in terms of what Allah prescribes. I want to tell Nigeria and the world that we give them the gift of these two policemen, this sergeant and corporal. We want to give these men the judgement of Allah.' Abu Sa'ad lifted up a book he was holding. 'I am going to read from this book,' he said, showing the cover to the camera. It was an interpretation of the *Kitab Tawheed, the Book of Unification*, originally written by a conservative thirteenth-century Saudi Islamist scholar, then reworked by another Saudi scholar from the nineteenth century.

Abu Sa'ad began a long monologue, showing the pages as he quoted from them. 'We are going to do things in accordance with the book,' he repeated. 'We will do this to anybody we catch. In Kano, we entered the police headquarters and we killed them as they shat themselves. We did the same in Damaturu and Maiduguri. Let the world know that we will never compare anyone to God. No government, no constitution, can compare to God.'

Ten minutes later, Abu Sa'ad finished. 'Let's thank God and give him more bodies,' he concluded. He then pulled a knife from his combat vest, grabbed Corporal Daba and laid him on his side. The crowd started cheering. 'Allahu Akbar! Allahu Akbar!'

Two men held Daba's chest and legs. Abu Sa'ad held his head with one hand. He started sawing at Daba's throat with the other. Blood jetted onto the sandy ground. Abu Sa'ad kept sawing. He couldn't get through the neck bone. He switched to the back of the neck and started sawing again. Still the head wouldn't come

257

off. Abu Sa'ad dropped the knife and twisted Daba's head around a full 360 degrees with both hands, trying to snap it off. It didn't work. He picked up the knife and sawed again. Finally, after half a minute, Daba's head came free. Abu Sa'ad lifted it up by the hair and showed it to the crowd. Its eyes were closed. Flesh and ligaments were hanging loose. Abu Sa'ad placed the head on Daba's body.

Then he moved over to David Hoya, whom his men were already holding in place. This time Abu Sa'ad worked ferociously. He took David's head off in half the time.

I said nothing. The general was silent, too. He clicked on another video. A woman was being held on the ground, next to a newly dug grave. 'I didn't pass on any information,' she said. 'I didn't tell anyone anything.'

'Allahu Akbar,' said the cameraman.

The men set to work. The woman shrieked. She screamed again, then went silent. Blood spurted on the ground. Her head was off in 15 seconds. The men tried to arrange it on her body but couldn't balance it. They tried propping it on her hair. Eventually one man lost patience and punted her head sharply into the grave. The other men shoved her body in afterwards.

The general clicked on another clip. This time it was a young boy. I told the general I couldn't take any more and he froze the frame.

We sat there for a while, the two of us. The general was examining me for a reaction. Finally he said: 'We found over 200 graves like this in the area. All beheaded. A lot of them were young boys.'

Nigeria is a creation of colonial expediency. In 1914, its British rulers fused two of their existing West African protectorates, southern and northern, each of which already contained several kingdoms, scores of languages and more than 250 tribes. The amalgamation of this vast and diverse territory was overseen by Lord Lugard, one of the Empire's most industrious servants, who before his time ruling Nigeria had fought in Afghanistan, Burma and Sudan, mounted expeditions to Uganda, Benin and Botswana and been Governor of Hong Kong. Lugard justified the unifying of Britain's Nigerian possessions under the 'hinterland principle'. 'By this dictum,' wrote Lugard in *The Dual Mandate in British Tropical Africa*, 'a power in occupation of coast lands was entitled to claim the exclusive right to exercise political influence for an indefinite distance inland.'

It never occurred to Lugard to consult his subjects on their impending union. They were, after all, little more than 'attractive children' with minds 'nearer to the animal world' than other humans. 'Happy, thriftless, excitable, lacking in self control, discipline and foresight, with little sense of veracity, fond of music and loving weapons as an oriental loves jewellery,' he wrote.

Predictably, Lugard's union was contentious. Southerners were especially opposed since Lugard never intended a union of equals. Early in his career, Lugard had been posted to northern Nigeria and his time there had left him with a lasting admiration for the feudal northern dynasties. By contrast, he despised the 'Europeanised African' he found in the south who, he wrote, was less fertile, had worse teeth and was prone to lung problems – ailments he ascribed to southerners' taste for Western clothes, 'which [are] enervating and inimical to the health of the African'. Southerners' superior education, wrote Lugard, was a particular problem. 'Education has brought to such men only discontent, suspicion of others and bitterness, which masquerades as racial patriotism, and the vindication of rights unjustly withheld. As citizens they are unfitted to hold posts of trust and responsibility where integrity and loyalty are essential. They have lost touch with their own people. Some even appear to resent being called negroes.'

Far better suited to the backwardness of Africa, in Lugard's view, were the medieval northern emirates, dominated by the Hausa and Fulani tribes. 'We are dealing with the child races of the world, and learning at first hand the habits and customs of primitive man,' he wrote. 'The finer negro races' – by which he meant northern Nigerians – 'have reached a degree of social organization which, in some cases, has attained to the kingdom stage under a despot with provincial chiefs.'

Aside from prejudice, there were practical reasons why Britain might be disinclined to educate the natives. Imperial administrators in India and Egypt had learned to their cost that well-intentioned efforts to give their subjects a Western education could backfire. Irritatingly, the students' first act on graduation tended to be to demand their liberation.

Lugard would not make the same mistake in northern Nigeria. Schools there were pragmatic and conservative, producing clerks, engineers and technocrats, but not thinkers. Teachers stressed a respect for hierarchy, underwritten by white supremacy. Since education could be so dangerous, it was also strictly limited. At independence in October 1960, there were just 16 secondary schools in all of northern Nigeria.

Restricting enlightenment was not only shrewd colonialism, it was cheap, too. Lugard ruled through a handful of officials who co-opted the structures of the emirates. In this way, the emirs' interests were also protected. Several felt the added protection of British authority made them untouchable and became little more than tyrants.

The emirs also saw the value in maintaining their subjects' ignorance. They drew on their religious authority to give their anti-enlightenment stance some religious justification. Since education often came in the form of Christian missionary schools, it was to be resisted in the name of God. Islam had to be protected. The people had to be insulated. Western education was a sin.

Since a united Nigeria was a fiction founded on colonial convenience and prejudice, the idea might have been expected to die at independence. But by the time freedom arrived in 1960, the concept was ingrained in government structures and many southerners had developed a customary deference to northerners. Accordingly, the northern elite dominated the new Nigerian independent government and its army from the outset. It was more than three decades before a southerner became President.

Expediency and chauvinism are no foundation for a stable nation, however. Even before liberation, northerners killed thousands of southerners in Kano in a pogrom in 1953. After independence, once southerners discovered that, for them, freedom meant rather less than promised, it wasn't long before they rebelled. In 1967 Igbos from the south-east unilaterally declared the secession of a new country they called Biafra. More than a million people lost their lives in the civil war and mass starvation that followed.

The discovery of Africa's biggest oil reserves in the southern Delta in the 1950s only heightened the sense of grievance. The northern-dominated state quickly developed a habit of appropriating the billions of dollars that began flowing to Nigeria from foreign oil companies. So immense were the oil revenues, which by 2015 still accounted for 80–85 per cent of all government income, they allowed Nigeria's rulers to create new lives for themselves as detached from their countrymen as the offshore rigs that sustained them. An example was the state petroleum authority, which collected more than $40 billion a year from foreign oil companies but did almost nothing to build or maintain Nigeria's oil-refining capacity. Britain's biggest export to Nigeria was petrol and diesel, much of it originally extracted from Nigeria, then processed in Britain and shipped back. Making matters worse, every few months Nigerian importers throttled supply to hike prices – and Africa's largest oil producer ground to a halt as fuel stations ran dry.

So much larger were oil payments than domestic taxes, foreign businesses effectively replaced Nigerians as the government's constituents. The Nigerian state served them. It felt little need to work for a people who did not, in the end, pay it. Likewise, since the people did not pay for their government, they had few ways to make it accountable. And the riches on offer in Nigerian politics attracted the most venal kind of kleptomaniac. In 2007, Nigeria's own anti-corruption watchdog estimated that its rulers stole $300 billion in oil revenues between 1960 and 1999. More cash was leaving Nigeria for foreign banks than all the foreign aid being sent in the reverse direction to Africa.

This world-record corruption made oil a curse rather than a blessing. Nigerians resented the thieving, of course, but the state brooked no dissent from a people from whom it had largely disassociated itself. In 1993, military dictator Ibrahim Babangida held an election and then annulled it when the southern Yoruba leader Moshood Abiola won. In 1995, Babangida's next-but-one successor, the Kano General Sani Abacha, executed Ken Saro-Wiwa and eight other activists from the Delta who opposed the way their land was being polluted and sucked dry of its riches. In time a more violent group, the Movement for the Emancipation of the Niger Delta (MEND), stepped into the space left by Saro-Wiwa. Members of this loose alliance of heavily armed militant groups rode around the Delta in speedboats, attacking pipelines and army bases and, by siphoning off oil, managed to halve Nigeria's official output by the middle of the last decade. In the end, that rebellion led not to greater transparency and equality but more corruption: the state simply bought off the rebels with government posts and contracts.

But if the elite's riches largely insulated them from their country's poverty and their people's dissent, they did not live in gilded harmony. Rather, the rewards brought by power ensured the state was consumed by an intense and endless struggle for it. Nigeria's first coup was carried out by a group of Igbo majors in January 1966. A northern counter-putsch followed in July and there were more coups or attempted coups in 1975, 1976, 1983, 1985, 1986, 1990, 1993, 1995 and 1996. Democracy was revived in 1999 but in rigged form. Olusegun Obasanjo, a former military dictator and a southerner, oversaw a deal between north and south under which each would allow the other to rule alternately every eight years.

Naturally, Obasanjo reserved the first two presidential terms for himself.

Over time, lower levels of the Nigerian state learned to take their lead from their political masters. Government teachers played truant for years at a time. Government doctors required patients to pay a bribe before they were treated. Bureaucrats purchased their positions, and then set about earning the money back by charging for permissions and other paperwork. Customs came to see their job not as taxing imports but taking a cut. For policemen, the roadblock became a favoured bribe extraction point. The general who showed me the Boko Haram videos insisted the majority of the security services were good men earnestly battling to save Nigeria. But he admitted that, yes, some officers sold weapons and equipment to Boko Haram, yes, some political leaders backed the militants and, yes, the effectiveness of both army and government was crippled as a result. 'One bad apple can drag the whole country down,' he said. In the north-east, the damage done to the state's credibility was near-total. 'We're not in control of anywhere out there,' the general said. 'We are living in denial and have been for a while now. I'm convinced there is no greater threat to Nigeria in its 100 years of history.'

This vacuum inside the state left a hole where Nigeria's national heart should have been. Public interest was replaced by self-interest and, towards the people, disinterest. Left to fend for themselves, Nigerians retreated to their sectarian identities, to the delight of communal politicians, who stoked division further in their own narrow interests.

Perhaps the greatest damage done was to public trust. Politicians lied, banks stole, heads of industry bribed, even football players fixed – and the infection spread. Soldiers' salaries were pocketed by their commanders. Medicines turned out to be counterfeit. Cheaply serviced airplanes fell out of the sky. Email scamming was one of Nigeria's few growth industries. Even in 2015, few Nigerian businesses accepted anything but cash. Trust was experienced mostly in the negative: in the firm belief that it was every man for himself and everyone was out to con you. And in a country where crime equated to money, and money to status, and status to everything, all shame evaporated.

In this nation of a million conspiracies, all but the most sophisticated and devious explanations were dismissed as naïve. Every leader was said to be the puppet of a hidden hand, every businessman a money launderer or a tax dodger or secret stasher. Boko Haram was viewed alternately as a creation of northern power brokers, or of the presidency, or even of the CIA. The army was whispered to be co-ordinating troop movements to leave villages like Chibok undefended, or ferrying in new supplies to the militants, or even shipping in Delta militants as reinforcements. Shekau was in Saudi Arabia. Shekau was a guest of the government in Abuja. Shekau was dead. Prejudice, rumour and suspicion ruled. Certainty and knowledge were lost. This, to borrow a phrase, is how things fall apart.

When Portuguese explorers arrived in 1472, so scattered around marshes and lagoons was the settlement of Eko that they renamed it after the Portuguese word for lakes. Lagos first became a trading hub for slaves, then a British administrative city, then, after oil was discovered in the Bight of Benin in the 1950s, a boom town. As it was transformed into the biggest city and port in West Africa, Lagos became a destination for migrants across the continent. As we dropped out of the clouds, the city appeared below me and it was endless – a plain of dusty tile and tin roofs extending all the way to the horizon. Veins of traffic, electric-red and white, glittered prettily in the evening light. This was Africa's megacity, the biggest metropolis in its most populous country and the third largest in the world although, with a new resident arriving every minute, beyond a broad guess of 20 million, nobody could say how many people lived there, even to the nearest million.

The Dutch architect and urban theorist Rem Koolhaas has

eulogized this chaotic, crushing growth and the ingenuity it inculcated in Lagosians. The reality was less romantic. Almost every tree had been cut down and every garden built on. Offices and factories were squeezed into residential apartments. To cope with the gridlock, businessmen converted their car back-seats into offices, complete with phones, laptops and secretaries.

Oil's disconnecting effect on government exacerbated Lagos' decline. When oil prices collapsed in the mid 1970s, work on Lagos' infrastructure stopped. When prices recovered, no one thought to resume it. Instead, as the city began to buckle, the federal government abandoned it for a new purpose-built inland capital, Abuja. Soon, foreign investors and tourists were also staying away. As the city crumbled, 'Area Boys', self-proclaimed vigilante street gangs who ran protection rackets and mugging syndicates, began terrorizing neighbourhood turfs.

In the first decades after independence, a time when many southerners discovered they were effectively barred from national politics by their ethnicity, Lagosians found an outlet for their frustration in the music of a home-grown superstar, Fela Kuti. Fela was from a middle-class, southern and Christian background. But after a few months in 1969 spent with the Black Power movement in Los Angeles, he returned to Lagos a musical maverick. He set up a commune and recording studio in Lagos, which he called the Kalakuta Republic and later declared independent from Nigeria. Four nights a week at his club, the Shrine, he would castigate Nigeria's leaders to a musical style he called Afrobeat. 'Go Slow' cast Lagos' gridlocked traffic as a metaphor for Nigeria's spiritual standstill. 'Zombie' was a satire on the Nigerian military's unthinking brutality. 'Coffin for the Head of State' recounted how, in 1977, 1,000 soldiers attacked the Kalakuta Republic and the Shrine, burned both down, beat Fela and killed his mother by throwing her from a window. (The coffin was Fela's mother's, which he imagined dumping outside the gates of government.) 'I see see see all the bad bad bad things them dey do do do North and South,' sang Fela.

One Christian and the other one Muslim.
Them steal all the money.
Them kill many students.
Them burn many houses.
Them burn my house too.
Them kill my mama.

Fela tried to run for President in 1979 but was barred. In 1984, the regime jailed him for 20 months. In 1997 Fela, who had formalized his promiscuity in 1978 by marrying all 28 of his women composers, dancers and singers, died of complications brought on by AIDS. More than a million Nigerians attended his funeral at the site of the old Shrine.

'I'm depressed that it's happening, I wish we were not falling into this deep black hole, but as my father's son I'm not surprised,' said Femi Kuti. 'I do not see a way out for this country. The corruption is just too big.'

We were in Femi's backstage dressing room. After Fela's death, Femi took on his father's mantle, keeping Afrobeat alive at the New Afrika Shrine, which he and his sister Yeni built on a new site 14 years ago. Femi reckoned the need to speak out was more urgent even than in Fela's time. Unlike many Lagosians, 'who don't even know where the north is', Femi had visited regularly since 1985 when his father was sent to jail in Maiduguri, the town where Boko Haram was founded 17 years later. 'I was shocked,' said Femi. 'It was just flies everywhere.'

Femi thought Nigeria's divides – north-south, Muslim-Christian, rich-poor – had only widened since. 'It's been years and years of neglect now. The gaps have got larger. You see the number of children coming out of school and you have to be scared. Where are the jobs? Where is the future? They grow up begging on the street. They have been so deprived that they do not know respect. They do not have values. They do not care for human life. They do not care about anything. It makes it easy to brainwash them.'

Femi let out a long sigh. 'This country is in big trouble,' he said. 'Nothing works. We don't have good education, we don't have health, we have no electricity, we have bad roads, the airport is shit. And the Chibok girls – what about the military? They have the highest budget. Where's all that money? The truth is we don't have an army either, just generals with big stomachs.'

In Lagos, just as they did in Fela's time, the elite used their money to separate themselves from the rest of the country. This was the Lagos of Gucci boutiques, Porsche showrooms, 2,000-guest weddings, weekend beach house parties – and even the elite's own in-house magazine, a publication called *Luxury Reporter*. Somehow many foreign investors had taken this small band of super-rich, living apart and above like potentates, as an indication of Nigeria's national economic health. In this imagined Nigeria, the rich were the tip of a golden iceberg rather than what they were: inhabitants of a tiny, free-floating offshore haven. These foreign investors also used a string of superlatives to describe the country – the biggest population in Africa, its biggest economy, its biggest oil reserves and, at 7.3 per cent, among the fastest rates of economic growth in the world. The reality, said Femi, was that Nigeria was the ultimate example of how money hadn't fixed anything. 'Growing for who?' asked Femi. 'The multinationals, maybe. The telephone companies? The elite? Nobody else. The poverty is greater than before. Primary school education costs 10 times the monthly wage. Who can afford that?'

It was the lack of change that most depressed Femi. The same corruption and anarchy existed in his father's time. Now they had acquired a permanence, woven into the national fabric. In the end, said Femi, the damage was spiritual. Humanity became degraded. 'It gets into everybody this corruption. You cannot trust anybody. Today people in Nigeria are not brought up to love. Nobody reads them a bedtime story. They don't know how to take care of each other any more. Anybody who says they love you, you don't believe them.' The Chibok abductions might be 'finally waking people up' but, said Femi, too late. The country's soul had already been corroded. 'Because, you know, we've had kidnappings for years. My kids have to go to school with security guards. Here in Lagos you hear about children taken for human sacrifice.'

It sounded incredible. But I checked and Femi was right. In March 2014, a case of mass kidnapping and suspected ritual sacrifice was discovered outside Lagos when eight men and women were found in chains close to starvation in an isolated building in a forest. Near by was a well filled with bones and body parts belonging to an unknown number of people.

Femi said he hadn't always been this pessimistic. When he rebuilt his father's temple to Afrobeat, he intended it to improve on the original. There was to be less chaos and less of the sponging that came with commune living. More outreach. More social concern. Entry was free at least once a week. Drinks were kept cheap. Small food and jewellery stallholders were invited to set up inside the club. Staff would be encouraged to think of themselves as members of a family, with Femi more of a father than a boss.

The experiment had been a grinding lesson in disillusionment. Only that day Femi had discovered that some of his own bar staff had been ripping him off for years, hauling in their own beer and selling it rather than the club's. 'I was a big believer in pan-Africanism,' said Femi. 'I thought: "People love us. The Shrine is great." These are the people I fight for and work for. So I did everything for free. People come to the Shrine for free. I sacrifice my whole career for this. Fourteen years. And they stab you in the back.'

Femi had 12 children, some his own, some adopted. I asked him how it was to bring up a family in Lagos. 'I love my kids too much,' he said. 'But today I do not know if I made a big mistake. If I did not have all these kids, I would not remain here in this country of pain. But I'm stuck. How can I run with a family?' It was hard to think of anything more disheartening than a father who loved his children but regretted having them. I winced, and Femi caught me. 'I cannot lie to you,' he said. 'There are many times I wake up and I just want to be dead. I told my son the other day: "Some days I wish I would not wake up any more." Really. I wish I was dead.'

I hung around to watch Femi and his band, Positive Force. They played in front of a #BringBackOurGirls banner, the Chibok girls' social media hashtag. To one side was another poster: 'United we stand. Divided we fall. Africa must unite.' A thick cloud of weed smoke hung over the audience. The band, six guys on horns, three singers, two drummers, a congo player, two guitarists, two keyboard players and a bassist, hit its groove instantly. The chorus was simple and catchy.

One people.
One God.
One Love.
That's the way it should be.

After a few minutes, Femi came in on an organ. The chord he was playing was off-key and jarring, like a horror movie. It was deliberate, I realized. Femi held the chord, letting the discord and chaos swell. It became louder and louder. People in the audience began to stop and stare. Even the band started to lose its way. It was becoming agonizing. I noticed Femi was shaking, like a man with his finger in a power socket.

Finally, he let go. The drummer hit a cymbal and it was as if a bottle had been thrown against a wall. There was silence in the club. For a moment Femi stood alone, stage front, eyes down. Then he was gone.

In the Sokoto *jihad* of 1804–8, Nigeria's northern tribes rejected the rule of the northern Hausa dynasties, accusing them of un-Islamic corruption, elitism and self-indulgence. The *jihadis* were led by an Islamic scholar called Usman dan Fodio. His anti-authoritarian opposition to an avaricious, distant elite inspired several copycat revolutions across West Africa, and his influence endures even now. Several northern Nigerian emirates trace their lineage to commanders of the Sokoto *jihad*. Dan Fodio's writings, and those of his daughter, still sell well across northern Nigeria.

In the 1970s, a group of imams from a sect called the Izala blossomed in Maiduguri's deprivation. The Izala took a similar line to dan Fodio, preaching a purist morality in life and politics and denouncing the greed and corruption of Nigeria's rulers. By 2005, a young preacher called Mohammed Yusuf, who said he had studied in Saudi Arabia, was beginning to steal the Izalas' mantle. He too copied dan Fodio's anti-elitism.

Nigeria's divisions, corruption and suspicions, not to mention the north's history of *jihad*, were a gift to a northern Islamist revolutionary. Yusuf could also draw on popular dissatisfaction with foreign aid. The international humanitarian movement was founded for the Biafran war. In the years since, aid had become so entrenched that it was a permanent part of the state. Yet aid workers had done nothing to hinder the Nigerian state from becoming one of the world's most autocratic and most flashily uncaring. Nor had they done much to change the lives of millions of Nigerians who were worse off than they had been at independence or even, in the north-east, about as close to the bottom as a human being could be in the twenty-first century.

But, unlike dan Fodio, Yusuf did not campaign for more enlightenment but less. Dan Fodio's daughter had been one of the great progressive Islamic scholars of her age. Yusuf, however, had no tolerance for women intellectuals or any other modernizations. Why bother with Western-style education, Yusuf would ask in his sermons, when there were no jobs even for graduates? Hadn't money and oil given them a government that stole from its people? Hadn't Western influence given them Ali Modu Sherrif, a state governor who built himself a palace of marble pillars and golden gates in the centre of Maiduguri? Yusuf advocated going back to a purer, pre-enlightenment Luddite age, before 'so-called education, democracy and rule of law'. Yusuf called his group Jamaatu Ahlisunnah Lidawati wal *Jihad*, Arabic for 'People Committed to the Propagation of the Prophet's Teachings and *Jihad*'. It soon became better known by the nickname given it by Nigeria's journalists, Boko Haram, which translates loosely as 'books are blasphemous' or, in an ironic echo of Lugard, 'Western education is forbidden'.

By all accounts Yusuf was an impressive speaker. Many of his ideas, however, were half-baked, inauthentic imports. In line with his medievalism, he rejected all rationalism, denouncing as Godless ideas like evolution, the roundness of the earth and the evaporation of water. He copied other concepts wholesale from the Middle East and South Asia. He set up a camp he called 'Afghanistan' to instruct volunteers for his revolution against the evils of progress. Copying images of the *mujahedeen*, his followers began wearing the South Asian *kurta pyjama* and asking their women to wear the full veil.

The spark for violence came in late July 2009 when police officers watching a Boko Haram funeral procession saw some mourners riding motorbikes without helmets. In Maiduguri, helmets had become a point of contention. The security services insisted on them. Boko Haram resisted, since wearing one required a man to remove his traditional Islamic cap. 'It was not about safety,' said one Maiduguri elder recounting the story. 'People felt it was just a way to control them.'

The police watched the helmetless funeral cortège pass. Then they attacked. The mourners retaliated. Three people died. Riots erupted. A few days later, on 28 July, the army surrounded Yusuf's compound in Maiduguri, arrested him, then executed him. A bloodbath ensued. By nightfall on 29 July, barely 36 hours later, around 1,000 people were dead.

The killings briefly halted Boko Haram's rise. But within a year the group was operating as a 5,000-strong rebellion across all northern Nigeria that threatened to split the country in two. Boko Haram's response to state repression had been to elevate what had been an ideology of peaceful obscurantism to nihilist destruction. There was a connection between politicians' wives' $1 million shopping sprees and the high rate of malnutrition and death of pregnant mothers and children, the Islamists were saying. That was money that could have saved people. This was corruption escalated to murder. Worse, the people taking the money were the people entrusted with protecting those lives. They were killing the same people who voted for them. Everything was rotten. So everything, and everyone, had to die.

Boko Haram's apocalyptic vision had no room for freedom other than that promised by a *jihadi*'s death. Its men slaughtered whole columns of Nigerian soldiers, cleaved their way through Christian congregations with machetes, cut down moderate Muslim families as they left Friday prayers and staged co-ordinated attacks that wiped out small villages and devastated cities such as Kano and Damaturu. In June 2011, they hit the national government when a suicide bomber killed himself and an officer as he tried to assassinate the Director-General of Police at the national police headquarters in Abuja. Next on Boko Haram's target list was aid.

Created by decree in the 1970s when overpopulation first threatened Lagos' collapse, Abuja was somehow never finished. Today it remains less a capital than a collection of unfinished highways, empty lots and car parks in search of a city. Even Nigerians who have lived there for 30 years will tell you Abuja is not so much a place as a state of mind. What at first appears to be a resident population is in fact a slow-motion mass transit of visiting politicians, diplomats on three-year postings, travelling businessmen, itinerant traders and migrant workers.

In this city of strangers, Mohammed Abul Barra was able to drive his grey Honda Accord right up to the gates of UN House

Al-Shabab attacks: *(above)* the aftermath of the 2010 World Cup bombing in Kampala; *(left)* a bomb attack on Eastleigh, Nairobi, in 2011; and *(below left)* one of the victims of Al-Shabab's attack on the Westgate mall in Nairobi, 2013.

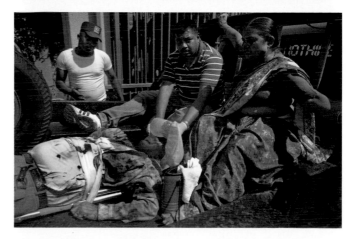

In the townships during the 2010 soccer World Cup in South Africa.

Re-greening in Ethiopia: turning desert into farmland.

(above right) A wall of remembrance
set up after Nelson Mandela's death
in Johannesburg, South Africa.

(right) The singer Youssou N'Dour with
a crowd of supporters during the protests
against the government in Senegal, 2012.

Flower farming in Ethiopia.

A new Chinese-built road in northern Kenya.

before anyone noticed him. In a second, he swerved off the road into the UN's 100-metre driveway and sailed past a guard-post at 30 kilometres an hour. He bounced over one speed bump, then another. Maintaining his deliberate unhurried pace, he drove straight at a three-metre sliding steel security gate, hitting the right corner so it popped off its rail and fell with a deafening clanging to one side. Mohammed drove on and repeated the manoeuvre with a second gate a few metres away.

It had taken perhaps 12 seconds for Mohammed to breach all the security between him and the UN's Nigerian headquarters. Five storeys high and shaped as a three-pointed star, the building's lobby was in a high glass atrium attached to its front. Mohammed drove at its glass doors and smashed into the lobby. Finally halted by a low wall, the car bounced back on its wheels.

Mohammed did not try to get out. In the lobby, security cameras captured a guard to one side, apparently frozen in shock. Perhaps a dozen others – UN staff, security personnel – ran away, then, unsure, stopped and turned back. Regaining his composure, the guard walked up to the car and peered in. Others also started edging forward. A full 12 seconds passed. 'Was he having second thoughts?' wondered the US Ambassador to Nigeria, Terence McCulley, after watching the video. 'Was he praying? Was he searching for the detonator?' Suddenly one of the onlookers seemed to see something. He turned and grabbed the man next to him. The pair started running. Inside the car, Mohammed leaned forward.

Flying bits of car and glass shredded most people in the lobby to a bloody pulp. Few of the rest of the 24 dead and 115 wounded had visible injury marks. Instead their insides were crushed by a blast wave so big it crumpled a water tower 90 metres away as if it were cardboard.

An FBI forensic team examining the 26 August blast later determined the bomb was colossal, and clever. Around 125kg of plastic explosives had been placed inside a metal cone – a shaped charge

– to focus its force. Nigeria's then National Security Advisor, General Andrew Owoye Azazi, was effusive about the professionalism of the attack. 'This was very, very carefully planned,' he said. 'They did thorough surveillance, they knew the weaknesses of the gates. And the materiel was very volatile, very specialized. This was not just a local guy from Maiduguri.'

What Azazi meant was: al-Qaeda. Despite a long history of Islamic militancy that stretched back centuries, this was Nigeria's first ever suicide attack. The Nigerian government immediately blamed international terrorism. This was 'just like other terrorist attacks in the world', said President Goodluck Jonathan. It was simply Nigeria's bad luck that it had become the latest battlefield in this global war.

The trouble was, as Azazi and President Jonathan well knew, Mohammed Abul Barra *was* a local guy from Maiduguri. Within days he was identified as a 27-year-old mechanic and father of one from Nigeria's north-easternmost city. A month after the attack, the French news agency AFP was sent a video of Mohammed shot immediately before the attack. In it, Mohammed was wearing the same black-and-white striped T-shirt and a white turban that looked too big for his head. He was standing in front of a sheet painted with Arabic slogans in a rough hand and as he moved, the camera revealed he was wearing a green canvas vest of the kind used in suicide bombings. Mohammed also had a Kalashnikov, which he apparently found unfamiliar and awkward to handle. Initially he held it by the barrel, then he folded it in the crook of his arm like a baby.

Mohammed smiled shyly at the camera and spoke so softly that the microphone struggled to pick up his words. 'I'm going to shed my blood,' he said. 'I am going there now. God willing, and I pray to Allah to make me steadfast. May He take me there safely.' The camera then showed two men, whose faces it did not reveal, embracing Mohammed. Perhaps because he was unaccustomed to the attention, Mohammed reacted stiffly, beaming and nearly knocking heads with the second man. These were Mohammed's last goodbyes. He looked like a boy setting off for camp.

Maiduguri stood out even amid the poverty of the Sahel. Its roads were lined with ancient rusted signs and broken street lamps and the surface had potholes the size of swimming pools. Behind the checkpoints of policemen and soldiers, in their roadside igloos of sandbags and barbed wire, were a few solid-looking buildings. But most houses and businesses seemed to have been patched together from whatever – wood, car doors, flattened oil drums – was to hand. The statistics described true destitution. More than three-quarters of Maiduguri's population lived in absolute poverty. Just 3.6 per cent of children were vaccinated against disease. Only one in five children went to school. The average girl managed three weeks of school in her lifetime.

Nigeria's army and police responded to the UN attack in August with a cruelty that matched Boko Haram's. They raided villages and towns, rounding up young men and executing them – even gutting them – and dumping hundreds of bodies in trenches and mass graves. They razed at least one town near Maiduguri, Baga, and massacred around 200 people. In Maiduguri a group of elders showed me a cell-phone video of 20 uniformed Nigerian soldiers using truncheons and whips to beat a crowd of young men, stripped and on their knees, in Maiduguri's market. 'They do this daily,' said one. 'They can just take you and shoot you. Whenever there is a bomb blast, they just call the youth and shoot some of them.' One time, he added, they shot an entire wedding party of 20. 'Does a young man need any other reason to rise up after this?'

Professor Shettima Khalifa Dikwa from Maiduguri University was unequivocal. 'Boko Haram is about injustice and freedom,' he said. Nigeria's economy and finances were in the hands of a few. Teachers' and doctors' salaries were stolen. Ordinary children were denied school, 'but the children of corrupt politicians rode around town in cars'. The professor continued: 'The system is as rotten as hell. It's like the people of Maiduguri are aliens in their own country.' The army only made things worse, he said, by using the war to make money in corrupt contracts for equipment. They built big hotels using contractors from the south. In these, 'they fornicate and they protect gay rights, which are an abomination. Instead of talking to people, they beat them with cowhide whips and kill them. They kill everyone, rape their children and burn the place. They want to Somali-ize Maiduguri: make it lawless and then make more money.' Bodies are not counted in a dirty war. By 2015, the dead were estimated at around 13,000, though nobody could be sure even to the nearest few thousand.

The Nigerian government was keen to present Boko Haram as an international threat – something it could do little about. Counter-terrorism officials briefed journalists on how some former Izala activists had formed a small group, Ansaru, with global ambitions. They added that the UN attack was carried out by a Boko Haram splinter with similar aims and that Boko Haram had also reached out to other militants in Somalia and Yemen.

The Americans shared this analysis, to a degree. In 2011, the then Commander of US forces in Africa, General Carter Ham, had warned of the emergence of a pan-African al-Qaeda that merged Boko Haram, AQIM and al-Shabab in Somalia and had 'very explicitly and publicly voiced intent to target Westerners and the US'. The US embassy in Abuja reckoned Ham's 'Africanistan' scenario was overstated but added that several hundred Boko men had travelled to Mali for bomb-making and propaganda training by AQIM.

In Maiduguri, Nigeria's army was also eager to endorse Boko Haram's link to al-Qaeda. Describing an attack on a police station at a village called Mainok the night before, Lieutenant Colonel Hassan Ifijeh Mohammed said it had been 'a bomb attack, an IED' and that was all the proof anyone needed that 'we are fighting ter-rorists'. 'Here they call it Boko Haram but Boko Haram is totally al-Qaeda,' he said. 'The name does not matter. The characteristics are the same. All the terrorists are in one group. They have one activity, one [way of] thinking. Al-Qaeda has no boundary. There are perfect links. It's exactly the same as al-Qaeda.'

I drove the 45 minutes to Mainok. There had been no bomb or IED. A small group of Boko Haram fighters had arrived by motorcycle, shot at the outside of a small hut belonging to the Federal Road Safety Corporation and a tiny adjoining police post. When a man stepped outside his house to investigate, they also shot him dead. The militants then burned a clinic inside the Road Safety Corporation's hut and slashed the tyres on a government jeep parked outside it. After 45 minutes, they left.

September 11 this was not. The colonel had initially dismissed Boko Haram as 'a bunch of nobodies from the countryside', and that was much closer to the truth. Boko Haram's concerns were local. They hated the Christian President and they hated the state government in Maiduguri even more. Without Yusuf to guide them, they no longer thought much beyond that. Killing had become the religion. Killing, in itself, was the end.

Such ideological weakness only underlined what hick town rebels they were. At times, they had a hard time even making sense. They said they wanted to be left alone in the purity of their poverty by an outside world that had long ago left them behind – but by taking up arms, they had forced the government to try to stop them. Their reasoning for attacking the UN was just as flawed. Several weeks afterwards, a Boko Haram spokesman called Abu Qaqa tried to explain. 'We are at war with infidels and all over the world the UN is a global partner in the oppression of believers,' he said. 'In Nigeria, the federal government tries to perpetuate the agenda of the United Nations.'

Boko Haram's cult of violence was exactly what bin Laden wanted to avoid. It made a nonsense of its claim to fight oppression. The group's behaviour and reasoning displayed all the wilful distortion and witless simplicity of fascism. But in the way it blew apart the dark mysteries of power in Nigeria, that was its appeal.

*

Boko Haram's tactics had another effect. They attracted attention. Its kidnapping of 276 schoolgirls in April 2014, in particular, drew worldwide notice. Among those moved to demand international action to #BringBackOurGirls were Jesse Jackson, Angelina Jolie, the Iranian government, the Coca-Cola company, the Prime Minister of Nepal and the cast of the Sylvester Stallone shoot 'em up, *Expendables 3*. Pakistani schoolgirl and Taliban attack survivor Malala Yousafzai called the girls 'her sisters'. Michelle Obama commandeered her husband's weekly address to tell Americans: 'In these girls, Barack and I see our own daughters.' The US, Britain, Israel and China offered drones, spy planes and advisors to assist Nigeria's government in the girls' recovery. French President François Hollande hosted a Paris summit for President Jonathan and four other West African leaders. The head of the Anglican Church, the Archbishop of Canterbury, Justin Welby, who once lived in Nigeria, flew to Abuja to pray with President Jonathan.

None of this did anything to bring home the girls, whose fate was a deepening mystery. Boko Haram initially said it would marry off the girls or sell them as slaves, then claimed 100 of them had converted from Christianity to Islam. Scattered reports located the girls as all together in Sambisa, a remote, roadless area of dry scrub close to Chibok, or split up and moved to different areas, in Nigeria and across the border in Chad and Cameroon. By their own efforts, more than 50 girls escaped.

And rather than buckling to outside pressure, Boko Haram responded enthusiastically to the publicity by stepping up its attacks. Northern Nigeria became a bloodbath. Almost 1,000 people were killed in seven weeks. More or less every day, it seemed, Boko Haram was massacring another village, slaughtering people and burning their huts to the ground. The attacks were often reprisals for the assistance the villagers provided to Nigeria's army, either in the form of intelligence or self-defence groups made up of village hunters. Further afield, hundreds more Nigerians died in a series of bombings in the country's cities, including in a twin blast in Jos, which killed 130, and another in Abuja, which killed close to 100.

Many of the attacks seemed designed to draw the same outrage as Chibok. Boko Haram staged two more mass kidnappings near the village. It began using girls as young as 10 as suicide bombers. Then in January 2015, it staged its bloodiest attack to date, massacring hundreds of people, possibly even up to 1,000, in and around the remote north-eastern town of Baga – the same village to which the Nigerian army had laid waste in April 2013.

The result was to force #BringBackOurGirls to confront an awkward suspicion: that by 'raising awareness' as the humanitarian imperative required, the campaigners might be giving Boko Haram precisely the global profile it wanted. Any time the limelight threatened to fade, the group would stage another atrocity to recapture it. Additionally, the campaigners' narrative was feeling increasingly forced. The promotion of girls' education was a favourite humanitarian rallying cry. But the idea that the Chibok girls' abduction was another example of how violent Islamism was, at root, a problem of sexism was given the lie by the revelation that the girls' gender may have saved their lives. In other raids on mixed schools, Boko Haram slit the throats of all the boys. Similarly, the notion that Nigeria was the latest battleground against international terrorism, as Jonathan, Hollande and United States Senator John McCain maintained, seemed increasingly off the mark when measured against the hyper-local focus of most of Boko Haram's atrocities.

The campaign did at least expose the corruption and indifference of the government. For close to three weeks after the girls first went missing, the government had appeared not to even notice. It then claimed they had been set free, then said al-Qaeda was to blame. After that President Goodluck Jonathan's wife Patience accused the girls' parents of inventing the whole affair to embarrass her husband; then had one of the #BringBackOurGirls organizers arrested; then told people not to criticize Jonathan since his presidency was the work of God; then, to press her point, went on live television to evoke God's presence, wailing, 'There is God-o!' over and over. The President's office later displayed the same sensitivity when it claimed, without any basis in fact, that it had a peace deal with Boko Haram, before going on to announce that the slogan for the President's re-election campaign would be #BringBackJonathan.

The drive north to Jos passed from dirty coastal swamps into thick forest and out onto wide river valleys and finally back into lush flatlands planted with yams and maize and small forests of giant mango trees. Out of the fields rose colossal single-boulder mountains of smooth, dark granite, as though the skin of the earth had been peeled back to reveal the bone beneath, which had been left to bake to black in the sun.

If Nigeria was going to disintegrate, it was a fair bet that the rupture would start in Jos. The southern half of the city was mostly Christian, the northern half mostly Muslim. Though the two sides had lived together for hundreds of years, both still described the Christians as indigenous and the Muslims as incomers. Christians accused Nigeria's many Muslim rulers of ripping off the country. Muslims complained of being marginalized in Jos – excluded from government jobs and schools and services and budgets. These communal grievances, and attempts to protect turf, found a focus at elections, which were often violent. Every few years Jos simply exploded. Mobs from one side ran wild through neighbourhoods belonging to the other, bombing churches and mosques, wrecking businesses and schools, and slaughtering families in their homes.

Two days before I arrived, two car bombs detonated 10 minutes apart in the city's central market. Around 130 people were dead, possibly more. Body parts were thrown hundreds of metres in every direction and rescuers were finding it impossible to put them back together. Sadeeq Hong, a 30-year-old former journalist who gave up the trade to focus on reconciling the two sides of his home city, agreed to show me around. We took a three-wheeled bike taxi to the market, ducked under the yellow police tape and walked in.

Where thousands of people had once crowded hundreds of stalls there was now an empty double-lane highway, perhaps 800 metres long. The road was flanked by wide, bare-earth verges and, to one side, a double-storey row of shops. Many of the shop windows were blown out. Every few metres there were the ashes of fire. We found the site of the second bomb: a small crater in the road, 30 centimetres deep and wide. Two hundred metres away was the hole made by the first bomb, twice as deep and the size and rectangular shape of a small car.

A policeman with a surgical mask draped around his neck walked up. 'The bodies were on the roof,' he said, pointing to the tin roof of a two-storey building a block away. 'Pieces, pieces, pieces,' he said. 'The women . . . it cut their neck and throw the head down. We pick them. Pick, pick, pick.' I looked over to where the officer was pointing. A wall perhaps three metres from the blast had ceased to exist, blown back to its stumps. Towering television aerials, 20 metres high, had been bent back by the explosion's force. Next to them was a palm tree. Three bras – maroon, white and beige – hung from a frond. Stuck in others were pink and green knickers. The policeman kicked at the rubble absently. 'The people who do this expect something from God,' he said.

'What do they know of God?' snapped Sadeeq.

After putting out the fires and removing the bodies and limbs, the clean-up team brought in bulldozers. The pile of detritus they pushed together was the height of a man and 30 metres long and wide. It seemed incredible, bigger even than the market that created it. How stacked were the stalls? How packed was the market? Tight enough to absorb a bomb, I realized. I couldn't see a single shrapnel hole in the buildings around us.

Sadeeq and I picked our way around the smouldering mess. Here were the remains of a bag stall: a brown and silver backpack, a black laptop case, a fake designer handbag. Here was a shoe stall:

black sandals, smart leather loafers, turquoise heels, a blue-suede zipped platform boot. A pile of mattresses had fused together in the heat. Next to them was a stack of kitchen flooring, melted like wax.

Here was a DVD stall. I could see covers for *Game of Thrones* and *The Walking Dead*. The blast had exposed a second, hidden business: there was porn everywhere. 'Indian professional prostitute extremely happy red beautiful women,' read one DVD cover. 'There was a boy selling these,' said the policeman, watching me sift through the boxes. 'He was killed.' The officer made an arc through the air with his hand, high and wide, tracing the boy's trajectory.

Sadeeq said the days after the blast had been nervous. 'They were out on the street straight away, right after the blast,' he said of Jos' Christian militias. 'They want to kill, maim and destroy. But our people informed us where the groups were moving and the security forces neutralized the forces who were about to attack.'

Sadeeq took me to Plateau Hospital, where some of injured were being treated. A list of 35 names had been pasted to the wall next to the entrance. There were Christian and Muslim names here. 'Goodness Chimedu; Joy Christopher; Patience Daladi; Mohammed Bashir; Umar Yusuf; Hadiza Ajiji.' One name, Elizabeth Musa, suggested a mixed family. We found Elizabeth surrounded by relatives on a ward in the back. There were bloody bandages around her left foot, her left knee, both her arms and around her head. One eye was obscured with a patch, the other closed by swelling. She looked unconscious, but when Sadeeq said a few words of introduction, she sat straight up and started talking all of a tumble, swaying alarmingly as though she might fall out of bed.

'BOH!' she said, throwing her arms up. 'Ra opposite me! BOH! And I can na see anything. Ma eyes are forever blind. De luggage from de luggage stall just fall on ma head. I ma covered. I said: "Oh help me! Oh help me! Oh help me!"'

The women in the room began to sway and murmur. 'Oh!' they said. 'Mmmm-huh!'

'Oh help me!' repeated Elizabeth. 'I can na move ma head. I see maself going down, down, down.'

'Mmmm-huh,' said the women.

'People were moving around,' said Elizabeth. 'I was shoutin'. Shoutin'! But they could na find me under de luggage.'

Elizabeth said that eventually she heard two men approach. They heard her shouts. 'No, dat one over there is much more in need,' said one. His companion disagreed. 'We might lose her if we just pass her,' he said. The second man won. 'Dey said: "Let's go, let's go." And dey carry me.'

Elizabeth was 50. She sold rice and beans in the market. She was a Christian, but her husband was Muslim. The bombers had found their target, I thought. Elizabeth's religious mongrelism was an affront to the purity they demanded.

Sadeeq told Elizabeth to rest and she sank back onto her bed. He asked the men and women in the room if the government was following up on its promise to pay for the bomb victims' treatment. 'We payin',' said one man. 'We see nuthin' from government.' Sadeeq grunted. 'Politicians!' he spat as we left. 'There are politicians who will try to make money even from this.'

Sadeeq and I walked back to my guest house. On the television behind reception the evening news was showing a portly man in uniform with gold and scarlet brass on his shoulders. It was the Chief of the Defence Staff, Air Chief Marshal Alex Badeh, strolling through the scene of the attacks. A reporter shoved a microphone in his face. The Air Chief Marshal smiled. The security services were like a well-trained goalkeeper, he said. They saved many goals but let one in and the whole team blamed them. The Air Chief Marshal beamed at his metaphor.

Sadeeq insisted his efforts to breach Jos' divide had had some success. Still, it was a daily and sometimes losing battle. It was not uncommon for priests and imams to carry Kalashnikovs in Jos, he said. Some had even led attacks. This sectarianism was not, Sadeeq insisted, unique to Jos. The city was merely where the rents in Nigeria's national cloth were most exposed. The stakes of what happened in Jos could hardly have been higher. 'Some people say the country will split apart even by next year,' said Sadeeq.

I asked Sadeeq to introduce me to figures on either side of the divide – community leaders and militiamen. By the next morning he had arranged for several to come in careful sequence to an office in an area of town considered neutral territory. The militiamen were mostly unemployed graduates in their twenties. They were careful about what they said. Though their members were routinely attacked or killed, they denied carrying anything more than machetes. They also claimed to enjoy semi-official endorsement. Their neighbourhood patrols were in constant contact with the police and army.

All sides described Nigeria as effectively two countries, north and south, Muslim and Christian, with Jos straddling the border. One 28-year-old Christian militia leader seemed almost to be looking forward to the day the country fell apart. 'The north contributes nothing to the economy of the nation,' he said. 'They are only parasites. I feel let them just go. Them be there and we be here. With this segregation, they cannot come between us and plant bombs.'

Both sides also agreed it was state failure – a government that did not provide security, or jobs, or education worthy of the name – that made vigilantes necessary. Abandoned by an indifferent and incompetent government, Nigerians had been forced to create their own services, setting up their own private schools, employing private security guards, plugging in their own electricity generators and digging their own water boreholes. 'The government has totally failed in its responsibilities to the people,' said Muslim militia leader Litty Omar, 32. 'In Nigeria, the people are on their own.'

Like many Nigerians, Sadeeq believed the failure went deeper than disinterest. The state was not just unfocused on its citizens, it was sometimes complicit in the violence. The bloodshed suited politicians, said Sadeeq, who found their contest for power made easier by forcing Nigerians into sectarian trenches from where they voted along communal lines. Violence also worked for the security services, whose national budget of $5.8 billion a year depended on them having a conflict to address. 'The whole thing is a creation,' said Sadeeq.

Sadeeq introduced me to Sani Mudi, a spokesman for an umbrella Muslim group called Jama'atu Nasril Islam. Sani agreed the authorities were 'deeply involved'. And Sani would have known. He was a former deputy chairman of north Jos and ex-assistant to the state governor. 'It's partisan, it's intractable, it's barbaric and it's callous,' said Sani. 'It's almost beyond imagination how the struggle for power could get this bad. It's the opposite of patriotism. And it's our rulers doing it.'

Next came a 51-year-old evangelist who worked with Sani in conflict mitigation and who had formed his own Christian-Muslim vigilante force, which gave early warnings of brewing violence in Jos. Yohanna Garba agreed that Nigeria's rulers stoked the country's divides for their own purposes. But he considered the security services most to blame. 'There has to be trouble for there to be money,' said Yohanna. 'The more crisis, the more money. So they allow trouble. They even make it.' Yohanna said he had a friend, a colonel, at army headquarters in Abuja. 'Some of the conversations there disturb him,' he said. 'A common opinion among the generals is that the insurgency may cost 1,000 deaths a month but there are 200 to 300 births a day. So it's not really a problem because there are replacements.'

The next day, I left Jos. That evening a suicide bomber killed himself and three others at the entrance to a crowded community hall on the outskirts of town. The following week the newspapers reported that a Boko Haram militant arrested in Jos had confessed there were six more devices and 100 more militants in the city.

The news reminded me of something Yohanna said about the other big Nigerian story that year: the country's surging economy. Yohanna seemed to share Boko Haram's dim view of Western-style development. 'Today people talk about a great, bright, wonderful future for Nigeria,' he said. 'But what they are saying is: "We will have more and more business and more and more power as we get people to support us."' Yohanna said this was not the path to progress that it was commonly held to be. 'The Bible says in the last days, we will be lovers of money, people will hate each other and brother will rise against brother. And I tend to believe the Bible. I tend to believe there is no brighter future for Nigeria. It will get worse and worse. I see the end of the world.'

ELEVEN

KENYA, SOMALIA AND UGANDA

In January 2007, a Pentagon spokesman named Bryan Whitman announced that somewhere in southern Somalia American
warplanes were carrying out air strikes against Islamists. Whitman refused any further details. 'I don't have anything for you
on Somalia,' he said. When the US attacked a second time two
weeks later, he was just as reticent. 'We're going to go after
al-Qaeda and the global war on terror, wherever it takes us,'
he said. 'The very nature of some of our operations is not con-
ducive to public discussions and there will be times when there
are activities and operations that I can talk to you about and
there will be other times when I just won't have anything for
you.'

Six years after 9/11, I was tiring of the US military's paradoxical
view of freedom: that it was dandy in peace but in war you best
defended liberties like freedom of information by restricting them.
The US had just declared war on a group of Islamic militants in
Africa but was refusing to account for it beyond a few sentences to
a small group of Washington journalists 13,000 kilometres away
– because it was Africa and nobody cared. That wasn't defending
freedom. It was contempt for it, and the same old contempt for
Africa too. By assuming authority for Somalia, by not considering
that *Somalis* might have something on Somalia, Whitman was
placing himself firmly in the tradition of arrogance and ignorance exhibited by so many foreigners in Africa. Whitman's sparse

statements did at least confirm what I'd been hearing in Mogadishu, however. The Americans were back.

The US military had nursed an allergy to any presence in Somalia
for more than a decade after 'Black Hawk Down'. That persisted
after 9/11. It endured even after the CIA located in Somalia three
fugitive leaders of the 1998 US embassy bombings – Comoros
Islander Fazul Mohammed, Kenyan Saleh Ali Saleh Nabhan and
Sudanese bomb-maker Abu Talha al-Sudani. Instead of pursuing
these three al-Qaeda men directly, in the years after 9/11 the CIA
outsourced, hiring four Mogadishu warlords to do the job for
them. And I'd just met one of them.

Mohamed Afah Qanyere was 65 and an elder from the Murosade
sub-clan of the Hawiye clan, Somalia's largest. When Bashir called
him, Qanyere asked us to drive out to his camp on the southern
outskirts of the city at the end of a broken and deserted coastal
road. The warlord had taken over an old, isolated villa whose
windows and walls were all shot up and which was surrounded
on all sides by thorn bushes that, after years without tending, had
grown as big as trucks. He'd ringed the building with artillery,
truck-mounted heavy-calibre machine guns and a few hundred
uniformed men. Satisfied he was safe, Qanyere had taken to dressing down. His hair out-shocked Don King and he met us barefoot
in a yellow and orange Hawaiian shirt and a thin *kikoi* wrapped
tightly around his pot belly.

Qanyere led us into the villa's main reception room, bare of furniture except for a large, deep-red Persian rug, a comfortable sofa
for Qanyere and a plastic chair for me. 'You're late,' said Qanyere
as we shook hands. 'You said five o'clock.' It was a few minutes
after. Qanyere didn't look busy. Still, I apologized. 'Don't ask too
many questions,' he snapped. 'I don't like too many questions.'

Qanyere's aggression extended to his pessimism over the
transitional government that had just replaced the Islamists in
Mogadishu. 'Clan war never ends,' he said. 'They fight over grass,
they fight over water. You rape my girl and I kill 150 of yours. There

is no reconciliation.' It seemed disingenuous for a clan warlord to complain about clan fighting. At the time, Qanyere was also refusing a request from the new government to disarm. I suggested Somalia's future might be brighter without so many guns. Qanyere snorted. 'If you have two people and you take a weapon from one, and I keep mine, then what will happen?' he asked. I said I didn't know. '*I* know,' said Qanyere, looking me in the eye. 'I will kill you.'

After half an hour of this, I ventured: 'You've always enjoyed close relations with the US.' Qanyere laughed. 'I think their involvement is confidential,' he said. 'But I am sure they're not far away.' The CIA's whereabouts in Mogadishu were actually no secret. Theirs were the first buildings you saw when you landed at Mogadishu airport, at the end of the runway, painted pink. Still, the Americans were careful to stay hidden in town and Qanyere, speaking against his own interests, was the first meaningful confirmation I'd had of their presence.

By that time, Qanyere had enjoyed a long and profitable relationship with the US. In 2006 a UN panel monitoring an arms embargo on Somalia published a report detailing how, in the first few years of the new millennium, the CIA paid him between $100,000 and $150,000 every month. In return he allowed the CIA and US Special Operations soldiers looking for the al-Qaeda trio to use his militia of around 1,500 men as well as the airstrip, south of Mogadishu, to where Qanyere flew in daily planeloads of *qat* from Kenya. Asked why the Americans had returned, Qanyere grew suddenly serious. 'The people who destroyed the US embassies in East Africa were here,' he said. 'These are bad people. They tried to kill me several times.'

Qanyere said he had known for years where the three embassy bombers lived. Initially he was puzzled when the Americans declined to act on the information. But Qanyere soon realized their timidity was his opportunity. He began doing the CIA's work for it, snatching what he said were al-Qaeda members off the streets of Mogadishu and handing them over in return for more money. Hearing how much Qanyere was earning, three other Mogadishu warlords began doing the same. For their part, the CIA was delighted. This was an unprecedented local buy-in. Apparently with a straight face, the CIA called its band of warlords the Alliance for the Restoration of Peace and Counter-terrorism.

The Agency's enchantment was short-lived. The US was paying millions of dollars to the men who were tearing Mogadishu apart. Predictably, the warlords used the money to buy more men and guns and wage yet more destruction. Mogadishu was already wrecked by a civil war that had raged since 1991. Now the warlords set about destroying what was left. Their mini arms race also helped transform Bakara Market into one of the world's biggest illegal arms bazaars, a market offering not just small arms and mines but artillery, surface-to-air missiles and even, I heard more than once, chemical weapons and dirty nukes. Asked to explain the chaos, Somalis liked to recite a proverb that celebrated the stubborn and self-defeating animus of the warlord:

> *I against my brother.*
> *I and my brother against the family.*
> *I and my family against the clan.*
> *I and my clan against Somalia.*
> *I and Somalia against the world.*

In addition to their appetite for self-destruction, the warlords turned out to be less than reliable contractors. In 2003 one of them, Mohamed Ga'modhere, abducted a Tanzanian, Suleiman Abdallah Salim, from Mogadishu and sold him to the Americans for several hundred thousand dollars, claiming he was the al-Qaeda commander Fazul. The Americans took Suleiman for interrogation in Nairobi, then on to a French-US Special Operations base in Djibouti, then Afghanistan, where he was held without charge for five years at Bagram outside Kabul. Finally, in July 2008, the US sent Suleiman back to Tanzania with a brief note saying America did not consider him a threat after all. A medical team from an independent US group called Physicians for Human Rights who examined Suleiman in Zanzibar reported he had been repeatedly tortured. 'Severe beatings, prolonged solitary confinement, forced nakedness and humiliation, sexual assault, being locked naked in a coffin and forced to lie on a wet mat, naked and handcuffed, and then rolled up like a corpse,' was their summary.

If the CIA was having doubts about the tools of its intervention, most residents of Mogadishu had long ago rejected them. By 2004, almost anything seemed better than a city run by homicidal clan gangsters. Out of this popular desire for law and order arose a rival alliance of Muslim clerics called the Islamic Courts Union (ICU). Aware that warlords recognized only muscle, the ICU formed a militant wing it called al-Shabab (The Youth).

The CIA's problematic outsourcing experiment had now graduated to full-blown catastrophe. Al-Shabab, like 'Taliban', was a common name in the Muslim world for zealous and uncompromising Islamist militias. The new group soon attracted a collection of exactly the kind of characters you might expect: thousands of young, ill-educated hotheads, sprinkled with a few hundred itinerant *jihadis* from the Middle East, plus the three embassy bombers. This was a disaster. For years the Americans had been too fainthearted to go after the bombers. For the sake of expediency, they had employed a group of warlords who exaggerated the size of the al-Qaeda presence in Somalia, duped the CIA into kidnapping and torturing innocent men, then screwed them for millions of dollars. The 'collateral damage' from this mess amounted to more or less the entire capital of Somalia and a large part of the rest of the country. Now the blowback from all that had empowered the very al-Qaeda group the CIA was meant to be pursuing. Al-Qaeda were part of a group championing Somali freedom. Bin Laden couldn't have wished for more.

The US was undeterred. It promptly labelled al-Shabab an al-Qaeda offshoot and Somalia a new hotspot in its war on terror. Again, this seemed to be giving bin Laden precisely what he wanted. But how true was the charge? Had a new member of an international Islamist conspiracy suddenly materialized in Somalia? Or did that perception reflect the old problem of foreigners in Africa: how assumption, extrapolation and imagination, in this case emanating in equal parts from Washington and Abbottabad, could conjure up an illusion more captivating than its reality?

Shortly after I met Qanyere, I asked Bashir to set up a meeting with an al-Shabab fighter. To meet me at the Peace, Ali Sayid stashed his gun, changed into jeans and a football shirt and walked across the city, through several battlefields and a series of militia and Ethiopian checkpoints. Just 15 years old, he was skinny, polite and mostly serious, though every now and then he would collapse in giggles, almost as though he'd caught sight of the man he was becoming and the boy he still was saw right through it.

Bashir brought Ali to the Peace and after we introduced ourselves I asked him why he had joined a group that the CIA regarded as a blood brother to al-Qaeda. Ali told me he was born in southern Somalia in 1991, the year civil war broke out. When he was 11 he left his village and travelled to Mogadishu to look for an education. Realizing he could not pay the school fees, he found a job as a porter, then graduated to selling shirts and *kikois* by the side of the road. In time, he was given a job inside a clothes store in Bakara Market.

By then, Ali was earning 80 cents a day, just enough to feed himself. Walking home from work, he was often forced to hand over his wages to clan fighters at roadblocks that the warlords had set up across the city. 'I was very angry with the militias,' said Ali. Ali could not speak English or Arabic – 'the warlords had done that to me' – and now his oppressors were robbing him too. They killed people, including one of Ali's friends, and made a business out of denouncing innocent men as al-Qaeda to the Americans. 'They took one of my neighbours to Addis Ababa and said he was a terrorist. But the Ethiopians said he was not and the man came back to Mogadishu and told us what happened to him. It was all just a business for these warlords.'

Al-Shabab fought back against the warlords on the people's behalf, said Ali. They were 'good people' who trained you to defend your neighbourhood, how to handle a gun, how to drive a car and endure pain and administer first aid. 'So I began to end my work then go for training with al-Shabab from four o'clock until midnight.'

Ali was describing the growth of a Somali popular resistance movement pushing back at tyranny sponsored from abroad, in this case by the US. There was no suggestion of international terrorism. Al-Shabab attracted sympathy even from its nominal enemies. In early May 2006, when al-Shabab attacked all the warlords' positions in Mogadishu simultaneously, the warlords found their own men were reluctant to fight what even they considered to be a legitimate revolt. Hundreds of them defected to al-Shabab. By 5 June, the Islamists had pushed the warlords out of the city. For the first time in nearly a generation, Somalis could walk the streets of their capital in safety.

Its success earned al-Shabab even wider support. One morning on the terrace of the Peace I watched a group of Somali clan leaders meet for coffee and, when they had finished their discussion, asked if I could join them. In the Byzantine constellation of Somalia's clans, all Somalis ultimately claimed to be descendants of Cush, son of Ham, son of Noah. Because Ugas ('King') Abdullah Ugas Farah could trace his ancestors back 24 fathers, further than anyone else, the others had made him their chairman. Though no Islamist himself, he took a pragmatic view of al-Shabab. 'They secured the city,' said Ugas. 'If that security had lasted, then Somalia would have had something we have not seen in 16 years: unity. Everyone believes that.'

By mid-2006, it was possible to believe a new, peaceful era was dawning for Somalia. But a resistance movement against oppression is a broad tent. Though al-Shabab attracted mostly nationalist Somalis, it also pulled in those with a more international and doctrinaire outlook. Those included the al-Qaeda trio and a former colonel in the Somali army who had fought in a war against Ethiopia in 1977, Sheikh Hassan Dahir Aweys. Aweys had also been friends with bin Laden during the al-Qaeda founder's years in Khartoum and even used bin Laden's money to form his own militia, al-Itihaad al-Islamiya, which carried out bomb attacks in Ethiopia in the 1990s.

If bin Laden considered al-Shabab ripe for hijacking, Aweys was the man to do it. Without consulting other ICU leaders, Aweys abruptly declared a *jihad* on his old enemy, Ethiopia. Aweys had few men at his command and, even if he had had more, the threat that a few thousand guerrillas posed to one of Africa's biggest and best-trained armies was empty. According to an Ethiopian intelligence officer, the US was also counselling Ethiopia against a strong reaction, stressing the dangers of giving Aweys the fight he apparently wanted and the risk that posed of bringing al-Shabab's more hard-line elements to the fore. The then commander of the US Central Command, General John Abizaid, flew to Addis Ababa in November 2006 to urge Prime Minister Meles Zenawi to reconsider what was, by then, a plan for a fully fledged invasion, banging the table and shouting that Somalia would become 'Ethiopia's Iraq'.

But Meles was adamant. Ethiopia was facing its own low-level ethnic Somali insurgency in the east of its territory and could not risk further escalation of a centuries-old conflict. On Christmas Eve 2006, Ethiopia invaded Somalia. In days, it killed more than a thousand al-Shabab fighters. 'They came at us in wave after wave after wave,' the Ethiopian officer said. 'We just cut them down.'

Ali was on the receiving end of the onslaught. Outgunned, outtrained and poorly equipped, most of his comrades were killed before they could fire a shot. But the slaughter only seemed to redouble Ali's commitment to al-Shabab. 'It was our duty to die at the front instead of being under occupation here in Mogadishu. Everyone prayed they would be killed at the front. It was excellent.' Ali stared off into the distance, his eyes dancing as he remembered the bright bloodiness of battle. 'I've never seen a government in my life and the Ethiopians took away the only security I've ever known,' he said. 'But to defend your religion and your country – it was excellent.'

Having glimpsed the subtleties at play in Somalia, Washington quickly forgot them. Once the Ethiopian invasion was under way, no longer did the US perceive a popular uprising against repression nor a patriotic resistance against a foreign invader. What it saw was an opportunity to settle its old score with three of its most wanted.

Within a week, the Ethiopians had captured Mogadishu and overthrown the ICU. Thousands of Islamists fled Mogadishu, driving south towards bases and camps on the Kenyan border. The Mogadishu exodus was the moment for which the Americans had been waiting. Somewhere in those convoys were the three al-Qaeda ringleaders. Suddenly Somalis began spotting small groups of bearded US Special Operations soldiers travelling with the Ethiopians.

This was the moment the rank and file of al-Shabab began to feel they might be engaged in a war with significance beyond Somalia. Ali, for one, had no doubts as to his ultimate enemy. 'It's the Americans who are now attacking us,' he declared. 'The Americans were supporting the warlords. Now Americans are using the Ethiopians to kill us. Why? Because America does many things against Islam.' That made the US his enemy, said Ali. 'If America is an enemy of Islam, then I am an enemy of America.'

It was all too neat. Too neat, and too nuts. In its hunt for three bombers, America had so inflamed Somali national pride that a patriotic fury was now coalescing around an anti-American, radically Islamist insurrection. Whitman's terse statements suggested that Washington hadn't even considered Somalis might object to a foreign power attacking their country but, rather, assumed that any sense of national sovereignty had been obliterated in Somalia along with everything else.

That misunderstood the stubborn nature of freedom, how people fight for it harder the more it is threatened. Ordinary Somalis, certain of the righteousness of their cause, were undeterred when the US described al-Shabab as part of al-Qaeda. If America wanted to unite al-Qaeda with a Somali popular resistance, if it wanted to fight Somalis in Somalia, they said, bring it on. The Islamists led the cheerleading. 'Bush must invade Somalia!' demanded Hassan al-Turki, a hard-line al-Shabab commander. 'Everyone in Somalia is a terrorist!'

Was everyone blood-crazy? Was Ali, the boy soldier? I tried an appeal to reason. Al-Shabab had allowed the embassy bombers to join. Al-Qaeda's No. 2, Ayman al-Zawahiri, had just released a video calling on Somalis to 'launch ambushes, landmines, raids and suicidal combats' against the 'crusaders . . . until you consume them as the lions eat their prey'. You had to see how this looked to Washington, I said. It appeared as though Ali and his friends were part of al-Qaeda, the group that had started the war on terror by attacking the US.

Ali sighed wearily and slumped in his seat. Saying America was his enemy had sounded good. Now the foreigner was taking it too far. 'People think our group is something else, that we're al-Qaeda,' he said. 'We're not. We fight for the people. We fight for Somalia. People need security. It has to come.' Zawahiri's broadcast didn't matter. It wasn't relevant. 'If someone called al-Zawahiri says the people should do this or do that, then it could be right or it could be wrong,' said Ali. 'I don't know and I don't really care. He is not from here, you see?'

*

When I returned to Mogadishu six months later, Ga'modhere's abduction of a random Tanzanian and selling him to the CIA for millions of dollars had become well known. Somehow that had not prevented Ga'modhere from being appointed Interior Minister. At his new office in Mogadishu, I was nervous about bringing up his ties to the CIA but I needn't have worried. Almost before we sat down, Ga'modhere said he was pleased to see me because foreigners needed to know they should be sending him all the cash they could. 'We are fighting al-Qaeda,' said the warlord. 'They are a danger to the whole world and it's the world's duty to give us support.'

Ga'modhere skipped to the next item on his wish-list: US assistance in rounding up troublesome journalists. 'The media here belongs to al-Qaeda,' said Ga'modhere. 'They demand freedom of expression but they use it to criticize the government. That means they are members of al-Qaeda. They are partners of them. We know this. We are following them. We have a lot of information on them.'

Ga'modhere's attitude struck me as not all that different to the Pentagon's. Whitman was also trying to shut down reporting on Somalia and Ga'modhere's reasoning was the same as his: that anyone not helping the US was against it. Ga'modhere's insistence that he was fighting al-Qaeda also bore striking resemblances to the rhetoric from Washington and his fellow warlord, Qanyere. The US and its warlords seemed to be drowning in group-think.

I decided to test the theory on a third Alliance warlord, Bashir Raghe Shiraar. In more reduced circumstances than his two peers, camped by the side of the road with a handful of men and a single artillery gun under a torn and oily tarpaulin, Raghe was even keener than Ga'modhere and Qanyere to stress the danger the Islamists posed and the need for millions more dollars to fight them. 'We know their dream was to have a nuclear bomb and they wanted to prepare it somewhere here in their safe haven,' he declared. 'So you see? There was that danger coming from them. This is not only to save Somalia. This is to save the world.'

Ali hadn't seemed like a global threat. Still, it was possible that a foot soldier would be unaware of his commanders' more diabolical ambitions. I asked Bashir to find me an al-Shabab commander, someone of rank, and within a day Mohamed Mahmood Ali appeared at my door at the Peace. Mohamed smiled a lot but he had the burning eyes of a zealot. He seemed torn between his duty to welcome a foreign visitor and his duty to kill a *kufr*.

Mohamed introduced himself with a brief sketch of his life. He was 41, had three wives and eight children. He was in charge of around 30 al-Shabab fighters. 'We are defending ourselves and our country against an occupation by our long-time enemy, Ethiopia, which is backed by the American government,' said Mohamed. 'This is a local war. But because of the American involvement, it is also a fight for our faith and freedom and that is an international war.'

Mohamed declared: 'We are against al-Qaeda.' But he added he was also against America because, 'in the war on terror, this government of America takes their weapons and uses this word "terrorism" to stop Muslim beliefs and eliminate Muslims from the globe. We want to implement *sharia* law. But even if a small town declares *sharia* law, America will make war.'

I asked Mohamed if he truly believed he was fighting America. 'We feel the suppression of America,' replied Mohamed. 'We feel the hostility of Westerners.' He followed events in Afghanistan and Iraq and felt al-Shabab shared the same beliefs and was fighting the same war as the Taliban and the Iraqi resistance. US aggression was a great recruiting tool, he added. 'That's one of the things we use to get more troops, to get their trust. America has the upper hand but we have people's moral support.'

As I had done with Ali, I asked Mohamed to see the situation from Washington's point of view. What were the Americans supposed to think of a group that had taken in the three embassy bombers? Mohamed replied that America knew there was no real al-Qaeda threat in Somalia. 'They know everything. Sometimes we cannot sleep at night because we hear their aircraft circling above us.' The US had allowed itself to be tricked by the warlords, he said, who wanted two things: 'to rule the country and to get money from Westerners'. Or maybe, he added, the US had its own agenda. He had heard talk that the US wanted to create a new state of Israel in Somalia. Mohamed's tone suggested he was sceptical of this particular conspiracy. He was like Ali. The big talk was rousing and fun. But no one took it very seriously.

No one, that was, except intelligence analysts in Washington and foreign journalists like me. Obsessed with al-Qaeda, we seemed almost determined to miss the point. As I circled back time and again to the subject of al-Qaeda, Mohamed became increasingly exasperated. Eventually he said that, as best as he understood it, 'America is fighting their own war across the world and, for now, they just happen to be fighting it here.'

It was that casual disregard for Somalia's sovereignty that Mohamed found unacceptable. Ali expressed similar senti-ments. So had Africans over the centuries. Caught up in their own ambitions or best intentions, foreigners looked right past African freedom as if it didn't exist. The arrogance offended Mohamed's patriotism. But it also violated his notions of plain common sense. 'Here is Africa,' he said. 'How far away is Amer-ica from here? What is their cause here? Can we disturb America from here?'

As a former officer with US military intelligence with 20 years' service including time in the Balkans and Iraq, David Snelson's charm, slight build and neatly parted blond hair always seemed unusual for a soldier until you remembered it was his job not to appear like one. Since leaving the services, David had freelanced as a security contractor in East Africa and often partnered with

Bashir. When I'd gone to see Qanyere, it was David who had taken me and we'd stayed in touch.

When the Pentagon announced its air strikes, I emailed David to see if he was interested in heading out to southern Somalia to look for the wreckage. If the CIA was mischaracterizing al-Shabab, the sparse information the Pentagon was releasing about its own operations felt like lying by omission. The strike site was solid proof of a US operation in Somalia and the wreckage was a good place to start unearthing the truth. The problem was the location, deep in al-Shabab territory close to the Kenyan border. David said we'd have to wait for a break in the fighting. Six months later he called to say there was a lull. We could go.

We caught a UN prop making a fuel resupply run from Mogadishu to a UN airfield outside the southern port of Kismayo. This was the northern edge of al-Shabab's newly reduced territory. Driving into town we heard gunfire, and when it continued through the afternoon and into the night, David set about making us look as forbidding as possible. By nightfall we had two pick-ups filled with a total of 20 gunmen that he hired off the street for $10 a day, guns and rounds included.

David also sought out the local MP for advice on routes. Abdirashid Mohamed Hiddig was a middle-aged man with a ready smile who asked people to call him Abdi. The Islamists had arrived in 1993, he said, the year after bin Laden moved to the region. They based themselves in an area of southern Somali swamp called Ras Kamboni. The place had no road, no airport and no communications but did have fresh water, fish in the sea and proximity to Kenya. 'You can do whatever you want there,' said Abdi. 'The people in the area are nomadic so no one knows who is who. There is just the ocean. If you're looking for a place to hide, you can stay there for as long as you want.'

After the Ethiopian invasion, a few hundred Islamists, among them numerous foreigners, regrouped in Ras Kamboni, said Abdi. 'They're waiting until things change. As soon as they get their chance, they will do what they're planning.' Abdi said the foreigners had attracted concerted attention from the US. 'At times, the sky was black with aircraft. Helicopters, jets, drones. I thought they would crash into each other.'

Also of interest to the US, added Abdi, were the thousands of fighters captured by the Ethiopians. Most were local Somalis but some were foreigners and neither the Americans nor the Ethiopians could tell them apart. 'The Americans asked me to go with them and sort them out,' he said. He flew with the Americans to a holding site where he stayed for five days, sifting foreigner from Somali. He identified more than 20 *jihadis* from abroad. Many were British, he said. After that, the Americans flew Abdi to a town called Kulbio, the site of the US air strikes where David and I were heading. There the Americans asked Abdi to sort out the dead. 'That was a last stand for an Islamist convoy,' said Abdi. 'The Ethiopians and the Americans killed all of them but they didn't know who was who.'

Just then there was a burst of gunfire outside our guest house gates and Abdi apologized and asked to be allowed to leave. We promised to talk again once David and I returned.

Starting the next morning, David and I made a long, lazy loop to the Kenyan border and back, 800 off-road kilometres in 36 hours. We kept our distance from towns and villages, driving through swamps and acacia thorns that, by the end of the trip, had scraped our pick-up's paintwork back to the metal. We saw partridge, guinea fowl, warthog, dik-dik and leopard tracks but, as David intended, very few people. When we did come across a farmer or a goatherd, David and I would hide on the back seat, our faces wrapped in headscarves.

That, and our gunmen, was enough to make anyone who saw us hesitate. Our plan was simple – get in, get what I wanted and get out – and we made only three brief stops during the trip: a couple of hours' sleep, an hour straightening a bent axle with a rock and a half-hour righting our pick-up after a passing tree snagged the front bumper and tipped us gently on our side. It was a hard pace. One of our gunmen seemed especially unhappy, complaining loudly that he was tired and enforcing our brief sleep stop by firing a single shot into the air and jumping off the back of the truck. The next day, when the same man wondered out loud what kind of ransom David and I might make, his commander walked him off to one side, then reappeared two minutes later, his arm around the man's shoulder, offering him a tissue for his broken lip.

We'd been driving for 24 hours when our dirt track opened out into a clearing littered with brass bullet casings, metal ammunition boxes and plastic mortar wrappers. Six burnt-out and rusted 10-ton trucks were scattered in a rough circle. Several had flipped on their backs. One had been carrying an anti-aircraft gun. Its three-metre steel barrel had been blown 30 metres from its mount. The ground was punctured with scores of fist-sized holes and, towards the centre, nine large craters, two metres deep and twice that distance across.

I had brought with me accounts of the RAF strikes of November 1920 ordered by the then British Minister for War, Winston Churchill, against the 'Mad Mullah'. Group Captain Robert Gordon, commander of the RAF's secret and experimental 'Z Unit', wrote that the attacks were a test run for an early form of shock and awe. The warplane was a new weapon that, it was hoped, would have the 'power to carry out, without warning, a form of attack against which no counter-measures could avail'. Captain Gordon added that 'this object was attained in full'. Six airplanes bombed the Mullah's forces, even singeing the Mullah's clothes. They then descended to 300 feet and engaged the Mullah's forces with machine-gun fire, which 'created the most profound impression on all'.

From the debris around us, I was able to reconstruct an air strike whose essential elements were unchanged since 1920. Going by the number of trucks, a group of 60 to 80 Islamists had been running south. The craters indicated the warplanes – US and Ethiopian, we later discovered – struck first with their largest weapons, 250lb and 500lb laser-guided bombs. Once they stopped the Islamists' trucks, they followed up with incendiary rounds, which filled the cabs and flat-backs with fire. Then, with the few surviving Islamists scattering for cover, the holes in the ground indicated the pilots had strafed them with cannon fire. They'd done it over and over. In parts, the ground looked ploughed. Most of the wreckage lay inside a rough rectangle the size of a football field, a kill grid, I read later, that was the signature of an American AC-130 gunship. No one had escaped.

We were still examining the wreckage when we heard the sound of a vehicle approaching. A pick-up entered our clearing. Our gunmen surrounded it. Three bearded men got out with their hands raised and lay face-down on the ground. 'Al-Qaeda,' hissed our militia commander.

He and David had a brief discussion. David turned to me. 'Our commander wants to kill them. He says they have a nice car and we could use the extra room. He says that if we just let them go, they'll only come back and try to kill us.'

David told the commander we weren't killing anyone and that we wanted to know who the men were. The commander asked them some questions. The men said they worked for Hassan al-Turki, the al-Shabab commander who had urged the US to invade. They were en route to one of al-Turki's camps. It seemed to be a supply run: next to the men's Kalashnikovs, the back seat of the car was full of tea and sugar.

David instructed our militia to let the three men go, minus their guns. The trio drove away slowly, until they disappeared out of sight – though for the rest of the trip our militia reported seeing the car following us from a distance. That was only more encouragement to get back to Kismayo as quickly as possible. Affronted by our squeamishness, our gunmen's opinion of us was also darkening.

*

We made it back to Kismayo in the early hours of the morning, paid off the gunmen and slept. In the morning I went to find Abdi. But he had left Kismayo and nobody knew when he would return. I cursed myself for not asking him more about the US operation when I'd had the chance. It wasn't like the Americans went around recruiting anyone who spoke English.

Sure they did, said someone. Within minutes I was talking to Haile Abdi Hakim, a 35-year-old sugar importer whom the Americans had also asked to assist them separate local al-Shabab fighters from foreigners. Haile said the entire operation, the bombing, the capture of prisoners and the sifting of the foreign *jihadis*, took around three weeks in all. 'The planes were moving day and night out of Kismayo airport,' he said. He listed the aircraft as helicopters, MIGs and lumbering AC-130s, American and Ethiopian. 'One AC-130 was bombing the vehicles, then others on the ground would attack the Islamists as they ran for cover,' he said. The Americans used phone signals to target their attacks. 'One time a local farmer found a satellite phone left behind by the Islamists and tried to make a call and they bombed him too.'

Haile said the Ethiopians had hundreds of Islamist prisoners. A group of Americans in civilian clothes went through their ranks, comparing their faces to pictures they had on their computers. Though neither the Americans nor the Ethiopians knew it for weeks, one of the three embassy bombers, al-Sudani, had already been killed. 'When the villagers went to loot the vehicles, they found him there,' said Haile. 'They buried him. His body is still there.'

A second man introduced himself as Hukun Abdi Koreye. He was 28 and worked as the UN's fuel manager at Kismayo airport, where he'd also got to know the Americans. Hukun said the operation had lasted 28 days. The Americans had flown in on Kenyan and US planes, up to 60 soldiers at a time. 'They took over one whole side of the airport,' he said. Hukun said he'd seen F-16 fighter-bombers, helicopters, including a Chinook, and drones. The planes arrived from Kenya. The helicopters came from a US aircraft carrier, stationed just offshore in the Indian Ocean. Later, studying US Navy ship deployments, I found the US had had five warships off Somalia that month, including the USS *Eisenhower*, which had 3,500 men and 60 aircraft on board.

Far from the two air strikes Whitman had announced, this had been a mammoth US military operation, a mini-invasion, lasting a month and involving thousands of US servicemen on land, sea and in the air. It was the biggest clandestine operation the US had undertaken since 9/11. That combination of size and its secrecy made its legality questionable.

The operation has continued in the years since. The Pentagon has maintained its policy of disclosing almost nothing about its operations. But even if you counted only the attacks it admitted to, by September 2014 the Pentagon had staged a total of 30. More even than the number, it was the range of armour used – drones, missiles fired from submarines and warships, helicopter gunships, fighter-bombers, AC-130s and Special Operations attacks by sea, land and air – that described the scale of the US effort in Somalia.

Mohamed and Ali had been right. They *were* fighting Americans. America was waging a covert war in Africa.

If you misread a problem, you can't fix it. If you misrepresent a local rebellion as global terrorism, that may eventually be what you'll face.

A conflict that had started with the CIA's blundering pursuit of three al-Qaeda men had led directly to the creation of a new anti-American Islamist force. If there was a war on terror in Africa, it was at least partly the self-fulfilment of a prophecy that originated in America. And as the conflict grew in size and reach, and with bin Laden taking such an interest, it was all but inevitable that one day al-Shabab would take the path others had already marked out for it.

In the early evening of 11 July 2010, as the world watched Spain beat the Netherlands in the soccer World Cup in South Africa, three men wearing black safari-style vests made their way through a warm, dusty evening in the Ugandan capital Kampala. The first man entered the Ethiopian Village restaurant, where a crowd of Ethiopians, Eritreans and Americans were sitting in front of an open-air screen. A second man slipped into the Kyandodo rugby club where another crowd had gathered to watch the game. Sometime on his journey across town the third man removed his vest and slid it into a laptop bag before entering the ICS nightclub, just south of the city centre.

During the first half of the game, each of the three men received a phone call. The first two reached into their vests. In an inside pocket they felt for a lighter and, sticking through the pocket lining, a short fuse. They both flicked the lighters. The fuses sparked and ran quickly to their other ends, where they disappeared into several pounds of plastic explosive wrapped inside a number of bags of ball-bearings.

Tesfalem Waldyes, a 27-year-old Ethiopian journalist on a Norwegian exchange programme to Uganda, was a few metres from the Ethiopian Village blast. 'I hear this sound, then this high ringing in my ears,' he said. 'I look around and people are screaming everywhere, jumping over the chairs. I have blood and bits of flesh all over my clothes, my arms, on my glasses. Three white people are on the ground covered in blood. This other white guy is saying to them, "Can you hear me? Can you hear me?" I am talking to them too. But they do not respond. They just stare up in the air.'

A total of 76 people died in the two blasts, mostly Ugandans, but also Ethiopians, Eritreans and a 25-year-old American, Nate Henn, of Wilmington, Delaware, who was working for Invisible Children. Around 85 more people were injured, among them five Americans.

Somehow – maybe the bomber lost his nerve, maybe his device malfunctioned – the third bomb did not detonate. A cleaner found the laptop bag the following morning leaning against a wall near the bar. Also in the bag was a cell-phone.

*

In the years after the Ethiopian invasion of late 2006 al-Shabab regrouped and counter-attacked. It beat back the Ethiopians. It beat back a Ugandan force sent by the African Union to replace the Ethiopians. By late 2008 it controlled most of Mogadishu and large parts of Somalia. That year also marked al-Shabab's international debut. It killed 30 people in a series of bombings in the autonomous state of Somaliland, to the north of Somalia proper.

By taking its war to the Ugandans 18 months after those first strikes, al-Shabab was finally graduating to what the US claimed all along it was trying to prevent: fully fledged international terrorism. But like humanitarians who could only advocate more involvement as a solution to their failures, the Kampala attacks were the signal for yet more US intervention. Within 24 hours of the blasts, a team of FBI agents arrived in Kampala. Handed the phone found by the nightclub cleaner, they bypassed its pin code and used the phone's call history to plot a network of numbers. The FBI agents then repeated the process with those numbers. Within hours, they had a phone tree connecting more than 100 people in Uganda and Kenya. The FBI men then handed their diagram to their counterparts from Uganda and Kenya.

Eleven days after the attacks, at 3.30 a.m. on 22 July, Mohamed Abdow, a 24-year-old Kenyan Somali street hawker, was asleep with his brother in their shack in the market town of Tawa, east of the Kenyan capital Nairobi, when there was a knock at the door. Mohamed opened it to find 20 men, some in police uniform, some in civilian clothes. They pushed past him.

'They ask for our phones,' said Mohamed. 'My phone is under my mattress so I ask my brother to call it. I say, "0. . .7. . .2. . .4. . .," and as soon as I mention those digits, one man says, "That's the number we're looking for" and they tell us to lie down on the floor, tie our hands behind us and say: "If you get up, we will shoot." Then they ransack the house as two officers hold guns to our heads.'

After several hours, the pair were taken to Nairobi and separated. Three days of interrogation followed. On the fourth day, Mohamed was bundled into a car with two other men and driven west. Several hours passed, then the trio reached an immigration post and Mohamed guessed they were entering Uganda. Soon they were transferred to a waiting Ugandan convoy and taken to Kampala, then nearby Entebbe.

More interrogations followed. On the third day there, three white men who said they were FBI joined Mohamed's interrogation. On 30 July, his ninth day of detention, Mohamed was taken to court in Kampala and charged with 76 counts of murder, 20 counts of attempted murder and terrorism. 'It is the first time I've heard that I am being accused of the Kampala bombings,' said Mohamed.

After his court appearance, Mohamed was taken to Luzira maximum-security prison in Kampala. There he was interrogated intermittently over the next few months by the Ugandans and more white men. What linked him to the bombings, it became clear, was his phone. Mohamed explained that he had bought it second-hand from a market in Nairobi on 8 July 2010, just three days before the bombings. He'd barely used it. The part it played in the phone tree had to be due to the previous owner.

But his interrogators wouldn't listen. One day Mohamed found himself being questioned jointly with Khalif Abdi Mohammed, the shopkeeper who sold him the device and who had arrived in Uganda after a brief spell at a secret prison in Mogadishu. 'If you do not tell the truth, you will never see your family again,' said one of the white men.

In East Africa, I often worked with Mohamed Ibrahim. Mo was an ethnic Somali born in Mogadishu, raised in Nairobi and educated in London, from where he retained an accent. Laid-back and easy-going, every now and then Mo would let slip hints of extraordinary journalistic endeavour. One day he mentioned how, at a time in 2008–9 when few journalists felt safe going to Mogadishu, he spent 18 months in the city photographing the front lines of al-Shabab's war with the Ugandans. Another time I discovered he had made more than 30 trips to meet Somalia's pirates and even acted as a go-between for them and the families of the hostages they were holding. Then there was the time when, walking down a street in Mogadishu, the convoy of the then Somali President, Sheikh Sharif, passed Mo on the street.

'One of Sharif's security guys stopped and asked me to come with him,' said Mo. 'I said I was a journalist, yeah? But they took me anyways to Villa Somalia and just next to the presidential palace is this prison. It runs deep underground, yeah? It's a secret prison. Everyone in Mogadishu knows if you go in there, you do not come out.'

It dawned on Mo that he had been taken to a clandestine CIA 'black site' prison. 'We could see some white men in Ray-Bans and khakis – military dudes – five of them going up and down into the prison. They took me into a room, got my fingerprints and mug shots, and then they started asking questions.' In American accents the men asked Mo who he was and for whom he spied. Then they told him they knew he worked for al-Shabab. 'You collect information for them,' said the Americans. 'But we can help you. We can put you in our witness protection program.'

Mo laughed. 'I said to them: "This is ridiculous, man. I need to make a call." And they said: "You can't call." And they took me to this room above the cells.' An hour later, the white men returned with more questions. They asked him again who he was. 'I said: "Listen, man, I am a journalist. I have a British passport."'

The Americans took Mo's shoes and belt, then marched him down a set of stairs leading underground and into a long, window-less corridor. Barred cells lined each side of the corridor, said Mo, all of them occupied by a total of perhaps 50 men. Mo was pushed into one cell already home to another man. Mo recognized him immediately as someone with whom he'd been at school in Nai-robi. 'Three classes above me,' said Mo. 'His name was Ahmed.

311

He had lost a leg.' The man looked at Mo and recognized him but, before Mo could say anything, murmured: 'We do not know each other.'

After a while, Mo persuaded Ahmed to talk. Ahmed said he had been in the prison for 19 months. His family had no idea where he was. 'They came to my home in Nairobi,' said Ahmed, 'knocked my door down, blindfolded me, took me to the airport and brought me to Mogadishu.' Mo began asking around the other prisoners. All of them had been kidnapped from Nairobi. They said that the Americans would interrogate them occasionally but mostly they were just kept in their cells. Like Ahmed, most had been there for months or years. Mo said he thought Ahmed had once been a member of al-Shabab but had retired a few years earlier after losing his leg in fighting. 'The Americans don't know what to do with him,' said Mo. 'He's not a fighter now and they haven't got anything on him. But they're afraid if they release him, he will go public. So he's still there.'

During the night, Mo managed to give his mobile number to a guard and asked him to pass it to a leader from his clan. The next day the man showed up with several trucks filled with armed men and demanded Mo be released. 'And suddenly it's, "Sorry, we did not know who you were,"' said Mo. Still, as they were letting him go, the Americans warned Mo: 'You cannot tell anybody what you saw or we will get you.'

Mo sighed. 'These guys, man,' he said. '*Serious*, I'm telling you.'

The Americans' brief detention of Mo, like their belief that a phone signal was sufficient grounds for an air strike, encapsulated how little care they took with the facts. What protected them was secrecy. With his brief detention in a US black site prison, Mo had pierced that. Keen to find out more back in Nairobi, Mo sought out Amin al-Kimathi, a former journalist who had founded the Muslim Human Rights Forum in Kenya and specialized in researching secret US prisons in Africa.

Amin was tall and broad, with a beard, skullcap and gold-rimmed glasses, a look that mixed traditional and modern Muslim. In Kismayo in 2007, I'd heard that once the Americans and Ethiopians sorted their foreign prisoners from locals, they took non-Somalis to Addis Ababa. Amin had heard the same, plus other testimony that more prisoners rounded up on the Somali-Kenyan border were also renditioned to Ethiopia.

Working with the British rights charity Reprieve, over several months Amin uncovered a system of black site prisons in Ethiopia, Kenya and Somalia, run by the CIA and FBI inside existing African jails. Detainees were held incommunicado, often without charge, sometimes for years. Most were interrogated by American and British officers. Eighty-six people had been renditioned from Kenya, either to Somalia or Ethiopia. Between 85 and 120 people, at least 11 of them children, had been taken from Somalia to Ethiopia. After years of campaigning, Amin and Reprieve helped get all the detainees home. None was ever charged with a crime. In 2010 Reprieve's East Africa representative was deported from Kenya.

After the Kampala bombings, Amin began hearing about another round of abductions and renditions, this time from Kenya to Uganda. 'People had been renditioned from Kenya and it was illegal,' he said. 'So I decided I would monitor the trial.' Amin first travelled to Kampala to visit Mohamed Abdow and around 50 other Kenyan prisoners in August 2010. In an email he sent to a colleague at the time, Amin wrote: 'I am advised that it will not be wise to make the trip now as the investigations into the bombing are giving the anti-terrorism operatives carte blanche to pull in anyone they may be having grudges with and I fall quite high up that premise. Kenya will definitely turn a blind eye/deaf ear and feign action as the Ugandans work on me in the Ugandan way, I am told.'

Despite his misgivings, Amin went. He was denied permission to see the detainees. A month later, Amin set off for a second attempted visit with a lawyer friend, Mbugua Mureithi. 'Just before

313

I boarded my flight at Nairobi, I got a call from this fellow, Andy,' Amin said. 'He said he had visited the Rapid Response Unit, the Ugandan security cell that was the lead agency in the investigation and which had a terrible human rights record. He told me to call him when I arrived. So I got to Entebbe and I call this guy and he said: "I really want to meet." It was 10.30 p.m., and he said he wanted to meet now, at a hotel en route to Kampala.'

Amin and Mbugua drove to the hotel. Andy was waiting in the car park, carrying a phone and a newspaper as arranged. As the two Kenyans pulled in, a car pulled up next to them, the doors opened and a group of heavily armed men jumped out. 'We were surrounded,' said Amin. 'They pushed me into their car. Andy got into the driver's seat and I saw that in the newspaper he was carrying a pistol. Andy drove the car. There were five other security officers in there with me. We were searched. Then one guy says: "Hood them."'

Unable to see where they were being taken, Amin said it felt as though they drove around the city for a while before turning onto some rough roads, country tracks. 'It was like they were waiting for instructions,' said Amin. At one point they were held for two hours in cells in a police station. 'All the time, these guys are shouting at us,' said Amin. '"You are terrorists! You have come to do what you did in Ethiopia! But we do not have human rights for terrorists in Uganda!" Mbugua asked them: "Are you going to kill us?" And they said: "That's up to you!"'

The driving continued until daybreak. Just before dawn, Amin was moved to a second car. 'Mbugua was screaming, thinking it was the end of me,' he said. 'But in the second car they were more friendly. They asked: "Why do you think terrorism suspects have human rights? You should let us do our work. You should not do what you did in Ethiopia. If you don't stop, we will put you on the charge sheet."'

Despite acknowledging that Amin was a human rights worker and Mbugua a lawyer, their captors eventually drove them to the headquarters of Uganda's Rapid Response Unit. Amin's legs were chained and he was led to a cell where he and Mbugua stayed for several days. Any attempts at investigation were amateurish. 'At one point they asked about a grant I received from the Open Society Institute,' said Amin. The organization, founded by billionaire George Soros, promotes democracy around the world. 'They said: "This is terrorism money,"' said Amin. 'I mean, what do you say to that?' Eventually Amin and Mbugua were taken to court with 31 other prisoners, 20 of them, like Mohamed Abdow, from Kenya. All were charged with terrorism, 76 counts of murder and 20 of attempted murder.

Over the next few months, Amin was able to observe the interrogation of other prisoners by Ugandan, American and British officers. At the end of November, 19 of them were released without charge. Neither Amin, Mbugua nor Mohamed Abdow was among them. 'We are not sure whether Kimathi really is a human rights defender or if he was involved in the attack,' said Kenya's government spokesman, Alfred Mutua. Mutua also claimed – wrongly that smuggling prisoners across borders was legal. 'We cannot have renditions among East African states,' he said. 'We have agreements on terrorism. This is a legal process.' Amin's Ugandan lawyer Ladislaus Rwakafuzi replied that the accusations against his client were absurd. 'If Amin took part in the bombings, would he really have come here to observe the court hearings?' he asked. 'It makes no sense.'

With just a blanket to sleep on and 45 minutes outside his cell every day, plus 15 minutes to empty his waste bucket, wash and eat a bowl of porridge, Amin found conditions in jail wearing. He tried to occupy himself by fighting to improve them, demanding more time to exercise, and books, and pens. Eventually, to stop torturing himself with hopes of his release, he forced himself to 'accept that these people wanted me there for the long haul'.

Finally, after 362 days in prison, his captors told him they were dropping all charges. Amin, Mohamed Abdow and Khalif Abdi

Mohammed, the shopkeeper who had originally sold him the phone, were all freed the same day.

Freedom and dignity are the marrow of the soul and a year in prison had starved Amin's close to death. It was five months since his release but he still had that jail look, like a cornered animal, all stress and humiliation. Amin was channelling his adrenaline into pursuing his tormentors. But even before he'd left jail, he had given up on calling the true culprits to account. 'In prison, the Ugandan authorities would complain the Americans were in total control,' he said. 'They would say, "The Americans treat us like children. They come here and interrogate *us*." Whatever the Americans wanted done would be done. Several times the Ugandans told me the decision to release me did not rest with them but with the Americans.'

Amin added that, since his release, a senior Kenyan minister had told him that the government in Nairobi repeatedly petitioned the Americans for his release, explaining who he was. But the Americans had insisted. 'They were not happy with your exposure of the Ethiopian renditions,' said the Minister. 'With you removed from the scene, they reckoned they were going to have an easier ride.'

Amin told the Minister flatly that such subservience to a foreign power was a disgrace to Kenya and Africa. 'You have opened yourself to the point of ridicule,' Amin said. But despite everything he now knew, despite everything he and Mo and hundreds of others had endured, Amin said there was no way to make a legal case against the Americans. 'They configured it all to make sure that would never happen.'

The lesson the US military seemed to have taken from its earlier prison scandals at Guantanamo and Abu Ghraib was simply to be more secretive. From Nairobi, I phoned Joseph Margulies, a Chicago attorney and former counsel for the Guantanamo detainees. Margulies had created many of the Bush administration's legal headaches by pursuing the rendition case of a British man taken from Afghanistan to Guantanamo to the Supreme Court, which ruled that it was for US courts alone, not the US government or its military, to decide whether inmates could be held indefinitely.

When I described the programme of renditions, detentions and black site prisons in East Africa, Margulies replied: 'This is counter-terrorism 2.0. It's very deliberate and reflects a learning curve from the perceived mistakes of counter-terrorism 1.0.' Guantanamo 'had had its own purpose', said Margulies. 'It created a sense of security. "We are keeping you safe because these guys are not on the street." But it ended up biting them in the butt. There were abuses, guys that didn't belong there. The whole thing became a symbol of an oppressive America all over the world.

'That led to 2.0,' continued Margulies. The rise of al-Shabab in East Africa was an opportunity to test some new ideas about how to wage the war on terror. Mostly these centred around out-sourcing. 'You reduce footprint and visibility, so there is very little risk to US life,' said Margulies. 'And by keeping it in the region, you reduce the risk of international legal pressure as a result of rendition flights, say, overflying Italian airspace.' It was crucial to keep the operation outside US jurisdiction, said Margulies. 'If it's run by Somalis, the expectation will be: "Were these guys treated according to local standards?"' Plus, with everything happening overseas in Africa, American lawyers like him had been completely shut out. Margulies said he almost admired the neatness of it. 'It's a very elegant solution,' he said. 'We used *habeas corpus* so effectively in Iraq and Guantanamo. But if these people are not in US custody, if Americans are present only as "advisors" and "observers", then there is no jurisdiction.' Abu Ghraib and Guantanamo looked amateurish by comparison, said Margulies. The US's new black site prisons in Africa were truly hidden. 'Democracy dies in the dark,' he said.

Especially ironic was how the US secret prison programmes were often dressed up as assistance programmes to help professionalize foreign armies – teaching developing-world allies a respect for the law and civilian authority. In reality these programmes were precisely and intentionally the opposite. The US was hiding its illegality in plain sight. The US liked East Africa's prison system *because* it was open to abuse. Inside it, the US could retreat from view and do in obscurity what it could no longer do in its own territory. Tellingly, the US persuaded African countries to go along with its plans by paying them. 'We buy them,' said Margulies. 'We call it "capacity-building" of local forces but the training, the offer of surveillance and intelligence, the sending of funds and weapons but particularly the money – all that makes an irresistible offer for local economies. It's what the US does best: throw money at the problem. It's what we've always done. And it always leads to foreign policy and moral bankruptcy.'

Amin said he had made the same point to the Kenyan minister. 'I told him: "The people who say they're coming to help you should not be trampling on your sovereignty as a nation. What they are doing could not happen in the US or UK. They tell you how bad your system is, how bad your President is, how they are trying to help them shape up."' But the truth was the reverse, said Amin. The US *wanted* Africa's prisons to be bad. It had a use for them. 'The more tainted it is, the better for them.'

The Kenyan minister agreed his government did it for the money, said Amin. 'There was a lot of infighting because of it,' said the Minister. 'The military intelligence took the largest share, the prison service complained they did not get enough, the joint terrorism force had a bigger share.' These arguments over money helped distract everyone from questions of sovereignty, the Minister said. 'Pretty soon the money was the only thing people talked about,' he told Amin. 'Nobody talked about what they were doing but what they were being paid to do it.'

In Rwanda, Paul Kagame had said the foreigners turned things upside down. In East Africa, the extent of the inversion outraged every African who knew about it. That wasn't many. The Ugandan newspapers ran regular stories warmly reviewing the co-operation between Kampala and Washington as proof of Uganda's clout and the professionalism of its security services. 'On the face of it, it looks like a very noble and lawful and helpful intervention, assisting poorer countries to improve standards of policing and intelligence,' said Peter Walubri, a Kampala lawyer for the detainees. 'But what they are actually doing is assisting the Ugandan, Kenyan and Tanzanian governments to break their extradition laws, to break the laws on pre-trial detention, to break laws against the use of torture, to break laws against the mistreatment of prisoners, to deny the accused prisoners access to their next of kin and lawyers, or doctors; to frustrate their attempts to get bail; and to assist in setting up a kangaroo court.'

Peter was most offended by the disrespect to his country's sovereignty. 'We should not allow them to run a Guantanamo in Uganda,' he declared. 'To whom are they accountable? This is a question of our liberty.'

There it was again. Freedom. Freedom had been al-Shabab's rallying cry in Mogadishu. Freedom was what motivated Amin in his work on secret jails and what, when it was taken from him, so humiliated him. Freedom was the continuing African fight on which bin Laden was trying to piggy-back. And the al-Qaeda leader was starting to look prescient, said Amin. America's abuse of African freedom would inevitably rebound on it. 'There is a lot of anger about what America is doing. Everyone thinks America is behind everything now, that they force their way into everywhere. This high-handedness, it radicalizes more than the radicals. It moves everyone to extremes. It makes people say: "It's us against them."'

It was, in the end, what had always outraged Africans about foreigners: the way they barged into a foreign land, proclaimed their self-righteousness, then relentlessly pursued their own narrow interests. It was the corruption of them.

*

In September 2007, at the start of the global financial crisis then gathering pace, bin Laden released a startling video address to the 'people of America' in which he declared Western democracy had failed them. 'The major corporations are the real tyrannical terrorists,' he said. Despite its slogans – justice, liberty, equality, fraternity, humanitarianism – bin Laden said the reality was that democracy was a con in which one 'class of humanity' laid down 'its own laws to its own advantage, at the expense of other classes – and thus made the rich richer and the poor poorer'. Any neutral observer would conclude that Western civilization was regressing, he added. 'The capitalist system seeks to turn the entire world into a fiefdom of the major corporations under the label of "globalization". If you were to ponder it well, you would find that in the end, it is a system harsher and fiercer than your systems in the Middle Ages. It is imperative that you free yourselves from all of that.'

This was another element to bin Laden's plan to restore al-Qaeda's standing. In places like Iraq, Afghanistan and Somalia, it would do that by confronting American military adventurism directly. Across Africa, it could confront criminal and venal government, especially when it was backed by the West. But Western capitalism – what Westerners called development – also offered a global theatre of war to the perceptive *jihadi*, said bin Laden. Not only did capitalism cover the world; as a system based on personal reward it inevitably involved greed, and that led to social injustice. 'Their laws make the rich richer and the poor poorer,' repeated bin Laden. 'Those with real power and influence are those with the most capital.'

Bin Laden's new thinking borrowed heavily from Karl Marx. Bin Laden proposed his fighters champion the oppressed, whether their subjugation was military, political or economic. The group would align itself with the righteous masses in the oldest of human divides, between rich and poor. It was an approach that has often been adopted by extremists. Adolf Hitler also attacked capitalism for exploiting the weak and mixed Marxism with racism to produce Nazism. To create his ideology, bin Laden mingled it with religious righteousness, depicting inequality as not just crooked and repugnant but a profanity and a sin. Though the Sheikh never spelled out what would take capitalism's place, he presented al-Qaeda as a purist and pious alternative. The holy mission, to which bin Laden returned repeatedly in his broadcast, was for the masses to cast off their chains. 'As you liberated yourselves before from the slavery of monks, kings and feudalism,' he said, 'you should liberate yourselves from the deception, shackles and attrition of the capitalist system.'

If al-Qaeda had once attracted only zealots and sociopaths, now bin Laden hoped its appeal would be almost unlimited. In his address, he extended his call to revolution beyond the *ummah*, speaking to the poor and neglected everywhere, even those inside the rich, capitalist, Christian US. The reach of America's military, political and economic power meant almost no one on earth was untouched by its hegemonic abuse, he said. 'Iraq and Afghanistan and their tragedies; the reeling of many of you under the burden of interest-related debts, insane taxes and real estate mortgages; global warming and its woes; the abject poverty and tragic hunger in Africa – all of this is but one side of the grim face of this global system,' he declared. The enemy was the US and its facilitators, including poor-world governments who took aid or investment from the West and, in doing so, made themselves slaves to it.

Foreign humanitarians wanted to save Africans from themselves. African nationalists wanted save Africans from foreigners. Bin Laden's strategy proposed saving the poor from both. After all, they represented the same injustice. They were rich.

By arguing that Westernization and elitism were one and the same, bin Laden was echoing the movement against globalization, a term he used several times in his speech. 'Globalization' is a term that describes how, more than 100 millennia after humanity first began dispersing around the planet, we have begun to reconnect in the past few centuries. In our modern interpretation of it, it describes the process of how, after the collapse of Soviet Communism in 1989, the West attempted to take liberal democracy and capitalism to the world. In the West, this was initially described as a wondrous uniting of humanity in a 'global village' whose new interdependence would underpin a new era of worldwide peace and prosperity. But critics, mainly from the poor world, saw it as a process of ever more Westernization.

The sceptics had plenty of evidence. There was the imposition, via the World Bank and the International Monetary Fund and foreign aid funding, of Western liberalism as the global political and economic orthodoxy. There was also the extension of Western culture and mores to the world. This took numerous forms: in economic behaviour, via the efforts of the World Trade Organization, the World Economic Forum and the G-20, G8 and G7, as well as the World Bank and IMF; in human rights, pushed by the International Criminal Court and Western pressure groups; in a liberal sexuality, transmitted via pornography and Western women's and gay rights groups; in sport via the English Premier League; and in cinema via Hollywood. All the while, Western military forces, UN peacekeepers and aid workers were shaping ever more of the world's nations into Western-style capitalist democracies.

From a Western angle, these were well-intentioned efforts to improve the world according to a set of universal human values. From others, they could look like a fiendish attempt to remake the world to a Western model, one whose design would ensure that power and money remained the preserve of a new global class of Westernized super-rich. Doubters argued that 'globalization' was a disingenuous misnomer hiding what, in reality, was a Western victory parade celebrating the super-rich's win in the great ideological battle of the nineteenth and twentieth centuries. Far from inaugurating a harmonious coming-together of equals, by this view globalization was a rigged game in which the rich and their

Third-World proxies were the sure winners and the rest of the world merely the spoils.

This is the great paradox of globalization: how it has provoked a backlash of anti-Western nationalism and cultural conservatism around the world. Strident opposition to the West is now consensus politics in much of the world, uniting governments, nations and rebels of all stripes. The West, in this shared view, is hypocritical, sanctimonious and dissolute. All the emerging powers – India, Brazil and South Africa – oppose the West on principle. Russia and China, and lesser powers such as Iran, Kenya, Venezuela and Zimbabwe, sometimes seem to talk of little else.

Bin Laden planned to ride this wave of anti-Western sentiment. His timing was excellent. He broadcast his speech just as the financial crisis was beginning to revive some long-buried suspicions inside the West about whether capitalism was striking the right balance between the haves and have-nots. The richest of the rich – the bankers – had managed to plunge the entire world into crisis. That raised doubts about whether anyone should wield such outsize influence in a civilized world and whether the West's cult of individuality had reached such heights that it threatened the whole. The crisis also prompted loud criticism of Western inequality which, after three decades in which stock markets boomed but average real wages failed to rise, had risen to heights not seen since the roaring 1920s. Resentment at this disparity swelled and spilled onto the streets. The G-20 protests, the Occupy Wall Street Movement, the *Indignados* in Spain – all were the acceptable face of this unrest. More questionable manifestations included the rise of far-right parties in Europe, sporadic riots across European capitals and, as bin Laden foresaw, a steady trickle of disaffected Westerners to radical Islamic causes.

Much of this has been minutely observed and analysed. Less attention has been paid to the accompanying widening of inequality in poorer parts of the world. In cities like Bombay, Johannesburg, Jakarta, Moscow and São Paulo, the arrival of unfettered capitalism led to the sudden emergence of some of the world's richest people, who promptly built themselves sky-high, multimillion-dollar apartments from where they gazed down on slums home to millions of the world's poorest. How long before the poor wake up one day and decide to tear them down?

Not long, perhaps. If the links between government and big business have spawned a rising public suspicion in the West, in the poor world the public is often openly hostile to ruling elites who seamlessly blend the two. The Arab Spring, the Indian Naxalites, the Nepalese Maoists, Peru's resurgent Shining Path, South Africa's mine and farm worker protests, Boko Haram, and the battles between riot police and government opponents that seemed to sweep the world in early 2014 from Bangkok to Kiev to Phnom Penh to Khartoum to Caracas – all have followed the same anti-elite, anti-corruption, anti-capitalist narrative.

It is an era ripe for the enterprising revolutionary, and in no continent more so than Africa. With the end of slavery in the nineteenth century, foreigners and African leaders stopped physically selling Africans – but they have continued to sell them out. Since African independence, the resource extraction business in Africa has been capitalism at its most raw: taking as much as possible – diamonds, gold, rubber, platinum, wood – for as little as possible, with scant regard for the people who live there.

The most notorious example of a neo-imperial industry was the global oil business. If post-independence Africa was a place of murderous dictators, billion-dollar corruption, epic poverty and environmental destruction, it was no coincidence that that coincided with Africa's first oil boom. For decades, in return for being allowed to keep most of the profits, oil companies paid billions of dollars directly into African leaders' foreign bank accounts while ignoring the environment, natural and human, in which they worked. It was oil cash that maintained so many of Africa's despots, funded their armies and stoked the inequality and resentment that sparked countless counter-coups and rebellions. The most infamous example was Nigeria and its crude-slicked, rebellious Delta, but there were others: Equatorial Guinea, Gabon and Angola, to name just three. So bad was the history of Western oil in Africa that the Africa-focused crude prospector and extractor Tullow built one of Europe's biggest businesses in 30 years largely on the proposition that it didn't screw Africans. 'The history of oil is pretty bad [in Africa],' CEO Aidan Heavey said. 'The bulk of the profits went to the oil companies and they really didn't care about the environment or local communities. They just went in, made as much money as they could and got out.'

Western business still short-changes Africans when it can. In February 2012, former South African President Thabo Mbeki kicked off a two-year investigation into foreign business in Africa by revealing that between 2000 and 2008 the continent lost $50 billion a year in illicit financial flows – that is, due to foreign companies under-reporting profits or manipulating prices or laundering cash so as to avoid tax and move money off the continent. Measured against foreign aid, the outside world was taking back from Africa almost as much as it was giving. If you included estimated losses to Africa of an additional $17.7 billion due to illegal logging and $1.3 billion in illegal fishing, Africa was down nearly $20 billion a year. As Mbeki, Kofi Annan and the African Development Bank all noted, Western business in Africa still follows an essentially imperial model. Partly because of resource extractors' habit of paying the ruler not the people, the top six most iniquitous countries in the world are all African. Even if Western aid mitigated the inequality stoked by Western capitalism, it did nothing to soften the impression of arrogance.

Bin Laden was adamant that al-Qaeda should show the poor the meaning of genuine altruism. As well as attacking the rich, al-Qaeda itself would guide the poor out of poverty and supplant Western aid. 'Some Muslims in Somalia are suffering from immense poverty and malnutrition because of the continuation of wars in their country,' he wrote in a letter to al-Shabab leader Muktar Abdirahman Godane, outlining a poverty alleviation strategy he recommended al-Shabab adopt alongside its military campaign. It was imperative that the brothers make time to 'support pro-active and important developmental projects'. In another letter, he wrote: 'The people have needs and requirements, and the lack of these requirements is the main reason for their revolt against the ruler. It is human nature that they will go with whoever better provides them with these needs.'

This was a modernization of Africa's conflict with colonialism. Once again it cast *jihadis* as the champions of Africa's freedom. Now it pitted them against Western humanitarians and Africa's Western-style economic rise – and positioned al-Qaeda as their true saviours. When Western diplomats described the deployment of peacekeepers to Darfur, South Sudan, Cote d'Ivoire, Mali, Somalia and the Central African Republic as noble missions to save lives, *jihadis* would note that all of those countries were Muslim and decry the interventions as yet more Crusades. If Western business looked at Africa's rising GDP as proof that the continent was finally coming right, *jihadis* saw it as evidence of Africa's descent into degeneracy. Aid's billion-dollar budgets might be touted as proof of generosity in the rich world, but on the other side of the planet *jihadis* argued the money showed how poorly Western materialism contrasted with Islam's ascetics and self-sacrifice. Aid was not a salve to inequality, they argued, but a tool of Western corruption, channelling billions to criminal African leaders and allowing them to shirk their responsibilities to their people. The true solution to inequality was not patching up the Western system that spawned it but replacing it.

There was an awkward accuracy to this analysis. It became even more uncomfortable if you examined how closely, in the age of mega-philanthropy, Western charity was linked to inequality. To be a billionaire philanthropist, after all, you had first to be a billionaire. When, in the early years of the millennium, the world's richest man, Bill Gates, emerged as the newest champion of Western aid, perhaps least surprised or impressed would have been the *jihadis*. When Gates unwisely began describing aid in religious terms, calling critics of it 'evil' and squaring off against groups such as the Taliban and Boko Haram who blocked foreign polio eradication programmes, the connection between the West's unjust wealth, its aid and its war on terror was never clearer to the *jihadis*. The manner in which the US created a famine in Somalia with aid group complicity would likewise have come as little surprise.

There was a clear solution to all this hypocrisy, argued bin Laden. Al-Qaeda was to show it cared.

The Westgate shopping mall in central Nairobi is aptly named. Owned by an Israeli company, home to designer boutiques, high-end fast food joints, coffee shops, an Apple retailer, a casino and the best sushi for hundreds of kilometres, to step through its doors is to walk out of the poor world and into the rich.

On 21 September 2013, five al-Shabab gunmen walked through those doors and shot and killed 67 people. The dead were a perfect cross-section of the cosmopolitan Kenyan elite: 48 Kenyans, including a nephew of President Uhuru Kenyatta and his fiancée, four Britons, three French, three Indians, two Canadians, one of whom was a diplomat, an Australian architect and his pregnant Dutch girlfriend, a 78-year-old Ghanaian poet, a Peruvian manager for Unicef, a South African, a South Korean and a 29-year-old Oxford economics graduate originally from Trinidad and Tobago. At least four of the dead were working in aid. Since two of the gunmen entered the mall through a rooftop car park where an Indian radio station was holding a kids' cooking contest, the dead and injured, an additional 175 people, also included several children.

Al-Shabab initially boasted that its men held off the might of the Kenyan armed forces for three days. Later, in a special edition of al-Shabab's magazine *Gaidi Mtaani* (*Street Fighter*), the Islamists crowed they caught affluent Kenyans unaware as they shopped and dealt a blow to the West, which was pursuing 'a crusade against Muslims' through its 'British slaves', Kenya and Uganda. 'If Westgate was Kenya's symbol of prosperity, it is now a symbol of their vulnerability, a symbol of defeat and overall Kenyan impotence,' the group wrote. 'Westgate was not a fight, it was a message. This will be a long, gruesome war.'

Soon, however, it emerged that many of Kenya's soldiers, far from being held off by the gunmen, had simply been having too good a time to pay them much attention. CCTV cameras caught soldiers looting the supermarket and designer stores. Photographs of scores of empty beer bottles strewn across the bar of a cocktail lounge bore witness to a legendary party. It was only when the soldiers tired of shopping and drinking and thieving that on the fourth day they fired a missile into the building and collapsed it on top of the attackers.

So many themes of the new Africa converged in the Westgate attack: the continent's rising prosperity; the greed and inequality that accompanied it; the way that made the aid and government elite targets of popular anger; the Islamists who wanted to co-opt that fury. *Gaidi Mtaani* was also an inadvertent reminder that what happened in Africa reflected a global phenomenon. The magazine alternated between Swahili and south London English. One article was illustrated by a photograph of a black man in a black coat and wool hat, a butcher's cleaver in one hand, his other covered in blood. Michael Adebolajo, an ethnic Nigerian from south London, had been arrested in Kenya in 2010 en route to receiving training from al-Shabab. Deported back to south London, in May 2013 he and another ethnic Nigerian ran over a British soldier, Lee Rigby, in a car on a busy street in Woolwich, then stabbed and partially dismembered him in an attack they encouraged passers-by to film on their phones. The photo, from one of the phones, showed Rigby's blood on Adebolajo's hands. 'Remove your government,' Adebolajo told onlookers. 'They don't care about you.'

Al-Shabab had been attracting *jihadis* to Somalia since 2007.

They came from the Middle East and Pakistan but also American, British and Scandinavian cities with large Somali populations like Minneapolis, Cardiff, London and Oslo. One day in a Nairobi hotel room I met a Kenyan al-Shabab deserter, Ali Warsame, who gave me a stunningly complete list of the globalized make-up of the group. Nationalities inside al-Shabab included Somali, Kenyan, Ethiopian, Eritrean; Sudanese, Tanzanian, Algerian, Libyan; Pakistani, Syrian, Saudi Arabian; British, American, Canadian, Australian, Swedish, Norwegian and Danish. Al-Shabab had been founded on patriotic Somali grievance. By Westgate, its growing international membership indicated how it saw itself as part of a worldwide struggle, and had ever more global ambitions.

I spent the days after Westgate talking to survivors, asking them why they thought they had been targeted. For most, it was too soon for reflection. A wedding photographer called Joe had braved the gunfire for seven hours to rescue people, but as he spoke the nerves danced so wildly under his skin that I cut the interview short and made him promise to see a doctor.

In any case, the attackers' backgrounds held clear clues to their motivations. All five were young Muslim men, Kenyans and ethnic Somalis. They came from all over Kenya, a reflection of how a young Muslim might find the inspiration to become a *jihadi* almost anywhere in the country. In the east, Kenya's Muslim coast had been ignored for decades by governments run by Kenya's inland tribes. Its main port, Mombasa, was now home to a group called the Muslim Youth Centre, later al-Hijra, which in 2012 declared it was 'part of al-Qaeda in East Africa'. In the north, 20 years of war in Somalia had produced the Dadaab refugee camp, three permanent settlements with a total population of 400,000 Somalis who were unable to work, vote, own property or ever really belong.

Kenya's marginalization of its Muslims was nowhere more visible than in Nairobi's Somali neighbourhood, Eastleigh, where at least two of the Westgate attackers lived. Home to 500,000 people,

Eastleigh was the wholesale capital of East Africa, attracting buyers of clothes, electronics, plastics and food from as far away as Rwanda and Congo and accounting for around a third of Nairobi's $9 billion-a-year economy. Much of the place was also a giant money-laundering machine. A couple of years before the attacks, I'd been wandering around Eastleigh with my Somali journalist friend Mo when I wondered out loud how much pirate cash was floating around. 'See that hotel over there?' Mo asked, pointing to a new-looking six-storey pile of purple and gold. 'We call that the "pirate money hotel".'

For all the money – licit and illicit – that Eastleigh brought into Kenya, the authorities had not returned the favour. The dirt-packed roads, open sewers and lack of state hospitals or schools gave Eastleigh a resemblance to parts of Mogadishu. And in the last few years, the mood in Eastleigh had soured. In October 2011, a small Kenyan army force had invaded southern Somalia, claiming it was acting out of frustration at Somali gangs who crossed the border and killed a British tourist and abducted a French one, who also later died. Al-Shabab sympathizers in Nairobi retaliated with home-made grenade attacks on bus queues and crowded markets, which killed around 100 people. Kenya's security services struck back in turn. In and around Mombasa they assassinated a dozen radical Muslim clerics. The Kenyan police harassed, beat, robbed and detained Somalis, at one stage rounding up more than 3,000 in a football stadium and holding them for weeks while claiming to be checking their identities. In Nairobi, MPs in the Kenyan parliament called for the mass deportation of all Somalis. In the streets ordinary Kenyans threw stones at Somalis. Slowly but inexorably, Somalia's war was moving south to Kenya.

A year before the Westgate attack, I got talking to Adan Mohammed Hussein as he sipped a counterfeit Coke in an Eastleigh café. An unemployed international relations graduate, Adan said the experience of living in Eastleigh could easily persuade a young man to join al-Shabab. 'The police harass us and make us feel like second-class citizens just because of the way we look and dress,' he said. They stopped ethnic Somalis from going to school, arrested them even if they had identity papers and demanded bribes to set them free. 'If there is any problem, they just figure, "It is Eastleigh. Let's get Eastleigh."

'So, sure there is anger. And when people feel excluded, when they feel furious and neglected and marginalized, people associate with extremists.' Imagine finishing school or university to find 'there are no jobs for you', said Adan. 'People feel they have no option but to go against the law. They become capable of anything. Maybe they even flee out of the country. Maybe they even join some group.'

Adan's words echoed those of John Githongo. John was a veteran anti-corruption activist who in 2006 fled from Kenya to London in fear of his life. His story had been the subject of a book on African corruption, Michela Wrong's *It's Our Turn to Eat*. And here he was back in Kenya, holding court in a city-centre coffee shop like a Big Man, dressed in a huge, expensive-looking white *babban riga* with four phones in front of him on the table. 'Africa is full of contradictions,' laughed John when I remarked on his appearance.

I laughed too. After a while I asked whether he thought that – contradiction, complexity – wasn't the real story of the new Africa? Africa wasn't dirt-poor any more. But to see the place as on a smooth path to prosperity was simplistic.

John agreed it was going to be a bumpy ride. Kenya had a growing economy, better health care, even a new IT industry. The number of Kenyan kids in primary school had doubled in the three years to 2006. 'But if you tell the average African that his economy is growing, he'll ask you: "Growing for who?"'

Inequality, not flat-out poverty, was now the biggest challenge in Africa, said John. And that would see 'some nations disappear under the wheels of a bus. Some countries will suffer tremendous convulsions. Some will sink. We will see an increase in coups.

There's truth to the optimism about Africa. But if you do not share the benefits, there is a price to be paid – and it's paid in blood.'

John said the new inequality would play out along Africa's existing divisions: tribe, race, religion. One group worried him in particular. 'Look at the Muslims,' he said. 'We've lost them. They're really marginalized and they're really pissed off. That's a bomb. It's going to explode.'

Westgate was that explosion. And after the attacks, whatever ways I once had of reaching al-Shabab fell away. I called Amin. The security services were right that he sometimes talked to the group. If I couldn't hear from al-Shabab directly, Amin might pass on what they were saying.

Amin lived just behind Westgate and had followed the battle by listening to the sound of gunfire coming through his window. The tenacity and discipline of the attackers disturbed him. Initially, Amin thought the attackers must belong to another group. 'I know al-Shabab,' he said. 'Most of these fellows are kids. They're goofers. I don't see them having the capacity to pull something like this off.'

As the Westgate siege went on, however, it dawned on Amin that the kids he once knew had become men. They'd had training. 'And look at the target,' he said. 'An Israeli property full of luxury and foreigners. It says they have changed their ways. Before, they used to target bus queues with little bombs. It was small and indiscriminate. Now they're saying: "We are going after the real owners of the economy."'

This new professionalism terrified Amin. 'They did this thing of separating out the Muslims by their dress and by asking them to recite parts of the Qur'an,' he said. The night of the attack, Amin received a call from a friend who had been inside the mall. 'She said she saw two of the gunmen. Both were speaking English with American-Somali accents. She said they were very controlled. They said to my friend: "You are a Muslim, you can go." The next lady was a Muslim but not in Muslim gear at all. The guy was very mad. "You are a Muslim! And you are dressed like this! It can't be true!" And he shot her. Blam! Blam! Blam!'

Just as worrying was the group's new class-consciousness. 'This is a progression,' said Amin. 'The inequality we have here is coming into play. All the previous targets have been in poor districts and that stirred animosity against them. Now they're trying to tap into people's feelings of being marginalized. And it's almost working. People don't support it, but what they do say is: "These guys deserve it. They are our oppressors. At least they got the right guys. At least they got the big Babas. Why should we care?"'

Amin reckoned that by aligning itself with the underdog, al-Shabab was finally implementing a strategy that had been long in gestation. Even four years earlier, he said, al-Shabab members had told him they wanted to remake their image into a humane anti-capitalist group. 'They wanted to be seen as more caring than they were depicted. They wanted to show they were in tune with the suffering of the masses. They identified with injustices and leftist causes around the world. They wanted to make Islam the identity of the dispossessed.'

After false starts in Mali and Nigeria, and two years after his death, bin Laden's last teachings were finally being put into practice.

Inevitably, Mo knew a leader of this remade al-Qaeda. Two weeks after Westgate, a group of US Navy Seals, coming ashore in rubber speedboats, stormed the town of Barawe in southern Somalia. As usual, the Pentagon revealed almost nothing about the raid beyond stating that it was intended to capture Abdikadir Mohamed Abdikadir, also known as 'Ikrima', a Kenyan of Somali origin said to be an associate of the 1998 bombers and 'a top commander in the terrorist group al-Shabab'.

Mo called from Nairobi. 'I used to play football with this guy Ikrima,' he said. 'He's older than me by about seven years. He grew up here and in Norway. He loved pets, especially pigeons. He loved children. He's really short, kind of skinny and smiley. I could wrestle him down and beat him.' Mo was talking fast. 'My head is still banging, man,' he said. 'He's such a humble, harmless person.'

Mo went over what he remembered about Ikrima. 'About a year ago all of my friends who he had visited in Norway and London and Nairobi were pulled in by the cops,' he said. 'That means a year ago this guy was on the radar. So the plan to capture this guy is something that they have been planning for a while now.' Mo reasoned that must mean Ikrima was indeed, as the Pentagon said, 'a top commander' in al-Shabab. Asking around Eastleigh, Mo said he heard Ikrima was the liaison between al-Shabab and other al-Qaeda groups, including the central leadership in South Asia. 'He's very well educated, from this middle-class family in Kenya,' said Mo. 'He can speak English, Swahili, French and Arabic.'

The Seal unit deployed to seize Ikrima had been Team Six, the same team that killed bin Laden. The Pentagon tried to put a brave face on the Somali operation, saying 'it demonstrated that the United States can put direct pressure on al-Shabab leadership at any time of our choosing'.

That was not how al-Shabab saw it. Dug in at Barawe with surveillance in all directions, they had seen the Seals coming and waited until they were in range before pouring fire down on the Americans. 'The Americans were lucky to get out alive,' said Mo.

After all the years of doubt and introspection, then the blow of bin Laden's death, Mo said the failure of bin Laden's killers had renewed the *jihadis*' faith in their cause. Maybe Allah was smiling on them once more. Maybe they were back on the path of miracles. 'They're saying, "We beat Team Six!"' said Mo. '"We beat the best in the world!"'

PART III

THE NEW AFRICA

TWELVE

ETHIOPIA, NIGERIA AND KENYA

'This is Africa's moment!' exclaimed Eleni Gabri-Madhin. 'This is catalytic! This affects millions!'

Eleni was sitting in a leather chair in her glass-walled office on the fourth floor of the Ethiopia Commodities Exchange in downtown Addis Ababa. She was wearing a black trouser suit and a gold necklace and earrings, and as she spoke she tucked her legs underneath her. I knew Eleni as a regular at Africa business conferences. For years, these events had had all the atmosphere of a palliative counselling session, with the experts confronting participants with the evidence of their condition, in this case depressing statistics on African poverty. But more recently they had become the forums for a different range of emotions: optimism, even giddiness and joy. In the excitement, few were pausing to ponder why Africa was taking off. Eleni's speeches suggested she had pondered little else for most of her professional life.

As we shook hands and sat down, I remarked that Ethiopia might not be the first place people would imagine setting up a food commodity exchange. Eleni laughed and shook her head. 'You're right, people don't understand,' she said. 'They ask, "Who is this crazy woman, creating a food exchange in a country where there isn't any food?"'

Well, quite. How did she explain it?

*

By the dawn of the twentieth century, two of the great suppressors of Africa's population had finally evaporated. Slavery had been abolished across all of Europe and the US. The late nineteenth century also saw the advent of modern medicine.

As a result, Africa's population doubled from 120 million in 1900 to 229.8 million in 1950, then accelerated further to half a billion in 1980 and finally a full billion in 2009. Africa was filling its empty spaces. The old ways – wandering, common land, *ubuntu* – didn't suit this increasingly crowded land. More appropriate was farming, private property and boundaries. This was the familiar path to development humankind had followed in other parts of the world. As individual rights replaced communal ones and capitalism overtook feudalism, this was how we had evolved a life based around individual freedom.

In the mid to late twentieth century, however, it became clear that Africa, once again, was breaking away from the norm. At independence, most of Africa was richer than most of Asia. But over the next four decades Asia soared while Africa slowed, stagnated and, in many places, shrank. By 2000, 11 African countries were poorer than they had been in 1960 and few Africans earned more than a few hundred dollars a year. In particular, African food production was not rising with population as it had in other parts of the world. Africans' growing numbers seemed to be leading their continent not into a new era of prosperity but into Malthusian catastrophe. Millions starved to death in Biafra, Sudan, Somalia and Ethiopia. More than ever, Africa was a place of poverty, hunger, war, dictators and disaster. What was wrong with Africa?

Eleni was born in Ethiopia in 1965. At the time, the country was still a feudal kingdom ruled by an Emperor, Haile Selassie, who traced his line to Noah. Eleni's family was connected to the old aristocratic order. That did not spare it from the turmoil of hunger. In 1974, the harvests failed and more than 300,000 Ethiopians died in a famine. Half-hearted efforts by Selassie to alleviate the suffering were the last straw for a group of young Communists

inside an army long frustrated by the deference and archaic tradi-
tions of the imperial court.

But the Derg and their leader, Mengistu Haile Mariam, did not
inaugurate the liberation for which Ethiopians had hoped. Consumed by Cold War paranoia, and so suspicious of freedom that
it even banned Ethiopians' beloved jazz, the new regime executed
100,000 people. Hundreds of thousands of Ethiopians fled into
exile. Eleni travelled with her mother and sister to Rwanda, where
her father was working for the UN Development Programme.
In reduced circumstances, it was in Rwanda that Eleni observed
small-scale African farmers up close for the first time. 'I saw this
agriculture with no tools by people who were uneducated and
living in grinding poverty,' Eleni said. 'It was clear to me that these
farmers were stuck.'

By the mid 1980s, Eleni was studying at Cornell University
in New York when a second Ethiopian famine changed her life
again. Mengistu's collectivist farms were failing, Ethiopia's food
production had plunged and in 1984–5 images of more starving
Ethiopians began appearing on television. 'I had this feeling of
grieving,' said Eleni. 'And I remember my university had a tradition
of kids' food fights in the cafeteria after the meal. So one night I
leaped out of my chair and I said: "Stop it! Stop doing this! People
in my country are starving!" And of course they didn't stop. In
fact, I'm pretty sure they threw food at me. But for me that became
a seminal moment. From then on, I was going to focus on this issue
of how to end hunger.'

Overcoming hunger would rescue Ethiopia from starvation and
the food aid dole. Eleni also understood from Ethiopia's experience
that hunger and dictatorship were connected. Despots were bad at
caring for their people. And maybe, Eleni began to think, moving
beyond famine was also a way of moving beyond autocrats.

A decade later, by which time Eleni was studying African grain
markets for her Ph.D. at Stanford, she finally returned to Africa
– and soon discovered something that surprised her. 'Wherever I

341

went in Africa,' she said, 'I kept seeing the same thing – people changing grain sacks. Each buyer and seller would check each and every bag, ton by ton, lorry by lorry. Then they would change the sacks. This would happen four to five times before the grain got to market. And there were millions of grain sacks in Africa.' Why was transporting and trading food so laborious? Why all the changing of sacks? 'Because there was no system of checking whether what you were buying was good stuff,' said Eleni. 'There was a high default rate. There was no transparency. Trading, basically, was high-risk. You had to be physically present.' Eleni later calculated the cost of this mistrust, in time and effort wasted, was adding 26 per cent to Africa's grain price.

When Eleni returned to Stanford, she told her professor about the sacks. 'How do we solve this?' she asked.

'It's called a commodity exchange,' her tutor replied.

If an early stage in human progress is moving from foraging to farming, a secondary one is graduating from farming to survive to farming for profit – and in that simple act the farmer sows the seeds of all the economies of the world. The dynamics are simple. A commercial farmer aims to make a surplus to sell beyond his family's immediate subsistence needs. When he takes his extra food to market, he connects to a commercial grid. When he trades his surplus, then returns again the next month, then invests the returns from these trips in better seed or fertilizer or a tractor so that he can produce an even bigger harvest next year, those are the beginnings of an economy.

These are the humble motivations that have guided humankind from cave to city. As Eleni suspected, as well as growing economic freedom, they contain the seeds of political liberty. By establishing an ability to live autonomously without the assistance or permission of higher authority, a man advances from living as a serf or an *ubuntu* foot soldier to what we would call a free man. Commercial farming was how we invented capitalism. And in the entrepreneurialism and self-reliance it required, the way it weakened the authority of others and strengthened our own, the way it brought people together and made them harder to push around, it was how the majority wrested their liberty from kings and chiefs and tyrants. Farming was freedom.

Human beings have also never found a better way to develop materially than farming. Studies by the International Food Policy Research Institute and the World Bank show that every 1 per cent rise in agricultural incomes reduces the number of people living in extreme poverty by 0.6–1.8 per cent. In Europe the transition from feudalism to the modern age was lengthy and contentious, running through several centuries of revolutions. In India and China it was faster and smoother. A 'green revolution' in India in the 1960s introduced more productive seeds and mechanization to farmers and moved the country from intermittent starvation to exporting $10 billion a year in food today. In China, from 1978 to 2011 farmers' incomes grew 7 per cent a year, the number of farmers needed to feed a population of 1.3 billion fell from 380 million to 200 million and, partly as a result, Chinese poverty fell from 31 per cent to close to 2 per cent today.

In Africa, where seven out of every 10 people still live off the land, the implications of moving to commercial agriculture are profound. On a continent where poverty has left hundreds of millions powerless before aid, tyranny or terrorism, the causal link to freedom is little short of electric. This was not living subject to the funding fashions of aid workers or the caprice of despots. Nor was it, as the *jihadis* would have it, being sucked into yet another subservient relationship with the perfidious West. Farming for profit was how Africa might leave behind an existence subject to the whims of any of its bullies. This was how a billion Africans might climb out of the Rift.

The problem for Africa's farmers, the reason they were 'stuck', in Eleni's phrase, was that their transition from subsistence growers to businessmen was incomplete. A fully functional agricultural industry required at least some ingredients of modern agribusiness: available and affordable seeds and fertilizer, the latest farming methods, farming insurance, clear land rights, and infrastructure like roads, warehouses, mills, irrigation and refrigerators.

Historically, African farmers had none of these. Even in 2015, 96 per cent of African farms were still rain-fed and use of fertilizers and tractors in Africa was about 10 per cent of the world norm. Thanks to *ubuntu* and the nomadic life, property rights and land ownership were often unclear – even in 2015, title was established over just 10 per cent of farmland – making it difficult to buy or sell land, which in turn discouraged investment. As a result, African land was around half as productive as land in Asia or Latin America.

This was what Eleni's tutor meant when he said Africa was missing a commodity exchange. Exchanges require a fully functional agricultural sector, everything Africa didn't have. Eleni decided to look at the problem not as a disability but as a challenge. 'Could a small, stagnant economy get all the pieces of a modern market together?' she asked. In effect, she was asking: was Africa ready for its future?

In 2007 Eleni gave up a well-paid job at the World Bank to find out. She set up a central trading house, the ECX, and a countryside network of 55 refrigerated food warehouses. To end the obsessive sack-changing, she hired inspectors to guarantee integrity. They would check goods for quantity and quality, then certify both in receipts. So that every farmer would know he was getting a fair price, Eleni erected scores of electronic price boards at markets across Ethiopia and introduced a mobile phone service to transmit the latest crop prices by text message.

By building the physical infrastructure for commercial farming, Eleni was also laying the foundations for its financial framework. That was needed because farming was risky. The vagaries of weather meant even good farmers had bad years and without spreading the risk via insurance or loans, all farmers eventually went bust. That was why small, developing-world farmers often stuck to subsistence operations. To grow more was to risk more.

Eleni's exchange allowed farmers to predict prices or even, via a futures market, guarantee them. And if farmers could accurately estimate future incomes, banks and insurance houses would share their risk. And if *that* happened, Ethiopia's farmers would suddenly have a brand-new incentive: to grow as much food as possible.

Before I spoke to Eleni, I'd spent an hour on the trading floor beneath her office watching buyers and sellers trade commodities in 10-minute sessions and, in the short breaks in between, swap stories about cars, girls and big nights out. The conversation quickly turned to the exchange's star trader, absent that day. 'The guy came from nothing,' the floor manager said, 'and he just bought a hotel. He buys five, maybe six million dollars a session. He sets the price for African coffee by himself.' I fell into conversation with a 38-year-old sesame trader. Takele Chemeda idolized Bill Gates and Gordon Gecko. He'd got his start in dried peas, then moved up to maize, then sesame, and said it wouldn't be long before he hit the big league: coffee. Before he could tell me more the bell rang for a new session and Takele was off, striding into the pit, yelling: 'I love this job! I love this money!'

In 1984–5, a million Ethiopians had starved to death. A generation later, Ethiopia's first yuppies were food traders. In only its third year of operation, the ECX turned over a billion dollars in 12 months. This was another reason why, a month later, the Somali famine would feel so strange to me. The success of Eleni and the ECX traders suggested Africa's future lay in feeding the world, rather than the other way round.

If Ethiopia's growth was part of a continental change, I should be seeing innovations like ECX appearing across Africa. And I *was* seeing those. Across the continent rice production was growing 8.4 per cent a year, partly due to the use of more productive strains of rice and partly because more land was being farmed. Government biotechnology engineers in Uganda, Kenya and Tanzania were experimenting with new types of disease-resistant banana and cottonseeds. Cote d'Ivoire was using a new type of cocoa plant that raised productivity three times. In Rwanda, the introduction of 116 basic washing stations catapulted the quality of the country's coffee from among the worst in the world to among the best, quadrupling earnings for Rwanda's three million coffee farmers. One of the world's poorest countries, Malawi, transformed its economy by subsidizing fertilizer and better seeds from 2006. For three years afterwards, economic growth was 6.5 per cent.

The results were especially evident in Africa's three cornerstone economies. In Kenya, hundreds of new kilometre-square poly-tunnel farms had sprung up along the floor of the Rift Valley from where farmers exported a total of $2.3 billion in vegetables and flowers in 2011, up 50 per cent in three years. South African farmers were sending lamb and ostrich, apples and oranges, wine and olives, even celeriac and quinces all over the world and had doubled their output to $6.3 billion in the same time. In Nigeria, in the five years to 2011, farmers tripled their exports to $1.8 billion and that figure was only expected to multiply: between 2011 and 2013 the government oversaw the investment of $8 billion in agriculture.

Foreigners used to the idea of feeding Africans sometimes had trouble with the notion that the reverse might be becoming true. But the proof was there on their food packaging. That fair-trade Cadbury's chocolate bar? Cocoa grown in Cote d'Ivoire. Starbucks' gourmet coffee? The Rwandan highlands. That out-of-season asparagus, those mange-tout peas and those oddly perfect midwinter roses? All from Mount Kenya. Quietly, in small print, those food labels were subverting the notion of Africa as a land of hunger.

Nigeria's Minister of Agriculture, Akinwumi Adesina, was a particular cheerleader for the idea of Africa as an agricultural powerhouse. Only 60 per cent of Nigeria's farmland was actually farmed, he noted, and only 10 per cent of it efficiently. What was needed was a change in attitude. 'Agriculture is not a social sector,' he declared. 'Agriculture is a business.'

Historically, Africa's great expanses had been too big for anyone to harness. Suddenly that was no longer the case. And with a total of 1.46 billion acres of unused arable land in Africa, compared to 741 million in Latin America and just 198 million in the rest of the world, Adesina's vision of Africa feeding the world only seemed to make sense. Farming was also helping foster a new continental cohesion to underpin this new Africa. Just as building the ECX required Eleni to create a national infrastructure, other initiatives to modernize farming did the same for Africa. Co-operatives sprang up such as the East Africa Dairy Development in Uganda, Kenya and Rwanda, which organized 179,000 farmers into collectives, giving them access to credit, insurance, refrigeration and veterinarians with the aim of doubling their incomes in five years. African banks, which had ignored farmers for decades, were suddenly tripping over themselves to offer loans and insurance. The boom in food production drove the formation of four African free-trade blocs – the Economic Community of West African States (ECOWAS), the Southern African Development Community (SADC), the Common Market for Eastern and Southern Africa (COMESA) and East African Common market (EAC) – the last three of which merged with each other in 2015 in the 26-nation Tripartite Free Trade Area that, echoing Rhodes, finally did run from Cape Town to Cairo. Common currencies in southern and eastern Africa, matching the one already in circulation in West Africa, were one likely result.

Farms, roads and markets; banks, exchanges and insurance; the uniting of individual farmers in businesses, co-operatives and trade federations – these were the building blocks of a connected, integrated twenty-first-century continent. No longer did Africa's wealth depend on the luck and skill of the hunter, whether an African with a spear or a foreigner with a drill. Now it was about a maturing and broadening economy. From 2000–8 natural resources like oil, diamonds and gold only accounted for a quarter of Africa's growth. After living for so long in the past, Africans were stepping into the future.

Eleni and I talked about much of this. I told her my theory about Africa's size being key to understanding it and how all that land seemed to make the most perfect reversal possible: from a continent of hunger to a land of food. Eleni replied that she'd spent her professional life trying to incite exactly that kind of continental Big Bang. So I was not surprised a few months later when I learned that she had left ECX to found a new company whose ambition was setting up exchanges across Africa.

Before we said goodbye, she told me that what was driving her wasn't so much the commercial logic of commodity exchanges or the financial rewards of running them but seeing the way they changed lives. She told me a story to show me what she meant. 'At ECX, we used to tell each other to be patient, that things don't change fast,' she said. 'And then there was this beautiful day in a village in northern Ethiopia when we convinced a food co-operative that instead of going to the old market, and haggling, changing sacks, maybe waiting weeks for payment and after all that probably being ripped off, they should put 200 sacks of grain in our system as an experiment.

'So the farmers brought their grain in on a tractor. They were given a warehouse receipt and told it would be sold the next day. The following morning, we had hundreds of these farmers lined up outside the bank to see whether their money would be there at 11 a.m., as we'd promised it would.

'And at precisely 11 a.m., they sent a man in. He walks in. And a little while later, he walks out. In his hand, he's got the balance of the co-operative's account on a piece of paper. And he holds it in the air, and he shouts: "It's there! It's all there!"

'And the crowd erupted. People were crying. People were laughing. The women were ululating. It was amazing. Just amazing.'

Eleni let the scene sit between us for a moment. Then she laughed, leaned forward and tapped me on the knee. 'This idea of yours about Africa being big,' she said. 'Imagine how big this will be!'

I once met a blind man who liked to walk clean across Lagos and said he was considering buying a car since he saw as well as 80 per cent of Lagos' drivers. It was a good joke and, like most good jokes, it held a truth. As with Africa's farmers, many of Africa's city dwellers seemed stuck – in traffic, in dead-end casual labour jobs, in sprawling ghetto townships. Africa's cities were less motors for advancement than stagnant poverty traps. Nobody seemed to know a way out. Like the blind man, everyone was just feeling their way around.

Lagos was the prime example of this anarchic inertia. It was the biggest city in the world's poorest continent and one of its fastest-growing: the population was expected to be as much as 25 million by 2015. When I first visited in 2009, Lagos represented a concentration of poor people unmatched anywhere on earth. Around 65 per cent of Lagosians – 13 million people – lived below the poverty line, earning $2 or less a day. This was chaos at its ugliest, deadliest and most colossal, a malarial megalopolis built of driftwood and tin, with little running water, electricity, jobs or law and order, where the ground was filled with garbage, the water with sewage and the air with the smog from a million unmuffled exhausts. Lagos was one of the world's first failing city states, a victim of what UN-Habitat, the agency for human settlement, calls over-urbanization, a concentration of too many people with too little money in too little space.

Farming was crucial to Africa's progress, especially in rural countries like Ethiopia. But with ever more Africans moving to cities, urban progress was becoming just as important. Nigeria was slightly smaller than Ethiopia but, at 160 million, had twice the population. In that sense, Lagos was a vision of Africa's future. And before city governor Babatunde Fashola took over in 2007, it was not a pretty one. 'If you have 20 million people, you are going to need more water, more roads, more jetties, more schools, more hospitals, more space for housing,' said Fashola in his city-centre office. 'And all of that literally stopped for about 30 years.' Lagos was a place, he said, 'of broken promises and very evident despair'.

Governor Fashola was not a conventional Nigerian politician. Rather than barge his way across town with sirens blaring and lights flashing, he chose to endure Lagos' traffic with his fellow citizens. Fashola also read economic theory for fun. On his bedside table: books by economists who saw potential in poverty, like the Indian C.K. Prahalad or the Peruvian Hernando de Soto. These poor-world academics argued that the underprivileged might lack money as individuals but together, in their billions, they represented a mighty untapped resource. This vision matched Fashola's own. When he looked around the city, he said, 'In everything I see, I see opportunity. The infrastructural deficit of Lagos [is also] a chance to relieve its poverty. If there is a bad road, it means we need an engineer and labourers, architects, valuers, land merchants, banks, merchandisers, suppliers of iron rods and cement, and food courts.'

Once elected governor, Fashola set about implementing his vision. His idea was simple and remarkable: take one of the world's worst cities and make it one of the best. He embarked on a comprehensive overhaul of Lagos' infrastructure, building new expressways, widening and resurfacing others, stringing street lights along all the main highways, integrating road with rail, air and even water.

The city was too big to transform overnight, but improvements were soon marked. Traffic slackened, garbage dumps were replaced with green parks, the proportion of Lagosians with access to clean water rose from a third to two-thirds in three years and flood defences covering 10.8 million people were strengthened. By the by, the amount of work generated by reconditioning such a vast city created tens of thousands of government jobs, 42,000 in waste and environmental management alone. New state skills centres trained a further 250,000 people in new trades, then offered them microloans to set up their own businesses.

The centrepiece of this new city was Eko Atlantic, an entirely new district being built from scratch out of the ocean by using sand dredged up from the ocean floor. It would be six and a half kilometres wide, extend one and a half kilometres out into the ocean and house 250,000 residents with offices for 150,000 commuters. A model at the offices of its developers featured gin-clear canals, giant malls, three marinas, trams, the island's own power station and a sail-shaped 55-storey skyscraper that would be the new headquarters for a Nigerian bank. 'It will be orderly development, linked transport – rail, water taxis and roads – improved law and order, a place to call home, a place to live and work and spend your leisure time, where things work, where there is electricity, water, health,' said Fashola. 'That's what I see: it will still be an African city state operating to global standards.' Lagos was to be the remade face of a new continent. An African Hong Kong. 'It's an amazing thing,' said a World Bank official, 'not least because it actually looks like it will happen.'

The purpose behind Lagos' new infrastructure was to put the city's teeming millions on a grid, just as Eleni's commodity exchange had done for farmers. But this wasn't just about roads and bridges and canals. Less tangible and more ambitious even than Eko Atlantic were Fashola's plans for Lagos' slums. To transform them, Fashola hired Hernando de Soto. De Soto's work focused on the unregulated, unmapped and illegal businesses in which the vast majority of poor people work. As individuals, argued de Soto, these people had little that could be described as wealth. But viewed together, they were a huge, overlooked opportunity. How to unstick them? Property rights, said de Soto. 'Since the Domesday Book, people have been linked to their assets and identified themselves through them. Property rights are the key to finding out how many citizens you've got, and who they are and what they're doing. Once you have that, then you can reform the city.'

When de Soto's team first went to work in Lagos in May 2009, they discovered the mother of all informal economies. Their survey revealed that 68 per cent of the city's property and 94 per cent of its businesses, with assets worth a collective $45.1 billion, functioned outside the law and any kind of formal registration. That handily beat annual foreign aid to Nigeria ($11.4 billion) and dwarfed foreign investment ($5.4 billion).

To banish the old anarchy and create an inclusive and orderly city that would be the guiding spear to Nigeria's future, Fashola had to pierce the murk, said de Soto. Rather than great, illegal slums where no one owned homes – and so could never leave or sell or rent them – he advocated giving residents property rights so they had the freedom to do all those things. Make the informal economy formal. End the free-for-all and the law of the jungle by legalizing, regulating and taxing. Squash suspicion and rumour. Create certainty. Rescue trust.

It seemed to be working. The city was coming together in a collective effort. 'We set out to demonstrate we can transform our-selves if everybody joins,' said Fashola. And they were. One result seemed to be a remarkable revival in community spirit. Armed rob-beries in Lagos fell 89 per cent one year and car theft and murder more than halved. The rising sense of citizenship revealed itself in another way. By 2010, the governor was raising 70 per cent of the state's income from local taxes. The government was accountable to its people once again.

The implications of Lagos' transformation were vast for a con-tinent where two-thirds of city residents lived in slums. Fashola saw his task in almost spiritual terms. A city that did not function according to rules, said Fashola, 'creates desperate conditions for people and reduces their ability to resist temptation'. The old Lagos left its people at the mercy of others. They became accomplices to criminals, victims for gangster politicians, beggars for aid workers and recruits for extremists. Fashola said the new Lagos offered its

people a way to break free from all of them. 'Corruption is a mani-
festation of frustration, a symptom of an economy that does not
work. What we did was suggest in very practical terms – in ways
that are touchable and can be seen – that things can be changed no
matter how bad they are. We restored hope. We restored belief.'

Fashola was giving every Lagosian a documented stake in the city's
future. His success ensured his methods were copied, particularly
by the governor of Nigeria's second-largest city, Kano in the far
north. But in other ways Kano felt as if it were in a different country. Built around a 1,000-year-old caravanserai where Africans and
Arabs had met on the southern edge of the Sahara for 50 generations, it was a desert oasis of somewhere between four and 10
million people. In the old quarter, behind arched gateways whose
stone entrances bore the marks of centuries of battle and wayward
carts, was a market whose narrow alleys still attracted Tuareg
nomads, Arab merchants and traders from as far away as China
to buy spices, beads, jewels, kohl, armadillo skins, black-spotted
serval coats and cotton dyed in Kano's 500-year-old indigo pits.

Tradition ran deep in Kano. With thousands of northern nota-
bles, French photographer Benedicte Kurzen and I had been invited
to a 'turbaning' at the Emir's palace, where Kano's 83-year-old monarch, Alhaji Ado Abdullahi Bayero, was due to ennoble five men.
At the palace gates, stallions harnessed with ornate silver-studded
faceplates and saddles stitched in yellow, red, green, black and
gold leather stood ready to parade the new nobles around the city.
The courtyard beyond was a vast, sweaty tapestry of thousands of
men dressed in *babban riga* of 100 different colours: orange, gold,
magenta, fawn, striped brown, sunburst-yellow, ochre, sky-blue,
navy-blue, indigo and purple. Their turbans were lace, cotton and
silk, flecked with black and gold. They wore embroidered leather
slippers from Timbuktu, Mombasa and Peshawar.

In a small hall beyond, sitting on the floor against one wall, was
a line of men in especially elaborate dress, the last of whom was

barely visible beneath what looked like a giant black-silk puffball decorated with red and silver polka dots. His face was hidden, his eyes concealed behind sunglasses and his head and chin wrapped in a black, red and gold turban tied in an elaborate topknot that resembled the ears of a Playboy Bunny. The man underneath rose to his feet and removed his sunglasses. His face was neat and small and his hair close-cropped. 'You made it!' he exclaimed in Queen's English. A hand was extended. 'Lamido Sanusi.' We shook hands and Lamido gestured at the crowd. 'Quite the show, eh?' he said. Then he addressed Benedicte in fluent French.

Nigeria's great flaw was its politics of division. To its persistent divides of north-south, Christian-Muslim and rich-poor, its elite-focused economic growth had added a newer identity crisis: modern-ancient. But Lamido transcended the identities that trapped so many others. He was a Muslim royal, the heir apparent to the emirate of Kano, but as a boy he had attended a Catholic prep school. He had studied economics and worked for Citibank on Wall Street but also read Islamic law and Greek philosophy in Khartoum at a time when a fellow foreign resident of the city was Osama bin Laden. He was a scion of the Nigerian establishment, but for the past five years he had hounded that establishment for corruption in his job as Governor of the Central Bank of Nigeria. 'I removed bankers from their jobs, I fought the national assembly over their pay, I put a captain of industry in jail, I said half the civil service should be fired, I said the petroleum minister was leasing her own private planes to the government, paying herself every time she took a flight,' he said. Finally, in September 2013, Lamido told President Goodluck Jonathan that around $20 billion was missing from Nigeria's national oil accounts. When the allegation was leaked, Jonathan suspended him. 'He took it personally,' huffed Lamido.

Formally, Lamido was in the last three days of his five-year term as Central Bank Governor. But already he was contemplating a new role as a 'public intellectual', holding forth on issues such as state corruption and incompetence. 'The government is full of sycophants, people who sit at the feet of the President and tell him the sun shines out of his back,' he said. The normal functions of government, he added, had been almost completely abandoned. 'We have people ready to be minister for eight years and achieve nothing. Even the President and Vice-President. Most of the politicians who get a job in government, they want the title, they want the salary and the privileges. They have no sense of shame. I used to ask them what is the power capacity of the country? What about national security? Health? Education? Culture? It drove them crazy.'

Days later, the ailing Emir died in his sleep, and Lamido was elevated to a post even better suited to goading the government. His accession made him king of one of the most influential fiefdoms in northern Nigeria. Though the position had no constitutional power, the high regard in which the Emir was held gave Lamido wide spiritual and moral authority. What was more, in contrast to his old job as Central Bank Governor, Lamido had no loyalty to the government and couldn't be fired. He had, in effect, become chief government critic for life. 'It's a remarkable thing in Africa,' Lamido mused. 'Technically the traditional leaders are not in the constitution but they are somehow the true leaders. There is a sense that politicians are only temporary.'

The same suspicion hung over Nigeria itself. It was the continental heavyweight – by population, economy, oil reserves and with its possession of Africa's largest city. And yet as it marked its 100th year, the big question was whether the government's failure would become the nation's. Was a government crippled by ineptitude and greed even capable of addressing the deprivation it had allowed in northern Nigeria and the ferocious rebellion that it had spawned? Would Nigeria fall apart? 'A state fails when its leadership fails,' said Lamido. 'Personally I am not very optimistic. Our citizens are left on their own to perform the functions of the state. I think we have all the symptoms of a failing state.'

The notion that Nigeria might be disintegrating just as foreign-investor excitement over it was peaking was not easy to digest. But neither was a country in which a group of militants could kidnap a whole girls' school and get clean away with it. I had been going to Nigeria for years, but I told Lamido I often left feeling as confused as when I arrived. He smiled. To understand Nigeria, he said, you had to accept you were entering a world where all truth was relative and all fact transient, and what seemed to be the most visceral and bloody reality could ultimately be revealed as artifice. 'It's about power,' said Lamido. 'Power, and the construction of truth.'

Lamido switched identities as easily as changing from a *babban riga* into a suit. To his mind, the solution to Nigeria's problems was to recognize the divisive and binary thinking of identity politics as the fiction it was. 'These identities are about a small elite that finds it useful to deliberately construct them, elevate them to the status of belief for their subjects and to take up positions around it,' he said. Such an identity might be 'forged around a sense of an exclusion' or around 'ethnicity or religion' or simply around 'a sense of opposition to "the other"'. Its purpose, always, was to accrue power. The British called it divide and rule. Their Nigerian successors called it politics. 'If you are able to place yourself as the mouthpiece of some imaginary identity you have created, if you create a whole theory about how you have been excluded and marginalized, then that's how politicians operate,' said Lamido. 'They make a blood sport of identity.'

Lamido rejected that. When he was fired as Central Bank Governor, he said, he could have made much out of how a southern president was getting rid of a northern leader. He refused, mainly because it would have offended one of his alternative identities: the economist. At its most fundamental, an economy is about working together. That co-operation spurs material progress. But it also implies political advances: individuals making choices and defining themselves, rather than being defined by others.

Most importantly, the way that an economy required and re-inforced popular cohesion, and could shape a scattered and even segregated people into a mighty whole – that was a way to create a nation that was connected and capable and resilient. That was the kind of country where the people were masters of their leaders, not the other way round. In Lagos, Fashola said corruption was in-stigated by economic frustration. Lamido saw a thriving economy as the foundation of a liberating patriotic spirit. 'You build a sense of loyalty to your country – of national identity – where people have a sense of belonging,' he said. 'And the best way of fostering belonging is providing economic opportunities. It's only when an economy stalls that identity politics kicks in and becomes about the other, about these immigrants and that religion.'

In the end, said Lamido, economic development was about free-dom. Nigeria's best hope of moving past the prison of its politics, off the aid dole, and leaving behind the nightmare of Boko Haram lay in growing the economy and transforming it from an apparatus of exclusion into one of inclusion.

Before he was forced out of the Central Bank, Lamido had un-veiled a project which had the potential to do just that: a biometric database for the entire Nigerian economy, the first of its kind in the world. After registering their fingerprints, Nigerians would be able to withdraw cash from ATMs or pay for goods at checkouts, gas stations or shops simply by presenting their finger to an electronic reader.

The system would be almost impossible to defraud. Businesses would also be able to see if their customers had a history of bad credit or crime. Should the database be rolled out across Nigeria, the room for forgery, fraud, bribery and money-laundering would shrink dramatically. Cash, especially suitcases of it, would become automatically suspect. Most significantly, with an indelible im-print at the heart of Nigerian life, the database would finally give Nigerians what they had lacked since the great colonial lie of

Nigeria was first promulgated: their own immutable and individual identity. This was how Nigerians could move past fearful and centrifugal tribal hate to a future of secure and confident citizenry. It was the grid that would connect every Nigerian to the nation and, at a stroke, diminish their politicians' monopoly on power.

Like Fashola, Lamido saw the database in almost mystical terms: as an attempt to light up the dark mysteries of money and power in Nigeria with facts, figures and records. 'It closes off opportunities for opacity and brings more clarity,' he said. 'It will be revolutionary.'

It was the most hopeful I'd heard Lamido be. His optimism was tempered by doubts over whether the database could be mothballed or his other reforms undone. He also saw no sign that the Nigerian state was climbing out of its hole of venality. 'The state just does what it wants, perpetuating itself in power using its monopoly on money and the army,' said Lamido. 'It's Louis XIV. *L'état, c'est moi*. Effectively, it's a monarchy.'

Lamido added that the number of people he knew who had met 'mysterious ends' suggested the Nigerian state would always try to destroy its critics. Still, he would not be cowed. And whether he was there to see it or not, he was sure liberty would win. As a student, he said, the Stoics taught him that 'even if I am jailed or killed, I am not going to lose. If you think of loss as the loss of freedom or loss of life, you miss the point. If you die for a just cause, you are free. They are the ones who are dead, lost, finished.' Whether you were an emir, a militant or the parent of a lost Chibok girl, Lamido was saying that freedom was defined only by the limits of your imagination. Nigeria's leaders had none. Even if they won, even if they killed him, they would never be free. 'What they think is important,' said Lamido, 'is not.'

It was possible Denis Karema had too much imagination. It poured out of him in a flood, and he often had trouble putting it into words. When I asked what his company did, he said: 'We create next-generation real-time anti-fraud solutions for near field communicators.'

Denis was sitting sideways on a bench, stirring sugar into a latte on the wooden table between us. We were on the open-air terrace outside a branch of Java House, Nairobi's own Starbucks. Behind us was one of Nairobi's handful of modern malls, the Junction, whose tenants included the Phoenicia Lebanese + Sushi Bar, Planet Yoghurt, an Apple iStore and a six-screen cinema. On the other side was a large car park full of new-looking European and Asian sedans.

Denis was 30, tall and had a neat moustache. He had arrived with an equally tall, younger-looking American called Connor McCarthy, who was on sabbatical from his management consultancy and had taken it upon himself to chaperone Denis. Not that Denis needed much minding. When Connor announced that there was 'a ton of opportunity' in Denis' company Usalama (meaning 'safety' in Swahili) and that he was considering an investment of '10 kay to 100 kay', Denis shot back: '200 kay'.

'Well, maybe 200 kay,' Connor conceded.

Denis' expression suggested that, even for 200 kay, Connor would be getting a steal. Usalama, explained Denis, would revolutionize the fight against electronic fraud. 'As money becomes easier to transfer, it becomes easier to compromise,' he said. 'If you look at the amounts lost to electronic fraud, Deloitte's says it's $4.8 billion a year but we think that that's 10 per cent of the true total.' Denis gave me a look that said: 'QED'.

In Addis, Eleni had showed me how Africa might move out of the past. In Lagos, Fashola had demonstrated how a city might win back its present, and in Kano Lamido had done the same for a country. I was hoping that Denis might give me some idea of what came next. But he was skipping too far ahead. I told Denis he would have to slow down and go back. He looked disappointed but sighed, gathered himself and, speaking slowly and checking that I was keeping pace with my notes, he began.

*

Denis told me he was born in September 1983 in the tea gardens on the southern slopes of Mount Kenya, close to the provincial market town of Murang'a, about an hour north of Nairobi. Famine was gathering pace in Ethiopia a few hundred kilometres to the north and Denis' early life was tough, though not in a way that a Live Aid audience would recognize. His parents were modestly paid provincial civil servants and they split up when Denis was seven. His mother Eunice raised him and his younger brother alone. Asked to describe life for three on a single government salary, Denis replied: 'Challenging.'

But difficulty only seemed to spur Denis on. 'I always knew I was bigger than my town,' he said. At 13, he persuaded his grandfather to pay for him to attend one of Africa's most prestigious schools, Maseno, near Kisumu on the shores of Lake Victoria in western Kenya. Maseno's students had included several future ministers, a number of African freedom fighters and Barack Obama Snr, economist and father of the first black US President.

But if it was history and prestige that attracted Denis to Maseno, it was a new gadget then arriving in Kenya that obsessed him while he was there. The year Denis started his studies, 1997, was the year the first mobile phones came to Africa. At the time, mobiles were new anywhere in the world. Denis remembers his mother visiting one weekend and showing him the first he had ever seen: a bulky German model with a green screen, an aerial and a hand-strap to assist with the device's considerable weight. Denis couldn't get over its tininess. 'Compared to a call box,' he clarified. 'I was amazed.'

The following year Denis bought a second-hand phone of his own, an early Nokia. Initially calls on Kenya's first mobile provider, Safaricom, were extortionate, 'so I learned how to communicate all my stories in seconds'. Denis also began to notice how his nerdiness – an addiction to chess and Pac-Man that, until then, had closeted him in geeky isolation – now transformed him into something else: cool. Or as Denis rather nerdily put it: 'The phone improved my social ratings.'

In the West and the Far East the arrival of the mobile phone was greeted with equal parts enthusiasm and annoyance. The convenience was undeniable, but people fretted about noise pollution, brain tumours and a decline in manners. Still, it soon became fashionable to talk about how the world was shrinking to a global village.

For a far larger proportion of the planet, mobiles were experienced as something that promised precisely the opposite. Where the world had once ended at the village limits, now it exploded beyond them – to the town, the port, the capital, even across borders and continents and oceans. Mobiles connected to anywhere and, with the advent of cheap prepaid pricing, to anyone. The effect on Africa was transformative. Overnight, Africa's great silent spaces began to shrink. Africans who previously had never used a light bulb or sent a letter or ridden in a private car found they could suddenly dial into our common existence. For the first time in history, it was possible not only to talk about all humanity, but talk *to* it too. 'Technology gave me access,' said Denis. 'The kind of access I could not have had without actually travelling to Europe or America.'

Unsurprisingly, demand for such an astounding innovation was unprecedented, all the more because Africa's rising population meant the continent now represented the second-largest mobile market in the world. In 15 years, Africans went from possessing a few million landlines to one billion mobiles at the end of 2015.

The knock-on effect on economic growth was as dramatic as the invention of farming. A series of studies by, variously, the London Business School, the World Bank and the consultants Deloitte found that for every extra one in 10 Africans who possessed a mobile, their country's national income rose by 0.6 per cent–1.2 per cent. Why? Because progress is a collective effort. The special significance of the mobile to Africa was that, uniquely, it let

Africans leapfrog the kind of heavy infrastructure that Africa's size had long made all but impossible. Mobiles – off-grid and able to operate remotely – conquered Africa's empty spaces in an instant. They tamed Africa's girth not by trussing it up in girders and wires but by effortlessly superseding it. Air-time did what land-line never could.

Such a stunning invention was hardly going to remain limited to calling home. Soon the mobile became the basis of a whole new African infrastructure. Mobile education – classes and lectures recorded remotely then delivered by website, email or text message – meant students no longer had to walk for hours to school and could even access teaching where none had previously existed. Mobile health services allowed patients to consult a doctor, learn about a disease's symptoms and prevention, even perform first aid – all without visiting a surgery or hospital and often for free. Because seven out of 10 Africans were farmers, hundreds of the most popular African apps related to agriculture: meat and vegetable prices were sent out by text message, as were reliable predictors of rain, sun and crop disease. A Kenyan app called iCow alerted herders to the vagaries of their beasts' oestrous cycle.

In the West, mobile and internet services formed a virtual grid which ran alongside the old, physical one and whose biggest selling point was convenience: online shopping or bill payment or email, an instant electronic postal service to replace letters. In Africa, the mobile installed a grid where none had previously existed. This was not expediency. This was plugging in, opening up and shouting out for the first time. This was what Africa's size had prevented for all human history. It was liberation.

The mobile also had a profound impact on perceptions of Africa. In his seminal *The Fortune at the Bottom of the Pyramid*, C.K. Prahalad wrote in a similar vein to de Soto about how most businesses were missing a huge pot of money by assuming the poor had none. Actually, said Prahalad, they did have a little. What's more, there were billions of them. For the right goods and services

– cheap, mass-market – they represented the world's biggest consumer market.

Mobiles proved Prahalad was right. If Africans didn't have phones – or pens or lights or shampoo or even much of a varied diet – it wasn't because of lack of demand but lack of supply. The key for a business wishing to unlock this vast and virgin territory was to adjust its view of Africans. No longer were they to be seen as penniless charity cases. Mobiles weren't pushed out of the back of a plane to the starving millions. They were bought, in shops, by millions of ordinary African consumers. What's more, it was becoming evident that there were enough of those to usher in a global financial revolution.

At Maseno, Denis saw mobiles take off. Instinctively, he understood the commercial promise of Prahalad's billions. 'In my heart, I had a feeling – which I still have even now – that tech is better than discovering oil,' he said.

Denis spent his last few years at school learning how to write computer programs. In 2005, he was accepted to study computer science at Kenyatta University in Nairobi. He began earning money almost immediately, and fell for technology all over again. 'I loved the way offering a little IT consultation would generate instant cash for me,' he said.

He wasn't the only one. Nairobi is East Africa's business hub and the headquarters for banks, insurers, manufacturers, food exporters and a large tourism industry. In the early twenty-first century, it desperately needed the skills Denis and a new generation of teenage African code writers could offer. For Africa's geeks, it was the perfect start-up environment. 'Money was never an issue,' said Denis. 'If I needed $1,000, I just developed a couple of websites and sold them.'

The young programmers shared a pioneering, hippy-ish spirit. As Denis described it, 'there was any number of people running start-ups. We'd meet and exchange information on where to get funding so that everyone had enough to build their own product. You looked out for other entrepreneurs. It wasn't a competition. They could access my methods and I could access theirs. The idea was for all of us to get the opportunities – and that would be good for all our businesses here.' In an article I wrote at the time, I drew parallels to the California tech explosion a generation before and gave its Kenyan equivalent a nickname that stuck: Silicon Savannah.

In 2008, his fourth and final year at Kenyatta University, Denis began to focus on his first big solo project. Taking data from police forces across Kenya, he developed Kenya's inaugural national missing persons database. His room-mate, meanwhile, built mzoori. com, an online market designed specifically for Kenyan shoppers, whose preference for examining what they were buying, and the seller too – like Eleni's grain traders – mitigated against the success of a site like Amazon. The idea of mzoori.com was to match buyers with sellers for a small fee. The site quickly became one of the biggest in Kenya. Looking back, Denis said he felt he and his classmates were at the forefront of a revolution. 'We thought technology could really change everything,' he said, 'the way we run businesses and institutions, the speed, the value, the transparency.'

Revolutionaries find it hard to stay out of politics. And an industry of people in their twenties, which valued entrepreneurs and collaborators and change, naturally had a pronounced anti-establishment edge. Denis got a particular kick out of befuddling Kenya's bureaucrats. 'They didn't understand what we were talking about,' said Denis. 'I'd say: "It's a development system to find missing people." And they'd say: "Oh. So it's a system. OK. Right." Then there'd be this long pause. Then they'd ask, "Is it something we can hold?"'

There was a more serious political edge to Silicon Savannah. On his weekends, Denis would return home to Murang'a to teach basic computer skills to his former classmates, some of whom he described as brilliant but plain unlucky victims of inequality. Among his most celebrated peers were four programmers who, in response to months of tribal violence after a disputed election in 2008, built the crowd-mapping platform *ushahidi* ('witness' in Swahili), designed to take information of attacks sent in by text, email, instant message or phone calls and plot it on a map of the country. One of the *ushahidi* four, Erik Hersman, went on to found iHub, a workspace in downtown Nairobi that became a base for 100 Silicon Savannah start-ups. iHub subscribed to two explicitly political goals. To build Africa's name as a source of tech talent. And to use technology to promote political freedom.

Surprisingly, perhaps, these were ambitions shared by Bitange Ndemo, the Kenyan civil servant in charge of technology. In July 2011, over the objections of bureaucrats who feared exposure for corruption or inefficiency, Ndemo released online millions of official documents, making Kenya's the first government in Africa and one of the first in the world to be completely data-open. Bitange's ultimate goal was free email and mobile phone calls for every Kenyan. 'The internet is a basic human right,' he liked to say. If physical infrastructure allowed Africans to move, connect, trade and prosper, mobiles took that to a new level. They put freedom in every African's hand.

As budget-conscious consumers, Africa's mobile users overwhelmingly preferred the cheapest form of communication: text. That prompted a range of text-based innovations including Mxit, a South African social network based on texting, txteagle, a developing-world outsourcing network and mPedigree, a Ghanaian service that offered a central number to which customers could text the barcode of a medicine packet and find out whether the drug was counterfeit.

To make sure it was profiting fully from text, in March 2007 Kenya's biggest mobile company, Safaricom, unveiled its own package of text services, which included a money transfer service the company called M-Pesa: 'm' for mobile and 'pesa' meaning money in Swahili. The idea was simple. A Safaricom subscriber would approach a Safaricom agent with some cash they wanted to transfer to another person, and that person's mobile number. The agent would take the money and, for a small fee, send the credit to the recipient's phone account. Soon the sender could upload credit to his own account, then send it directly to the other subscriber. It doesn't sound like much. It wasn't even original. By 2007, mobile companies in Japan and the Philippines had both been offering text-based money transfers for years.

M-Pesa's growth, on the other hand, was extraordinary. Hundreds, then thousands of M-Pesa agents sprang up across the country, reaching 19,000 within a year. After eight months, a million people were using M-Pesa. By June 2010, 10 million were. In 2013, 17 million Safaricom subscribers – close to half the Kenyan population – were using M-Pesa to transfer $2 billion a month. That was equivalent to a third of Kenya's national income and about 40 per cent more than all the coins, notes and current account balances in Kenya put together. Simply put: in Kenya, M-Pesa was bigger than cash.

Why? M-Pesa was more proof of Prahalad's principles. Kenya's banks had historically deemed most Kenyans too poor for an account. Why did the poor need a bank? As it happened, almost every poor Kenyan disagreed with that. Soon after Safaricom launched M-Pesa, it began to notice Kenyans were using M-Pesa not just to send money but as a substitute for a fully fledged bank. They would take their phone shopping and use it to transfer money to their grocer, their hairdresser, even their travel agent, in the same way a shopper would use a debit card in the rich world. They would also use it in places where plastic was useless, such as paying their gardener or buying a bus ticket or tipping the neighbourhood beggar a few cents at the traffic lights.

They used M-Pesa to save, too. That prompted Safaricom to link its M-Pesa accounts to actual bank accounts offered by Equity Bank and Kenya Commercial Bank. It was a neat reversal of the way credit checks worked in the West. There your bank account acted as the credit record necessary to obtain a mobile phone. In Kenya your prepaid mobile was your credit record and your passport to a bank account – and savings, loans, interest and plastic.

In the West, banks were brick-and-mortar institutions. In Africa, they were in the air. It took such a leap of imagination to grasp how such a startling amount of financial freedom had arrived in Africa almost instantly that, for half a decade, the rich world didn't get it. By 2013, there were 50 mobile money services in Africa and Kenyan-style mobile banking was available in almost any developing country in the world, from Mexico to Iran to Nepal. The number of mobile banking users in the world had reached 600 million and was predicted to cross a billion by 2017. But in the US and Europe, mobile banking was still in its infancy.

The contrast between the crashing of American and European banks, however, and the rocketing fortunes of an African bank that was really a mobile phone company made Safaricom and its competitors impossible to ignore. Carol Realini, boss of a Californian mobile-banking company, Obopay, was emphatic. 'Africa is the new Silicon Valley of banking,' she said. 'The future of banking is being defined here. The new models for what will be mainstream throughout the world are being incubated here. There are 100 countries around the world looking to Kenya and asking: "How do we do that?" Africa is going to change the world.'

The bigger mobile banking grew, the keener each new Kenyan developer became to write the code that would shape its next evolution. Shortly before I met Denis I attended a two-day mobile technology conference in Nairobi. As the first day began, the dozen or so European and Californian venture capitalists in the audience affected studied scepticism about the whole idea of African tech. But as the presentations proceeded, it became steadily less clear who, exactly, was out of their depth. Many of the Kenyan developers were focused on the future of money – or rather a future without money, as most of their audience understood it.

The Kenyans were sure the phone would soon replace the wallet. 'Our mobile money system is the alternative to cash in Africa,' announced the 24-year-old vice-president of business development at a start-up called Kopo Kopo. The boss of a company called Zege Technologies said his rival cashless banking system went one better, offering 'business at the speed of thought'. At first there were no questions. Then there were a lot.

After the conference, Denis told me he had decided not to make 'just another mobile wallet', as if that were the dullest thing in the world. Instead he proposed to secure every single mobile wallet against fraud. Eventually, predicted Denis, he would be protecting hundreds of millions of customers and handling trillions of dollars. He imagined Usalama as the Group 4 of the financial internet. 'All our solutions are global,' he said. 'One of our products reduces ATM fraud by 90 per cent. We have an anti-credit-card-scamming product. We can report fraud live, as it happens.'

Almost as an advertising gimmick, Denis had developed a personal panic button that could be downloaded as a mobile app and which, when activated, would send an alarm to private security companies, banks and family, giving time and location. The high demand for that had turned it into a whole separate business that Denis hoped to roll out next in Nigeria and Ghana. 'Everyone in the world needs security,' said Denis. 'And we can give it to them.' Carol Realini was right, said Denis. 'It's Africa's time to change the world,' he said.

A growing population, commercial farming, remade cities, mobiles – these were the drivers of Africa's growth. There were other factors common to rising prosperity anywhere: better education, health and democracy; diminishing conflict and corruption; cheaper wages than China; better language skills than India; and Africa's physical proximity to pacey economies in Asia, the Middle East and Latin America.

By the turn of the twenty-first century, it was no longer accurate to regard Africa as a huge void. It was a waking giant. But every time I took a night flight across Africa's blackened spaces, one question would return. When would Africa finally turn on the lights?

One day I drove out of Nairobi before dawn, heading west over the lip of the Rift and away from the city. By mid afternoon I was close to the Ugandan border, and in the midst of a patchwork of green maize fields ringed with sagging papaya trees I found the tin-and-grass-roof village of Kokete. I was there to meet 39-year-old Gladys Nange. We shook hands and she showed me around the maize plantation and chicken coops on her half-acre plot. Then she led me into the two-room, windowless hut that she shared with six children and her husband. 'You hear about government plans to bring power cables here but it never comes,' she said. 'I can't afford the $400 connection charge anyway.'

It was a perfect poverty trap. Gladys couldn't afford power. Lack of power had, in turn, kept Gladys and her family poor. No light prevented her children from finishing their homework, so they did badly at school. No power meant that to charge her mobile phone, on which she checked maize and chicken prices, she had to walk five kilometres to the nearest working plug, whose owner charged $3 for the service. Even when Gladys could afford paraffin for her lamps, the fumes inside the tiny hut sometimes made the family so ill they had to stay home sick.

Spain, with a twentieth of Africa's population, produces as much electricity as the entire continent. In 2014, a full 700 million Africans – two-thirds of the population – had no power lines and for them night still meant what it did when mankind first stepped out onto the savannah four million years ago: darkness and silence, an end to work, a time to sleep. The collective implications of life without power are grave. Economists reckon every 1 per cent shortfall in a country's energy supply shaves 0.7 per cent off its economic growth. Kokete's village chief, Francis Morogo, told me no one from Kokete had been to university, many had never

369

even left the village and almost everyone lived on what they grew. 'People here are really on the edge of nothing,' he said. 'They still have a hungry season between harvests.' The chief waved a walking stick in a wide arc. 'What you see here,' he said, 'is lives lived in the dark.'

I'd come to see Gladys because, two months before, in an experiment then unique on the continent, she'd swung a small solar panel onto her roof and run a cable back to a central yellow junction box linked to two LED lights and a mobile charger. It was an adaptation of prepaid mobiles to electricity, transcending the need for a national power grid. Gladys paid an initial $12 for the kit, made by a start-up spun out of Cambridge University in Britain. She paid off the rest of the $93 cost in weekly payments of $1.20 spread over 18 months by buying scratchcards and punching their code into a keypad on the junction box. At the end of her payments, Gladys could choose either to enjoy free power for as long as the panel lasted or upgrade to a better pack with more lights and power points.

The idea was simple. Its effect was close to miraculous. Gladys' children could finish their homework, the house was no longer filled with noxious fumes and Gladys was saving money and planning to expand her chicken-farming business with bigger, electrified hatcheries. This was a change big enough to be seen from 30,000 feet.

Before I left, I asked Gladys to imagine her future. She thought for a moment, then laughed and opened her arms wide across the electric light falling all around her.

'Brighter,' she said.

THIRTEEN

CHINA IN AFRICA

• Kinshasa

• Lusaka

Mathis Xu was standing by the side of the Boulevard 30 Juin in central Kinshasa, capital of Congo, watching giant bulldozers stamped with the word 'CREC' obliterate a small hill. 'Before the road was only 10 metres wide,' Mathis shouted as a giant palm came crashing down. 'Everybody tells me that 30 years ago China was just like Congo. We bring a new conception. Modern engines, modern techniques, modern thoughts. This road, it's going to be huge. It's going to be fantastic.'

The size of Western Europe but, in 2009, with barely a kilometre of unbroken road, Congo was the broken heart of Africa. Congo was where the Belgians introduced Africans to hand amputations and where Joseph Conrad set *Heart of Darkness*. In return, Congo gave the world AIDS, Ebola and, with the CIA's help, Mobutu Sese Seko, the ultimate African despot who ruined his people for 31 years while chartering Concorde for shopping trips to Paris. His overthrow by Rwanda in 1997 ushered in a civil war that killed tens of thousands, made child-soldiering and rape routine and which, in one form or another, has continued ever since.

The Western way of helping Congo had been aid. Success had been mixed. Emergency aid let hundreds of thousands of war refugees eat and find shelter. Health and education programmes delivered basic care and teaching to millions more. Foreign-funded wildlife and forest conservation efforts saved some gorillas and

373

chimpanzees and prevented the extinction of the okapi, a jungle horse with a zebra's legs and a giraffe's face.

But the aid world didn't build or maintain hardly any of the roads or railways needed to reach across Congo's vast interior and unlock its potential. The world's loans to the dysfunctional Congolese government, which might have gone to such projects, were a disaster: corruption soared, repayments were missed and by 2009 the government was $10 billion in debt. And despite the UN assembling the world's biggest peacekeeping force in the east of the country, it had consistently failed to keep any kind of peace. Meanwhile the West's appetite for diamonds, gold and coltan, used for batteries in mobiles and laptops, gave Congo's wars a commercial incentive.

This corrosion found some of its fullest expression in Kinshasa, a megacity of somewhere around 10 million – like Lagos, nobody could really say – and one of the most lawless metropolises anywhere in the world. The Congolese nickname for Kinshasa at independence was 'Kin la Belle', Kin the Beautiful. By the time I first visited in 2008 that had been changed to 'Kin la Poubelle', Kin the Bin. Terrifying gangs of stoned children with Kalashnikovs ruled different neighbourhoods. At night gunfire echoed across the city. To drive around Kinshasa, without the benefit of street lights or any light from its buildings, felt like venturing out after the apocalypse. My abiding memory of Kinshasa was a moment at the city's airport. Waiting for my bags to appear on the carousel after returning from a trip up-country, I watched as 20 cloth sacks emerged, leaking dark, sticky blood, the last of them tied in a cinch around a crocodile's tail that was curling up out of the bag.

This was where the China Railway Engineering Corporation (CREC) had chosen to make its fortune. Where others saw a sucking vortex, Mathis saw a greater need for his services. At times, his enthusiasm ran ahead of his language skills. 'The first one who eats the crab is really a hero!' he exclaimed at one point. I must have looked confused. 'We will transform this city!' translated Mathis. 'It will be fantastic!'

Mathis was not the first Chinese to set out for Africa with high ambition. The Silk Road linked Alexandria to Beijing more than two thousand years ago. Records of the Tang dynasty (AD 618–907) mentioned gifts from rulers in Africa such as a rhinoceros and bird's eggs, as well as knowledge of the cities of Berbera on the Somali coast and Malindi in Kenya. In AD 750, a Chinese army officer called Du Huan was captured by Arab soldiers during a battle in modern-day Uzbekistan. He travelled widely with his Arab masters and, after eventually escaping, returned to Guangzhou 12 years later to write a book in which he described visiting what appeared to be Ethiopia, which he called 'Molin'. Steadily, exchanges between Africa and China became more frequent and formal. By the ninth century, Arabs living in Guangzhou were importing East African slaves to China, where fashionable and wealthy merchantmen used the imposing, dark-skinned *kunlun* as doormen. Envoys from Zengdan ('Land of Blacks') were also visiting China from the eleventh century. Sung dynasty porcelain (AD 960–1279) found in Zimbabwe and South Africa suggests long-distance trade around this time.

As China and the West compete for Africa's resources in the twenty-first century, this history of seemingly friendly pre-European contact between Asia and Africa has assumed strategic significance. Of crucial importance to China is rewriting the history of foreign exploration of Africa to emphasize that China arrived first, something about which there is already no doubt. In 1320, 26 years before Jaume Ferrer even set out from Majorca for West Africa, a Chinese cartographer called Zhu Siben drew a map showing Africa as an inverted triangle, suggesting China already knew of a southern passage around the Cape. Though Zhu's map has not survived, a second map based on it in 1402 filled in more detail, including the existence of Lake Victoria and Madagascar.

In 1417, the Ming dynasty explorer Zheng He, who had already made six voyages across the Indian Ocean with a fleet of up to 300 ships, sailed to Mogadishu, then tacked south to Malindi and possibly Zanzibar, Madagascar and South Africa. Here European and Chinese explorers might have met one day had not China's exploration ended abruptly in 1424 when a new isolationist emperor ascended the throne and closed China off from the world.

China's efforts to establish its pre-eminence centre on Zheng He's exploration of East Africa. It claims samples of hair and skin from villagers in Lamu, an ancient Arab trading post turned tourist resort between Mogadishu and Malindi, contain DNA with traces of Chinese ancestry. China has also paid several million dollars for a team of Kenyan and Chinese archaeologists and divers to search for the wreck of one of Zheng's ships, which, according to legend, struck rocks off an island near Lamu. Around 20 surviving crew were said to have swum ashore, married locally and built a village, which they named Shangha, supposedly after Shanghai. American and European historians tend to dismiss the story as fanciful. And it is easy to see the leaden hand of Chinese propagandists in the story of the 'China Girl', a 19-year-old from Shangha called Mwamaka Sharifu. In 2005, claiming their DNA tests showed she was, in fact, Chinese, Beijing's diplomats whisked Sharifu to a university in China, then a series of television chat shows, film premieres and mall openings. The *China Daily* reported the girl was delighted to be 'home'. 'China is far better than I thought,' said Sharifu, apparently suddenly fluent in both platitude and Mandarin. 'It is so beautiful and well planned. The scholarship will change my life and the lives of the rest of my family. I believe that through hard work – a characteristic of the Chinese – I can make a better living.'

The sceptics had a point. But they missed a bigger one. The importance of this history is less in the details than in the broad facts of what appeared to be a flourishing fifteenth-century friendship – and which, by implication, might yet be again. Herman Kiriama, lead archaeologist at the National Museums of Kenya, said: 'We're discovering that the Chinese had a very different approach from the Europeans to East Africa. Because they came with gifts from the emperor, it shows they saw us as equals.'

China's recent success in Africa had much to do with the way it projected itself as the opposite of the West. Unlike aid agencies, the Chinese didn't pay much and working conditions could be dire. But everywhere you went in Africa you could see with your own eyes how, unlike aid, the Chinese were changing the continent with extraordinary speed. The Chinese could be seen pumping oil from Sudan to Angola, logging in Liberia and Gabon, mining in Zambia and Congo and Ghana and Zimbabwe and farming from Kenya to Nigeria. Where they were not digging or farming or cutting down trees, the Chinese were buying, from a $5.5 billion stake in Africa's largest bank, South Africa's Standard Bank, to a $14 million investment in a mobile phone company in Somalia. China was quickly becoming part of the African fabric. Cheap Chinese knick-knacks filled street markets, Asian fusion was the fashion in high-end African restaurants, and news stands sold the *China Daily* and cheap Chinese cigarettes.

China's presence was most visible in the way it was bringing Africa the one gift the continent had always needed from foreigners: infrastructure. Overnight, it seemed, Chinese contractors in hard hats were standing over construction crews on every road from Equatorial Guinea to Ethiopia, and building dams, hospitals, universities, sports stadiums, airports and presidential palaces across the continent. The new experience these roads and buildings created – and the Chinese engineers in luminous jackets now at work at seemingly every thoroughfare and chokepoint in Africa – ensured that China's presence on the continent was unmissable.

China also liked to package its infrastructure projects in outrageous, headline-grabbing barters. Between 2004 and 2007, China offered Angola $7.5 billion in soft infrastructure loans in return for oil concessions; the money was earmarked for new transcontinental railways linking Angola's coastline with Congo and Zambia. In 2010, China said it would build three oil refineries and a petrochemical complex in Nigeria – where it already had several billion dollars invested in oil production – for a stunning $23 billion. When I asked Mathis how he'd ended up in Congo, he told me that, as a French-language student in Beijing in 2008, he was plucked from class to translate negotiations between the French-speaking Congolese government and the state-owned CREC. CREC was proposing to build thousands of kilometres of roads and railways, 31 hospitals, 145 health centres and two universities – an overhaul of Congo's national infrastructure estimated at $6 billion – for which, as part-payment, China would receive $3 billion in concessions to mine copper and cobalt.

China's infrastructure was the final element in the conquest of Africa's open space. Farming was filling Africa's rural voids. Off-grid innovations like mobiles and solar were doing the same in the gap left by much heavy infrastructure, just as innovations such as mobile banking and biometric citizenry were for more intangible hollows. But much of Africa's economy was still accounted for by raw materials, and those needed roads, railways, ports and airports.

Inevitably, the dramatic changes wrought by the Chinese in Africa raised questions about the rich world's approach to the continent. Chief among them: did West really know best?

CREC's vision of a remade Kinshasa was certainly more impressive than any aid project. Laid out as a model at the Kinshasa offices of the young government spokesman for the public works, Barnabé Milinganyo Isombya, the new capital as envisioned by CREC would have tree-lined boulevards, gracious shopping malls, luminous green grass and a Congo River whose muddy rapids would somehow become placid and sparkling-blue. It was Singapore transplanted to central Africa. After taking 30 minutes to reach Barnabé's office in a decrepit taxi bouncing across Kinshasa's garbage-compacted streets, my expression may have betrayed some scepticism because Barnabé suddenly shrieked: 'You think it is unbelievable! It is not unbelievable! It is believable!'

The atmosphere had changed in an instant. Suddenly I was just another white man insulting Congo. Barnabé, I saw, was rounding on me, trembling and bunching his fists. I decided to pretend I hadn't noticed.

'We did 50 years with the Europeans and the IMF and we did not succeed!' shouted Barnabé, wagging a finger in my face. 'Before that there was 100 years of colonization! And we got nothing! Not even any roads! The Belgians – *they* got roads. *They* got rich!' Barnabé steadied himself and became calmer. 'Now we are beginning a new method with the Chinese,' he said. 'We will see.'

The remaking of Kinshasa was part of President Joseph Kabila's vision, explained Barnabé. The idea was to finish by 2016. 'We are working day and night for seven years to achieve that. Anyone can dream but when a chief dreams, it counts. Joseph Kabila dreams of rehabilitation and modernization. Are you going to refuse his dream?'

Carefully, I asked Barnabé why he thought the Chinese were helping the President realize his grand ambitions when the Europeans and others were not. But Barnabé had regained his composure. 'The difference is in the Chinese approach,' he replied. 'The Europeans give donations or credit totalling $3 billion to Congo but now, with interest, they calculate the total as $11–12 billion. We cannot pay that. Then the Europeans come, and they are paid very well, they always have holidays, they have villas, Blackberries, five women each. *Vraiment!* And at the end of it, they only finance 12 kilometres of road on this plan while always saying they are going to cut us off.

'The Chinese are completely different. There is no debt. Everyone always tells us that Congo is rich, so the Chinese come with their engineers and calculate the value of our minerals. And once they do that, whether it's $3 billion or $9 billion, we say: "We keep that for you. Bring money." And they bring money. But you cannot eat cash. So we say: "Make a hospital, make a school, make a road." And they do.'

Barnabé's outburst was a reminder that in Africa development was not a dry, technical subject but a source of burning shame and big dreams. His description of the difference between Chinese and Western behaviour in what had become a new twenty-first-century Scramble for Africa was also as good as any I had heard. This time round, the old colonial powers and the US were united against the emerging upstarts led by China. There was no doubt China was the coming force. Two-way trade between Africa and China stood at $3 billion in 1995. By 2000, it was $11 billion, by 2006 it was $55 billion and in 2008 it hit $107 billion, ensuring China overtook the US as Africa's single largest trade partner.

China's spectacular entrance soon prompted jealous head-lines in Europe and the US about a Chinese takeover of Africa. Apparently without irony, European and American businessmen, diplomats and journalists lined up to accuse China of imperialism. The Chinese were said to be 'grabbing' resources, spreading cor-ruption and neglecting to share the benefits of a country's natural riches with the population. Philippe Maystadt, President of the European Investment Bank, said he was in 'clear competition with the Chinese banks' and complained his opponents weren't playing fair. 'They don't bother about social or human rights conditions,' he said. Western diplomats began describing China as a 'rogue donor' dispensing 'toxic aid' and briefing journalists with apocry-phal rumours of China importing forced prison labour. In a cable released by Wikileaks, US Assistant Secretary for African Affairs Johnnie Carson described China as 'a very aggressive and perni-cious economic competitor . . . [with] no morals'. In 2011, the US Secretary of State Hillary Clinton warned on a visit to Zambia: 'We saw that during colonial times, it is easy to come in, take out natural resources, pay off leaders and leave . . . When people come to Africa to make investments, we want them to do well but also want them to do good . . . We don't want to see a new colonialism in Africa. We don't want them to undermine good governance in Africa.'

It was unclear how patronizing Africans and insulting the Chinese would persuade them to turn against each other. Clinton's warnings were, in any case, too late. By 2011 China's spectacular deals, coming at a time when liberal capitalism was looking distinctly tired, had transformed the narrative of foreign engagement in Africa. A senior IMF banker once told me through gritted teeth how in 2007 he had been close to agreeing a new $5 billion loan to Angola – after years of talks centred on how the IMF could ensure Angola used the money properly – only for Angola to tell the IMF one day that it didn't need its money. Beijing had offered it $5 billion soft loans and infrastructure deals in return for oil concessions. What's more, the banker spat, it had agreed its deal 'over a single bloody weekend'.

China's deal in Congo dismayed the West almost as much. The IMF argued that a Congolese guarantee to China that it would recoup at least $3 billion in minerals was an IOU on Congo's national assets and, therefore, a new debt. That fell foul of conditions for writing off Congo's foreign debt, which require the debtor take on no new loans. 'If the Congolese take the Chinese deal,' an American diplomat in Kinshasa told me grumpily, 'they will not get any more of our support.' He missed the point. If Barnabé was any reflection of national sentiment, the Congolese were hoping not to need any.

China was outwitting the West so deftly because it moved quickly and didn't tell Africans what they needed but simply asked, then gave. By backing private business with state support, it could also accept far greater risk and a far longer return on investment than Western businesses that were prisoner to quarterly shareholder reports.

Almost none of this seemed to have registered with American and European diplomats in Kinshasa. One talked airily about the day when China joined the top table as 'more of a player'. Another sniffily dismissed Chinese construction as of dubious standard. 'The Chinese do work quickly so it's an easy way to get your infrastructure built,' she said. 'But is it the right way? Will we be repairing these roads in 50 years?'

For its part, China was keen to project itself as the new foreign power in Africa. As an indication of its growing confidence, in 2009 its normally secretive ambassadors suddenly became visible. In Kinshasa, I was ushered into the Chinese embassy – as vast, red and spartan as any Party building in Beijing – and given a cup of green tea and an hour's chat with Ambassador Wu Zexian. Wu was charming and cheerful and instructed me to ask anything I wanted. 'We Chinese need to speak more if we want to be understood,' he explained.

I asked Wu whether investing $9 billion in Congo wasn't plain crazy. Wu laughed. 'Yes,' he said, 'there is a risk. In the short term, there are lots of problems.' It had taken him six months just to extract CREC's giant machines from Congolese customs, he said. 'But in the long term, not much risk. In 50 years, we will still be here. And so will all those mines.'

This was, he added, a 'new way of aid'. 'This country needs infrastructure now. It cannot wait. That is why we offer this new model of development assistance. Before, African countries never profited from their resources. Some even said they were *un malheur*, a curse. Now they help them build infrastructure. The mines will pay us back little by little, so it's also profitable for Chinese banks and contractors. It's a co-operation that will last 20 or 30 years. And if it goes well, we can find more mines and continue like this.'

What did Wu make of the West's mistrustful reaction to China's plans? I asked. 'It's a big problem. The West is *méfiant*,' he said, using the French for 'suspicious'. 'They say: "This co-operation will increase Congolese debt." We tell them: "You are mistaken. This is not debt but a guarantee. And we are spending hundreds of millions of dollars and we need this." But the West doesn't listen. It manufactures a situation where the Congolese are forced to choose between China and the West. And the Congolese get very annoyed. I think it's a shame for the West to try to stop the Congolese from pursuing development how they wish. It's a great pity, because this is a country that needs to develop.'

The ambassador paused to sip his tea, then carefully placed his cup back on its saucer. Foreigners' different behaviour in Africa revealed their different attitudes to Africans, said Wu. 'The West says: "This country has a lot of problems." We think that does not help. We try not to criticize their problems so much. We try to encourage them to work hard to fix their problems.' China preferred to stress how a country had huge potential, said Wu. And it wasn't as if aid was an unqualified good. It was not efficient. It was not a solution. 'Sometimes aid workers spend a lot of money and achieve nothing. If they had achieved anything here, would Congo be where it is now?'

The ambassador took another sip. 'This is not, in the end, a problem of finance or economics,' he said. 'It's a problem of dignity. There is this Western distrust of China. There is the way they tell Africa it is poor.' Europe and the US had to 'change its mentality and its way of analysing things. Always telling everyone how to be. We are offering the Congolese a new way out, a new way for them to move forward. But the West makes them feel *coincées*. They are squashed again.'

Wu watched quietly as I took my notes. Then he said: 'You know, China used to be locked away. But then we said we must open the country and contribute to building peace and harmony and a world where everyone develops together. That other way, that old way – it's just not all that effective. *On a changé*.'

*

China would thrive in Africa, above all because it provided an alternative to the West – and one that didn't lecture Africans on the virtues of rich-world civilization. Africans now had a choice not to listen to those presuming to tell it what to do – and in that moment China found opportunity, the West lost half a millennium of authority and Africa glimpsed its freedom.

For the same reason, Western ideas of a Chinese takeover of Africa fell short. China's advances in Africa were about Western loss and China's gain, inasmuch as Africa reflected a new global reality. But to imagine that Africa was being passed from one power bloc to another was to think of Africa in outdated, imperial terms. Africa was still a trove of raw ingredients, whether for farming, industry, energy or construction. But in a post-colonial world that drew suitors, not conquerors. The new African dynamic was not subservience but assertion. Africans were no longer spectators to their own destiny but directors.

Again, the crux was freedom. Eleni was making money, but what truly interested her was building a nation. Denis was profiting too, but he was helping change the lives of his old friends in Murang'a. One day, in the departure lounge of Entebbe airport in Uganda, I stopped at a new kiosk called Good African Coffee. More striking even than the excellent espresso was the company slogan: 'Trade not Aid'.

When I called the boss, Andrew Rugasira, he told me he had set up his company as a commercial and political concern. Andrew conceded that aid had made Africa more populous, healthier and better-educated, and helped create the conditions it needed to take off. There was also still plenty of suffering in Africa, he said, which emergency aid could help alleviate. But beyond that, Andrew argued, aid could and should do no more. Aid was about allowing people to live longer. Economic development was about allowing people to live better, and that was very different. The fuel in an economy's engine was not assistance but autonomy and sovereignty and freedom – entrepreneurs like him running their own show, making their own decisions, plotting their own futures. Aid had helped, once. But Africa's new path lay in leaving aid behind. Those who talked about a Chinese takeover of Africa had yet to rid themselves of the old assumption that Africa couldn't lift itself out of poverty. He wondered whether such a view wasn't ingrained in Westerners. Looking back at the history of their involvement in Africa, he questioned whether the West's entire purpose hadn't been to 'undermine the creativity to lift Africans out of poverty, and the integrity and dignity of the people. It says, "These are people who cannot figure out how to develop".' That, in the end, was the most exciting thing about Africa's new reality, said Andrew. It gave Africans the chance to prove the Westerners flat wrong.

This new African assertiveness also meant China's presence was tolerated only as long as it suited Africa. Often it didn't. In Ethiopia in April 2007, eastern rebels killed nine Chinese workers and another 65 labourers at a Chinese oilfield installation, accusing them of propping up a repressive state. The same year workers protesting pay and conditions killed their Chinese manager at a stone-crushing plant in Mombasa, Kenya. In West Africa, when Ghanaians found their goldfields flooded with 12,000 illegal Chinese gold miners, they too reacted violently. In 2012 a 16-year-old Chinese miner was killed in one government crackdown and the following year the state began a mass deportation of Chinese. Whatever Wu said about a 'new way of aid', Africans perceived some rather old-fashioned attitudes behind China's operations on the continent. Writing in the *Financial Times* in March 2013, Lamido Sanusi said: 'China takes our primary goods and sells us manufactured ones. This was also the essence of colonialism. Africa is now willingly opening itself up to a new form of imperialism.'

Among the most contentious of China's initiatives in Africa were its investments in Zambian copper. In 2005, 49 workers died in an accident at a Chinese copper mine in Chambishi in the centre of the country. The following year a panicked Chinese manager shot and wounded five Zambian workers who stormed the bosses' compound. After that, China became the central political issue in Zambia. Populist opposition leader Michael Sata, who accused the Chinese of paying slave wages and shoddy safety practices – when he wasn't being overtly racist – won power in 2011.

In Lusaka, I was granted an audience with Ambassador Li Qing-min. When I asked about the safety standards in Chinese mines, Li replied, brightly: 'Some Chinese people [in Zambia] and some companies are criminal.' Still, Li insisted, Zambians and Chinese were 'just like brothers'.

Just without much brotherly love between them, it seemed. In the years since, Zambian workers have murdered two more Chinese managers at two different mines. At a third, a pair of Chinese managers opened fire on protesting workers, injuring 11 of them.

If China was overstating its good relations on the continent, it was also exaggerating the size of its presence. That $23 billion investment in Nigeria? Never happened. The $9 billion Congo deal? Quietly reduced to $6 billion. In February 2013, a US Congress report found the US was still the bigger investor in Africa, putting $16.6 billion into Africa between 2007 and 2011 to China's $12.8 billion. A UN report found China wasn't even the biggest Asian investor in Africa. The foreign country with most investment in Africa was France ($58 billion), then the US ($57 billion), then Britain ($48 billion), followed by Malaysia ($19 billion) and South Africa ($18 billion). China came sixth with $16 billion, around a quarter of France's total.

If there was any lingering doubt about where power now lay, a second set of figures scuppered any last suspicions that Africa was any foreigner's to own. In 2011, China invested $4 billion in South Africa. South Africa, on the other hand, invested $12.8 billion in China. Who owned whom?

China wasn't taking over Africa. Nobody ever would again.

FOURTEEN

THE NEW AFRICA

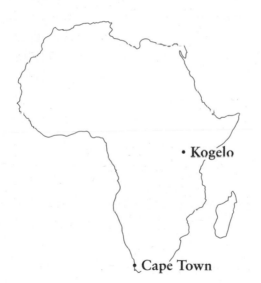

In his memoir, *Dreams from My Father*, Barack Obama wrote how, visiting his father's ancestral home in Kogelo in western Kenya in 1988, he found his relatives living in timeless peace. 'I began to imagine an unchanging rhythm of days, lived on firm soil where you could wake up each morning and know that all was as it had been yesterday, where you saw how the things that you used had been made and could recite the lives of those who had made them.' Twenty years later, in the days before Obama's election as US President, I stayed in Kogelo with Malik Obama, Barack's half-brother and head of the Obama clan, the Jor'Obama. Malik had invited me sleep on the floor outside his bedroom in his grass-roofed hut and watch the election with him and the rest of the clan, who had been arriving for weeks from their farms around Lake Victoria.

It turned out Malik had a hidden agenda for asking me to stay. Around 50 members of the extended Obama clan, the Jor'Obama, had made the trek to Kogelo and they were expecting Malik, clan headman, to feed them meat and beer for weeks. Within hours of my arrival, Malik took me on a tour of Kogelo in his battered 20-year-old Toyota, pausing every now and then to bargain briefly with the owner of a goat, truss the animal and sling it onto the back seat. Malik would then nod expectantly at me. I bought three goats on that first excursion. Before I left Kogelo I'd paid for several more goats and two colossal bulls, which Malik had me hold down while he slit their throats.

The better I got to know the Jor'Obama, drinking Tusker around a giant fire at night, the more astonished I became at the unlikeliness of Barack's ascension. This was a family that had gone from barefoot farming to the White House in two generations. There were so many improbabilities in this story – so much audacity, to use Barack's word – that it took a peculiar skill even to imagine it was possible. The family themselves had no doubt. But on the eve of the vote, I confessed to Malik that the long odds of his brother's story were making me increasingly unsure.

Malik said I needed to adjust my perspective. I regarded Kogelo and Washington as different worlds, separated by their distinct positions on a linear scale of development. The Jor'Obama, he said, took a three-dimensional view. All humanity was connected. If there were different levels of material or political or educational advancement in the world, through people, these were still linked. Malik himself was a case in point, spending half the year in Kogelo as village chief and half in Washington, where he worked as an accountant. He held these two different realities in his head simultaneously and could switch between them as easily as he would change from pants into a *babban riga*. By my two-dimensional Western view of the world, said Malik, 'my brother is not meant to accomplish half of what he's done. It's meant to be impossible.' Yet it would happen, said Malik. And a day later, it did.

That mental agility, a kind of heightened imagination, freed from space and time, is essential to understanding the new Africa. Africa is no longer one place at one at one time. It is third world and first world, Cape Town and Kogelo, talking drums and mobile phones. Change in Africa is fast and deep but above all uneven – and the size of the continent means it can accommodate all these degrees of advancement simultaneously.

I'd seen this benign schizophrenia at work elsewhere in Africa. In the richer neighbourhoods of Lagos, Nairobi or Johannesburg, young executives would tell me how they had gone to school under trees and college in Europe or the US. During the holidays they would abandon their white-walled, white-floored apartments and travel a dirt road home to the old village where they'd swap their suits for T-shirts and sandals and cook over a fire. Just after South Africa hosted a triumphant soccer World Cup in 2010, I saw Desmond Tutu again in Cape Town and found all trace of his earlier uncertainty gone. 'I wish you could meet some of the young people I've been meeting,' he said. 'They take your breath away. Man! You sit there with your mouth agape, listening to these young people. They really can make this country hum! They do not see themselves as handicapped. They see all the opportunities, all the things they can become. The sky is the limit now! I get the sense we are a scintillating success waiting to happen! It's like, it's like . . .' Tutu trailed off, searching the heavens for inspiration. 'It's like we've become *Americans*!' he said.

Africa is not yet in danger of losing its African-ness – it hasn't had the time. It also doesn't have the need. In West Africa, just as Western banks were nosediving in 2008, I came across Ecobank, which had added 200 branches across the continent in three years to make a total network of 620 in 26 countries, and a workforce of 11,000 managing a balance sheet of $8 billion. When I queried CEO Arnold Epke on his choice of headquarters location – the tiny West African country of Togo – he replied that success made my question redundant. 'Warren Buffet comes from Nebraska,' he said. 'It's not where you're from, it's what you do.'

Sometimes Africa's new complications had an almost circular symmetry. Like the way the birthplace of mankind was also the place most likely to discover aliens. Africa had eight space programmes. Most were still in their infancy. But since 2003 Nigeria had launched five satellites. In 2012 South Africa won a global contest to host the world's most ambitious astronomy project. With thousands of radio dishes to be built across Africa by 2017, the Square Kilometre Array (SKA) was to be 50 to 100 times more powerful than any previous telescope. It would have two main missions: solving the Big Bang and finding extra-terrestrials. At the SKA's data analysis centre in Cape Town, which one day will require more computing power than in 2010 powered the entire internet, telescope manager William Esterhuye held up a printout of the SKA's first readings. 'The origin of life is one thing,' he said. 'This is the origin of everything.'

Foreigners often find this diverse and complicated Africa confusing. Much of it, like the space programmes, they ignore. Sometimes Africans assist them in this maintenance of old stereotypes. In Kenya, for instance, it is the Africa of Karen Blixen's *Out of Africa* – safaris, savannahs, sunsets, all overlaid by imperial glamour – that draws hundreds of thousands of tourists every year. So, naturally, that is the Africa the Kenyan tourist industry gives them. Planes arriving from Europe disembark hundreds of Europeans and Americans, Japanese and Chinese ready-dressed in safari suits, as though they expect to step off into the bush. Working from century-old photographs, Kenya's decorators have ensured that the big hotels in Nairobi – the Norfolk, the Fairview, the Stanley – remain wedding-cake affairs with high ceilings, wood panelling, bellboys in scarlet tunics and verandas appointed with rattan planters and fans fashioned from ancient airplane propellers. There is even a Karen Blixen museum in the author's old house and a Finch Hatton game lodge, which takes its lead from Blixen's lover's 'refusal to abandon home comforts, culture and cuisine while on safari' and insistence on 'fine china and crystal, [and the] gramophone recordings of Mozart'.

The same accommodating approach can be heard in souvenir shops, where the staff play the *Lion King* soundtrack on a loop but listen to punk-rap (South Africa), heavy rock (Botswana) and Goth rock (Nairobi) in their own time. It explains why waiters serve crocodile and warthog in tourist lodges but eat sushi or pizza or pumpkin risotto when out on the town themselves. It accounts for how burly Afrikaner Dutchmen in safari shorts can guide tourists around game parks and vineyards near Cape Town, then change into even tighter shorts to enjoy Africa's biggest gay scene by night.

Risotto, gay bars, billion-dollar banks – this blossoming complexity is what you might expect when a people climb out of the narrowness of the Rift. It illustrates a final way that the new Africa will change the world. In time, humanity will no longer view itself as split according to the accident of birth between developed and undeveloped, rich and poor, American and African. Instead, our differences should come to feel less as sources of division than of diversity. It's the same richness in unity that, half a century after the civil rights struggle, allowed the US to elect its first African-American President. On a visit to Africa in 2013, Obama told students in Cape Town that it once seemed inconceivable 'that a prisoner [could] become a President [or that] an African-American President might address an integrated audience at South Africa's oldest university. It would have seemed impossible.' What it took, like the new Africa, was a little imagination.

I also began to think there was an alternative way to look at Africa's suffering. A part of freedom is ripping away. Even as it is inspiring and triumphant and enriching, it is bloody and uncertain and destructive. Freedom should mean peace, eventually. But you often have to fight for it.

Perhaps, then, adversity has been good for Africa. To survive in a continent with little security, almost no guarantees and few formal jobs, where governments were often a hindrance, you have to hustle. Eight out of every 10 Africans work for themselves. To be born in Africa is, in many ways, to be born an entrepreneur.

In the aftermath of another African disaster, rich-world economists typically predict doom. But that is to misunderstand how trouble forges resilience. In the days after the Westgate attack, my Silicon Savannah friend Denis Karema surprised me by predicting a golden future: the market for his panic button had just exploded, and the attack had given him an idea for another app that stored vital data like blood type and next of kin. Talking about the Rwandan genocide one day, Kagame said: 'All these challenges, these injustices, I have found they tend to strengthen us rather than weaken us. I think my life really prepared me. I never run away from a problem. I just get up and move towards it.'

In the two weeks after Africa's most mythic freedom fighter died, I took a 5,000-kilometre road trip around South Africa visiting the prisons, courtrooms, townships and protest sites that were the backdrop to Nelson Mandela's long struggle. I spoke to his former comrades, his former jailers and even, sitting on the floor of a bottle store in the village where he was born, a litre of beer between her legs, a 98-year-old woman who wailed that she should have been his wife. My last stop was a small *Highveld* town called Brandfort in the rolling plains about an hour north of the old Afrikaner capital, Bloemfontein. This was where the apartheid government had 'banned' Winnie Mandela for 10 years in the 1970s and 1980s.

In a letter to Winnie soon after the apartheid authorities first imprisoned her in 1970, Mandela wrote:

You may find that the cell is an ideal place to learn to know yourself, to search realistically and regularly the processes of your own mind and feelings . . . Internal factors may be even more crucial in assessing one's development as a human being: honesty, sincerity, simplicity, humility, purity, generosity, absence of vanity, readiness to serve your fellow men – qualities within the reach of every soul – are the foundation of one's spiritual life. The cell gives you the opportunity to look daily into your entire conduct to overcome the bad and develop whatever is good in you. Never forget that a saint is a sinner that keeps on trying.

It was an unusual reaction to privation. Being denied freedom, Mandela was saying, being stripped of all things and all choice, was a useful aid to introspection and to the imagining of a new and better future path. It was the beginning of a process of mellowing that would allow Mandela to emerge from 27 years of prison in 1990 with a message of forgiveness and reconciliation, of how freedom was meaningless without peace – an extraordinary about-turn for which Mandela came to be seen, almost unanimously, as the finest ever articulation of the human spirit.

What is often forgotten is that Mandela's conversion did not come easily. In a section of his diary edited out of his ghostwritten autobiography, *Long Walk to Freedom*, Mandela wrote that in the 1950s, 'I was bitter and felt ever more strongly that SA whites needed another Isandlwana,' referring to the 1879 battlefield where 20,000 Zulus wiped out 1,350 British soldiers. As he travelled around South Africa as an underground agitator, Mandela wrote that he imagined rural landscapes as battlefields where 'the sweet air will smell of gunfire' and cities as front lines where 'elegant buildings will crash down and streets will be splashed with blood'.

Perhaps unsurprisingly, many of Mandela's comrades were suspicious of his later transformation to an icon of peace. It was the rebel's old dilemma: romantic revenge versus the dull pragmatism of peace. Other ANC leaders argued that peace and freedom were one thing, but that without justice, punishment and restitution, without giving full vent to their righteous anger, such things were pointless. In 2013, Mandela's fellow liberation leader Robert Mugabe told an interviewer: 'Mandela has gone a bit too far in doing good to the non-black communities, really in some cases at the expense of [blacks]. That is being too saintly, too good, too much of a saint.'

One of those who disagreed most fiercely with Mandela was Winnie. The pair separated soon after Mandela was released from prison in 1990. Twenty years later she gave an interview to the writer V.S. Naipaul and his wife Nadira in which she said: 'Mandela let us down. He agreed to a bad deal for the blacks. Economically, we are still on the outside. So many who gave their lives in the Struggle have died unrewarded. Mandela was not the only man who suffered. There were many others, hundreds who languished in prison and died. Mandela did go to prison and he went in there as a burning young revolutionary. But look what came out.'

The gulf between Winnie and Nelson was the difference between having the courage to fight in the Rift and having the wisdom to perceive a way out. I drove to Winnie's old home in the township outside Brandfort. Hut 802, where Winnie was under house arrest from 1977 to 1985, was actually half a hut, a tiny three-roomed semi-detached place with bare breeze-block walls, a tin roof and no electricity, running water or indoor toilet. Next door was a small, burnt-out wreck of a building. As I pulled up, four elderly women were holding a service of remembrance for Nelson Mandela in front.

I introduced myself and Nora Nomafu shook my hand. She had lived in Hut 806 all her life. Winnie had been her best friend, though not, said Nora, at first. 'We were not even allowed to speak to her when she arrived. The women who worked in town told their children: "Don't go near this certain Communist woman. She is very dangerous." So when she called to the children, they would run away and scream.' Nora's idea of community was offended by such behaviour. 'I could not tolerate it,' she said. 'So I asked my little boy to help her fetch her water in a bucket. And then Winnie got ill and her lawyer got permission for me to help her and it was then that we discussed so many things.'

Winnie used her standing in the ANC to bring food, blankets and clothes to Brandfort's township. Later she built a clinic and a crèche. It was the clinic in front of whose remains we were standing. The apartheid police burned it down one night. Winnie ordered it be left derelict as a monument to their thuggery. 'She was not even angry,' said Nora. 'She was so strong. She would just say: "I know these dogs. They can kill you any time."'

Nora said Winnie relished confrontation. She often defied her banning order by going to funerals and receiving visitors. At a time when whites refused to handle money touched by blacks and ordered them to leave it on the counter where it could be wiped down, Nora remembered a day when Winnie spent an hour trying on expensive dresses and shoes at a whites-only store in town. 'When she came out, all the police from Bloemfontein were outside,' laughed Nora. 'Madiba was forgiveness and reconciliation. But Winnie was *strength*.'

Strength can be terrific. With her husband and hundreds of ANC leaders in jail or exile, Winnie kept the ANC alive from Hut 802, welcoming journalists and leaders like Jesse Jackson and Ted Kennedy. But strength can be terrible, too. Even as Nelson began to talk peace with his apartheid oppressors, Winnie was urging the ANC to kill them all. 'With our boxes of matches and our necklaces we shall liberate this country,' she told a crowd in 1986, a reference to the practice of 'necklacing' suspected informers with tyres filled with burning petrol.

The violence of those years has haunted Winnie ever since. In 2013, the bodies of two men killed by the Mandela Football Club, a militia she kept around her in Soweto in the last years of apartheid, were exhumed for re-examination. I asked Nora whether she thought all the fighting damaged Winnie. 'She did not show her suffering,' said Nora. 'She would say she needed us to be strong so as to face the Boers.' To Nora, by burying her suffering, Winnie had shown true courage. That was how the brave dealt with injury. But when I pressed her, Nora sighed and said, yes, she thought Winnie was deeply wounded. The pain had made a twist in her soul. 'I think she was bitter,' she said. 'Because they took Madiba from her when she was still young with that burning love.'

After I said goodbye to Nora I drove into Brandfort to meet Charmaine Albert. Charmaine was 52 and owned a farm on a gentle hill outside town surrounded by cattle plains and thorny scrub.

On it were several monuments to South Africa's past wars. One recorded where Afrikaner settlers defeated the Basotho tribe in 1858. There was also a cemetery commemorating those who died in Kitchener's concentration camps during the 1899–1902 Boer War. Brandfort had been the third-biggest camp in the country, holding thousands of Boers. British officers were said to have looked on, sipping sherry and whisky on the balcony of the Brandfort Hotel as their wretched charges starved and succumbed to disease.

In 1993 Charmaine bought the hotel, turned it into a cavernous family home and set about creating a small publishing business dedicated to uncovering what had happened in the war and especially in the camps. Charmaine gave me three of her books. The broad outlines of the history were familiar. The commanders of the British Army, Lord Roberts and Lord Kitchener, introduced a new way of war, the scorched earth campaign. Families thought to be providing support to the Boer guerrillas were interned in camps. Somehow my English education recalled this episode as a decent and sensible policy to keep the innocent out of the way while the men sorted out their differences. Now I read that it was nothing of the sort. Families were given five minutes to gather up their belongings and leave their homes before their houses were torched and their livestock – millions of animals – shot. Charmaine had found several photographs of the evictions, beautiful homesteads in flames surrounded by great plains of dead cows and sheep. Just as their commanders seemed to be trying to torture their enemy into submission, British soldiers appeared to have been given free rein inside the camps, sometimes raping at will. Roberts and Kitchener also insured the camps were overcrowded, with little shelter, food or water. Typhoid and dysentery were soon rife. Children died in their thousands.

I asked Charmaine if I could see the camp cemetery on her farm and she gave me directions. I drove out of town, turned onto a dirt track, passed through two gates and then, as Charmaine had instructed, parked and set out on foot across a wide field towards a small copse. Inside the trees was a raised white-marble plinth about the size of a soccer field. A few solitary headstones stood out from the stone. Almost everyone seemed to have died in October or November 1901. Most of them were children. To one side was a headstone the length of a bus on which was written *Kinders 15 Jaar En Onder*: children aged 15 and under. On it I counted 1,260 names. Many shared the same surnames. There were 10 de Klerks, 12 Barnards, 15 Krugers, 17 Bothas and 26 du Plessis.

I knew the facts about apartheid's origins, but its emotional pull had always eluded me. How could anyone dream up such a hateful system, and as late as 1948? Here was my answer. Apartheid was an act of revenge, cold and deliberate. Imagine the hate those concentration camps could inspire. Imagine being the only surviving son of a family whose children had been wiped out. The names on the Brandfort monument were the names of the men that had created apartheid. Why did they loathe blacks? Because most blacks signed up with the British, who could pay them. Never again would Afrikaners and blacks live together, the survivors decided. What the English had called the Boer Wars, the Afrikaners called *Vryheidsoorloë*. The Freedom Wars. If the Afrikaners ever won their freedom back again, they decided, never again would they share it.

This, also, was the difference between Winnie and Nelson. The Afrikaners had been oppressed, beaten, murdered and tortured. When their chance came, in the name of their freedom, they had oppressed, beaten, murdered and tortured in revenge. Winnie reckoned it was now Africans' turn. She would right all the wrongs done to her and to Africa, way back to the first greedy and ignorant European to set sail for the continent.

Nelson wanted, finally, to move beyond that cycle. Winnie burned for revolution but Nelson wanted to end all revolution. He wanted to leave behind fighting and revenge, all the racists and tyrants and fanatics. He hadn't succeeded, as his fellow comrades' disappointing record showed. But the miracle was that he was even

399

able to imagine it. To take his suffering and use it as a chance to meditate, to look out from prison at 650 years of subjugation and not be bent by it, to see not just black and white but to perceive liberation instead – to 'be able to look through everything', as Charmaine put it – that was Mandela's unique gift. Through a single barred window in an icy prison cell on a godforsaken island off the bottom of the world's most troubled continent, Mandela had spied how Africans might win their freedom.

Like Mandela's successors in the ANC, some African leaders were still using the memory of imperialism's oppression to further their own careers.

Approaching his fourth decade in power, Kagame's old commander Yoweri Museveni managed to take an ever tighter grip on power in Uganda by persuading his countrymen that their big problem was not his family's looting of the state but white homosexuals bent on sodomizing their children. In Kenya, Uhuru Kenyatta performed a similar trick by turning charges by the International Criminal Court that he stirred up tribal violence in 2008 in which more than 1,000 people died into an issue not of his unsuitability for power but of Western interference. He was duly elected President in April 2013.

But others were finding it hard to control Africa's appetite for freedom once they lit the spark. Senegal was one of Africa's more prosperous nations. In early 2012, an alliance of students, rappers and the singer Youssou N'Dour forced the 85-year-old President, Abdoulaye Wade, from power after he tried to change the law to give himself a third term. The protesters saw their victory in epochal terms. 'We are building a new Africa founded on legality and democracy where power is returned to the people and we don't have these tyrants,' said Youssou. His fellow protest leader, Kilifeu, from the Dakar group Keur Gui (whose song 'Y'en a Marre' – 'I've had it' – was the movement's theme) said Senegal was changing not just its leader but also its mindset. Out was the subservience of the past. In was a new, courageous sense of citizenry that extended into all areas of life, even to such minor issues as punctuality and littering. 'We call it NTS: New Type of Senegalese,' said Kilifeu, in the tiny, bare-walled apartment he shared with 40 other activists in Dakar's back streets. Senegalese had to seize responsibility for their country and destiny, said Kilifeu. 'It's the fight of a new generation. It's what Kennedy said. "Don't ask what your country can do for you, but what you can do for your country."'

This new sense of bottom-up self-assertion spelled the beginning of the end for Africa's tyrants. It did the same for old-style aid. Some aid workers were learning to adapt. A new campaign against malaria, which saved the lives of several million Africans between 2005 and 2015, embodied the new innovation. The campaigners pulled in aid groups but also business, African governments and religious leaders by coming clean about aid's inherent self-interest and appealing to bottom lines. For business, they argued, fixing malaria improved worker productivity. For governments, a healthier population boosted GDP. For imams and priests, malaria treatment raised their standing in the community. Kagame singled out a new type of philanthropy personified by former US President Bill Clinton and former British Prime Minister Tony Blair. Both used their contacts to encourage not donations but investment. Blair, in particular, instructed his small teams of managers not to tell African governments what to do but instead trust them to know best what their countrymen wanted, then work with them to achieve those goals most efficiently. 'You have to assume that on the whole they have a better idea of what they want than you do,' Blair told me.

One day I received an email detailing a startling example of this more deferential aid. In 2012, on a visit to rebel areas in southern Sudan, I'd written about a 14-year-old, Daniel Omar, who'd run behind a tree to escape a government bombing, wrapped his arms around the trunk – and had had both his arms blown clean off. Daniel's life had been saved due to the skill of the only surgeon working at the only hospital in the Nuba Mountains, an American called Tom Catena. I wrote at that time: 'Even for a surgeon who is, by now, most likely one of the world's most experienced amputators, there are things he can't fix.' After a month, Daniel's arms had healed into neat, smooth stumps but there seemed to be no repairing his mind. 'Without hands, I can't do anything,' Daniel had said. 'I can't eat. I can't even fight. I'm going to make such hard work for my family in the future.' He looked me straight in the eye. 'If I could have died, I would have,' he said.

Two years later, Elliot Kotek sent me an email from California. 'Hey Alex,' he began. 'Wanted to let you know that just three weeks ago, my business partner, Mick Ebeling, inspired by your article, returned home to California from Sudan's Nuba Mountains where he set up the world's first 3D-printing prosthetic lab and training facility with Tom Catena. Named for that boy in your article, Project Daniel successfully taught people barely familiar with computers to utilize the printers.' Daniel was now 16, said Elliot. Mick found him living in a refugee camp home to 70,000 people. 'On 11/11/13 he received version 1 of his left arm by virtue of a consumer-grade 3D printer. As a result, Daniel was able to feed himself for the first time in two years. We just today sent more 3D filament to Tom and his team so that they can continue to print arms and hands.' Elliot had attached a picture of a smiling Daniel.

It was hard to imagine something more enabling than printing a pair of new arms for a double amputee. Even better, Elliot and Mick hadn't hung around to set up an aid group and weren't asking for money to fund it. They read my article, realized they knew how to help, took a 3D printer somewhere it was badly needed, showed a group of Sudanese nurses how it worked by printing an arm – and left. I was delighted for Daniel, whose story had depressed me more than most. I was just as happy at this faultlessly selfless aid. Elliot didn't even ask me to write a story. He just thought I should know.

*

With each passing year I came across ever more Africans taking back their freedom. Sometimes all it took was a simple question about the future and, right before my eyes, it seemed, people would step forward and be bathed in the bright light of their own possibility. At first these great changes happened mostly quietly and one by one. But over the years the phenomenon grew as whole families, then whole streets, then whole towns lifted off before you. A new dawn was breaking across Africa and the land was blossoming in its warmth and glow. There were even a few miracles. One was Mogadishu.

On the sandflats next to Mogadishu airport, inside a three-metre-high fence, behind two security checks and a stone berm was a small, nameless bar. Playing darts under its open roof or on its terrace on any given night in the past few years you might have found French Special Forces, CIA paramilitaries, Turkish commandos or UN officials. Drinks were limited to beer but the bottles were cold and nobody minded if you brought your own whisky. Conversation was low and conspiratorial. Everybody in the bar had secrets and if this was a place to chew them over, that was because it was a rule that they were forgotten the moment you left.

About a year after the 2011 famine, a friend picked me up, signed me in, bought us both a beer and walked me over to a white plastic table where a handsome middle-aged man with thin, blond, receding hair was sitting in front of a bottle of Johnnie Walker Red. Richard Rouget was a former French commando, a mercenary with two decades of experience in Africa and an officer for one of the strangest aid groups in existence. Bancroft Global Development began as a de-mining operation in 1999. By the time I walked into the company's Mogadishu bar, it had become two divisions coupled together: a non-profit mercenary group – Guns Without Borders, if you like – and a for-profit war-zone property developer. Bancroft the soldier group would venture into a conflict and train one side to win, generally whichever one the West was backing. As Bancroft's new protégés advanced, Bancroft the construction consortium sent in a wave of builders behind them to construct the apartments, pools, golf courses and beachside bars that would soon be needed by the resource wildcatters and aid types expected to flood in. 'We directly align our interests with those of conflict-affected communities by investing,' read the company website. Like other aid groups, Bancroft earned money from war. Unlike them, it ultimately fought for peace – because there was more cash in it.

Rouget was a Bancroft trainer. In 2007, the year after their invasion, the Ethiopians began pulling out and handing over to an African Union force (AMISOM) of several thousand Ugandans and Burundians. Initially, AMISOM fared poorly. Al-Shabab fighters in Mogadishu would position themselves in civilian areas, especially Bakara Market, and fire a couple of mortars or RPGs at an AMISOM base – at which point AMISOM would rain a barrage of artillery on the city's central market or flatten whole streets of private homes.

Arriving in 2010, Rouget stopped that immediately. 'We stopped using armour and mortars,' he said. 'This was human terrain, moving through houses and gardens.' The Ugandans, who made up the bulk of AMISOM, were Rouget's focus. When they arrived in Mogadishu they were, he said, 'only an army of bush fighters' with the training and character of the former rebel army they were. Now they were being called to fight in the city. Rouget immediately formed a squad of 100 snipers. Bancroft's other trainers began instructing the rest in urban warfare. So as not to alienate Somalis, the Ugandans were told to advertise where they were going in advance, giving civilians time to move. They were also told to open their field hospitals to all Somalis. Above all, they should have enough confidence in their superior skill to allow them to be disciplined and patient. 'It's block by block, corner by corner, metre by metre,' said Rouget. 'You have to be trained, not scared. You don't just pull the trigger. You don't treat people here like second-class citizens in their own town. There's very few people in the world who can do that.'

In August 2010, al-Shabab mounted what it assumed would be a final offensive to take the last blocks of Mogadishu it did not already rule. To the Islamists' surprise, Uganda's sharpshooters cut them down. 'Al-Shabab took more than 1,000 casualties,' said Rouget. Then AMISOM began advancing through the city according to Bancroft's plan, street by street, neighbourhood by neighbourhood. The fighting was painstaking and bloody. Out of a force numbering 7,000, Rouget reckoned he had seen 1,000 body bags shipped back to Kampala in two years. But by early 2012 AMISOM had pushed the last al-Shabab fighters out of Mogadishu and captured a string of satellite towns. With the Ethiopians providing support from the west and the Kenyans from the south, plus reinforcements from Djibouti, Ghana, Nigeria and Sierra Leone, al-Shabab was soon penned into its southern stronghold once more. The Ugandans were also seeing a sight never before witnessed in Mogadishu: smiling children waving at passing soldiers. It was an extraordinary accomplishment, said Rouget. 'Today the Ugandans are one of the best urban fighting armies in the world.'

This was more than Africans taking care of African problems. It was Africans taking care of the biggest, most insoluble African problem. At the cost in a year of less than what the US spent in a week in Afghanistan, a few thousand Ugandans had achieved what the UN and US had failed to do in close to two decades. 'For the first time, Africans have shown they can solve African problems better than anyone,' said Rouget. 'They've done it by building trust with the population and projecting confidence. They've done it because they have the one thing that *mzungus* can never have. A black face.'

Mogadishu revived with astonishing speed behind AMISOM's advance. A few months later Dominic and I returned to profile the first Somali President for 20 years to take power without killing someone. A former teacher called Hassan Sheikh Mohamud, the new President, entered politics out of frustration that the university he built into a 4,000-student institution had to shut down whenever the fighting became too dangerous. 'We're starting everything from scratch,' he told me over a family lunch of curried chicken and rice. 'We lost everything in the war. Everything has been destroyed. We're walking in the dark. But there is no doubt about our will.'

Out in the city, the change even in a few months was arresting. Al-Shabab still launched regular bomb attacks. But all but two or three of the 60 or so neighbourhood militia checkpoints had gone. Shop owners had patched up their broken walls, plastered over the bullet holes, repaved their sidewalks and thrown open their doors once more. They were being joined by a mass of returning expatriates from Britain, Canada, the US, Australia and Scandinavia who were crowding the city's hotels and bringing in hundreds of millions of dollars to fix up their old homes and invest in new businesses. Where once there had been an empty harbour there was now a queue of ships arriving with concrete, televisions, cars and mobile phones, and taking away camels, mangoes and bananas. That was also proof of another improvement: the pirates were gone. International hotel chains were buying up seafront property, whose price had tripled in a year. Coca-Cola had reopened its factory. A team from the backpackers' guide, *Lonely Planet*, was talking to Bashir about researching a guidebook.

Our experience of Mogadishu was transformed. Where Dominic and I used to race down deserted streets, now we were slowed to a crawl by thousands of Somalis walking in the road and sitting in roadside cafés sipping coffee and smoking shisha pipes under street lights late into the night. Dominic, incredibly, began shooting a series on Mogadishu at night.

Most impressive of all was the self-reliance. Though Hassan needed aid to fund his government, he insisted it would be received on Somalia's terms only. Gone were the days when foreigners could expect to run their Somali programmes from the safety of Nairobi. 'We need a shift, a change of mindset within ourselves and within the international community,' said Hassan. 'From now on, it will not be that when we need even the smallest funding, we go to the outside world. No. Now we will do all we can by ourselves. We say: "Stay with us, great. Assist us, great. But we will do it."'

I met David Snelson, my old guide around southern Somalia, for a glass of sweet tea at a café in the ruins of an old garden next to the airport. David was now running an upmarket guest house in the city for aid workers and UN contractors. He worried that the major donors, the US and Britain, were making the same old mistakes. 'There's this overwhelming desire to change the culture and remodel it as more Western,' he said. 'It took hundreds of years for the West to make a transition that they're asking Somalia to make overnight.' But David had hope that the new Somalia wasn't going to allow others to tell it what to do any more. 'Nobody wants to go back to the old days,' he said.

Later that day Dominic and I went out with two of the President's aides to a former al-Shabab stronghold, a stunning white-sand beach in the north of the city. It was a Friday, the Muslim day of rest, and perhaps 10,000 Somalis were crowding the shoreline swimming, playing football and buying ice creams. Dominic busied himself in the crowds while I sat in a new beachside seafood joint built inside what used to be an al-Shabab compound. I ordered grilled lobster. My two companions allowed me to eat in silence, looking out at the scene. Eventually I confessed I was finding the whole experience slightly surreal.

Malik Abdullah, Hassan's press aide, had recently returned from California. He hadn't been sure whether to stay at first, he said. But every day he grew more convinced. 'Maybe after doing so badly for so long, Somalis really only had one option left,' he said. Malik grinned. 'Doing great,' he said.

*

Soon after I arrived in Africa, I bought a copy of Gill's Simplified Wall Map Series *Africa: Rainfall and Its Causes* by the early-twentieth-century geographer Laurence Dudley Stamp and hung it on my wall in Cape Town. Stamp's lifework was a series of maps of the British Isles, whose scale, six inches to one mile, required him to mark every hill, every house and every bend in every creek in the United Kingdom, a task which took him 15 years. Stamp drew the rest of the world with a colonialist's regard for detail. He drew Africa as a single country on a single page. He divided all the continent's weather into just four zones: always rainy, never rainy and sometimes rainy (two separate areas). Africa's winds he separated into four sets, his impatient triple arrows sending desert storms and cyclones skittering thousands of miles across the continent.

Initially I thought *Rainfall and Its Causes* was quaint. But the more trips I took into Africa, the more I began to think of those arrows, screaming towards a convergence on the southern edge of the Sahara, as indications of something else. With the kind of broad-brush strokes of which Stamp would have approved, it was possible, by transposing other dynamics onto his map, to make the arrows into opposing armies and give them names and characteristics. Desert, nomads, Islam and Arabs advancing south. Pastures, farmers, Christians and Africans pushing north. Stamp's dry zones marked many of my conflicts with uncanny precision and his red hot-spots had neat double meanings: battles, bombings, pirate attacks, drone strikes. The arrows were pointing me to where I needed to be.

Because story by story, year after year, I was pulling together a puzzle as large as the Sahara itself. It began with my first assignment in Mogadishu. Within a year it had grown to include the thousands of kilometres of sand, scrub, dust and thorn of the Sahel where Arabia meets Africa. My cast of characters expanded beyond Islamists, aid workers and counter-terrorism types to presidents and Christian rebels, oil prospectors and Hollywood actors, high-seas kidnappers and cocaine smugglers. Together they made up a giant band of instability that held the entire continent in its cinch.

What was it about the desert? The deeper into it I went, the more violence there was. That made some sense. The desert was Africa's last big void, a vast nothing where to survive was to fight, where there were no rules and only notional government, and peace was generally a misread pause. By that logic, the more desert there was, the more violence there would be. And by some reckoning, there was more desert every year.

Four million years ago, when human beings first walked out onto the plains of northern Kenya and Ethiopia, the Danakil Depression in the northern Rift Valley in Ethiopia was watery grassland. Ten thousand years ago, the earth tilted slightly on its axis and concentrated the sun's rays on Africa, creating a giant desert that stretched from the Mediterranean to the Equator. When the earth shuddered a second time around 8,000 BC, it inaugurated the last Ice Age, rainfall patterns changed again and the desert disappeared. But around 5,000 years ago the planet's axis shifted a third time, the ice melted and the rains slackened, and the Sahara advanced once more. The Danakil Depression in the centre of the Afar is once again the hottest place on earth with temperatures that can hit 63° C. Reminders of its very different past are preserved in the fish fossils that litter the valley floor and the small, inbred population of crocodiles that survives in its few oases.

In places, the Sahara is still expanding. Whereas droughts occurred every decade half a century ago in Somalia, now they come every other year. Across the width of the Sahara, an area equivalent in size to the whole of Somalia has become desert in 50 years. The United Nations Environment Programme says 14 African countries experience water scarcity or stress and predicts that to rise to 25 by 2025.

In modern parlance, this is called climate change. In its effects, it is analogous to the great droughts that propelled the first migrations out of Africa more than 100,000 years ago. Some African leaders describe the changes as environmental neo-imperialism – and in the rich-world origins of climate change, and the displacement and conflict accelerated in Africa, they have a point. The National Center for Atmospheric Research in Boulder, Colorado, has tracked half a century of declining rainfall on the continent. The Intergovernmental Panel on Climate Change says that although Africa produces just 2 per cent of greenhouse gases, it feels the bulk of its effects. Of the 80–120 million people estimated to go hungry because of desertification, rising sea levels and more locust plagues, around 80 per cent will be African.

Thirst kills. But it makes killers too. As millions of Africans retreat before the desert's advance, so hundreds of small climate wars erupt between them over the remaining good land. Across the Sahel, conflict breaks out wherever it finds a difference. Often the divisions are long-established: tribe against tribe, nomad against pastoralist, Arab against African, and Sunni Muslim against Christian, Sufi or pagan. The wars in Darfur, Somalia, Mali and Sudan all have roots in the competition for fertile land. During an extended drought from 1968 to 1974 in which more than 100,000 people died, disgruntled military men seized power in Burkina Faso, Ethiopia and Niger, and attempted several coups in Mali. The experts often describe that as a mere warm-up for what is to come. In 2007 Luc Gnacadja, Executive Secretary of the UN Convention to Combat Desertification (UNCCD), called efforts to stop desertification in Africa an attempt to 'help ensure humanity's survival'.

Most of the hundreds of thousands of Africans who try to cross the Mediterranean every year come from Africa's troubled dry zone: from Somalia, Eritrea or Sudan. The birth of at least three al-Qaeda-allied groups in the Sahel – al-Shabab in Somalia, Boko Haram in northern Nigeria and AQIM in Mali – means the connection between climate and conflict is also of interest to counter-terrorism types. In April 2007, 11 former US admirals and generals described desertification as a 'threat incubator' in a report for a military think tank. The next day at a debate on climate change and conflict at the UN Security Council in New York, then British Foreign Secretary Margaret Beckett asked: 'What makes wars start? Fights over water. Changing patterns of rainfall. Fights over food production, land use. There are few greater potential threats to our economies but also to peace and security itself.'

This marriage of desert and violence adds urgency to the work of scientists trying to predict how far the Sahara will expand. Will it once again reach Zanzibar? How many wars might that start? Just what is the danger of a desert?

Anthropologists would say: an innate one. An exhaustive study of more than 500 traits of more than 400 cultures by Robert Textor in 1967 found a historic split in humankind between people with ancestors in the rainforest and the desert. Rainforest people have many gods. Desert people have one. Rainforest communities are consensual. Desert society tends to be hierarchical and militaristic. Rainforest husbands treat their wives as equals. Desert husbands subjugate and denigrate their women, and restrict nudity and sex. While the rainforest provides in easy abundance, the harshness of the desert inculcates a cruel life. Desert people live on the move, following the rain and fighting rival groups they meet, hence the warrior code in all nomad culture from Berber to Tuareg to Turkana. All of which might make life as an inhabitant of the rainforest sound preferable. But in fact we are a world of desert people. Go back far enough and all of us are descended from migrants who, like today's refugees, wandered out of Africa in search of richer lands – and all human history has flowed from that.

All of which poses a question. What if we made the land wetter?

One day I arrived in Niger to look into AQIM's kidnapping of one of Canada's most senior diplomats, Robert Fowler. It was a strange few days. I wandered the capital, Niamey, without finding anyone to help me. At one point I was riding in a government car when 20 young men holding bricks and steel poles ran out of a side street and smashed every window as we passed. 'What the hell was that?' I yelled to the driver once we were clear. 'Kids,' he said, brushing the glass out of his hair.

In desperation one morning I walked into the national police headquarters and asked to see the boss – and within five minutes I was in his office, sipping a cup of tea and reading the confidential file containing everything the police chief said he had on Fowler and his abduction. None of it, sadly, was very enlightening.

Maybe my attention was already wandering. Dropping into Niamey through the brown haze of the Sahel, I'd caught sight of something unusual. As we descended, dark shapes had begun to appear on the desert floor below, stretching in ordered rows to the horizon. A few thousand feet off the ground, these dark outlines revealed themselves as crescent-shaped shadows. At a few hundred, it became clear they were the shadows of millions of trees.

Niamey was on the edge of the Sahara and as I drove across town in my search for anyone who knew anything about Fowler, I was surprised to see several government departments devoted to forestry. When I had been attacked, it was in a Forestry Ministry car taking me out of Niamey to see on the ground what I had glimpsed from the air. We drove on for an hour, then turned off the main road towards a village named Kareygorou. As we approached, I began seeing neat crescents and trenches made of stones in the dusty fields on either side of the road. As we entered the village, I felt a cooling in the air and looked up to see an avenue of acacias was shading us. I'd scarcely seen an animal in Niamey but now I saw pigs, ducks, goats and chickens. By the side of the road, women were selling maize and sorghum. Behind the houses I saw a sand dune, perhaps 90 metres high and latticed all over with a mesh of brushwood fences. The villagers had trapped the desert in a net. 'For years I watched the wind sweep the soil and sand off our land and into the river,' said the chief of Kareygorou, Moussa Sambo, 57. 'Then we stopped the desert. And everything changed.'

In the early 1980s in Burkina Faso, a farmer called Yacouba Sawadogo had an odd idea. Maybe the desert wasn't dead land, he thought. Maybe it was just very dry. For as long as anyone could remember, farmers had coaxed harvests from barren land by using *cordons pierreux* – lines of gathered stones – and *zai*, narrow, crescent-shaped fields with high sides. The stones stopped the soil from blowing away. The hollowed fields concentrated what water there was.

Sawadogo began experimenting, deepening and widening his *zai* to stop more of the sand, digging foot-deep sunken pits, building his *pierreux* into lattices and stirring rotten vegetables and manure into his plots. The manure attracted termites, which further broke up the soil. It also turned out to contain tree seeds. With water, these sprouted. Yacouba protected them by growing fences of millet around them.

It was a slow process. But after two decades, Yacouba could look out at a 25-hectare forest containing more than 60 types of trees, right in the middle of the Sahara. The shade from his trees protected his crops and animals. Some of them attracted bees, which made honey. Some had medicinal uses. The rest of the plants he used for firewood, which he sold for cash. Unsurprisingly, word of Yacouba's desert forest spread. He was, as he said, 'the only farmer from here to Mali who had any millet'. Farmers across Burkina Faso, then Mali, then Niger, then Sudan, then Ethiopia, then as far south as Zambia and Malawi were all soon building *zai* and watching crop yields and herd sizes rise.

Yacouba made his innovations at a critical time. In Burkina Faso and Niger, they coincided with the advent of private property rights. Frustrated by years of shortages and deaths, both countries had given up trying to decree better farm production or tree plantation. In the 1990s, pre-empting Eleni's commodity exchange and Hernando de Soto's work in Lagos, the state in both countries began allowing farmers to own, buy and sell their own land. This initially caused some violent disputes. But it also created opportunity. Since farmers could now plan on long-term returns, years of labour spent working a ditch became not just socially worthwhile but individually profitable. Returns were good. In Niger each hectare of rescued land brought in an extra $70 per head in a country where, according to the IMF, average per capita income was $185. Farmers who previously harvested one crop from every four sowings were now reaping each time they planted. Collecting firewood would take minutes instead of hours and there was often a surplus to sell. Farmers even began buying new patches of desert to rehabilitate and expand their fields.

The farmers were reversing the downward spiral of desertification and powering up a new virtuous cycle of life. Grassland and trees trapped the desert. Fruits and vegetables grown in their shadow provided food for people and animals. Animals made manure for the soil. That created bigger, healthier fields. As a result of the changes the forests wrought on Africa's climate, rainfall actually increased and the average daytime temperature fell from 45° C to 40° C. Hunger had also fallen. Niger's farmers now had enough surplus food and cash crops like wood to see them through the bad years. Two poor harvests in 2009 and 2010 prompted an international emergency operation to feed 4.3 million people. But in the areas where farmers were using *zai*, very few died. Aid agencies continue to announce every year that millions are at risk in the Sahel. But in fact in the last three decades, only one famine has been recorded in the Sahel – in Somalia in 2011 – and that, as we know, had its own special causes.

I wanted to find out how big re-greening had become. I emailed Chris Reij, a Dutch scientist who had been studying the phenomenon for years. Chris told me he had cautioned himself not to get too excited when he first noticed what was happening in Niger on a visit in 2004. 'I thought maybe they had re-greened a few hundred, perhaps 1,000 hectares,' he said.

The total turned out to be five million hectares, accounting for 200 million new trees. Nor were the changes limited to Niger. In neighbouring Mali, farmers had re-greened another 450,000 hectares. In Burkina Faso the figure was 300,000, in Ethiopia another million and in Tanzania 350,000. More than five million people were farming their way out of starvation. When I asked Chris to send some before-and-after photographs, he sent me slides taken by the US Geological Survey using satellites borrowed from NASA. The only way to see the scale of the change, said Chris, was from space.

The implications were giddy. A single African farmer had found the solution to desertification. Yacouba had invented desert farming and desert infrastructure. Out on the edges of a capitalist world, he had created his own capital from trees, soil and water.

This was not just filling Africa's empty spaces. It was filling the biggest empty space on earth. Yacouba was fixing the original problem that caused the first human beings to migrate out of Africa millions of years ago. He was finally kick-starting the process of development and modernization in one of the last great expanses in the world that it had not touched. That signalled an end to starvation and the coming of a day when even Africa's desert people might feed the world, not the other way around. It also heralded an end to the wars nurtured by the hardness of the desert. Chris told me that in areas where *zai* were common, conflict between farmers and herders was down 80 per cent.

If that wasn't enough, Yacouba had also found an answer to climate change and global warming. I'd felt the plunge in temperature. Chris said the average decline due to re-greening was 5° C. Moreover climatologists estimate that, because new plants suck in carbon dioxide, turning desert into farmland cut by a third the emission of carbon gases into the atmosphere. Africa had 60 per cent of the world's fallow land. That was enough to suck in all the excess carbon dioxide in the world. Yacouba had shown the world that fighting climate change didn't need to be in opposition to development. In Africa, fighting climate change was development.

I told Chris I'd never heard a story like it, and we began a correspondence. Years later, at a business conference in Cape Town, I told him about the Somali famine and described how that had come about.

Chris was quiet for a while. Then he said he wished Yacouba's ideas had spread to Somalia. They might have ensured the famine never happened, he said. They were, finally, the way out of a past crippled by foreign aid and foreign armies, and home-grown dictators, warlords and *jihadis*. 'This re-greening is the greatest environmental transformation in Africa, maybe even the world,' said Chris. But the biggest change was in how it came about. This wasn't something imposed from above by dictators or religious warriors or even well-meaning outsiders. In a new and different Africa, Africans were changing in ways that would be felt around the world. And best of all, said Chris, 'they did it for themselves'.

ACKNOWLEDGEMENTS

There are scores of colleagues and friends I should single out for special thanks but cannot because confidentiality remains essential. I hope you know who you are and please consider my thanks merely delayed until we meet next.

Among those I can name are Kassahun Addis, Richard Bailey, Andrew Belcher, Alan Boswell, Ryan Boyette, Allen Yero Embalo, Aurélie Fontaine, the late and much missed Tim Hetherington, Drew Hinshaw, Sadeeq Hong, Albert Kambale, Angelique Kidjo, Benedicte Kurzen, Reuben Kyama, Alexia Lewnes and Patrick Mehlman, Columbus Mavhunga, Yolande Mokolo, Mading Ngor, Adriane Ohanesian, Loki Osborn and Lucy Welford, Josh and Alissa Ruxin, Alisha Ryu, Munir Sanusi, Trevor Snapp, Mamadou Tapily, Amadou Thiam, Chris Tomlinson and Bram Vermeulen. All freely gave crucial assistance without expectation of reward. A special thanks to Max Askew, Richard Brown, Jessica Hatcher, Andrew Lebovich, Julian Marshall, Colin Perry and Tom Pow, who spent far more time than they should have reading and critiquing various drafts. Jessica's exemplary reporting from Congo in 2012 also informs much of the closing section of Chapter 5.

The cost of many years of travel across Africa was borne mostly by my former employers at *Time* magazine and, more recently, by my new editors at *Newsweek*. In particular I would like thank my old *Time* editor Michael Elliott, who was hard with my writing and generous with my expenses, Howard Chua-Eoan and Simon

Robinson, who among other assistance helped extract me from jail in Zimbabwe, and the late and deeply mourned Jim Frederick, who encouraged me to write this book. Much of the reporting in this book was undertaken for *Time* and I am grateful for the permission to use it. More recently, Richard Addis and Cordelia Jenkins at *Newsweek* have not only given me joyous, unprecedented freedom in where I go and how I write, they also granted me permission to use material gathered for their stories. In particular, parts of the chapters on South Sudan, Nigeria and Mali appeared in *Newsweek* and the *Newsweek* e-books *Clooney's War*, *The Hunt for Boko Haram* and *Cocaine Highway*.

This book owes its existence to my agent, Patrick Walsh at Conville and Walsh, the most charming, energetic and generous champion for whom a writer could hope. Patrick sowed the seeds of an idea and nurtured it until it became *The Rift*. My thanks to him, and to his staff: Carrie Pitt, Alexandra McNicoll, Kinga Burger, Jake Smith-Bosanquet and Henna Silvennoinen. Thanks also to Hari Kunzru for the introduction.

My editors, Bea Hemming at Weidenfeld & Nicolson, and Judy Clain, Amanda Brower and Vanessa Mobley at Little, Brown, displayed great enthusiasm from the start, heroic levels of optimism when I handed in several rough drafts, great insight in how each successive effort might be improved and extreme patience as I went repeatedly back to work. Thanks also to Geoff Shandler, and to Barend Wallet at Spectrum in Amsterdam, Nina Sillem at Fischer in Germany and Oriol Alcorta at Ariel in Spain, who all gave early support.

Dominic Nahr provided all the photographs in this book and I hope the layout has done justice to his visual genius and signature style. Dominic accompanied me on many trips in Africa and my failure to mention him more in the text is slightly unforgivable but explained by the fact that Dominic was normally so far ahead, around some dangerous-looking corner or over the next hill, that we were rarely together on the scene.

Acknowledgements

My wife, Tessa Laughton, has not only allowed me to roam freely in unsung places for large parts of our life together, she, too, encouraged me to quit my job to write this book, then turned her editor's eye to several drafts, all the while looking after our three beautiful girls. None of it, Tess, works without you.

FURTHER READING

Daron Acemoglu and James A. Robinson, *Why Nations Fail: The Origins of Power, Prosperity, and Poverty* (Crown Business, 2012)

Chinua Achebe, *There Was a Country* (Penguin, 2012)

Chris Alden, *China in Africa* (Zed Books, 2007)

John Allen, *Rabble Rouser for Peace: The Authorised Biography of Desmond Tutu* (Chicago Review Press, 2008)

Michael Asher, *Khartoum: The Ultimate Imperial Adventure* (Penguin Global, 2008)

Abhijit V. Banerjee and Esther Duflo, *Poor Economics: A Radical Rethinking of the Way to Fight Global Poverty* (PublicAffairs, 2011)

Adriaan Basson, *Zuma Exposed* (Jonathan Ball, 2012)

Mark Bowden, *Black Hawk Down: A Story of Modern War* (Grove Press, 2010)

Rukmini Calamachi, al-Qaeda papers, www.ap.org/media-center/secrets-of-the-al-qaida-papers

Ha-Joon Chang, *Bad Samaritans: The Myth of Free Trade and the Secret History of Capitalism* (Bloomsbury Press, 2008)

Nigel Cliff, *The Last Crusade: The Epic Voyages of Vasco da Gama* (Harper Perennial, 2012)

Paul Collier, *The Bottom Billion: Why the Poorest Countries are Failing and What Can Be Done About It* (OUP USA, 2008)

Rob Crilly, *Saving Darfur: Everyone's Favourite African War* (Reportage Press, 2010)

Angus Deaton, *The Great Escape: Health, Wealth and the Origins of Inequality* (Princeton University Press, 2013)

Daniel Defoe, *A General History of The Pyrates* (Dover Publications, 1999)

Hernando de Soto, *The Other Path: The Economic Answer to Terrorism* (Basic Books, 2002)

Alex de Waal and Julie Flint, *Darfur: A Short History of a Long War* (Zed Books, 2008)

Richard Dowden, *Africa: Altered States, Ordinary Miracles* (PublicAffairs, 2010)

William Easterly, *The Tyranny of Experts: Economists, Dictators and the Forgotten Rights of the Poor* (Basic Civitas Books, March 2014)

William Easterly, *The White Man's Burden: Why the West's Efforts to Aid the Rest Have Done So Much Ill and So Little Good* (OUP Oxford, 2007)

Stephen Ellis, *Season of Rains: Africa in the World; External Mission: The ANC in Exile 1960–1990* (University of Chicago Press, 2012)

Andrew Feinstein, *After the Party: A Personal and Political Journey Inside the ANC* (Jonathan Ball, 2009)

James Fergusson, *The World's Most Dangerous Place: Inside the Outlaw State of Somalia* (Da Capo Press, 2013)

Fiona Forde, *An Inconvenient Youth: Julius Malema and the 'New' ANC* (Portobello Books, 2012)

Howard French, *China's Second Continent: How a Million Migrants Are Building a New Empire in Africa* (Knopf, 2014)

Mark Gevisser, *Thabo Mbeki: A Dream Deferred* (Jonathan Ball, 2013)

John Ghazvinian, *Untapped: The Scramble for Africa's Oil* (Mariner Books, 2008)

Peter Godwin, *The Fear: The Days of Robert Mugabe* (Picador, 2011)

Peter Godwin, *When a Crocodile Eats the Sun: A Memoir of Africa* (Picador, 2007)

Philip Gourevitch, *We Wish to Inform You That Tomorrow We Will Be Killed With Our Families: Stories from Rwanda* (Picador, 1999)

Matthew Green, *The Wizard of the Nile: The Hunt for Africa's Most Wanted* (Portobello Books, 2012)

Robert Guest, *The Shackled Continent: Power, Corruption and African Lives* (Smithsonian Books, 2010)

Rebecca Hamilton, *Fighting for Darfur: The Wonks Who Sold Washington on South Sudan* (Palgrave Macmillan, 2011)

Graham Hancock, *Lords of Poverty: The Power, Prestige and Corruption of the International Aid Business* (Atlantic Monthly Press, 1994)

Mary Harper, *Getting Somalia Wrong? Faith, War and Hope in a Shattered State* (African Arguments, 2012)

Adam Hochschild, *King Leopold's Ghost: A Story of Greed, Terror and Heroism in Colonial Africa* (Houghton Mifflin, 1999)

Heidi Holland, *Dinner With Mugabe: The Untold Story of a Freedom Fighter Who Became a Tyrant* (Penguin, 2010)

Tom Holland, *In the Shadow of the Sword: The Birth of Islam and the Rise of the Global Arab Empire* (February, 2013)

Calestous Juma, *The New Harvest: Agricultural Innovation in Africa* (Oxford University Press, 2011)

Tracey Kidder, *Strength in What Remains* (Random House, 2010)

Stephen Kinzer, *A Thousand Hills: Rwanda's Rebirth and the Man Who Dreamed It* (Wiley, 2008)

Michael Klare, *Blood and Oil: The Dangers and Consequences of America's Growing Dependency on Imported Petroleum* (Holt, 2005)

Chuck Korr and Marvin Close, *More than Just a Game: The Most Important Soccer Story Ever Told* (St Martin's Griffin, 2011)

Rian Malan, *My Traitor's Heart: A South African Exile Returns to Face His Country, His Tribe and His Conscience* (Grove Press, 2000)

Rian Malan, *Resident Alien* (Jonathan Ball, 2009)

Nelson Mandela, *Long Walk to Freedom: The Autobiography of Nelson Mandela* (Back Bay Books, 1995)

Nelson Mandela, *Conversations with Myself* (Picador, 2011)

Greg Marinovich, *The Bang-Bang Club: Snapshots from a Hidden War* (Basic Books, 2011)

Greg Marinovich, *The Murder Fields of Marikana*: http://www.dailymaverick.co.za/article/2012-08-30-the-murder-fields-of-marikana-the-cold-murder-fields-of-marikana

Andrew Marr, *A History of the World* (Pan Macmillan, 2013)

Philip Marsden, *The Chains of Heaven: An Ethiopian Adventure* (HarperCollins, 2006)

Bryan Mealer, *All Things Must Fight to Live: Stories of War and Deliverance in Congo* (Bloomsbury USA, 2009)

Bryan Mealer and William Kamkwamba, *The Boy Who Harnessed the Wind: Creating Currents of Electricity and Hope* (William Morrow, 2010)

Martin Meredith, *The State of Africa: A History of the Continent Since Independence* (Simon & Schuster, 2011)

Martin Meredith, *Mugabe: Power, Plunder and the Struggle for Mugabe's Future* (PublicAffairs, 2007)

Martin Meredith, *Diamonds, Gold and War: The British, the Boers and the Making of South Africa* (PublicAffairs, 2008)

Greg Mills and Jeffrey Herbst, *Africa's Third Liberation: The New Search for Prosperity and Jobs* (Penguin Global, 2012)

Nina Munk, *The Idealist: Jeffrey Sachs and the Quest to End Poverty* (Doubleday, 2013)

Dervla Murphy, *In Ethiopia with a Mule* (Eland Books, 2012)

V.S. Naipaul, *The Masque of Africa: Glimpses of African Belief* (Knopf, 2010)

Barack Obama, *Dreams From My Father: A Story of Race and Inheritance* (Broadway Books, 2004)

Dayo Olopade, *The Bright Continent: Breaking Rules and Making Change in Modern Africa* (Houghton Mifflin Harcourt, 2014)

David Olusoga and Casper W. Erichsen, *The Kaiser's Holocaust: Germany's Forgotten Genocide and the Colonial Roots of Nazism* (Faber and Faber, 2010)

Thomas Pakenham, *The Scramble for Africa: White Man's Conquest of the Dark Continent from 1876 to 1912* (Avon Books, 1992)

Thomas Pakenham, *The Boer War* (Random House, 1979)

Linda Polman, *War Games: The Story of Aid and War in Modern Times* (Viking, 2011)

Samantha Power, *A Problem from Hell: America and the Age of Genocide* (Basic Books, 2013)

C.K. Prahalad, *The Fortune at the Bottom of the Pyramid: Eradicating Poverty Through Profits* (Wharton School Publishing, 2009)

Gerard Prunier, *From Genocide to Continental War: The Congolese Conflict and the Crisis of Contemporary Africa* (Hurst, 2005)

Alec Russell, *Bring Me My Machine Gun: The Battle for the Soul of South Africa, from Mandela to Zuma* (PublicAffairs, 2009)

Peter Russell, *Prince Henry the Navigator: A Life* (Yale University Press, 2001)

Jeremy Scahill, *Dirty Wars: The World is a Battlefield* (Nation Books, 2014)

Deborah Scroggins, *Emma's War* (Vintage, 2004)

Amartya Sen, *Development as Freedom* (Knopf, 1999)

Nicholas Shaxson, *Poisoned Wells: The Dirty Politics of African Oil* (Palgrave Macmillan Trade, 2008)

Allister Sparks, *Beyond the Miracle: Inside the New South Africa* (University of Chicago Press, 2009)

Jason Stearns, *Dancing in the Glory of Monsters: The Collapse of the Congo and the Great War of Africa* (PublicAffairs, 2012)

Jonny Steinberg, *The Number: One Man's Search for Identity in the Cape Underworld and Prison Gangs* (Jonathan Ball, 2010)

Jonny Steinberg, *Thin Blue: The Unwritten Rules of Policing South Africa* (Jonathan Ball, 2010)

Jonny Steinberg, *Three Letter Plague: A Young Man's Journey Through a Great Epidemic* (Jonathan Ball, 2008)

Joseph Stiglitz, *Globalization and its Discontents* (Norton and Company, 2002)

Joseph Stiglitz, *Making Globalization Work* (Norton and Company, 2006)

Michela Wrong, *In the Footsteps of Mr Kurtz: Living on the Brink of Disaster in Mobutu's Congo* (Harper Perennial, 2002)

Michela Wrong, *I Didn't Do It for You: How the World Betrayed a Small African Nation* (Harper Perennial, 2006)

Michela Wrong, *It's Our Turn to Eat: The Story of a Kenyan Whistle-Blower* (Harper Perennial, 2010)

INDEX

Index

Index

429

Index